CIVIL DISOBEDIENCE FROM NEPAL TO NORWAY

This volume explores the shifts in how civil disobedience has come to be theorized, defined, understood, and practised in contemporary politics. As social activism takes increasingly global forms, the goals of individuals and groups who view themselves as disobedient activists today can be defined in broader cultural terms than before, and their relationship to law and violence can be ambiguous.

Civil disobedience may no longer be entirely nonviolent, its purposes no longer necessarily serve progressive or emancipatory agendas. Its manifestations often blur the lines established in "classic", philosophically justified, and self-regulatory forms as epitomised in mass nonviolent protests of Mahatma Gandhi and Martin Luther King and theories of Arendt, Rawls and Dworkin. How civil disobedience operates has changed over the years, and this volume unpacks its many contemporary lives. It discusses new theoretical and political dilemmas and paradoxes through empirical cases and practical examples from Europe, the United States, and South Asia, which enables a "mirroring" perspective for the challenges and complexities of civil disobedience in different parts of the world.

Bringing together innovative and introspective perspectives on people and protests in contemporary political contexts, this volume will be of great interest to scholars and philosophers of political science, international relations theory, political philosophy, peace and conflict studies, sociology, and cultural studies.

Tapio Nykänen is University Lecturer in Political Science at the University of Lapland, and an Adjunct Professor at the University of Jyväskylä, Finland.

Tiina Seppälä is Senior Researcher in International Relations at the University of Lapland, and an Adjunct Professor of International Development Studies at the University of Jyväskylä, Finland.

Petri Koikkalainen is Professor of Arctic Politics and Governance (on leave of absence from the University of Lapland) and an Adjunct Professor of Political Science at the universities of Helsinki and Jyväskylä.

Ethics, Human Rights, and Global Political Thought
Series Editors: Aakash Singh Rathore and Sebastiano Maffettone
Center for Ethics & Global Politics, Luiss University, Rome

Whereas the interrelation of ethics and political thought has been recognized since the dawn of political reflection, over the last sixty years – roughly since the United Nation's Universal Declaration of Human Rights – we have witnessed a particularly turbulent process of globalizing the coverage and application of that interrelation. At the very instant the decolonized globe consolidated the universality of the sovereign nation-state, that sovereignty – and the political thought that grounded it – was eroded and outstripped, not as in eras past, by imperial conquest and instruments of war, but rather by instruments of peace (charters, declarations, treaties, conventions), and instruments of commerce and communication (multinational enterprises, international media, global aviation and transport, internet technologies).

Has political theory kept apace with global political realities? Can ethical reflection illuminate the murky challenges of real global politics?

This Routledge book series *Ethics, Human Rights and Global Political Thought* addresses these crucial questions by bringing together outstanding monographs and anthologies that deal with the intersection of normative theorizing and political realities with a global focus. Treating diverse topics by means of interdisciplinary techniques – including philosophy, political theory, international relations and human rights theories, and global and postcolonial studies – the books in the Series present up-to-date research that is accessible, practical, yet scholarly.

Deprovincializing Habermas
Global Perspectives
Edited By Tom Bailey

Civil Disobedience from Nepal to Norway
Traditions, Extensions, and Civility
Edited By Tapio Nykänen, Tiina Seppälä and Petri Koikkalainen

For more information about this series, please visit: www.routledge.com/
Ethics-Human-Rights-and-Global-Political-Thought/book-series/EHRGPT

CIVIL DISOBEDIENCE FROM NEPAL TO NORWAY

Traditions, Extensions, and Civility

Edited by Tapio Nykänen, Tiina Seppälä, and Petri Koikkalainen

LONDON AND NEW YORK

Cover image: Courtesy of Tapio Nykänen

First published 2023
by Routledge
4 Park Square, Milton Park, Abingdon, Oxon OX14 4RN

and by Routledge
605 Third Avenue, New York, NY 10158

Routledge is an imprint of the Taylor & Francis Group, an informa business

© 2023 selection and editorial matter, Tapio Nykänen, Tiina Seppälä, and Petri Koikkalainen; individual chapters, the contributors

The right of Tapio Nykänen, Tiina Seppälä, and Petri Koikkalainen to be identified as the authors of the editorial material, and of the authors for their individual chapters, has been asserted in accordance with sections 77 and 78 of the Copyright, Designs and Patents Act 1988.

All rights reserved. No part of this book may be reprinted or reproduced or utilised in any form or by any electronic, mechanical, or other means, now known or hereafter invented, including photocopying and recording, or in any information storage or retrieval system, without permission in writing from the publishers.

Trademark notice: Product or corporate names may be trademarks or registered trademarks, and are used only for identification and explanation without intent to infringe.

British Library Cataloguing-in-Publication Data
A catalogue record for this book is available from the British Library

Library of Congress Cataloging-in-Publication Data
A catalog record has been requested for this book

ISBN: 978-1-032-01300-8 (hbk)
ISBN: 978-1-032-34086-9 (pbk)
ISBN: 978-1-003-32049-4 (ebk)

DOI: 10.4324/9781003320494

Typeset in Bembo
by SPi Technologies India Pvt Ltd (Straive)

CONTENTS

Acknowledgements   *vii*
Notes on contributors   *ix*

1 Introduction: civil disobedience from Nepal to Norway   1
  Tiina Seppälä, Tapio Nykänen, and Tiina Harjumaa

PART I
Civil disobedience then and now   **9**

2 The concept and practices of civil disobedience   11
  Petri Koikkalainen, Tapio Nykänen, and Tiina Harjumaa

3 Experiments with civil disobedience during Norwegian
  environmental struggles, 1970–2000   27
  Stellan Vinthagen and Jørgen Johansen

4 Civil disobedience and artistic protests – the Álta and
  Deatnu disputes and the development of Sámi resistance   47
  Tapio Nykänen, Veli-Pekka Lehtola, and Birgitta Vinkka

5 Drugs, disobedience, and democracy: civil disobedience and
  drug policy   64
  Mika Luoma-Aho

vi Contents

PART II
Alternative insights and extensions of civil disobedience   83

6 Open source disobedience – rise of civic hacktivism in Taiwan   85
Sami Kotiranta

7 Masked struggle: uncivil disobedience on the streets of Finland   104
Johan-Eerik Kukko

8 Is there an alternative tradition of civil disobedience in Europe?   122
Taru Haapala

9 Different forms of dissent in anti-deportation activism
in Finland: from refugee protests to civil disobedience   139
Tiina Seppälä

10 Dissenting civil society, hunger strikes, and the transitional
justice process in Nepal   160
Neetu Pokharel, Som Prasad Niroula, and Tiina Seppälä

PART III
Defending civility in civil disobedience   177

11 Academic freedom, resisting intellectuals, and the idea
of university in South Asia   179
Arun Gupto

12 Understanding whistleblowing: civil disobedience
or uncivil action?   197
Manohar Kumar

Index   *217*

ACKNOWLEDGEMENTS

We would like to express our sincerest gratitude to the series editor Aakash Singh Rathore and the commissioning editor Aakash Chakrabarty from Routledge for their continuous support and encouragement. We are thankful to the external reviewers who provided us with important and constructive feedback. We give our heartfelt thanks to Tiina Harjumaa for her excellent editorial work and invaluable technical help. We would also like to thank Wendy Jo Dymond for editing and proofreading assistance.

We are very grateful to the authors of this volume. We thank them for their insightful contributions and their critical reflections, as well as their patience and solidarity when working together on this book during a global COVID-19 pandemic that influenced the editing process in several ways.

We would like to thank all the participants and communities of research, non-governmental organisations, and organisations, as well as the funding institutes, that made the publication possible. This book has been undertaken at the University of Lapland in Rovaniemi, Finland, with the framework of the Rethinking Nordic Democracy: Civil Disobedience in Exceptional Times (REND) research project (2018–2022), funded by the Academy of Finland (grant number 316443).

CONTRIBUTORS

Arun Gupto teaches at the Institute of Advanced Communication, Education and Research, Kathmandu, Nepal. He has been part of the faculty at the Central Department of English, Tribhuvan University. His areas of study are literary theory, postcolonial studies, and South Asian studies. His recent publications include *Goddesses of Kathmandu Valley. Grace, Rage, Knowledge* (Routledge, 2019) and *Theory and Criticism: Recent Writings from South Asia* (Routledge, 2022). He also dedicates his time to making cultural documentaries.

Taru Haapala is a Tomás y Valiente Senior Researcher at the Madrid Institute for Advanced Study and the Department of Political Science and International Relations of the Universidad Autónoma de Madrid (UAM), Spain. She also holds the title of docent in political science at the University of Jyväskylä, Finland. Previously, she was a Marie Curie fellow within the InterTalentum MSCA-COFUND programme at UAM. Her publications include *Tracing the Politicisation of the EU: The Future of Europe Debates Before and After the 2019 Elections* (Palgrave Macmillan, 2022).

Tiina Harjumaa is a university lecturer in cultural history at the University of Lapland, Finland. Her research interests include war memory, cultural reconstruction, history politics, oral history, mnemonic communities, and religious movements and people. She is a co-editor and contributor of *Reconstructing Minds and Landscapes – Silent Postwar Memory in the Margins of History* (Routledge, 2021; co-editors Marja Tuominen & T. G. Ashplant) and a contributor to *Conservative Religion and Mainstream Culture – Opposition, Negotiation, and Adaptation* (Palgrave Macmillan, 2021; eds. Stefan Gelfgren & Daniel Lindmark).

x Contributors

Jørgen Johansen is an independent peace researcher, bibliophile, and trouble-maker living amongst the trees in southern Sweden. He is the co-editor of the *Journal of Resistance Studies* and runs Irene Publishing. After 40 years of work in more than 100 countries, he has settled and is inspired by Cicero: "If you have a garden and a library, you have everything you need."

Petri Koikkalainen is a professor of arctic politics and governance (on leave of absence from the University of Lapland) and an adjunct professor of political science at the universities of Helsinki and Jyväskylä. His research interests include political theory, history of political thought, and Finnish party politics. Currently he works as a counsellor of science and education in the Embassy of Finland, Washington, D.C.

Sami Kotiranta is a PhD student of political sciences at the University of Helsinki, Finland, and currently works as a researcher at the University of Lapland as a member of the "Rethinking Nordic Democracy" research team. His work focuses on digital transformation in the public sector and the necessary governance reforms related to this process. He believes that civil disobedience is a core component of a free and democratic society and that one of the most important roles of the public service is to use this momentum for the benefit of society as a whole.

Johan-Eerik Kukko is a doctoral candidate in political science at the University of Lapland, Finland. He works with the "Rethinking Nordic Democracy" research project, funded by the Academy of Finland, and he is doing a PhD about vigilantism in Finland in the 2010s. His research interests include vigilantism and civil disobedience.

Manohar Kumar completed his PhD in political theory at the LUISS University, Rome in 2013. He has held postdoctoral fellowships at the IIT Delhi and Aix Marseille School of Economics, Aix-Marseille University. He is the co-author of *Speaking Truth to Power. A Theory of Whistleblowing* (with Daniele Santoro; 2018). His articles have appeared in *Philosophy and Social Criticism* and in edited volumes from Routledge. He is now finishing (with Arundhati Virmani and Jean Boutier) an edited collection on the role of social scientists in the civic space (forthcoming, 2022).

Veli-Pekka Lehtola (born 1957) is a professor of Sámi culture at the Giellagas Institute at the University of Oulu, Finland. Lehtola is a (North) Sámi from Aanaar or Inari in northern Finland. As a researcher, Lehtola specialises in the history of the Sámi and Lapland and in modern Sámi art, as well as in the development of the Sámi representations.

Contributors **xi**

During the daytime, **Mika Luoma-Aho** (University of Newcastle upon Tyne, 2002) works as a university lecturer in political sciences at the University of Lapland, teaching courses to do with political issues like ideology, rhetoric, and civil disobedience. During the night, he is a drug policy activist fighting for human rights and social justice for people who use drugs and defending policies of decriminalisation and legalisation in Finland. He serves on the executives of both the Finnish Cannabis Association and the Finnish Medical Cannabis Association.

Som Prasad Niroula is a human rights defender working in Nepal. He has a decade of experience working in the field of human rights, and he previously worked at the South Asia Forum for Human Rights based in Kathmandu. His research interests are peacebuilding, migration, and social justice. He holds a master's degree in peace education from the United Nations Mandated University for Peace, Costa Rica. He is the co-author of *Confronting the Federal Sphinx in Nepal: Madhesh-Tarai* (Sage, 2015).

Tapio Nykänen is a university lecturer in political science at the University of Lapland and an adjunct professor at the University of Jyväskylä, Finland. His research interests include politics of identity, reindeer herding cultures, human-nature relations, Finnish party politics, and political theory. He is interested in ethnographic methods and works also as a photographer.

Neetu Pokharel is a women's rights activist who has worked in the areas of justice and women's rights for more than 10 years in Nepal. She has been working as a program officer in the Alliance for Social Dialogue Nepal, being responsible for the Access to Justice Portfolio with a particular focus on legal empowerment and women's rights. She has engaged in policy advocacy, human rights campaigns, and research related to access to justice, government accountability, and rights of women and marginalised groups in Nepal. She holds a master's degree in conflict, peace, and development studies from the University of Ruhuna, Sri Lanka.

Tiina Seppälä is a senior researcher in international relations at the University of Lapland and an adjunct professor of international development studies at the University of Jyväskylä, Finland. She has engaged with women's rights and slum activists in Nepal and Bangladesh, anti-eviction movements in India, asylum seekers in Finland, and anti-war activists in the UK. She is interested in activism, social movements, development, displacement, post/decolonial studies, feminist theory, ethnography, and arts-based methods. She is the author of *Globalising Resistance against War?* (Routledge, 2012) and co-editor of *Arts-Based Methods for Decolonising Participatory Research* (Routledge, 2021).

xii Contributors

Birgitta Vinkka is a doctoral student in sociology at the University of Lapland. In her master's thesis, she studied the political traditions of the Indigenous Sámi activism. Her current research interests lie in the sociology of climate change, loss, and the human–nature relations of the urbanised arctic.

Stellan Vinthagen is a professor of sociology, a scholar-activist, and the Inaugural Endowed Chair in the Study of Nonviolent Direct Action and Civil Resistance at the University of Massachusetts, Amherst. He is the editor of the *Journal of Resistance Studies* and co-founder of the Resistance Studies Network (www.resistancestudies. org). His research is focused on resistance, power, social movements, nonviolent action, conflict transformation, and social change. Since 1980, he has been an educator, organiser, and activist in several countries and has participated in more than 30 nonviolent civil disobedience actions, for which he has served in total more than one year in prison.

1
INTRODUCTION

Civil disobedience from Nepal to Norway

Tiina Seppälä, Tapio Nykänen, and Tiina Harjumaa

Some of the most significant theoretical groundwork on the concept of *civil disobedience* took place in the 1960s and 1970s, often reflecting the contemporaneous ideologies of social liberalism and the welfare state. In the Western context, the philosophical justifications of the concept followed the work of scholars such as John Rawls, Hannah Arendt, and Ronald Dworkin. These theoretical ideas resonated particularly well with the goals of new social movements of the 1960s through 1980s, which introduced the concept of civil disobedience to wide public audiences.

Civil disobedience in this "classic" and self-regulatory form was inherently a state-centric concept, as its primary targets were either national legislation or government policy, and essential to its accepted practices was recognition of the state's ultimate monopoly of violence. The mass protests of Mohandas Karamchand Gandhi (better known as Mahatma Gandhi) against British colonialism in India in the 1930s, and the black civil rights movement led by Martin Luther King Jr. in the US in the 1960s were nonviolent, as were the theories of Arendt, Rawls, and Dworkin later. Their notions of legitimate civil disobedience included also several other preconditions, such as the political nature of the deed, unavailability of other means of influence, publicity, and acceptance of legal consequences. Engaging in this kind of "regulated" or "enlightened" form of civil disobedience that largely followed the philosophical ideals became a common political strategy for Western progressive, left, and green movements aiming to challenge unjust national legislation or government policies.

Nowadays, these conditions no longer necessarily apply. The goals of individuals and groups who view themselves as disobedient activists can be defined in broad cultural terms, for example, as defence of "national values", and their relationship to law and violence can be ambiguous. Moreover, as social activism takes increasingly

DOI: 10.4324/9781003320494-1

global forms, it can be asked whether the old, regulated form of civil disobedience remains feasible if the target of activism is no longer national legislation or policy but, for example, the global climate crisis. In the middle of such contradictions, it can even be asked whether the concept of civil disobedience is already fragmented beyond any reasonable use. In other words, the emergence of civil disobedience as a philosophically justified and somewhat clear concept with practical ways of telling which lines not to cross was possible in a certain historical context, and when that context changes, also the justifications and means of regulating disobedient behaviour may lose their original force. While this may offer opportunities for new solutions, special attention must be paid also to new theoretical and political dilemmas and paradoxes that come along with these justifications and actions of civil disobedience. What are the acceptable "limits" of disobedience? How do they change in different contexts?

The world of ours is of course in constant turmoil. Contentious politics, resistance, and activism are influenced not only by processes of globalisation and changes in the international political economy, global politics, and governance but also by other border-crossing developments such as digitalisation and digital surveillance, migration flows, the rise of populism, and narratives of the so-called post-truth era. Moreover, while new social movements are born, old movements are reinventing themselves – consider, for example, the emergence of movements such as Black Lives Matter, Extinction Rebellion, Greta Thunberg's Fridays for Future school strike, as well as other new forms of the environmental movement, the feminist movement, and various anti-racist and post/decolonial movements. Some of these developments have had very practical impacts on the utility of civil disobedience, and they have also shaped the theoretical debate on its role and effectiveness in a globalised world (see e.g. Brownlee, 2012; Cabrera, 2021; Celikates, 2014, 2016; Çıdam et al., 2020; Cooke & Petherbridge, 2016; Hidalgo, 2019; Scheuerman, 2019, 2021a, 2021b; Schock, 2021).

Simultaneously, there is empirical evidence which suggests that civil disobedience has been an effective strategy of nonviolent resistance also in these times of fragmented, globalised, and perhaps a bit confused social realities. While it seems also to have worked as a sole strategy, civil disobedience has been particularly effective when combined with other means of resistance, such as lawsuits, lobbying, and protests (Thiri et al., 2022). On the other hand, activists that engage in civil disobedience fall in danger of facing violent repression and criminalisation somewhat often, when compared to other means of resistance (Thiri et al., 2022). Despite this, civil disobedience clearly has a significant role in the toolbox of social movements yet in the seething 2020s.

This edited volume addresses and explores three key themes. First, it introduces and discusses classical civil disobedience as a theory and practice. Second, it asks whether the concept of justified civil disobedience should be broadened in order to understand both alternative theoretical traditions and contemporary forms of dissent. Third, it explores ways to unpack the "civility" aspect of civil disobedience

Introduction **3**

further. In sum, the aim of the book is to continue the discussion on the importance and nature of civil disobedience in the contemporary context and beyond.

Our aim is not to rethink or re-evaluate the already existing extensive literature on civil disobedience and its "extensions" as such (see e.g. Delmas & Brownlee, 2021), but rather to complement it with some new cases and slightly different examples. One of our primary objectives is to provide the readers with a nuanced understanding of diverse but partially little-known empirical forms of dissent and resistance which are either defined as or resemble civil disobedience. Many of the chapters also critically engage with recent theoretical and conceptual debates on civil or "uncivil" disobedience (see e.g. Delmas, 2018).

The title of the book, *Civil Disobedience from Nepal to Norway*, refers additionally to a further particular nature of the volume. As the name suggests, our empirical examples come primarily from Asia and Europe, especially Nordic countries. This choice is intentional: instead of concentrating on cases that originate from the United States, and thus building on Western mainstream debates, the book offers an alternative perspective of the past and present of civil disobedience. As stated, the book focuses on cases that may not be too well known to the global audiences but offer interesting insights to the variety of resistance. This does not mean that the United States would be absolutely forgotten. One of the chapters examines, for example, whistleblowing in the case of Edward Snowden, and several American theorists have a central place in the book.

The title also illuminates another central perspective of the book. Several chapters show how political and theoretical ideas have travelled from country and region to another. This movement of ideas happens constantly when people across the globe read each other's texts or hear about their deeds and become inspired. However, as the book demonstrates, it has always been very important to meet people in real-life situations and see with one's own eyes how injustices are fought elsewhere.

The first section of the book elaborates on the history of classical civil disobedience, as well as new practices related to it. Chapter 2 serves as the main conceptual introduction to the theme – it discusses the concept of civil disobedience in detail while outlining a mainstream (Rawlsian) theoretical description of civil disobedience and examining how it can be justified within the wider context of the Western tradition of representative democracy. The last part of the text also introduces paradoxes or tensions that may occur when applying theory to practice. In all, the chapter offers an introduction to the theories and empirical examples of civil disobedience and, hence, sets up the scene for the later chapters of this book.

In Chapter 3, Stellan Vinthagen and Jørgen Johansen advance our understanding of how the strategic use of civil disobedience has developed in the Norwegian environmental movement. Their focus is on the main changes in the use of civil disobedience from 1970 to 2000, and the driving forces that made it possible that the use of civil disobedience changed from a small experiment to an advanced political strategy. Four key cases of environmental struggles are analysed. They represent different phases in the development and show how leading activists tested a series of

4 Tiina Seppälä et al.

new strategies of resistance, where civil disobedience was a key element. All cases relate to the opposition of large-scale systems for electricity production. The chapter's main argument is that thanks to a creative and sustained combination of serious philosophical research work and the application of strategies and tactical principles in campaigns over a period of 50 years, it has been possible to shift the political culture in Norway. Today, civil disobedience is recognised as a potent and potentially democratic tool for ordinary citizens when the environment is under threat. Civil disobedience is now so established that there exists specialised knowledge among educators, organisers and authors, and different versions of the tactic: small-scale, mass-scale, constructive, and deterrent civil disobedience.

In Chapter 4, Tapio Nykänen, Veli-Pekka Lehtola, and Birgitta Vinkka examine two disputes concerning nature exploitation that have provoked open resistance among the Indigenous Sámi people in Nordic countries. The first one is Álta Controversy that took place at the end of the 1970s and early 1980s, and the second is the Deatnu fishing dispute, which revolved around the question of fishing regulations in and around the River Deatnu in the late 2010s. The chapter describes the course of the two disputes and the forms of resistance used by the Sámi protesters involved in them, with civil disobedience in particular focus. The chapter demonstrates that those engaging in acts of resistance first sought to defend everyday life as they lived it. However, both processes of resistance soon took a constructive turn. The protesters sought to build structures that would help in imminent resistance but would also strengthen the political position of the Sámi for the future. Moreover, the chapter discusses the nature of civil disobedience in Álta and Deatnu. It shows that the participants emphasised the importance of law, even if they broke it when engaging in civil disobedience. Finally, the chapter illuminates the central role of art and artists in the events.

Chapter 5 evaluates claims of civil disobedience made in the contemporary and the global drug policy context. According to Mika Luoma-Aho, previous literature identifies two claims or kinds of claim. For one, the clandestine practice and ideology of harm reduction, which basically means offering health care and different kinds of services to people who use drugs to minimise the negative health, social, and legal impacts of drug use. For another, the civil disobedience of cannabis activism, which protests against policies of prohibition by openly violating drug laws during the Global Marijuana March, among many other similar public gatherings. Luoma-Aho considers these claims in light of Rex Martin's definition of justifiable civil disobedience in a democracy. His analysis is based on previous case studies (harm reduction) and autoethnography (cannabis activism).

The second section of the book takes some distance from the concept of classical civil disobedience by exploring new alternatives to it. In Chapter 6, Sami Kotiranta discusses the recent civil society driven shift towards a more participatory system of governance in Taiwan. Social unrest that grew out of widespread frustration towards the secretive and elitist political culture led to weeks-long mass protests and the occupation of the parliament in 2014. The so-called Sunflower Movement was a watershed moment in Taiwanese politics that made the transformative agenda of

Introduction **5**

hacktivist communities a key component of the ongoing public governance reform. This reform is characterised not only by the rapid digitalisation of Taiwanese public service but also by the deepening inclusion of Taiwanese public in decision-making and the use of open-source civic technology. Governance reform carries on the spirit of the Sunflower Movement in a unique way as the developers included in this work previously applied their expertise in the Sunflower Movement protests, and this process is overseen by a power figure within this community, Audrey Tang, who in 2016 became the first digital minister of Taiwan. The chapter looks into the use of digital civil disobedience to understand what factors contributed to a positive societal impact, which in Taiwan can be seen as a transformative process that moves through stages of civic action, from empowerment to engagement to establishment.

Johan-Eerik Kukko analyses in Chapter 7 messages that are connected to masks and other symbols in the short history of the Finnish anti-immigration street patrol group Soldiers of Odin (SOO). He also compares their use of masks to the ways in which another Finnish activist group, the Loldiers of Odin, has used masks and symbols in their activism. Kukko describes how the SOO started its street patrol activity in 2015 to "safeguard" Finnish cities from the alleged threat of asylum seekers and how one year later, in 2016, the Loldiers of Odin were founded to oppose the SOO's vigilante activity. The Loldiers of Odin carnivalised the anti-immigrant group by appearing in their demonstrations and harassing their street patrolling while dressed as clowns. The chapter analyses the dynamics of these two groups and the ways in which they used the masks and symbols in their activities. In the SOO case, Kukko focuses on situations in which the group uses Guy Fawkes masks and, in the case of the Loldiers of Odin, on situations in which they use clown makeup. Additionally, he asks whether their actions with masks can be understood as "uncivil disobedience", a term that has been discussed, for example, by Jennet Kirkpatrick and Candice Delmas. The chapter concludes by demonstrating that both groups have two kinds of masks – one to wear and another to hide their real purposes.

Chapter 8 by Taru Haapala examines civil disobedience in Europe from a conceptual and historical perspective. Reflecting on Hannah Arendt's definition of civil disobedience that places it in the American tradition of voluntary associations, Haapala seeks to answer the question: Is there an alternative tradition of civil disobedience in Europe? First, she discusses the ongoing scholarly debate about civil disobedience in which the Rawlsian (liberal) concept has become challenged. Second, she examines how civil disobedience has been recently used in the political rhetoric of Catalan independentists and by French MEP Manon Aubry in attempts to justify freedom of rights. Third, she explores the postwar European integral federalism, focusing primarily on the Union of European Federalists, insisting on creating an alliance, also inspiring the "Europe of the Regions". Haapala concludes that there is a potential alternative tradition of civil disobedience in Europe which can be traced back to the Proudhonian principle of a voluntary pact.

In Chapter 9, Tiina Seppälä explores different phases and forms of anti-deportation activism in Finland since the beginning of the so-called European

6 Tiina Seppälä et al.

refugee crisis in 2015. In analysing various forms of dissent, she demonstrates that while anti-deportation activists have utilised a wide variety of methods in different phases very creatively, there have been only a few explicit cases of civil disobedience. For her, this invites the question of why it has not featured as a more attractive form of dissent in Finnish anti-deportation activism, given that it is more commonly used elsewhere and by some other Finnish social movements. Therefore, in her chapter, she also discusses the potential reasons behind the limited utilisation of civil disobedience, based on thematic interviews conducted with anti-deportation activists and solidarity actors. Seppälä's analysis concludes that civil disobedience is not necessarily considered an efficient form of dissent in anti-deportation activism as it is not always practically possible to utilise it in stopping deportations; it may result in decreasing the already low public support for the anti-deportation cause through negative publicity; and, as a controversial method, it is considered risky also in terms of movement or organisational image, as well as individual safety and well-being of the disobedient subject, especially if a female activist.

Chapter 10 by Neetu Pokharel, Som Niroula, and Tiina Seppälä elaborates on the Transitional Justice movement in Nepal that seeks justice for victims of human rights violations and crimes committed during the internal armed conflict (1996–2006) of which only a small fraction has been properly investigated or prosecuted. To combat the culture of impunity, the conflict victims have actively worked together with human rights activists and civil society organisations. In exploring different phases and forms of their activism, the authors demonstrate that civil society actors in Nepal have creatively utilised a wide variety of methods, including peaceful protests, sit-ins, non-cooperation, hunger strikes, as well as civil disobedience to demand justice and challenge laws and policies they consider unjust or discriminatory. The authors conclude that even though the conflict victims have not been able to compel the state to fulfil its responsibilities in making the perpetrators of the conflict era accountable, they have succeeded in articulating their dissatisfaction clearly in the public arena while building important networks and alliances and gaining support also from the international community. They also emphasise that it is remarkable that despite the long legacy of violence, the conflict victims, human rights activists, and civil society actors have continually chosen to pursue justice through the nonviolent approach.

In the third section of the volume, the focus is on the "civility aspect" of civil disobedience. Here, civility refers to the style and decorum of civil disobedience, rather than evaluating, for example, under what circumstances it should or should not be used (see e.g. Delmas, 2018), or if the disobedient subjects are citizens or non-citizens, as for example Finnish translation *kansalaistottelemattomuus* (lit. "disobedience of citizens") would suggest. In Chapter 11, Arun Gupto draws from his personal history as a teacher with long-term experience working in South Asian universities, as well as his conversations with fellow academics, students, and teachers alike. Gupto's chapter can be considered a philosophical attempt to describe the nature of resistance in universities in general and South Asian universities in particular. On one hand, he regards it very important that universities retain their peculiar epistemological position but, on the other hand, he is partially pessimistic about whether this is actually possible, as the establishment and authorities are directing universities into different directions and at times, suppressing the dissent by force. The chapter connects with several other chapters in the book through its emphasis on artistic resistance. Gupto highlights this dimension in his discussion on the "poetics" of resistance – according to him, poetics is a "rule and method" behind dissent – something that resembles a grammar. However, by using the word poetics, he also implies that there is aesthetics in the events of resistance: something that appeals to emotions and not only to reason.

Chapter 12 by Manohar Kumar discusses whistleblowing as a form of civil disobedience, while it also weaves some insights from other chapters together. The chapter begins by discussing the resurgence in the debate on civil disobedience. While on one hand, emerging forms of dissent like hacktivism, whistleblowing, and unauthorised economic migration make claims of civil disobedience, sceptics argue that they are mistaken as they neither accurately capture the nature of dissenting action, the claims of the activists, nor do they qualify the demanding requirements of civil disobedience. Sceptics claim that these protests should be seen in their own right, sometimes as instances of uncivil disobedience. Against sceptics, Kumar argues that whistleblowing is a form of civil disobedience and that the confusion in accepting it as one arises due to a conception of civility that is borrowed from the dominant Rawlsian theory of civil disobedience, which he considers demanding for forms of dissent that, although democracy-enhancing, need not demonstrate features similar to classic forms of civil disobedience. According to Kumar, whistleblowing challenges us to reconsider the shifting lines between civil and uncivil forms of disobedience and the fact that any theory of civil disobedience needs to be sensitive to the changing historical contexts of political action. The deviance of whistleblowing from standard models is no testimony to a lack of sincerity and seriousness but rather represents a response to the demands of the specific situation, the changing nature and forms of political engagement and governance, and a personal regard for individual circumstances.

Civil disobedience is a last-resort, radical, often controversial form of civic activism, and it always is a conspicuous way of making a political statement. This book works to demonstrate that empirical studies of civil disobedience can reveal much about the prevailing ideological climate around civil society and activism and about the current condition of "the political". Given that there is a lot of variance in the usage of the concept, we feel that it is especially important to distinguish between its standard Western and non-Western heritages, and between its historical birth contexts and the current politically diverse circumstances. We hope that the volume offers academic inspiration and encourages readers to reflect on the ever-important questions of one's opportunities and duties in the face of injustice.

8 Tiina Seppälä et al.

References

Arendt, H. (1972). Civil disobedience. In H. Arendt (Ed.), *Crises of the republic* (pp. 49–102). Harcourt Brace Jovanovich.

Brownlee, K. (2012). *Conscience and conviction: The case for civil disobedience*. Oxford University Press.

Cabrera, L. (2021). Global citizenship, global civil disobedience and political vices. In W. E. Scheuerman (Ed.), *The Cambridge companion to civil disobedience* (pp. 313–337). Cambridge University Press.

Celikates, R. (2014). Civil disobedience as a practice of civic freedom. In J. Tully (Ed.), *On global citizenship: James Tully in dialogue* (pp. 207–228). Bloomsbury Academic.

Celikates, R. (2016). Rethinking civil disobedience as a practice of contestation – beyond the liberal paradigm. *Constellations, 23*(1), 37–45. https://doi.org/10.1111/1467-8675.12216

Celikates, R. (2021). Radical democratic disobedience. In W. E. Scheuerman (Ed.), *The Cambridge companion to civil disobedience* (pp. 128–152). Cambridge University Press.

Çıdam, Ç., Scheuerman, W.E., Delmas, C., Pineda, E. R., Celikates, R., & Livingston, A. (2020). Theorizing the politics of protest: Contemporary debates on civil disobedience. *Contemporary Political Theory, 19*, 513–546. https://doi.org/10.1057/s41296-020-00392-7

Cooke, M., & Petherbridge, D. (2016). Civil disobedience and conscientious objection. *Philosophy and Social Criticism, 42*(10), 953–957. https://doi.org/10.1093/acrefore/9780190228637.013.114

Delmas, C. (2018). *A duty to resist: When disobedience should be uncivil*. Oxford University Press.

Delmas, C., & Brownlee, K. (2021). Civil disobedience. In E. N. Zalta (Ed.), *The Stanford encyclopedia of philosophy* (Winter 2021 Edition). https://plato.stanford.edu/archives/win2021/entries/civil-disobedience/

Hidalgo, J. S. (2019). *Unjust borders: Individuals and the ethics of immigration*. Routledge.

Scheuerman, W. E. (2019). Constituent power and civil disobedience: Beyond the nation-state? *Journal of International Political Theory, 15*(1), 49–66. https://doi.org/10.1177/1755088218806642

Scheuerman, W. E. (2020). Civil disobedience as an essentially contested concept. In Ç. Çıdam (Ed.), Critical exchange: Theorizing the politics of protest: Contemporary debates on civil disobedience. *Contemporary Political Theory, 19*, 517–522.

Scheuerman, W. E. (2021a). Political disobedience and the climate emergency. *Philosophy & Social Criticism*. https://doi.org/10.1177/01914537211040566

Scheuerman, W. E. (2021b). *The Cambridge companion to civil disobedience*. Cambridge University Press. https://doi.org/10.1017/9781108775748

Schock, K. (2021). Consequences of civil disobedience. In W. E. Scheuerman (Ed.), *The Cambridge companion to civil disobedience* (pp. 407–428). https://doi.org/10.1017/9781108775748.017

Thiri, M. A., Villamayor-Tomásad, S., Scheidela, A., & Demaria, F. (2022). How social movements contribute to staying within the global carbon budget: Evidence from a qualitative meta-analysis of case studies. *Ecological Economics, 195*. https://doi.org/10.1016/j.ecolecon.2022.107356

PART I

Civil disobedience then and now

2
THE CONCEPT AND PRACTICES OF CIVIL DISOBEDIENCE

Petri Koikkalainen, Tapio Nykänen, and Tiina Harjumaa

Whether we look at examples from history or contemporary politics, violating or ignoring the law for political reasons is nothing too rare or exceptional, but usually it is not taken to be a signal of healthy and functional political life. In well-ordered democracies, any attempt to circumvent the official channels of political representation can be considered suspicious or worse, whereas widespread political protests or civil unrest, especially when including violence, are often regarded as signs of major systemic problems, potentially anticipating serious difficulties or even downfall of the existing regime.

The specific notion of "civil disobedience" – that there could be a way of breaking the law and still staying on the morally speaking "right side" – constitutes an exception to the general rule according to which open public debate and free democratic institutions contain all means necessary for citizens to exercise political influence. What is more, when political acts against existing laws are recognised as "civil disobedience", their acceptability often increases and they may even become idealised expressions of civic activism, as in the famous mass protests utilising passive resistance and nonviolent action that were led and inspired by individuals like Mahatma Gandhi and Martin Luther King Jr. or, more recently, Greta Thunberg. In short, the concept of civil disobedience justifies deeds that might otherwise be unjustifiable, and unlike some other forms of protest, they do it in ways that appear to respect at least some of the "core values" of the given political community, instead of challenging their existence, as insurrectionist or revolutionary movements do.

In addition to the roles that "civil disobedience" may play as a political ideal, there are other ways in which the existence of that particular concept itself is noteworthy. First, insofar as "civil disobedience" is understood as a political act that follows a known pattern or procedure consisting of elements such as publicity, non-violence, and the acceptance of legal sanctions, it also provides practical guidance for political

DOI: 10.4324/9781003320494-3

activism.[1] If political campaigns utilising such "civil disobedience" prove successful, their exemplary force probably increases the likelihood of civil disobedience as a future political tactic. Second, and as already implied, the positive value associated with the concept can make it a powerful legitimation device. Deeds that follow the example set by civic leaders like Gandhi or King Jr. only in some part, or are even completely, against their spirit may be justified by associating them with just the name of the acts that such famous persons did. Third, the existence of a somehow fixed political concept is usually a starting point for its further theorisation and contestation. Various aspects of civil disobedience, such as nonviolence and the acceptance of legal sanctions, have been debated intensively among theorists since at least the 1960s and 1970s, which was the heyday of famous theoretical formulations by authors such as John Rawls, Hannah Arendt, and Ronald Dworkin. As can be noted from the history of several other key political concepts, the successful introduction of a major concept almost invariably leads to various competing interpretations of it.

While it may not be possible to give a final and absolutely correct definition of civil disobedience (and the purpose of this chapter or book is not to provide one), it is certainly possible to observe its practical uses and the various contexts in which it has been used. Following, for example, Candice Delmas, we may speak about 'public understandings' of civil disobedience (Delmas, 2018, pp. 23–24), which derive from observing its known public uses; the kinds of deeds that have been justified by it; ideologies it associates with; and behaviours that have been successfully justified by using the concept. In trying to grasp the content of such public understandings, there are at least two obvious contexts that must be considered: first, actual political life, for example, those social and political movements that have introduced civil disobedience and related concepts as their political strategies or "tools", and, second, the written formulations of the idea by various theorists and thinkers. The history of civil disobedience both as a practice and as a theorised concept goes back to at least the 19th century. Arguably, acts of civil disobedience have generally preceded at least their more elaborated theoretical and philosophical definitions (Delmas, 2018, pp. 25–26), as has been the case with many other central political concepts (see e.g. Pocock, 1975; Vinthagen, 2015, p. 3), but it also has to be acknowledged that in the case of civil disobedience, activism, and writing have been closely interconnected in the life of some central figures such as Henry David Thoreau, Gandhi, and King Jr.

While theoretical formulations may often come "after practice" in this sense, their role should not be underestimated as "only theoretical". Concise definitions of a political concept or "principle" are often also blueprints for practical action (consider Extinction Rebellion; see Smiles & Edwards, 2021). They allow quick and easy communication of ideas into new contexts and, for example, their translations into different languages. This, in turn, can enable the quick spread of novel political "tools" in the hands of activists to new areas. As will be shown in the later chapters of this volume, the history of crafting disobedient strategies "from Nepal to Norway" has for more than a century involved complex dialogues and networks

The concept and practices of civil disobedience **13**

between Asian, European, and American political activists and thinkers, leading to mutual learning of theoretical insights, concrete practices, and their justifications (Haapala, in this volume; Nykänen et al.; Vinthagen & Johansen, in this volume). Also, these theorisations allow the critical discussion and development of the concept, which can help in its more general justification and in developing new versions of the concept, which under changing circumstances can be converted back to practice as new forms of political action.

Given the modern history of more than one hundred years of civilly disobedient politics and thinking, providing brief examples of its "relevant public understandings" or "highly influential theorisations" almost necessarily leads to some kind of bias or injustice. Very simply put, the problem is that, if we grant that many of the leading theorists of civil disobedience during the last half a century or so have been Western and Anglo-American, they would probably not have been theorising the phenomenon in ways that they did unless some other individuals in other times and places (say, South Africa or India) had not thought and acted as they did. Another matter is whether they interpreted such events correctly, or even events that had happened recently in their own country.[2] With these caveats, we may acknowledge that since the latter half of the 20th century, Anglo-American philosophy and political theory, and within it especially John Rawls's formulations in his *A Theory of Justice* (1971/1973), are a very frequently quoted theoretical source. As a highly systematic philosopher, Rawls incorporated in his definition of civil disobedience many of the aspects discussed earlier, and despite its rather technical vocabulary, it can also be followed as a practical guideline for action – what things to do and what not to do. The definition also included many elements such as nonviolence and publicity that were already familiar from earlier thinkers.[3] In all brevity, civil disobedience, according to Rawls, was

> a public, nonviolent, conscientious yet political act contrary to law usually done with the aim of bringing about a change in the law or policies of the government.
>
> *(Rawls, 1971/1973, p. 364)*

Soon after this passage, Rawls (1971/1973) added several other important qualifications, including that there must be nothing "covert or secretive" about the disobedient act; that it must rest on "deeply held convictions" which address the sense of justice of the majority and "the commonly shared conception of justice that underlies the political order"; that it must be accompanied by "willingness to accept the legal consequences of one's conduct", and that civil disobedience is used only after "the normal appeals to the political majority have already been made in good faith and they have failed … civil disobedience is a last resort" (pp. 364–366, 373).

As Rawls himself openly acknowledged, this list of defining criteria was in large part a synthesis of influences from other thinkers that he accommodated to meet the needs of his general theory of justice. As such, it was also his interpretation of an existing "public understanding" of civil disobedience, highlighted by his insistence that all elements of his theory should be acceptable to "the majority of the community", which he believed really was the case. Against the backdrop of practical and theoretical influences that were then available to Rawls, it should also be noted that his collection of criteria was fairly extensive and stringent; Rawls notes the existence of alternative definitions (especially Howard Zinn's, Rawls, 1971/1973, pp. 364n, 366n), but remarks that they were broader and, in a way, more superficial than his. Because of its systematic and comprehensive nature and its later influence, Rawls's definition continues to be a decent starting point for analysing the mainstream views of civil disobedience in Western Anglophone political theory and, at least to some extent, political practice.

This is not to say that Rawls's is the best definition of civil disobedience, but that the term is even today used in public discourse in ways that in some significant part resemble the previously described "Rawlsian" notion of public, political, nonviolent, conscientious acts used as last-resort means to promote some higher good accepting the legal consequences that ensue. When politicians, scholars, lawyers, journalists, and other commentators praise or condemn disobedient activists because of their methods, their list of "accepted" behaviours often closely follows that definition. In other words, the public understanding of the term still overlaps with the "Rawlsian" theoretical heritage. Certainly, many activists and thinkers have not agreed with the whole list or the meaning of its individual items, but those who disagree have often done it explicitly against some parts of the "Rawlsian" definition, which they have seen for example as too narrow (see e.g. Brownlee, 2012; Celikates, 2021; Delmas, 2018; Scheuerman, 2021b). In terms of the more general history of ideas, the "Rawlsian" version of disobedience, which was regulated and "civil" in its practical expressions and philosophically followed the modern traditions of rationalism and enlightenment, resonated well with the student, anti-war, environmentalist, feminist, and other progressivist "new social movements" of the late 1960s and 1970s, which then figured prominently in the political scenes of various countries.

As a final note on Rawls's (1971/1973) definition, it should be added that in his theory of justice, civil disobedience is a meaningful concept only in well-ordered democratic societies where "the basic structure of society is nearly just" and there exists a "nearly just constitutional regime" (in contrast to for example Joseph Raz, who speaks on civil disobedience also in the context of illiberal regimes; see Raz, 1979). Under such circumstances, civil disobedience exercised within the previously discussed limits does not according to Rawls threaten the stability of constitutional democracy but merely reminds citizens of their shared underlying conception of justice (which according to Rawls should include equal liberties and sufficient equality) and thereby strengthens its moral basis and institutions. In the absence of just democratic institutions that could benevolently respond to civil disobedience, or a shared conception of justice that a disobedient minority could successfully invoke, civil disobedience properly speaking cannot exist or function. Rawls does not go very far in elaborating citizens' opportunities in less than nearly just societies or in clearly undemocratic or autocratic societies, but he does allow that "in certain circumstances militant action and other kinds of resistance are surely justified". In such cases, however, we are no longer discussing civil disobedience that seeks to support key democratic institutions, but "a more profound opposition to the legal order" in conditions that are so unjust that "one must try to prepare the way for even radical or revolutionary change" (pp. 351, 367–368).

Some notes on democratic theory and civil disobedience

In a democracy, the highest power by definition resides with "the people", but the opinion of the people about any significant political issue is usually divided. That is why democracy has, since the invention of the word in antiquity, been operationally defined as the power of the majority (Aristotle: the power of "the many"). In practice, the "will of the people" is construed from the multiplicity of individual opinions as the will of an arithmetic majority of individuals in the face of some choice or decision-making situation, for example the majority of all citizens in a popular vote, as in direct democracy, or the majority of their representatives, which is the case when a government rules with the support of a parliamentary majority. Majority rule may include formal safeguards for the rights of individuals and minorities such as bills of human rights and requirements of qualified majorities (e.g. two-thirds or three-fourths of votes), but the final say regarding legislation still stays in the hands of a majority. In modern political theory, it is also a very mainstream opinion to think that a fundamental aspect of *legitimacy* of a political regime is that it can be somehow demonstrated that laws and policy enjoy the majority's consent.

In majoritarian democracies, the crack in the edifice that opens up the route to civil disobedience (and obviously several other types of political activism) comes from the following consideration: while observable majorities can guarantee the *procedural soundness* of democratic decision-making, they are not a guarantee of its *substantial* or *moral soundness*. As, for example, Theo van Leeuwen has put it, majorities provide legitimation by way of "authorisation", but they are not a sufficient condition of legitimation by "morality" (van Leeuwen, 2007). Majorities do not necessarily make "right" or "fair" decisions, or, as Rawls (1971/1973) put it, "[t]here seems to be no way to characterize a feasible procedure guaranteed to lead to just legislation" (p. 360). Even if political institutions were designed perfectly, nothing can guarantee that decisions made by the majority would be optimal solutions for existing problems, that they would be the best protection against future risks, or that they would even treat all social groups and minorities in fair and non-discriminative ways, be *just*, to put it in a single word. Warnings of a "tyranny of the majority" in democracies have been sounded for more than 150 years by liberal political thinkers, in particular. The gradual historical evolution of political institutions through steps such as the constitutional division of powers, parliamentarianism, universal suffrage, constitutionally guaranteed basic human rights, transparency of government, and the like, may increase citizens' opportunities for participation and the procedural legitimacy of decision-making, but they cannot guarantee that all citizens would perceive the decisions as morally just.

16 Petri Koikkalainen et al.

These are all reasons why probably few modern political thinkers (or individual citizens, for that matter) would say that obedience to a law means surrendering one's judgement regarding the laws that one obeys. Obeying a speed limit need not always mean that one agrees with that speed limit but could result from other considerations, such as fear of punishment. Even Thomas Hobbes (1651/1962), whose political theory is often regarded as authoritarian and who recommended censorship of opinions that went against the sovereign's will, admitted in *Leviathan* that no one can really control what subjects think – but, of course, the sovereign was fully entitled to punish those subjects who made their unfitting thoughts public. Kant, in his essay "What Is Enlightenment", allowed freedom of speech in addition to the freedom of thought, as long as it did not lead to actual disobedience. In words that he put into the mouth of Prussia's enlightened absolutist king Frederick the Great, "Argue as much as you please, but obey!" (Kant, 1997). If thinking critically and publicly discussing the quality of the laws of one's country can be counted as steps towards breaking those laws, then Kant would allow them all except the real act of (civil) disobedience.

Following a similar logic, modern constitutions and declarations of human rights not only recognise the right of individuals to freely express their opinions about laws and policy, but they also grant citizens explicit political rights that allow public assemblies, demonstrations and pressure, and other ways of acting politically in order to change laws or policies. It could even be said that there are few things more *democratic* than the idea of people getting organised and acting collectively in order to replace an unjust law by a more just law or getting rid of a corrupt head of state or government in the hope of getting a fresh start under more virtuous leadership (see also Celikates, 2021). Especially the Rawlsian (and Arendtian) reading of civil disobedience also takes place in this generally speaking constitutionalist, democratic, and rationalist framework, where reason gradually replaces tradition and prejudice, and politics and laws obtain more humane and enlightened forms. While laws are meant as permanently standing rules at the time of their making, the state and its legislation as a whole are a historically changing and evolving entity in this greater scheme of things.

So, laws made by majorities may be imperfect, and the mere existence of laws is not generally considered to be a sufficient precondition of a good political community if they are not designed with the realisation of some higher good in mind – for Aristotle, the perfection of the *polis*; for modern utilitarians such as Bentham and Mill, the greatest public utility; and for the social-contractarian Rawls, his two principles of justice. When related to such higher goods, laws play the role of a tool. This observation opens the choice between obedience and disobedience from yet another angle. If an imperfect law serves a higher good only to some insufficient degree, at what point is the requirement to obey that law overridden by the need to disregard it in order to achieve greater justice? When can we ignore a badly functioning tool for the sake of the thing that the tool was designed for? Is there a point when one even has a *duty* to resist, via for example civil, or perhaps, ultimately, "uncivil" disobedience (Delmas, 2018)? And, if we follow the rationalist

The concept and practices of civil disobedience **17**

spirit of Enlightenment thinkers or their socially conscious progressivist later followers, we might also add: What if *history* seems to be on our side and law is clearly a result of some past prejudices or misunderstandings that reasonable persons would immediately fix?

Of course, the simple legalist or proceduralist answer to all these questions is that citizens (just as well as authorities) must always respect the laws, and if they are not content with them, they can try to change them through the channels of representative politics by voting and lobbying and using other forms of political pressure. In practice, the issue may not be as straightforward as this kind of "simple legalism" might assume. Even when not counting civil disobedience, there are many other occasions when individuals or authorities can "legitimately" do otherwise than follow the general law. As discussed earlier, authorities may withhold normally inviolable basic human rights in cases of emergencies such as a military threat or the spread of a pandemic. Also, individual citizens have for example the right to use reasonable (what is "reasonable" obviously varies) force, which in extreme cases can be lethal, as in self-defence to protect one's own life or the life of others. Depending on time and place, conscientious objectors have been treated as criminals and even executed, but in other jurisdictions, they may be legally exempted from military service. A head of state can grant amnesty to a convicted criminal who according to the general law should sit for life in prison. Other exceptional and borderline cases could be listed, but the main point here is that they testify of public understandings that recognise that laws sometimes lose in comparison against higher goods. The understanding that law cannot always be the final guide of action is also expressed in sayings such as *necessitas non habet legem*, "necessity knows no law", known in many languages, and, for example, in the Swedish theologian Olaus Petri's rules for judges from the 16th century and still printed in the preambles of Swedish and Finnish law books, the best known of which reads "what is not just and fair cannot be law either" (Tontti, 2000).

Now, while the examples listed earlier may support the view that the law is not even "officially" always the supreme guide for action, most of them are not truly extra-legal or extra-constitutional (Feldman, 2008). The use of emergency powers can be constitutionally justified even if it represses basic human rights, and if a citizen's otherwise illegitimate use of force in self-defence has been "reasonable" according to a court, then no law has been violated. An example of true extra-legalism on part of the government would be the "ticking bomb" case: officials torturing a suspected terrorist in the hope of gaining information that could prevent hundreds of deaths. This example (not only theoretical in light of for example recent American controversies on "waterboarding") provokes not only legal questions but also complex and open-ended political and moral considerations on means and ends (Feldman, 2008, p. 552, esp. n9). Civil disobedience, which in form and intent may be in complete opposition to the ticking bomb example, takes place in a similarly complicated area regarding the question of whether an act that breaks the law can be justified by the good it produces. The case of conscientious objection may elucidate some of the existing options. If a conscientious objector is officially

18 Petri Koikkalainen et al.

granted exemption from national service, then everything has gone according to the law and no disobedience occurs. In some other circumstances, courts sentence individual objectors to prison following ordinary crime case procedures. However, if there were several pacifist objectors who organised collectively and publicly explained their acts as a protest against an unjust war that their government has started or against its unfair conscription laws, then we would approach a case that could be classified as "civil disobedience" following even all items of the regulated and detailed Rawlsian definition. Legal sanctions could follow for the activists, but it is also conceivable that the publicity achieved could result in a change or reassessment in government policy or conscription laws or, at least, in a change of public opinion so that peaceful alternatives could stand a better chance in the future.

On justifications of civil disobedience: political judgement and the finiteness of time

How, then, can the decision be made that civil disobedience (or even uncivil disobedience) is the right course of action and that sufficient conditions for its justification exist? It must be obvious at this point that there are no universally accepted standards for those individuals who consider it, and relying on outside advice could be hazardous since an external advisor faces none of the risks of the situation. When governments face an exceptional crisis and consider the costs and benefits of declaring a state of emergency, they at least know that there is a possibility of "doing it legally" with the help of existing legislation, expert workforce, predesigned administrative procedures, and significant material resources from the taxpayers. None of these comforts is available to the disobedient citizen, and in addition to that, the threat of legal sanctions exists even if the act was conducted following for example the Rawlsian textbook definition, and the harms caused by sanctions can often reach beyond just suffering the immediate penalty. Engaging in civil disobedience must be one of the paradigmatic cases of exercising *political judgement* in the Arendtian sense (e.g. Biskowski, 1993; Schwartz, 2014), where there are no authoritative standards provided by the natural, technical, legal, economic, or other sciences, but agents must rely on their necessarily (at least partially) subjective assessments of every aspect of the situation, including the perceived strength of oneself against the others, direction and strength of public opinion, timing and other situational factors, and the possibility of unanticipated consequences. Why is an individual who considers civil disobedience so alone (at least judicially – socially she may be not alone at all) in this situation? In light of everything said so far, the answer seems to be that it could not be very much otherwise in the existing framework of liberal democratic and modern constitutional thinking. Once one *disobeys* the law, one leaves behind those institutional and moral supports that are associated with law and obedience, and even if legislators would sometimes feel sympathy for those who break laws for very good reasons, they cannot write into laws permits for overriding them because of personal judgement (and if legal exemptions exist, such as the conscientious objector

The concept and practices of civil disobedience **19**

example, they always occur within the law). As Rawls (1971/1973) put it in his *Theory of Justice* when discussing the justification of civil disobedience:

> In a democratic society, then, it is recognized that each citizen is responsible for his interpretation of the principles of justice and for his conduct in the light of them. There can be no legal or socially approved rendering of these principles that we are always morally bound to accept, not even when it is given by a supreme court or legislature.
>
> *(p. 390)*

Behind the philosophical formulation, these sentences recapitulate some very basic theoretical ideas of what it means to be a citizen in a democracy. As individuals, we have the capability of independent moral judgement regarding laws and values. We probably do not want to give up that judgement, the option of thinking otherwise, even if there are such things as supreme courts and legislatures that take normative decisions on our behalf. That is because even supreme courts and legislatures may sometimes err. We have individual capabilities for action, for example, to speak out our opinions and to obey or disobey the law. Therefore, it is ultimately our own decision how we morally judge things such as laws and whether we somehow change our conduct in light of those judgments. As citizens, we are aware that there can be social and other consequences that result from our actions. If our conduct puts us outside of the law, then it does leave us alone in this juridical respect, but the available support, comfort, and sense of community might come from another, political direction: our connection to other people who agree and sympathise with our case and could even join it, if they perceive it as genuine and important enough.

A central factor when considering the justifiability of civil disobedience is *time*, or in other words, the difficulty of political and judicial institutions to respond to urgent issues quickly enough. Political time can be counted as the time before the next elections, which can be far too long in an urgent crisis, or more generally, as the finiteness of human life and the permanent and irreversible harms that can be caused if issues are not responded to soon enough. "We have waited for more than 340 years for our constitutional and God given rights", wrote Martin Luther King, Jr. in 1963 in a letter smuggled to his supporters from the Birmingham city jail (King Jr., 1963). This was part of his response to those who urged the civil rights movement to "Wait!" (for the Birmingham city administration to act) instead of engaging in direct action including civil disobedience. On the other side of the balance, King Jr. argued, was the concrete and continuous experience of seeing "vicious mobs lynch your mothers and fathers at will and drown your sisters and brothers at whim … hate filled policemen curse, kick and even kill your black brothers and sisters", and more (King Jr., 1963). As King Jr. very clearly understood ("This 'Wait' has almost always meant 'Never'"), sticking to institutional procedures can be a way of playing time and delaying reforms almost indefinitely.

Moreover, insofar as the issues concern the interpretation of the law, there is the argument about the "inherent conservatism of the legal profession" (Bodenheimer, 1948),

20 Petri Koikkalainen et al.

suggesting that judges and lawyers are comparatively slow in adopting new or radical views about politics and morality and that new ideas are often accepted widely before their existence is legally recognised and regulated. So, if the law is "a force holding back rather than pushing forward; that it operates as a brake upon the dynamic forces in human society" (Bodenheimer, 1948, p. 233), then the conclusion for the disobedient activist must be that relying on judges and lawyers is not nearly always the wisest choice when trying to move ahead. If the existing laws or their interpretations are perceived as harmful, then the reactive and conservative nature of jurisprudence creates additional pressure to move ahead faster than official institutional time. Activists often remind that today's minority opinions are often held by tomorrow's majorities, and the purpose of those authorities who urge us to wait can be just to uphold the existing status quo. Still, many of the classical theorists of civil disobedience such as Gandhi and Rawls did not usually recommend rapid action but cautious political judgement also regarding the timing of disobedience. For Rawls, famously, civil disobedience is justified only as a last resort action, which means that one is required to try legal means until it is completely obvious that they are fruitless.[4]

It is typical for the classical theorists to perceive civil disobedience as a kind of *right* that citizens are morally and politically justified to use when certain conditions are met (e.g. Brownlee, 2012; Dworkin, 1978; Rawls, 1973; Raz, 1979). An important alternative way to approach justification is to see resistance as a *duty*, a political obligation, when facing injustices that are grave enough. For example, Candice Delmas (2018), following Gandhi, Dworkin, and others, claims that we have several morally binding reasons to consider resistance as a duty and not just as a right. Delmas introduces principles of justice and fairness, Samaritan duty, and our responsibilities to the political community as such reasons. According to her, these ethical principles create a strong political obligation to resist oppression.

If one sees resistance as a moral duty, then it is perhaps tempting to open a door not only to civil disobedience but also to other possibly effective extra-legal means to resist oppression. For example, Delmas defends what she calls "uncivil disobedience", a way of resistance that may include "incivility", that is a lack of decorum, but also for example violence for self-defence and limited destruction of property, if that seems to be the least harmful way to achieve legitimate and justified goals (Delmas, 2018, pp. 49, 58–71). According to Delmas, also this kind of disobedience strengthens a rule of law, as it in the long-term bolsters law's integrity just not unlike civil disobedience and stabilises the society (Delmas, 2018, pp. 54–55). Uncivil disobedience is discussed further in this volume later, both in a positive and a more critical tone (Kukko, in this volume; Kumar, in this volume).

The tensions and paradoxes of civil disobedience

The previous sections introduced mainstream definitions of civil disobedience that arguably are close to relevant Western public understandings of the concept and examined some ways of justifying it within the Western constitutional and liberal democratic traditions. While it is important to know such definitions, also because

The concept and practices of civil disobedience **21**

their justifications bear some practical relevance, one purpose of this book and finally also this chapter is to gradually move away from theory towards observing civil disobedience in practice. This also entails studying the fit between theory and practice, acknowledging that Rawls's vision of civil disobedience is only a particular and limited view of political action in which disobedient action could be present. While it is possible to imagine a well-ordered society normatively based on a nearly just constitutional regime, where the function and practices of civil disobedience are regulated according to Rawls's theory, the reality is usually much fuzzier. Rawls himself acknowledged that his entire theory presented (a normative) "general framework" to be approached, in other words not a strict description of reality (Rawls, 1971/1973, p. viii). One of the relevant questions that could be addressed to Rawls himself could be, whether for example the activists of the 1960s' Black civil rights movement who inspired his theory really believed that they lived in a well-ordered, nearly just society? Was the intent of their disobedience really the defence of the basic structure of their society, or were their goals actually much more socially transformative, even radical or revolutionary?

Critics of civil disobedience often invoke the apparent tensions and paradoxes within the concept. Probably the most obvious and common of these paradoxes is the following: If people make laws for themselves in democracies, why should some individuals feel justified to break them? The practical benefit of the philosophical definitions is that they address precisely that question. They attempt to answer why disobeying the law can be morally acceptable or recommendable, or even a duty, even if the act itself remains punishable. Such answers have no legally binding power, but under certain circumstances, they may have significant powers of moral and political persuasion that could make an appeal even to the majorities. Nevertheless, some other potential tensions and paradoxes remain. We discuss three of them briefly in order to reveal some of the tensions and contradictions that can emerge in the actual uses of the concept and theories of civil disobedience.

a. *Organisation and skills.* While the philosophical accounts of civil disobedience emphasise individual moral reasoning (because there is always an individual and social component in the decision to disobey, even if one belongs to a group), the practice of civil disobedience often follows interactional dynamics that are typical of social movements. If civil disobedience is portrayed as a means of democratic politics that serves especially the disenfranchised and marginalised, then its successful practice requires considerable skills and resources that few individuals possess alone. Successful disobedient groups, too, probably need (self-)education and experience. They must be able to judge the gravity of the situation, successfully articulate the values or principles one is invoking, stay connected to the public opinion, design tactics so that they minimise the threat of violence, choose the right moment for action, and so on. The public nature of civil disobedience requires excellent communications skills and possibly legal skills (see Nykänen et al., in this volume). Since civil disobedience is often a collective undertaking, a large-scale mass protest, leadership and organisational skills may be needed not only for mobilisation but also for giving guidelines for the action and managing it. Deviations from the "civil" and non-violent approach could ruin the image of the protesters in the eyes of the public opinion (even nonviolent civil disobedience can possibly do that in some situations; see Seppälä, in this volume). Once there are leaders and followers, criticisms can emerge from both inside and outside of the group, for example, accusations of elitism or avant-gardism that may result in internal fractions that are typical of social and political movements.[5] When discussing civil disobedience, the dynamics and tendencies that generally apply to social movements are often worthy of consideration. The potential professionalisation, centralisation, or fractionalisation of disobedient movements may not directly result from the nature of disobedient acts themselves, but effective collective disobedience does require mobilisation and organisation to the degree that can make a collective protest resemble a more conventional social movement, whether it wants to call itself one or not.

b. *Goals.* While it is almost a practical necessity to justify civil disobedience by some higher goals or principles, there is considerable disagreement about what such goals could be. Rawls's "two principles of justice" are a systematic philosophical attempt to formulate precisely such goals, but their usability as a practical political guideline is rather limited. Many activists appeal to universal human rights, such as minority rights as recognised in national or international documents and declarations (Luoma-Aho, in this volume; Nykänen et al., in this volume), which might be understood as a fairly accurate approximation of the idea of invoking generally or even universally recognised principles of justice. Still, even if one would choose to strictly follow Rawls's definition, the individual interpretations of whether one lives in a "well-ordered society" and wants to defend its basic social structure are likely to deviate much from each other. In other words, even under the regulated mainstream definitions, some ambiguity remains over when *exactly* civil disobedience is justified. Moreover, the regulated definition is certainly not the whole picture. Thoreau, who introduced the term "civil disobedience" into Anglophone debate, deviated from it in his perception of pre-Civil War United States as not a legitimate government.[6] Gandhi, too, regarded South Africa and India in the early 20th century as countries that demanded fundamental social and political change and the same applies to large parts of the Black civil rights movement in the United States in the 1960s and 1970s. These movements were more radically transformative than what Rawls later proposed, but if we take the notion of public understandings of civil disobedience seriously, then it would not make much sense to claim that their actions could not be morally justifiable or that they do not fall under the concept of "civil disobedience".

There are, of course, alternative ways of formulating the moral principles or political-social goals that would justify (nonviolent) resistance and especially civil disobedience, such as Gandhi's *satyagraha* (Vinthagen, 2015); Hannah Arendt's emphasis to the collective consent, social contract and "spirit of laws"

(Arendt, 1972, pp. 85–102[7]; see also Arendt, 1970); and Delmas's justice, Samaritan duty, fairness, and political membership (Delmas, 2018). By following these ideals, one is likely to be able to separate at least some rights from wrongs. However, some possible paradoxes remain. What if, for example, different oppressed minorities disagree on the nature of just social contract or the "true" spirit of laws? Maybe they have different views on fairness, the gravity of injustices or even on truth? If this is the case, it gets at least more complicated to decide which goals exactly justify the action, even if the participants would agree on the importance of principles like justice and fairness on some general level (it is worth considering, of course, that it is *enough* that people agree on these principles in general level).

Another paradox may arise if the "higher goal" behind civil disobedience is based on values associated with a national or ethnic identity, as shared by a majority of the population. Of course, reading carefully the definitions by theorists such as Rawls, Arendt, or Dworkin would not endorse civil disobedience with an appeal to the "sense of justice" of a religious, national, or ethnic majority, but it is possible to construe cases which come uncomfortably close to the "justifiable" examples.[8] One of the relevant considerations is that in this area there can be grey zones and slippery slopes and one really needs the ability to practise political judgement in Hannah Arendt's sense. Moreover, one should be aware that there are possibilities to mislead by using the good name of civil disobedience for purposes that are much narrower than its previously described spirit. Therefore, one should be careful about the uses of "civil disobedience" as a blanket justification for protests and resistance on the grounds that they "tick many of the boxes" in its prevailing public understanding. In other words, even if protesters themselves define their actions as civil disobedience, it is not always clear if the definition is correct in a relevant theoretical respect.

c. *Differences in historical context.* If we look at actual historical examples of civil disobedience, we perceive many different forms and examples of political action. Some of them, such as Gandhi, were parts of anti-colonialist or anti-imperialist movements that sought political independence. Martin Luther King Jr. and Nelson Mandela sought to rectify the status of legally underprivileged groups in racially segregated political communities. In marked contrast to these examples, the archetypal Rawlsian civil disobedient enjoys fully recognised citizenship in a political community the basic structure of which he or she perceives as just. Therefore, the resulting image of disobedient activism is different: the ideal type might be a 1960s–1970s' anti-war, civil rights, feminist or environmentalist "new social movement", organised by students and academic intellectuals, who possess the skills and resources required for "regulated" civil disobedience. These movements were often close to the parties of the left, and later the green parties, and many of their leaders later rose to prominence in mainstream national politics (consider Joschka Fischer or Finnish president Tarja Halonen). The question then is, How historically particular was this climate of 1960s to 1980s progressivist politics, which was generally sympathetic

24 Petri Koikkalainen et al.

to social movements, and how much, for example, Rawls's theory depended on its existence (see also Arendt, 1970; Haapala, in this volume)? If that mindset provided a "shared sense of justice" that at a certain point in time provided opportunities for social activism including civil disobedience, do we have it any longer? Does the perceived moral polarisation and fragmentation of societies prevent any successful attempts to appeal to any single shared conception of justice? (According to Rawls, civil disobedience did not apply to "morally fractured" societies where there is no shared moral basis.) Another important issue to consider is globalisation. If it was enough for the activists of the previous generations to address national laws and governments, the current protests often address global problems, such as climate change, where the need to appeal to people, raise awareness, and produce a change in norms and institutions cannot be made effectively in national contexts only.

For the future

There are tensions and paradoxes in contemporary civil disobedience, but we believe the concept has not lost its explanatory nor normative power. The world is not fair; many societies are not just; the political-environmental problems the globe is facing are tantalising in scale. Moreover, there is no absolute way to guarantee that laws and regulations made by states and their alliances are just more than there were in the 1970s. The need for political judgement and moral considerations has not disappeared. This applies also to the world where there is simultaneously an obvious need to defend the importance of constitutions and fidelity to the lawful democratic processes.

However, it seems likely that the content of "civil disobedience" needs reflection and reconsideration in order to stay as a practically meaningful concept. Such reconsiderations have already been done by scholars such as Kimberley Brownlee, William E. Scheuerman, Candice Delmas, Robin Celikates, and Maeve Cooke, among others, and this book gives its own contribution to the discussion. It introduces empirical examples of civil disobedience and asks what has been meaningful in them, both for the participants and for the results that followed. Moreover, it not only seeks to find viable extensions to the concept in the 2020s but looks also for classic elements that are worth holding on to for the struggles to come.

Notes

1 As seen clearly in the actions of Extinction Rebellion, for example. See for example Smiles and Edwards (2021); for a more critical approach, see Scheuerman (2021a).
2 Delmas (2018) for example argues that Rawls downplayed the radical and revolutionary character of the United States' Black civil rights movement, which clearly was an inspiration to his theory (pp. 26–29).
3 As direct influences to the definition below, Rawls (1971, p. 364n) mentions H. A. Bedau, Thoreau, and King Jr., with Howard Zinn giving a definition that is broader than what Rawls wanted to commit himself to.

The concept and practices of civil disobedience **25**

4 Third perspective to time in civil disobedience can perhaps be found from Gandhi's *satyagraha*. It encourages firmness, and hence, patience: one should not give up in the face of continued injustice. (See Vinthagen, 2015.)
5 Among others, Extinction Rebellion has aimed to create as non-hierarchical and "leaderless" organisations as possible. This aim has been criticised as "fantasmatic endeavour", as there are power structures in any form of organised endeavour (Fotaki & Foroughi, 2021).
6 Also, Thoreau did not start his tax boycott in public and the main justification he gave for it was "what I think is right", which are other issues that could separate his version of civil disobedience from many current definitions.
7 On Arendt's important term "political responsibility", see Herzog (2004).
8 This is feedback that many Central and Eastern European colleagues gave when Petri Koikkalainen was presenting the research project *Rethinking Nordic Democracy. Civil Disobedience in Exceptional Times* in the conference "Visions of Democratic Europe under Debate", Second Workshop of the COST Action RECAST at the University of Bucharest, 29 to 30 May 2019. An imaginable case could be a group of citizens organising a "peaceful and public" blocking out of an ethnic minority outside of the nation's territory in order to defend widely shared national values.

References

Arendt, H. (1970, September 4). Reflections civil disobedience. *The New Yorker*, September 12, 1970 Issue. https://www.newyorker.com/magazine/1970/09/12/reflections-civil-disobedience

Arendt, H. (1972). *Crises of the republic: Lying in politics; civil disobedience; on violence; thoughts on politics and revolution*. Mariner Books.

Biskowski, L. J. (1993). Practical foundations for political judgment: Arendt on action and world. *The Journal of Politics, 55*(4), 867–887. https://doi.org/10.2307/2131940

Bodenheimer, E. (1948). The inherent conservatism of the legal profession. *Indiana Law Journal, 23*(3), 221–235. https://www.repository.law.indiana.edu/cgi/viewcontent.cgi?article=3838&context=ilj

Brownlee, K. (2012). *Conscience and conviction: The case for civil disobedience*. Oxford University Press.

Celikates, R. (2021). Radical democratic disobedience. In W. Scheuerman (Ed.), *The Cambridge companion to civil disobedience* (pp. 128–152). Cambridge University Press.

Delmas, C. (2018). *A duty to resist: When disobedience should be uncivil*. Oxford University Press.

Dworkin, R. (1978). *Taking rights seriously* (5th ed.). Harvard University Press.

Feldman, L. C. (2008). Judging necessity – Democracy and extra-legalism. *Political Theory, 36*(4), 550–577. https://www.jstor.org/stable/pdf/20452651.pdf?refreqid=excelsior%3Abfb3fd5dbae50ac0cae0cf968bb0fc30

Fotaki, M., & Foroughi, H. (2021). Extinction Rebellion: Green activism and the fantasy of leaderlessness in a decentralized movement. *Leadership*, 1–23. https://doi.org/10.1177/17427150211005578

Herzog, A. (2004). Hannah Arendt's concept of responsibility. *Studies in Social and Political Thought, 10*(3), 39–52.

Hobbes, T. (1962). *Leviathan or the matter, form, and power of a commonwealth, ecclesiastical and civil*. J. M. Dent & Sons Ltd. (Original work published 1651)

Kant, I. (1997). What is enlightenment? (Trans. Halsall, P.) *Modern history sourcebook*, Fordham University. https://sourcebooks.fordham.edu/mod/kant-whatis.asp (Original work published 1784).

King, Jr., M. L. (1963, April 16). [Letter from a Birmingham Jail] Online resources. African Studies Center, University of Pennsylvania, USA. https://www.africa.upenn.edu/Articles_Gen/Letter_Birmingham.html

Pocock, J. G. A. (1975). *The Machiavellian moment: Florentine political thought and the Atlantic Republican tradition.* Princeton University Press.

Rawls, J. (1973). *A theory of justice.* Oxford University Press. (Originally published in 1971).

Raz, J. (1979). *The authority of law: Essays on law and morality.* Clarendon Press.

Scheuerman, W. E. (2021a). Political disobedience and the climate emergency. *Philosophy & Social Criticism.* https://doi.org/10.1177/01914537211040566

Scheuerman, W. E. (2021b). *The Cambridge companion to civil disobedience.* Cambridge University Press. https://doi.org/10.1017/9781108775748

Schwartz, J. P. (2014). *Hannah Arendt's theory of political judgment.* [Doctoral Dissertation, Duke University]. DukeSpace, Duke University Libraries. https://dukespace.lib.duke.edu/dspace/bitstream/handle/10161/8798/Schwartz_duke_0066D_12520.pdf?sequence=1

Smiles, T., & Edwards, G. A. S. (2021). How does Extinction Rebellion engage with climate justice? A case study of XR Norwich. *The International Journal of Justice and Sustainability, 26*(12), 1445–1460. https://doi.org/10.1080/13549839.2021.1974367

Tontti, J. (2000). Olaus Petri and the rules for judges. *Associations – Journal for Social and Legal Theory, 4*(1), 113–128.

van Leeuwen, T. (2007). Legitimation in discourse and communication. *Discourse & Communication, 1*(1), 91–112. https://doi.org/10.1177/1750481307071986

Vinthagen, S. (2015). *A theory of nonviolent action: How civil resistance works.* Zed Books.

3

EXPERIMENTS WITH CIVIL DISOBEDIENCE DURING NORWEGIAN ENVIRONMENTAL STRUGGLES, 1970–2000

Stellan Vinthagen and Jørgen Johansen

Introduction

From the 1950s, the Norwegian environmental movement drew from two important sources of inspiration: the writings and practice of nonviolent activism of Mohandas Karamchand Gandhi, and the eco-philosophical traditions of Peter Wessel Zapffe, Arne Næss, and Sigmund Kvaløy Setreng (with the last two being heavily influenced by Gandhi). The Norwegian environmental movement has combined a serious theoretical interest with the practice of ideas during societal conflicts. Groups, networks, and campaigns have continuously developed strategies in the spirit of nonviolent Gandhian traditions. Civil disobedience has frequently been an integrated part of the strategies.

This chapter aims to improve our understanding of how the strategic use of civil disobedience (CD) has developed in the Norwegian environmental movement. The questions we want to focus on are (1) What are the main changes in the use of CD from 1970 to 2000? and (2) What were the driving forces that made it possible that the use of CD changed from a small experiment to an advanced political strategy? This is done by analysing four key cases of environmental struggles. They represent different phases in the development and show how leading activists tested a series of new strategies of resistance, where CD was a key element. All four cases relate to environmental opposition to large-scale systems for electricity production.

One of the authors, Jørgen Johansen, was engaged in the movement from the early 1970s, and much of the material used in this chapter is from his own archives of unpublished notes, internal newsletters, and letters from other activists. Three documentary movies are additional sources for the first three cases: *Kampen om Mardøla* (The struggle for Mardøla) by Oddvar Einarsson (1972), *La elva leve* (Let the river live) by Bredo Greve (1980), and *Prognose Innerdalen* (Prognosis Innerdalen)

DOI: 10.4324/9781003320494-4

28 Stellan Vinthagen and Jørgen Johansen

by Oddvar Einarsson (1981). For the last example, there are mainly personal notes, two books and newspaper articles used as sources.

Before we look at these four cases, we need to trace the use of the concept and practice of CD in Norway.

Roots of nonviolent action and CD in Norway

The Norwegian philosophy and practice of nonviolent action is influenced by other countries and traditions but is, to a large extent, its own unique and domestic exploration. The roots of the modern environmental movement in Norway can be traced back to the doctoral thesis *Om det tragiske* (On the tragic) Zapffe wrote in the years prior to the occupation of Norway on April 9, 1940. The thesis argues that humans are born with an overdeveloped skill of understanding and self-knowledge, which does not fit well into nature (Zapffe 1941). The human craving for justification regarding matters such as life and death cannot be satisfied. Destruction of other forms of life and essentially the existential platform we need for survival (nature) can be seen as a consequence of this. His supervisor Arne Næss got inspired and later combined parts of Zapffe's perspectives on the relation between nature and humans with Gandhian philosophy, in his writings on "deep ecology" from the 1970s.

Two people came to be important partners with Næss in the introduction of Gandhian thinking in Norway and globally. The first was Johan Galtung, who was key to establishing *Peace research* as an academic field in the world, and the other was Sigmund Kvaløy, who became a key person in the experiments with CD in Norway. Næss and Galtung early on laid the foundation in arguably one of the best books on Gandhi ever written, *Gandhis politiske etikk* (The political ethics of Gandhi; Galtung & Næss, 1955). Although it was never translated into English (it is hard to understand why this has not yet happened), it is still in print in Norway and had a strong impact on two generations of politically minded Norwegians who later become key figures in civil society.

When Gandhi's birth anniversary in 1969 arrived with conferences, new books, and multiple events worldwide, Næss, Galtung, and Kvaløy travelled through Europe and the Middle East to India in a VW bus to participate, discuss, and learn (Setereng, 2010). They took part in a conference and one month of research at the Gandhian Institute in Varanasi. As they returned, they felt inspired and ready to continue their "mission" to disseminate Gandhian ideas in Norway and beyond.

One key, and controversial, element in the Gandhian strategy was what today is labelled CD: the tactic of intentionally, openly, and peacefully taking the risk to violate a law, norm, or order and facing the consequences (Vinthagen, 2015). This type of resistance goes back a long way in human history, although in the last 150 years or so, it has received the attention of authors and researchers. The term and its meaning have developed over time, and the definition is still contested, as we have seen in the introduction to this book. A foundational text that outlines the approach of CD was written by Henry David Thoreau in 1849. This booklet was originally titled "Resistance to Civil Government", but some years after Thoreau's death, it was retitled and the term "civil disobedience" was coined. Thoreau (1849, p. 6) argued that if an injustice of a government is "of such a nature that it requires injustice to another [you should] break the law [and] let your life be a counter friction to stop the machine". Since then, CD has been used in a number of very different contexts.

Of particular interest in the context of this book is that another root of the concept goes back to the Finnish struggle against Russification around the turn of the century (1899–1906). Viktor Theodor Homén published *Passiivinen vastarin-tamme: poliittisia kirjoituksia 1899–1904* (Homén, 1907) and used the term "passive resistance". This is also the concept used by Gandhi when he started his struggle in South Africa in the same period. To what degree this Finnish experience was important for the thinking and use of this particular form of struggle in Norway, we do not know for sure. But the experiments with passive resistance inspired Arne Næss to start researching how it was possible to use these means in group conflicts. The aforementioned *Gandhis politiske etikk* (Galtung & Næss, 1955), and Naess' (1974) book *Gandhi and Group Conflict: An Exploration of Satyagraha, Theoretical Background*, carefully analysed power relations, ethics, and the more philosophical sides of the different nonviolent actions used by Gandhi.

Etymologists have traced the first written use of the term, and its German equivalent "Passiver widerstand", back to 1819. Steven Huxley (1990) discusses the etymology of passive resistance in *Constitutionalist Insurgency in Finland: Finnish "Passive Resistance" against Russification as a Case of Nonmilitary Struggle in the European Resistance Tradition* (see especially pp. 52–53). It was applied mainly to constitutionalist and nationalist struggles and was initially used for different kinds of peaceful pressure within existing laws, but later also to openly disobey laws through mass noncooperation. The term was also used during Hungary's struggle against Austria. The Hungarian campaign influenced many similar struggles in the decades to follow. Ireland and Finland are two such cases (Randle, 1994). The book by Homén was published in both Finnish and Swedish and is the first known example of its use in Nordic languages. However, after the successful fight against the Russification of Finland (Huxley, 1990), it seems like the term disappeared from the vocabulary for a long time. Those that took up the ideas and tradition were then Næss, Galtung, and Kvaløy from the 1950s onwards but then as "nonviolent action" and "civil disobedience." Arne Næss invited Gene Sharp to join them in Oslo in the mid-1950s, and Sharp interviewed many who took part in the nonviolent struggle against the Nazi regime (Johansen, 2021, p. 45). Sharp later became the leading authority on studies of nonviolent actions, where CD was a crucial part of his research.

As we have seen in this section, while the ideas of "passive resistance" had circulated earlier, the thinking and writing on the topic took a sharp turn from the 1950s with the Gandhian influence on three young men: Kvaløy, Naess, and Galtung. They all brought the ideas into different disciplines and areas. With them the Gandhian approach to "civil disobedience" became influential on a new generation of activists, particularly from the 1970s onwards when these philosophical ideas were put into practice in concrete campaigns. And, despite that the practice of CD has deep roots in popular struggles for democratic rights and freedoms in Norway,

30 Stellan Vinthagen and Jørgen Johansen

going back hundreds of years, as described in *Den nødvendige ulydigheten* (Johansen & Persen, 1998), it was in the environmental movement that explicit and different tactical approaches to CD emerged and was developed. That period of 50 years of experimentation with CD is what this chapter focuses on.

Four cases illustrate the strategic development of CD

For many years, Norway has produced and consumed more electricity per capita than any other country in the world, except Canada. Most of the electricity comes from waterfalls with enormous destruction to nature, culture, fauna, and flora. Opposition to building huge hydroelectric power stations in Norway goes back more than 100 years. The botanist Hanna Resvold-Holmsen argued strongly against it already in 1917 (Esmark & Steele, 2020). She was one of many who saw the negative impact these constructions had on nature. From the early 1970s, Norway was in a unique situation with many informal networks of non-governmental organisations, political parties, trade unions, farmers' and women's organisations, and environmental groups. These networks formed when the first referendum on membership of the European Economic Community took place in 1972, leading to an unexpected defeat for EEC membership. Those networks made it easier for later campaigns to mobilise people and resources.

In the following, we show how the use and strategic thinking of CD have developed in Norway over the last 50 years. The leading persons in the CD campaigns were all Gandhians and have followed his principles when making experiments. The subtitle of Gandhi's autobiography is "My experiments with truth" and shall be understood as one of the most important conclusions he draws from his life as an activist. He wanted people to test out new strategies and techniques to resist injustice and violence (Gandhi, 1927). This was an important message for those who wanted to try out CD in societal conflicts in Norway.

Within these case studies, we can also detect a variation of specialised forms of CD. From the first *small-scale civil disobedience*, the blockade of a construction site in 1970, the main lesson was that there were too few participants to make a difference. Ten years later, a *large-scale civil disobedience* campaign was carried out. And almost simultaneously, a *constructive CD* occupation was experimented with. Although the last example included in this chapter occurred almost 20 years later, it still builds on the previous experiences, and it can be labelled *deterrent CD*. Here thousands of people signed a pledge to use CD if two planned huge gas-powered stations were built.

Each of the cases is briefly described and some conclusions are drawn. We also discuss the specific impact CD had in these four campaigns.

Mardøla – small-scale civil disobedience

Introduction and organisation

After returning from India in 1969, Kvaløy and Næss introduced the idea of CD to a network of environmental activists. They wanted to avoid a huge bureaucratic organisation and aimed for small groups connected in a loose network. This network of cooperating groups for nature and environmental protection was written in small letters and in parentheses (snm)[1] to show that the organisation was less important than the activities and campaign work (Kvaløy, 1984).

The Mardøla waterfalls were impressive, with more than 700-metre cascades of water falling down from the mountain. Mountainous Norway has many waterfalls and the industrialists in the Parliament saw these as sources of cheap energy. "Collect the water in pipelines and let a generator produce electricity" was the mantra (Regjeringen, n.d.). Nature was not seen as having a value in itself. And threats to biodiversity were not on the agenda. Arguments from those who opposed the destruction of nature were ignored, and few of the people in power bothered to participate in a serious discussion.

The CD component

The Gandhian idea to place your own body on the line inspired the activists, which they used to prevent the construction of dams and infrastructure. They viewed it as an interesting experiment to get attention. The activists wanted to force parliamentarians, media, and a wider audience to participate in a serious discussion about the value of preserving nature. This form of *conflict escalation* had never been used in Norway earlier (Sørensen & Johansen, 2016). (snm) hoped that openly and nonviolently violating laws, refusing to follow orders from the police, and presenting arguments for why such actions were necessary should persuade enough people to stop the dam construction and prevent the destruction of the waterfalls (Fadnes, 2020).

In the summer of 1970, from July 25 to August 6, several actions took place. Small groups of activists from (snm) sat down on the roads, blockading transports and preventing heavy machinery from working. Local people joined and supported the CD. This immediately attracted media attention, first, in local news outlets, and soon the actions reached the headlines in national newspapers, as well as radio and TV. When a counter-demonstration was organised with banners like "Hippies go home. If you have any?" the media attention escalated.

An additional element of escalation was when the recognised professor Arne Næss joined the activists and participated in the blockade. This was done in the tradition of the world-famous philosopher Bertrand Russell, who participated in CD against nuclear weapons in the 1950s and 1960s and argued there is sometimes a case for breaking the law (Russell, 2013). When world-famous and well-respected academics use CD, it gets more attention. During one of the actions, an iconic photo was taken of two policemen carrying Arne Næss to the police car.

Part of the story is that as a true follower of Gandhi, Arne stressed that the police officers were not the target of the actions, as they were just doing their job. He urged all activists to show respect for the police. In the rough terrain, Næss gave instructions to the police about how to carry him without risking injuries to their backs (Interview 1979 with Kvaløy by J. Johansen). The real target group of the CD was the Parliament, which gave permission to build the dam, and the companies making a profit from it. However, more than anything else, the aim was to educate

32 Stellan Vinthagen and Jørgen Johansen

ordinary citizens about the importance of preserving nature and the ecosystems for future generations. That the waterfalls were impressive and attractive for tourists was an additional argument used by the activists.

Discussion

The actions by (snm) in 1970 did not prevent the dam construction in Mardøla. There were too few participants and no experience of how to handle media. Sigmund Kvaløy enjoyed telling the story that in order to look like a huge crowd, each activist was asked to bring more than one tent to the protest camp (Interview 1979 with Kvaløy by J. Johansen).

Despite not achieving their main goal, in retrospect it is clear that these actions paved a new path for a more radical approach within the broader environmental movement. The actions opened up the development of a better equipped tool-box for environmental groups. Radical actions like CD moved from the fringe to becoming a central technique for groups who opposed the industrial exploitation of nature. When respected people participated, it was not easy for the establishment to dismiss them as extremists. And those who thought violation of laws was too extreme could support by engaging in more traditional civil society activities. This resulted in mainstream environmental organisations getting more members in the following years. The biggest one, the Norwegian Society for Nature Conservation, saw a 50% increase in members in 1970 (Norges Naturvernforbund, 1971, p. 3). In some way, it could be argued that the struggle contributed to long-term changes. Two years later, the first minister of the environment was established in the Norwegian government, and in 1973, a national plan for protection of rivers was passed in the Parliament.

It cannot be proved to what extent the increased focus on environmental issues was caused by the use of CD. But public discussions increased when arrested activists covered the front of newspapers and got attention from TV and radio stations. Two themes of that debate can be identified: one concerning the use of CD and one concerning the environmental and political issues at stake. These two discussions are still central in Norwegian society, 50 years later. Therefore, we can conclude that Mardøla was a key part of that formative process of environmental awareness and that the novel use of CD was a key part of making Mardøla into a symbol.

Alta – large-scale civil disobedience

Introduction and organisation

In the late 1970s, the next huge conflict about energy production in Norway entered the scene. Again, the plans by industrialists and politicians were to build a huge dam, fill a canyon with water and produce electricity, this time in Alta. Since 1973, a group named the Alta committee for the perseverance of the Alta-Kautokeino[2] waterways had been documenting the detrimental effects on salmon and the nature of the Alta canyon (Parmann, 1980). When it became clear that the Sámi reindeer herders in northern Norway were under threat, the conflict escalated.

In July 1978, an organisation was founded: the People's Action against the Development of the Alta-Kautokeino waterways.[3] With a formal structure, board and annual meetings, it functioned like a conventional civil society organisation. But one unconventional aspect was that from day one, they decided to include CD in their repertoire of political tools. The same people who organised the struggle in Mardøla joined the group. Based on the experiences from Mardøla, they decided to aim for an escalation of nonviolent means by increasing the number of activists participating in CD. In Alta, the opposition among the Sámi people made it easier to mobilise many more participants.

The CD component

The Detsika Camp in Alta was established in the summer of 1979. In the fall, as construction was ready to start, protesters performed two acts of CD; at the construction site itself in Stilla, activists sat down on the ground and blocked the machines, and at the same time, Sámi activists began a hunger strike outside the Norwegian parliament. The conflict dominated the media coverage. Sámi people were key players in these actions, but thousands of others travelled to Alta to join the actions (Hjorthol, 2006). 6,500 people from 20 nations attended. Many of the visitors participated in CD and were arrested. So many students and professors from universities and colleges around Norway took part that some classes had to be cancelled.

In February 1981, a group of Sámi women asked for an audience to discuss the situation with Prime Minister Gro Harlem Brundtland. When they felt the prime minister did not take their arguments and complaints seriously, they decided not to leave her office. They occupied the office for 19 hours until police arrested them. This CD got wider attention in mainstream media (Mandall, 2011; see also Nykänen et al., in this volume).

Compared to Mardøla, the struggle in Alta involved two kinds of escalations. One was the number of people involved in disobedience. The other escalation was the new technique utilised in Alta. Some activists tried to chain themselves together and to the ground, using chains so solid that it seemed impossible for the police to cut them and arrest the people. Specially made chains were forged for each person. All sorts of commercially available cutting pliers were tested, and none of them managed to break the chains.

The site for the blockade was far away in the wilderness, and some of the actions took place during the arctic winter when the sun never rises above the horizon. It was down to −30°C, and the activists made holes in the snow and poured water over the "icecaves" to construct very solid shelters. It was meant to protect them from both the harsh weather and the police they expected to come and try to arrest people.

The situation grew more tense as the actions continued and multiplied. We know from now declassified documents that the government was desperate enough to plan to use military forces as logistical support for the police. However, as it turned out, only troops and equipment from the Norwegian Civil Defence Forces were requisitioned as support.

When the main mass arrests started in the early morning of January 14, 1981, 10% of Norway's total police force arrived with diesel-powered electric generators and angle grinders (Mortved, 2021). They managed to break through the ice barricades and cut the robust chains without problems. Late in the evening, the last arrest was made. During the day, a huge media crowd had covered the arrest of about 800 activists. Some of the activists returned to the action site as soon as they could leave the police station. Several got prison sentences and huge monetary penalties.

Again, although we cannot prove the cause and effect, there seems to be reasonable evidence to claim some kind of success. The activists clearly lost the "battle" but did advance to a stronger position in the "war". Or, put alternatively, the activists made progress on the environmental issues involved but failed to stop the Alta dam project. Ultimately, the construction and building of the dam continued, and eventually, the dam could produce electricity, despite the serious consequences for the ecosystem in and around the river. Many years later, the former environmental minister and later prime minister, Gro Harlem Brundtland, confessed that the main argument from the activists was correct; the need for energy was exaggerated. Brundtland told the Norwegian Broadcasting Corporation in 1990:

> If you look back at the 70s and 80s, the expectations, and the belief that a very strong power development was necessary, were not fully justified. It has thus turned out, quite simply, that the energy forecasts have been lower. But that is only something you can say in retrospect, when you know how the development then later in the 80s was.
>
> *(Altaposten, 2019)*

However, regarding the long-term effects, it seems like the activists gained something. Regarding the two main issues driving these confrontations, namely (1) protecting the rivers against industrial exploitation and (2) respect for Sámi rights, the consequences turned out to be substantial.

The protection of all the other unexploited rivers was taken seriously by the Parliament, which created new legislation to guarantee better protection. "The overall plan for watercourses" was first presented to the Parliament in 1985 (Stortinget, 1985). The aim was to have a more unified, national management of the watercourses. This was seen as a major victory for the environmental movement.

Furthermore, Sámi rights received a boost in the aftermath of the Alta struggle. When Norway got its first Constitution in 1814, Sámi people were not allowed to vote. Norway acted as almost all other states with a minority nation of Indigenous people; they wanted complete destruction of the culture, religion, language, and almost every part of their identity. One hundred years after the constitution was signed, a Sámi convention was held in Trondheim and a struggle for their rights intensified. Many of the Sámi activists in Alta had experienced punishment for speaking the Sámi language during school breaks in the 1970s. After the Alta struggle, the Sámi population was recognised as an ethnic minority and as Indigenous people. As such, they got respect and specific rights according to international conventions. Norway also established a Sámi Parliament in 1989. The Sámi Parliament of Norway is the representative body for people of Sámi heritage. It acts as an institution of cultural autonomy for the Indigenous Sámi people.

Thus, the dam was built, although many demands for environmental and Sámi rights were fulfilled in the years to come. Moreover, CD was now established as a powerful tool in the environmental struggle.

Discussion

The dam was constructed on the Alta River, with the court cases finding all the activists guilty. In that sense, the Alta struggle was clearly a failure. But as we have seen, on another level, the years of confrontation resulted in public attention on environmental issues, and Sámi rights were lifted to the top of the political agenda in Norway. With hundreds of convictions, the circle of people who had dared to confront the authorities with CD grew immensely. The actions and court cases followed by the public discussions in the media and among people functioned as an educational process for those involved, as well as for bystanders. Arguments *pro et contra* of how to view dam constructions, ethnic minorities, ecosystems, democracy, the role of media, Sámi culture, international conventions, and a number of other topics dominated the public discourse when the confrontations took place.

Activists from all over Norway and many from abroad got direct experience of using CD and how to relate to the police force, the media, the courts, and several people also got a first experience of the prison system. For many, this was a game-changer in their political lives. The impact on Norwegian politics was dramatic; a new political tool was added to the acceptable ones for consideration in societal conflicts. Not since the times of the early workers' movements and their confrontations with the people in power had so many citizens been punished for political activities. To violate laws and confront opponents with CD moved from a fringe activity to becoming a widely accepted instrument for "underdogs" against power holders.

Within the activist community, some issues were discussed more in detail, with the aim of drawing lessons from this important experience. Much focus was on various ideas of how to obtain chains strong enough to prevent police from cutting people loose, the need for nonviolent training prior to participation in CD, how to have an impact on media coverage, and so forth.

In the preparations for confrontations in Alta, Arne Næss argued strongly against more solid chains and claimed that activists could never win the physical battles against states. He claimed that protesters' advantage was their moral upper hand and that they should learn how to improve their ability to utilise the power of good arguments and behaviour (Johansen in meeting with Naess, 1979). This leads us to

36 Stellan Vinthagen and Jørgen Johansen

the next example, Innerdalen, where the behaviour was planned to be very different than in Alta, aiming to be more constructive and therefore also more convincing for a general population.

Innerdalen – constructive CD

Introduction and organisation

Almost simultaneously with the plans to build the dam in Alta, another similar project was prepared in the middle of Norway (section based on Johansen's personal archive). A huge river system called *Orkla Grana* was targeted for exploitation to deliver water to a number of dams and generators for electricity production.

One part of the Orkla-Grana project was to build a huge dam in Innerdalen and fill it with water from a number of smaller rivers in the vicinity. Innerdalen was a valley that had up to the 1960s been used by local farmers for cow and sheep grazing during the summer season. The modernisation of agriculture policy had made it less profitable to continue. The valley, despite its high altitude, had good conditions for producing fodder. Since Norway is one of the countries with the least agricultural land and most electricity production per capita, the campaign to stop the dam construction in Innerdalen aimed to shift the discussion and bring the value of soil and land to the centre. This was not done by directly preventing the building of the dam as in Alta but instead by occupying the valley and starting to use it for food production. The idea was that such a creative CD, what we today would call a *constructive CD* or *constructive resistance*[4] (Lilja, 2021; Rigby, 2022; Sørensen et al., in press), would be difficult for politicians and industry to ignore. The campaign was led by the same informal network that was engaged in Mardøla in 1969–1970, and many of the same individuals participated. The leading figure was Sigmund Kvaløy, and his vision was inspired by the Gandhian *Constructive Programme* during the liberation of India. Gandhi saw the power of the villages as the main building blocks for a liberated India. In Innerdalen, the idea was to build a sustainable society in the valley that was threatened with submersion.

The "Green Action Innerdalen" started by repairing old farmhouses and organising a wide variety of positive activities in the valley. Local farmers allowed the occupiers to take their sheep and cows up in the valley and start production of cheese, butter, and meat. If, despite the constructive actions, the dam was built, the activists imagined working on the farms and milking the cows as the water rose up to their knees. That would be a powerful way to show what the "developers" were destroying. A central slogan was "Soil gives food, the world is starving". During wintertime, some 40 sheep and a young activist stayed in Innerdalen with more than a metre of snow on the ground. Many supporters visited him and helped with the work in periods. In the summer of 1979, the campaign arranged a "Green People's University" with lectures in ecophilosophy, alternative energy, nonviolent actions, courses on how to spin and weave, dyeing wool with plant colours, building timber houses, producing cheese, and numerous political and strategic discussions. Several hundred "students" from Norway and the rest of Europe participated. All members of the Norwegian Parliament were invited to visit the camp, only one turned up.

The organisers of the campaign soon realised that the media had no interest in a "bunch of activists" living in the mountains. When there were confrontations and arrests in Alta in the same period, all national media covered those incidents but, acting constructively, never received attention. Since some activists spent some weeks in Alta and other weeks in Innerdalen, there were plenty of opportunities to compare and discuss the two strategies.

One summer, the campaign ploughed new fields to grow more fodder for the coming winter. The soil turned out to be very easy to make into fields; neither stones to be removed, nor wetlands to drain. Again, the activists tried to get the message out about the values that were about to be destroyed forever, but there were no reactions from those in charge of the project or from the politicians. Almost in desperation, a small group then decided to fill a tractor-trailer with soil and drive it 500 km to the parliament in Oslo to show them in a very literal way what they were responsible for destroying. The idea was that, after the tractor had emptied the trailer in front of the main entrance, those in power would be forced to get dirt under their shoes when they walked to work. During the long drive to Oslo, the driver had a lot of time to think, and he changed his mind about what to do with the soil. In his view, it would create a bad image if the valuable soil would be wasted on the stairs of the parliament. So, after driving to the parliament for a photo session, he drove to a nearby kindergarten and gave it to them as a gift to build their own garden. "The six year old kids are acting more responsible by taking care of the soil for future food production than the elected politicians" was the conclusion of the driver Per Aschjem (Langmyr, 1979).

After three years of constructive resistance in Innerdalen, with close to zero attention from authorities and media, the occupiers lost their patience and decided to "force" the media to recognise what was going on. One early morning they walked the 3 km down to the dam area and blocked the construction road. A few hours later national media was on their way to cover a story "about some activists blocking the road." The large media corporations rented an aeroplane to be first with the spectacular photos of confrontation between police and activists. The result was huge headlines and coverage of people being arrested in all national media. Not a single media representative bothered to walk the 3 km up to the camp, the Green People's University, to see the sheep and farm. The activists' assumptions regarding the media's obsession with confrontations were confirmed and cemented those days (Aktive Debatt, 2020).

Discussion

The constructive and illegal occupation of the valley was very demanding when it came to time and resources. At times, it was difficult to have enough people present 24/7 to take care of the animals and keep all the activities of the campaign running. It was also a factor that the actions in Alta were going on simultaneously. Some were commuting between the two campaigns, but Alta got much more attention due to the media focus on arrests, spectacular actions, hunger strikes, and so forth. The constructive actions in Innerdalen almost never made it to the headlines in the national media. It can be discussed to what degree the involvement of more committed people over a longer period of time would have changed the situation, especially if a group of activists had been prepared to stay on also when the water was pouring in and threatening the valley. It is clear, however, that when the construction road was blocked the spectacular confrontations with police were what the media wanted to cover.

FAG – deterrent CD

Introduction and organisation

The best prepared and most successful large scale CD action in Scandinavian history was never implemented. In the end, the government had to resign.

In 1996, the Norwegian Parliament decided to build two large power stations to produce electricity from natural gas. With a company ready to build and a decision made by the authorities, it seemed almost impossible to prevent it. Natural gas had for years been presented as "clean" and "friendly to nature." To promote the project the company behind the plans took the name "Naturkraft" (The Power of Nature).

The traditions for organising nonviolent resistance, CD included, were during this time period broad-based and well known, although this time organising seemed to start too late. It took a long time before decisions were taken and a budget approved.

The civil disobedience component

Activists from the radical and environmental youth organisation Natur og Ungdom (NU; Nature and Youth) took the initiative and began a campaign against the proposed new power stations. In February 1997, the first meeting took place in secrecy. The idea was to build a strategy prior to any media attention. The planned campaign would be based on two pillars: first, educating politicians and the public about CO_2 emissions and the consequences of climate change and, second, preparing large-scale CD. The educational part was necessary since during this period, climate change was not widely acknowledged outside the specialist circles of scientists and environmentalists. Moreover, the large-scale CD built on the lessons from the Alta struggle. The group adopted the name the Common Action Against Gas Power Stations (FAG).[5]

With members from NU, elderly activists and local people from the planned sites, FAG was launched and the struggle begun. The Kyoto Protocol was finalised those days, so environmental discussions in the media were focused on the climate-altering greenhouse effect. FAG developed a small number of arguments around this issue that it used at every opportunity. FAG trained its members to reply to any question posed by a journalist that the "dirty and old-fashioned power stations polluted as much as 700,000 private cars." Eventually, almost every politician and journalist used the formulation of "dirty and old-fashioned power stations" and used the example of 700,000 private cars. Those who wanted to sign the Kyoto protocol and take the greenhouse effect seriously could not accept the power stations.

The campaign's other pillar was preparation for CD done in a very public way. First, FAG created a small group of experienced activists to work out the strategic plan for large-scale mobilisation by preparing training and organising the actions. The leading tactic was to collect signatures of people who promised to participate in any necessary CD. This collection of signatures was presented as a *pledge of resistance*,[6] where the names represented more than a list of supporters and those who signed knew what was expected. They knew that the list would be made public and that it would be known they were committed to taking serious actions if necessary. In addition to the usual crowd of young activists, FAG made a special effort to get famous people to sign. In this way, FAG tried to show how seriously these people viewed the power stations and how broad-based the movement was.

The number and names on the list became a regular media topic. When some members of Parliament signed the list, it made the headlines, of course. The same happened when leaders of trade unions and some priests and bishops signed and, again, when Grandmas against Gas Power Stations began to knit socks and collect warm clothes for the activists. When the number of signers passed 1,000, the media made a big thing out of it and again when the number passed 2,000 and at 3,000.

Local constructive work

FAG did not only put lots of energy into mobilising people all over the country, they also sought to build alliances with locals at the sites of the planned power stations. Well aware of previous experiences with a hostile local population, they contacted people at an early stage and invited them to become part of the leadership of FAG. Furthermore, inspired by the Gandhian idea of constructive work, FAG organised a summer camp close to one of the building sites and helped the residents with cleaning the beaches, painting the local church, and repairing some of the buildings used by fishers. The effect was two-fold. First, they were seen as serious and hard-working individuals, rather than a bunch of troublemaking activists. Secondly, many new friendships were formed between "guests" and people from the neighbourhood. Because of these good relations with people in the area, FAG picked up lots of information and rumours about what was happening in the district, including preparations for the start of construction, training by the police to arrest hundreds of demonstrators, and the local authorities' perspectives on the situation.

40 Stellan Vinthagen and Jørgen Johansen

Making large-scale CD probable

The next task for FAG in implementing their strategy was to convince the government that those that signed the list were serious about their commitment. Therefore, an action committee prepared people for massive CD. Week-long training camps took place in several parts of the country, while activists, in public view, mapped the areas of planned actions. Also, meetings with local people and the local police were done publicly. In this way, almost all the preparations became media events with TV teams reporting on the activists' preparations for all eventualities.

Tent camp exercises took place both night and day, anticipating possible surprise "attacks" by the police. FAG aimed to show political parties and the power station company that if they started construction work, they would have to face well-trained and -prepared activists. This action was not going to be just a symbolic blockade. Before any construction could take place, the government would have to mobilise huge police forces and arrest thousands of environmentally concerned citizens, some of them known, well connected, and with resources to make their voices heard in the public arena. Since nearly all the political parties competed for "green" voters, they found themselves in a dilemma.

The Social Democratic government faced opposition from among its own members (*Fædrelandsvennen*, 2002). The party's youth organisation even took part in the campaign against the "dirty old-fashioned power stations." Some in the parliamentary opposition had their own reasons to criticise the government, but most tried to act responsibly, making "green" environmental and future-oriented arguments. The liberal-centre parties and the Socialist Party talked about the greenhouse effect, the Kyoto Protocol, and the need to think of future generations (Rønning, 2020). Increased CO_2 emissions did not fit into this framework.

Because of intense professional lobbying and media work, gas power became one of the most discussed issues during the 1997 election campaign. When FAG called a meeting, all parties had to send prominent representatives or face criticism for not taking environmental questions seriously. Previously, such invitations to debates had often been ignored. Now FAG representatives had easy access to newspapers, radio, and television. At the May Day demonstrations, FAG printed thousands of small handheld posters to be carried on sticks and came to dominate the whole demonstration. Any meaningful picture from that day showed a large number of posters saying "No to Gas Power."

As the elections approached, opinion polls showed that about one-third of the people supported FAG and their struggle, while one-third were against it (and the rest undecided; NTB, 2000). All candidates were asked about their position on gas power, making sure the voters would know. The prime minister, Jagland, decided to delay the necessary "go ahead" for the project from the government until after the election, in a vain attempt to prevent the debate about gas power from dominating the elections completely.

Unsurprisingly, a coalition of liberal parties opposing the gas power stations got enough votes to form the new government. They did not have a majority by themselves but hoped to survive with support from other parties on individual issues, since no other coalition could agree to form a government. In the coalition's first declaration to the parliament, they promised to oppose the two planned power stations.

FAG expressed hope but did not trust that the battle was won. They continued with preparations for massive CD. Large numbers of activists took part in practical training with the explicit aim of preventing construction with massive blockades. The winter weather on the west coast of Norway is extremely hard, often with temperatures of $-20°C$ for days and hard wind and snow. Sitting in a blockade outdoors for hours or days, with few possibilities for moving into protection, requires careful preparation. People who had signed the pledge of resistance took courses on how to dress and what sort of food to bring, while supporters across the country took part in a campaign to collect necessary equipment. FAG set up tents in central squares in the main cities, collecting tools, cooking equipment, tents, sleeping bags, warm clothes, and other gear for a long winter camp with CD.

Those who accepted more responsibility for the actions took special training in decision making, consensus, first aid (specifically for frostbite and exposure), managing media relations, and the history of nonviolence. Activists who had taken part in earlier CD actions from 1969 onwards helped with training, strategic planning, and tactical decisions. It was unique that CD in Norway had been so well prepared, planned, and public.

The pressure on the newly elected government now mounted from two directions. FAG demanded a clear decision to cancel the plans for the two power stations, while Naturkraft (the company that planned to build the stations) argued that there was no way it could be stopped, since all the legal agreements were already in place. The government needed to find a way out. Aware that the parliament had originally accepted the plans and that formal laws offered little support for stopping the construction, the government introduced a change in the environmental law. The main change was in defining CO_2 as a pollutant that would require a special permit before it could be released into the atmosphere (Forseth, 1997). Thus, environmental authorities could now stop the planned construction. The power company had to submit an application for the emission of CO_2 and was required to use "the best available technology" to reduce CO_2 emissions (Gauslaa, 2000).

Leading social democrats and right-wing parties joined with the industrialists, saying that the process was a setup to win political points. They pledged to pressure the government through the majority in Parliament to force the government to reverse its decision. They also criticised the government for giving in to activists. They built a large enough majority in the parliament in favour of ordering the government to give the "go ahead" to the power plants. Then after three years, in 2000, the government resigned. One consequence was that the two power stations never came into existence (for more about the campaign, see Johansen, 2001).

In retrospect, the FAG campaign was an example of successful deterrent nonviolence. Even if no politicians would confess that the planned CD made the difference, it is obvious that without FAG the power stations would be up and running today. We argue it was possible due to a combination of factors that made this

42 Stellan Vinthagen and Jørgen Johansen

campaign victorious: a good media strategy, serious preparation for the largest CD actions in Norway in the last 50 years, the introduction of "climate change" on the international agenda, high electricity consumption, and many committed people. The organisation NU had a critical impact on FAG. Many of their most experienced leaders took on important roles in FAG. The importance of their skills, experiences, and commitment cannot be overestimated. Most of them were experienced nonviolent activists who were also familiar with how to "treat" media. In addition, NU used its whole organisation, including its financial strength and local groups, to support and work with FAG (Tjernshaugen, 2007).

When representatives from the church, trade unions, political parties, universities, and other parts of the civil society regularly and openly supported the arguments and strategy opposing the power stations, FAG received a strength that few campaigns in Norway had ever enjoyed. Time also worked in favour of the movement. Every delay to the start of the project made alternatives appear more realistic and convincing. The fact that the government felt forced to resign over the question of the gas power stations shows the force in this campaign. Outgoing prime minister Kjell Magne Bondevik stated:

> A government must consider where the boundaries go for what a government can take responsibility for. We have assessed it so that we cannot take responsibility in a situation where one can weaken one of the pillars of Norwegian environmental policy, namely the Pollution Control Act.
>
> *(Kommunal rapport, 2000)*

In the end, about 3,500 people signed the pledge of resistance, less than one per 1,000 of Norway's population. Why should any government care about a campaign that never came even close to a majority of the people? Most likely, they knew that if a large number of people were willing to use CD to stop the construction of the plants, the number of people who opposed the plans must be many times higher, a fact also reflected in opinion polls. The minority coalition government of Liberals, Christian Democrats, and the Centre Party that was formed in 1997 were against the building of gas power stations in Norway, partly because they realised the strength of the opinion supporting the activists. Still, the Social Democrats, the Progressive Party, and the Conservatives did not care about the opinion and wanted to build the stations. So, in 2000 they forced the government to resign through a vote of confidence in the Parliament. Therefore, it became the first Norwegian government ever to resign on an environmental issue.

Discussion

Can we draw any general conclusion from the struggle against the power stations? In any situation, a number of factors are at work, among them a country's political situation, history, media, culture, and civil society organisations. On this occasion in Norway, these factors came together in a unique way. Nevertheless, the history of FAG tells us that the combination of well-planned strategy, serious preparation for large scale CD, constructive work and good relations with the local community, openness about the plans for action, convincing arguments, and sufficient human and financial resources can make a difference.

If construction had started and the blockades had been organised, it is impossible to predict what might have happened. Few believe that FAG could have resisted the power of the state and police for very long. Still, the political costs of arresting thousands of Norwegians committed to "save the planet from [the] greenhouse effect" would have been very high. Moreover, the long-term impact on social change movements is also impossible to predict. Thousands of individuals in the environmental movement experienced a sense of empowerment through this effort, something that potentially had consequences much later on.

Discussion of the four cases: developing a culture of CD

These four cases illustrate a process of experimenting with different kinds of strategies in order to protect the environment and nature from exploitation. All campaigns are connected through a core group of people who have played a crucial role in the planning and promoting of them all. Meanwhile, in all four cases the use of CD was central. However, all of them also utilised other forms of nonviolent tactics and political tools.

One key question is to what degree the correlation between CD and outcome is a causal one. To answer that question, it is important to discuss what makes sense to count as an "outcome." But let us first be clear; when these four campaigns took place, they all received media attention due to the use of CD. The main headlines in the news came when people got arrested or made it public that they planned to refuse to follow orders from the police. Public meetings, op-eds in newspapers, production of books, lobbying, picket lines, and protests with police permission never elevated these cases up the political agenda. It was when the activists escalated the conflicts with CD the issues got attention in the Parliament and governmental bodies (Sørensen & Johansen, 2016).

A key question is: did the campaigns achieve their outspoken goals? In Mardøla, the waterfalls were destroyed. The Alta dam was constructed. In Innerdalen, the valley was filled with water. The struggle against the gas power stations actually prevented the planned construction. But to state that only one out of four campaigns was successful is too superficial a conclusion. First of all, the issues were taken much more seriously by those in power after the campaigns. The possible negative consequences with electricity production were taken into consideration in a way that was unthinkable prior to these actions.

Even more important, we would suggest that a "democratic education" has occurred, in which a combination of the writings of intellectuals and the struggles of radical activists have changed the political culture of Norway. Not only has Norway become a more environmentally friendly country that now recognises more Sámi rights, but Norwegian civil society has also come to develop a political culture where the use of CD by ordinary citizens is recognised by many as a key part of democracy. This is not a small achievement, and it has been possible only after decades of writings and campaign work where thousands of people have been involved.

During two decades from the 1950s, Arne Næss, Johan Galtung, and Sigmund Kvaløy Setreng brought in a novel Gandhian approach towards political conflicts in Norway, one in which nonviolent action and CD were key. With time, an ecological philosophy ("ecosophy") was developed. These writings had an influence on radical activists within Norwegian civil society, but even more important was that Naess and Kvaløy also initiated and organised practical campaigns along this new Gandhian approach, beginning in Mardøla in 1970.

Despite the first three campaigns being "failures" in a sense of objective results and stated goals, they all achieved important things that made this long-term democratic education possible. In Mardøla, two novel ideas were introduced. First, the idea that "civil disobedience" could be a nonviolent, democratic, meaningful, and honourable way of articulating opposition. Second, and simultaneously, is the novel idea of "nature" having its own, intrinsic value, beyond the profits and extractions of humans.

Ten years later, in the Alta struggle, thanks to a strong mass mobilisation of CD in defence of nature and the Sámi people, it became possible for not only both of these ideas to become accepted, established, and recognised in the wider society but also the rights of Indigenous Sámi people. This new acceptance of ideas that were very new in Mardøla ten years previously, became visible when the Norwegian state, despite the movement having used massive CD, gave new and unique legal protection and rights for waterways and Sámi people.

While the unique struggle at Innerdalen did not set off any mark in the history of Norway, few remember it today, it did at least influence some of the activists and intellectuals that continued to experiment with CD. The constructive CD in Innerdalen did not lead to any victory in that particular struggle, but it did influence the approach to CD applied against the planned gas power stations almost 20 years later. A constructive element of work with local communities became key to the mobilisation of local support for the campaign.

In an innovative way, the FAG introduced and showed how a "pledge" of CD could evolve into an effective deterrent. The FAG struggle against gas power succeeded on all accounts, but its victory against the threat of CO_2-emitting stations did rest, at least partly, on the impact of thousands of CD activists in the Alta struggle. The Norwegian state knew what it would mean if the FAG organised thousands of well-trained activists to obstruct the construction of the power stations. Ultimately, it was Alta that made them know the potential political costs.

Thus, our argument is that thanks to a creative and sustained combination of serious philosophical research work and the application of strategies and tactical principles in environmental campaigns over a time period of some 50 years, it has been possible to shift the political culture in Norway. Today, CD is recognised as a potent and potentially democratic tool for ordinary citizens when the environment is under threat. And the means of CD are now so established that there exist different versions of the tactic (small scale, mass scaled, constructive, or deterrent), and specialised knowledge among educators, organisers, and authors.

At least in this case, it has become clear that it is possible to transform a political culture of a country to adopt and accept CD, but it takes decades and demands several tactics being used simultaneously and thousands of people dedicated to the work of democratic education. CD is not a universal tool that will always deliver good results, yet it has become a widely recognised tool in the political toolbox for many sectors of society.

Notes

1 The Norwegian name of the network: Samarbeidsgruppene for natur- og miljøvern (snm).
2 The Norwegian name of the group: Altautvalget for bevaring av Alta-Kautokeinovassdraget.
3 The Norwegian name of the organisation: Folkeaksjonen mot utbygging av Alta-Kautokeinovassdraget.
4 *Constructive civil disobedience* is a new term with a long history. Several books are published on this, and the authors of this chapter have written one together with Majken Jul Sørensen to be published in late 2022 with Rowman and Littlefield (Sørensen et al., in press).
5 The Norwegian name of the group: Fellesaksjonen mot Gasskraftverk (FAG).
6 This concept is not new. In the 1980s, the *Central American Pledge of Resistance* (POR) created a widespread coordinated horizontal movement that was successful in preventing an all-out US war in Nicaragua and El Salvador.

References

Aktive Debatt. (2020, March 11). *2 Medienes dekning av Mardøla aksjonen i 1970 Ingrid Fadnes OsloMet* [Video]. YouTube. https://www.youtube.com/watch?v=EygWZIzuvnQ

Altaposten. (2019, March 23). Det har altså vist seg rett og slett at energiprognosene har ligget lavere. https://www.altaposten.no/nyheter/2019/03/23/%E2%80%93-Det-har-alts%C3%A5-vist-seg-rett-og-slett-at-energiprognosene-har-ligget-lavere-18718045.ece

Esmark, M. & Steele, C. (2020, December 14). La elvene våre leve! *Harvest.* https://www.harvestmagazine.no/pan/la-elvene-vare-leve

Fadnes, I. (2020, July 25). Kampen om Fossen. *Klassekampen.* https://klassekampen.no/utgave/2020-07-25/kampen-om-fossen

Fædrelandsvennen. (2002, March 21). Uro i Arbeiderpartiet. https://www.fvn.no/mening/i/be0eg/uro-i-arbeiderpartiet

Forseth, R. (1997, June 4). Bellona fikk rett om CO2-juss. *Bellona.* https://bellona.no/nyheter/olje-og-gass/1997-06-bellona-fikk-rett-om-co2-juss

Galtung, J. & Næss, A. (1955). *Gandhis politiske etikk.* Grundt.

Gandhi, M. K. (1927). *An autobiography or the story of my experiments with truth.* Navajivan.

Gauslaa, J. (2000, June 29). Mange løse tråder i gasskraftsaken. *Bellona.* https://bellona.no/nyheter/olje-og-gass/2000-06-mange-lose-trader-i-gasskraftsaken

Hjorthol, L. M. (2006). *Alta: kraftkampen som utfordret statens makt.* Gyldendal akademisk.

Homén, V. T. (1907). *Passiivinen vastarintamme; poliittisia kirjoituksia, 1899–1904.* Otava.

Huxley, S. D. (1990). *Constitutionalist insurgency in Finland: Finnish "passive resistance" against Russification as a case of nonmilitary struggle in the European resistance tradition.* SHS.

Johansen, J. (2001, January 1). Deterrent nonviolence. *War Resisters' International.* https://wri-irg.org/en/nonviolence/nvse11-en.htm

Johansen, J. (2021). *Hvem var Gene Sharp? Tyranniet kunne ikkje knuse dei!* Irene Publishing.

Johansen, J. & Persen, Å. B. (1998). *Den nødvendige ulydigheten.* Fmk.

Kommunal rapport. (2000, March 9). Regjeringen går på gasskraftsaken. https://www.kommunal-rapport.no/politikk/regjeringen-gar-pa-gasskraftsaken/85626!/

46 Stellan Vinthagen and Jørgen Johansen

Kvaløy, S. (1984). *Fra kraftrom til elvetid. To kulturer på norsk jord. Kraftutbygging, konflikt og aksjoner.* Oslo Universitet forlag.

Lilja, M. (2021). *Constructive resistance: repetitions, emotions, and time.* Rowman & Littlefield.

Mandall, R. (2011, February 6). 30 år siden okkupasjonen. *NRK Sápmi.* https://www.nrk.no/sapmi/30-ar-siden-okkupasjonen-1.7494956

Mortved, O. M. (2021, January 28). Politifolkene i Alta. *Politiforum.* https://www.politiforum.no/altaaksjonen-finnmark-historisk/politifolkene-i-alta/209522

Næss, A. (1974). *Gandhi and group conflict: An exploration of Satyagraha, theoretical background.* The Norwegian Research Council.

Norges Naturvernforbund (1971). *Årsmelding 1970.* Norges Naturvernforbund.

NTB. (2000). *Jevnt i meningsmåling om gasskraftverk* [Equal in the opinion poll about the Gas Power Plant]. Stavanger Aftonblad. https://www.aftenbladet.no/lokalt/i/Gj4qV/jevnt-i-meningsmaaling-om-gasskraftverk

Parmann, G. (1980). *Kampen om Alta: en trusel mot vårt demokrati?* Dreyer.

Randle, M. (1994). *Civil resistance.* Fontana.

Regjeringen. (n.d.). Norsk vannkrafthistorie på 5 minutter. https://www.regjeringen.no/no/tema/energi/fornybar-energi/norsk-vannkrafthistorie-pa-fem-minutter/id2346106/

Rigby, A. (2022). *Sowing seeds for the future, exploring the power of constructive nonviolent action.* Irene Publishing.

Rønning, M. (2020, February 17). 30 år med norske klimamål. Grønt håp – brutte løfter. *Dagbladet.* https://www.dagbladet.no/nyheter/gront-hap---brutte-lofter/72130747

Russell, B. (2013). Civil disobedience. *New Statesman, 142*(5183), 35.

Setereng, S. K. (2010). With Johan Galtung to India – on the road. In J. Johansen & J. Y. Jones (Eds.), *Experiments with Peace. Celebrating Peace on Johan Galtung's 80th Birthday* (pp. 338–343). Pambazuka Press.

Sørensen, M. J. & Johansen, J. (2016). Nonviolent conflict escalation. *Conflict Resolution Quarterly, 34*(1). https://doi.org/10.1002/crq.21173

Sørensen, M. J., Vinthagen, S. & Johansen, J. (In press). *Constructive resistance.* [Unpublished manuscript]. Rowman and Littlefield International.

Stortinget (1985). *Stortingsmelding no. 63 (1984–85).* The Norwegian Parliament.

Thoreau, H. D. (1993 [1849]). On the duty of civil disobedience. Original title "Resistance to civil government". The Project Gutenberg EBook.

Tjernshaugen, A. (2007). *Gasskraft: tjue års klimakamp.* Pax.

Vinthagen, S. (2015). *A theory of nonviolent action. How civil resistance works.* Zed Books.

Zapffe, P. W. (1941). *Om det tragiske* [On the tragic]. Dissertation. Oslo University.

Documentary movies

Kampen om Mardøla [The struggle for Mardøla] by Oddvar Einarsson (1972).

La elva leve [Let the river live] by Bredo Greve (1980).

Langmyr, A. (1979, n. d.). *Innerdalen: Nydyrker Per Aschjem.* [Video] Norge Rundt. NRK. http://www.norge-rundt.no/video/524

Prognose Innerdalen [Prognosis Innerdalen] by Oddvar Einarsson (1981).

Other sources

Johansen's personal archive

Kvaløy Setreng, S. Personal communication, July 15, 1979. Interviewer Jørgen Johansen.

Meeting between Arne Naess and Jørgen Johansen, August 1, 1979.

4

CIVIL DISOBEDIENCE AND ARTISTIC PROTESTS

The Áltá and Deatnu disputes and the development of Sámi resistance

Tapio Nykänen, Veli-Pekka Lehtola, and Birgitta Vinkka

In this chapter, we examine two disputes concerning nature exploitation that have provoked open resistance among the Indigenous Sámi people.[1] The first one is the Áltá Controversy, a series of protests in response to a project to dam the Áltá-Guovdageaidnu River towards the end of the 1970s and into the early 1980s. The second one is the still ongoing Deatnu fishing dispute, which revolved around the question of fishing regulations in and around the River Deatnu in the late 2010s. Both rivers flow to the Arctic Ocean in Sápmi, the historic dwelling area of Sámi. In terms of states, the Áltá-Guovdageaidnu River is located in Finnmark, Norway, and the Deatnu River is the border river of Finland and Norway.

Our chapter describes the course of the two disputes and the forms of resistance used by the Sámi protesters involved in them. Our particular focus is on using civil disobedience as a form of resistance. Unlike some other chapters in this book, our chapter does not address the moral justification of the action. Instead, we examine the motives and inspirations of chosen strategies and see if the strategies were effective from the perspective of the goals of the resistance. In other words, we trace the motions of political ideas and see what kinds of impacts their local applications had.

Our use of the concept of civil disobedience is based on theoretical discussions. In other words, it is not decisive whether the protesters themselves regarded their actions as civil disobedience or not. However, we do pay attention also to the notions that protesters themselves held. Especially in our material on the Deatnu fishing dispute, there are interesting and illuminating reflections on how the concept of civil disobedience was understood.

In our analysis, we apply the classic – but relatively loose – definition of civil disobedience. By *civil disobedience*, we refer to resistance on conscientious grounds that intentionally breaks the law (or takes the risk of breaking the law; see Vinthagen, 2015, p. 72) but is characteristically nonviolent and public. As the word *civil* implies,

DOI: 10.4324/9781003320494-5

48 Tapio Nykänen et al.

civil disobedience may also be a "civilised" form of resistance, meaning that activists may, on one hand, use art or other "poetic" means to draw attention and bolster the message (see Gupto, in this volume) or, on the other hand, follow a decorum that follows "conventional social scripts that spell out displays of dignity and ways of showing respect in their society" (Delmas & Brownlee, 2021). Furthermore, the objectives of the action are relatively moderate in that they are targeted towards bringing about change in legislation and provisions and not, for example, inciting a revolution (Koikkalainen et al., in this volume). Despite this, unlike, for example, demonstrations, civil disobedience has features that are, by definition, illegal or take a risk of being illegal.

Alongside civil disobedience, we examine other forms of resistance applied to the context of the Álta and Deatnu disputes. Some of these come close to civil disobedience and/or the forms of nonviolent resistance typically adopted alongside civil disobedience (see Vinthagen, 2015). For example, the hunger strike organised by the Sámi activists in conjunction with the Álta dispute in Oslo is – historically at least – linked to the idea of civil disobedience. One of the best-known hunger strikers of the 20th century was Mahatma Gandhi, whose thought has influenced the development of the theory of civil disobedience heavily. Also, fishing without permission in one of the tributaries of the Deatnu River closely resembles civil disobedience action: the fishers intentionally acted against the provisions on fishing and then voluntarily self-disclosed their misconduct to the police. Their purpose was to test whether the agreements and provisions on fishing in the Deatnu River were constitutional. This kind of process is often called *judicial review* and not considered an instance of civil disobedience proper (although the line between the two may be fluid; see Arendt, 1972). However, also the fishers intentionally took the risk of committing a nonviolent crime and did so on moral grounds, and in this respect, their actions strongly resembled civil disobedience.

Both examples addressed here indicate that in real-life contexts, various forms of (nonviolent) resistance are generally interlinked and overlapping. Resistance is, thus, dynamic and processual: it is seeking socially and politically acceptable – but effective – forms. Practitioners of impactful resistance have good situational awareness, which is also illustrated by the example cases discussed in this chapter.

The Álta controversy: chains, art and hunger strikes

The Álta Controversy is a major event in the political history of the Sámi and a widely discussed topic in the research literature and in other contexts (e.g. Garcia-Antón et al., 2020; Hjorthol, 2006; Vinthagen & Johansen, in this volume; Lehtola, 2015; Somby, 2016). In this chapter, we outline the main events of the dispute without going into greater detail about the complex chain of events related to it. Instead, our focus is on the resistance practised by Sámi activists and the impact of the resistance during the Álta events and in the long term after them.

One of the main sources used here is the memoir *Gumppe Diimmus* by Niillas A. Somby (2016), an activist who is considered to have led the Oslo hunger strike in

1979, and other written sources on the Alta dispute. Moreover, Veli-Pekka Lehtola, one of the authors of this chapter, participated in Áltá protests himself and later reported on the events as a journalist and researcher. We utilise the autoethnographic knowledge of Lehtola as our material as well as in the text.

As mentioned earlier, the controversy was sparked in response to the plans of the Norwegian government to dam the Áltá-Guovdageaidnu watercourse for the purpose of constructing a hydroelectric power plant. The local Sámi were against the development project and demanded that the issue regarding their traditional land-use rights to the region be properly addressed. The early stages of the planning encompassed a vast area of land. For example, the Sámi village of Máze would have been entirely submerged by the reservoir planned in the area. The resistance that emerged in 1968 in Máze led to planning more restricted alternatives in the 1970s.

The new plans made by the Storting (Stortinget, the Norwegian Parliament) in 1978 gave rise to a social movement among people opposing the development project. The movement was active from 1979 to 1981 and had two unofficial but recognisable strands. The "environmental strand", led by Norwegian Alfred Nilsen, had as their priorities especially ecological factors but also reasons related to the livelihoods and historical-cultural factors – all of which were unified under the environmental theme, although not very clearly articulated. The "Sámi strand" of the movement, which was led by two key bodies within the Sámi community – the Sámi Reindeer Herders' Association of Norway (NBR) and the Norwegian Sámi Association (NSR) – viewed the question of protection of their traditional livelihoods and the environments in which these are embedded as key issues.[2] They emphasised that damage to the livelihoods and the environments in which they are practised would threaten the very underpinnings of the Sámi way of life. Among the priorities of the Sámi were questions of land use and justice, which placed emphasis on legal arguments.

Among the most significant protest actions at and around the Áltá River was the Detsika Camp established in 1979 and the protests at the Stilla Camp in the autumn of 1979 and during the period 1980 to 1981. The protesters engaged in visible forms of civil disobedience at the Stilla Camp, where they, for example, chained themselves to each other, thus interrupting the progress of the construction work. The activists also organised protests in the Norwegian capital Oslo, led by a smaller and more radical group of young activists, called the Sámi Action Group. The protests in the capital included, for example, two hunger strikes and a spontaneous demonstration in the prime minister's office by fourteen Sámi women and gathered a great deal of publicity in the Norwegian media.

The Norwegian government paused the construction project several times but finally proceeded with executing the plan. In January 1981, the Stilla Camp was disestablished in a massive police intervention involving about 600 police officers. The new hydropower plant was finally opened in 1987, although to a smaller extent than was originally planned.

To understand the strategies of resistance during Áltá it is useful to look at the developments in previous decades. From the 1960s onwards, the political Sámi movement had been building its own image of the Sámi, articulating a novel sense of community through different networks. It was based both on localities and on the "pan-Sámi" (*buotsámi*) perspective of the Nordic countries, which emphasised the idea of the Sámi as "one people" undivided by state borders. It, thus, seemed natural that Sámi from Finland and Sweden participated in the Detsika and Stilla Camps, and the Oslo hunger strikers also invited Sámi from across the Nordic countries to join them (Somby, 2020, p. 30). Demonstrations were also organised in Finland and Sweden in front of Norwegian embassies and consulates.

Moreover, Nordic and European minority politics had embodied a significant current in the Sámi politics since the 1950s. It was first, in particular, "the friends of the Sámi" (*samevenner*) – themselves non-Sámi – who played an important role in publicly promoting these policies. From the 1960s onwards, the young and educated Sámi people started to become visibly more active in Sámi politics. Many of them were influenced by leftist political currents and global human rights movements such as anti-colonialist efforts in the third world and the civil rights movement in the United States – that is, minority movements that used civil disobedience as part of their political strategies. Towards the mid-1970s, the international Indigenous peoples' movement became a significant background network for the communal activities of the Sámi (see e.g. Nykänen, 2019). The Álta Controversy further strengthened this dimension in Sámi politics. For example, the World Council of Indigenous Peoples (WCIP) and the International Work Group for Indigenous Affairs (IWGIA) appealed to the Norwegian government to draw attention to the rights of the Sámi people (see e.g. *Charta79*, p. 8).

The emergence of the Sámi in the international arenas was beginning to influence the attitude of the Norwegian state already prior to the Álta events. Already back in the 1970s, the state was experiencing pressure to reform its Sámi policy and legislation. The aspirations of the Sámi towards improving their status internationally were first confronted by the conventional mindset of nation-state thinking and the traditional policy of assimilation of minorities. Despite this, the mindset for the change in Sámi politics had already started to develop, especially among Sámi political actors and activists (see e.g. Valkeapää, 1972).

The background for the protests in the capital city of Oslo can be traced in further different sources. First, although the Sámi issues were among of the demands articulated by the environmentalist strand of the movement, and the significance of nature was emphasised among the Sámi strand of the movement, the alliance between environmentalists and Sámi was above all strategic and the interaction between the parties and their objectives were not always aligned. Niillas Aslaksen Somby, a prominent figure of Sámi Action Group, seems to have had even quite strong suspicions over the environmentalists led by Alfred Nilsen. According to Somby, the environmentalists did not "genuinely" want to discuss the concerns of the Sámi unless they "were forced to do so" (Somby, 2020, p. 30). It might be that the reason behind Somby's irritation reflected some kind of a division of labour among the Sámi strand and the environmentalist strand, but Somby was, nevertheless, motivated to expand the demonstrations to Oslo:

We were beginning to realize that we must step in as leaders and refrain from doing what the Sámi have always done ever since the colonialists gained [a] foothold in Sápmi: submitting to the Norwegians and believing in their wisdom.

(Somby, 2016, p. 37; see also 2020, p. 30)

The hunger strikes, a strategy that was new for Sámi political action, had an immediate paragon. At the International Indigenous Festival Davvi Šuvva organised in the summer of 1979, Niillas Somby had become acquainted with Kurds who told about having organised a hunger strike in Stockholm in support of their demands. This gave Somby an idea to utilise the same strategy in Oslo as well.

One should emphasise the role of artists during the controversy. It was perhaps most strongly visible in particular in the Oslo protests, which were an artistic performance as such (Somby, 2020, pp. 32–35). The demonstrators erected a traditional Sámi dwelling *lávvu* right in front of Norway's Storting (Stortinget), the parliament building. The demonstrators wanted to voice their views not only verbally but also symbolically. Somby – who was a photographer – said that he was sure that, due to their extraordinariness, the pictures of the *lávvu*, including the ones taken by himself, would receive wide media coverage (N. A. Somby, personal communication, 10 October 2004). Other conscious symbols associated with the Sámi were traditional Sámi clothing (*gákti*) and Sámi musical expression (*joik*). Loudspeakers spread joiking by well-known Sámi artists in the neighbourhood, and among prominent visitors to the camp was Buffy Sainte-Marie, a world-renowned Cree singer-songwriter, whose performance received a great deal of attention in the context of the hunger strike (Somby, 2016, pp. 40–41; 2020, p. 33). The Sámi Action Group published also two numbers of a magazine called *Charta79*, which introduced the Álta case and the demands of the Sámi and emphasised repeatedly that the protesters did not accept violence as a political means.[3] Editorial team of the magazine consisted of well-known artists and political activists.

What were the effects of civil disobedience and other forms of resistance in Álta and Oslo? On one hand, the struggle was lost: the dam was built, even if the reservoir became smaller than in original plans, and for example, the village of Máze was not submerged. In particular, the environmental strand of the resistance saw the result as a bitter defeat. On the other hand, despite the protests not yielding any immediate results, the fight against the dam is considered an important turning point, especially in Norway's Sámi policy. During Álta, the Sámi demanded a democratically elected political representative body. The Sámi also demanded that the Sámi language be given an official status and that the Sámi be acknowledged as an Indigenous people under the Constitution of Norway. All these demands were fulfilled within about ten years of the Álta Controversy. The inauguration of Sametinget (the Sámi Parliament of Norway) took place in 1989 and Norway's Sámi Language Act was enacted three years later. Legislative measures affecting Indigenous peoples from the 1990s onwards have considerably

52 Tapio Nykänen et al.

improved the status of the Sámi in Norway. In these respects, the Áltá struggle was at least a defensive victory for Sámi.

Many prominent Sámi actors have been somewhat satisfied with the results of the struggle. Ole Henrik Magga, a famous Sámi leader involved in the dispute, later commented on the events, saying that the dispute "changed the Sámi from a post-card motif to a political force". According to Ivar Bjørklund, the Áltá Controversy "started as an environmental issue and evolved into an indigenous one". The artist Synnøve Persen, a participant in the Oslo protests, saw that the events made Norwegians realise that the Sámi are not a tribe or a group of people inhabiting a certain area but a people or a nation. (For the comments, see *Alattionjoen puolustajat* documentary, 2011; also Bjørklund, 2020.)

However, not all Sámi were content, and some seem to have had contradictory feelings. For example, in 1986, Synnøve Persen wrote that "the dream of Sápmi" was left behind at Stilla and "sealed within a wall of concrete" (Persen, 2020, pp. 52–55). In this context, Persen sees that the political system wanted the Sámi to live on but *not* as a people. When Veli-Pekka Lehtola travelled to Áltá and Kautokeino in the 1990s to write an article on the impact of the Áltá events, he also encountered disappointed Sámi people. Ture Bongo, one of the prominent figures in the protests, agreed to guide Lehtola and the photographer to the last boom barrier on the road leading to the hydropower plant but not all the way to the power plant, which was a place he had never been to. He said, "In vuolgge geahččat olbmuid jállosiid" (I have no desire to go and look at the folly of man). Bongo never went to look at the power plant.

The loudest critic of the outcome has been Niillas Somby. In his view (2016), the Sámi leaders lost the guiding principle of the demonstrators and the advantages that had been gained through civil disobedience and other forms of resistance. Somby stresses the role of the hunger strikers in particular and states that the subsequent Sámi politicians "failed" them and "left them to the wolves" for decades. Particularly hard for Somby was his stigmatisation by some Norwegians and Sámi as a wrongdoer:

> The same people think highly of the heroes of the wartime resistance movement who are known to have killed people. I destroyed property of the state, but I have not killed anyone and I caused damage only to myself.[4]
>
> *(Somby, 2016, pp. 140–143)*

In his memoir, Somby (2016) cites his friend Nils Magnus Tornensis, who expressed the view that without the hunger strikes, advances such as the inauguration of Sametinget would not have been achieved. The hunger strikers had paid a price for their actions both in the bodily sense (*rumaš lea nohkagoahtán* – "the physical body is coming to an end") and in the social sense because the Sámi politicians had abandoned them. For Tornensis, Sametinget was like his own offspring, born of his actions – but the child did not accept him, and he did not recognise the child as his own (p. 149). Somby (2020) admits, ironically, that although many have not been satisfied with the operations of Sametinget, "most of us must admit that it has stimulated much more permanent employment than the damming of the Alta river did" (p. 36).

The Ellos Deatnu! movement: civil disobedience or artistic protests?

In this section, we examine resistance targeted towards the 2016 agreement on fishing in the Deatnu River area (see Agreement between Finland and Norway relative to fishing in the Tana river fishing area 2016). Our particular focus is on the Ellos Deatnu![5] (in English, Long live Deatnu!) movement which, starting in the summer of 2017, has been protesting against the fishing agreement. The data consist of interviews conducted with eight Sámi persons who as part of the movement actively opposed the agreement. The interview data is augmented with information from the website of the movement, blog postings of members of the movement, and other information available via social media.

The Deatnu River (in Norwegian, Tana; in Finnish, Teno) is a border river between Norway and Finland, which means that fishing agreements need to be negotiated between the two countries. Fishing in the river and its tributaries has been regulated by means of state fishing agreements from the late 19th century onwards. The fishing agreement has been modified in the course of the years, and prior to the latest agreement in 2016, the 1989 Fishing Act was in force. Negotiations for the new agreement were held between 2012 and 2016. Observations of weakened salmon populations in the Deatnu River provided a backdrop for the renegotiations. The agreement explicitly aimed to ensure

> ecologically, economically and socially sustainable fishing in the river and safeguarding the fish stocks of the river based on the best available knowledge, including traditional knowledge, in order to enable exploitation of salmon stocks and ensure diversity of fish stocks .
>
> *(Valtiosopimukset, 2017)*

In practice, the aim meant that fishing was to be regulated in such a manner that allowed a fishing-related decline in salmon populations by one-third (Turunen et al., 2020, p. 9).

Proportionally, the agreement affected the traditional Sámi fishing methods – weir and drift net fishing – the most. Fishing permits issued for the purpose of practising these fishing methods were reduced by 80 percent compared to the previous situation. In addition, the fishing rights of the Sámi who are non-permanent residents of the Deatnu River Valley were further restricted. Local inhabitants who reside in the river valley less than seven months per year became not eligible to apply for a fishing permit for residents, but they must purchase a fishing permit for non-residents, known as the tourist fishing permit (Centre for Economic Development, Transport and the Environment, 2020). The change was particularly felt by the local residents who spend part of the year elsewhere, especially due to seasonal work or studies. Issuance of non-resident fishing permits was reduced by 40 percent compared to the previous situation and permit prices were increased. In 2017, in some parts of the watercourse, the prices for tourist fishing permits have nearly doubled compared to the fishing season of 2016 (Finnish Federation for Recreational Fishing, 2020).

The agreement was experienced as culturally, economically, as well as constitutionally unjust by the local Sámi community and opposed widely (Holmberg, 2020; Kuokkanen, 2020; Turunen et al., 2020, p. 9). However, this does not imply that locals were not interested in protecting nature and the salmon themselves. Instead, they emphasised that even if the fishing is to be temporarily reduced, Sámi constitutional rights as Indigenous people, their traditional knowledge and their culture are to be considered (Holmberg, 2020, pp. 144–145; see also Hiedanpää et al., 2020; Joks & Law, 2017). As activist Aslak Holmberg (2020) put it, the effort to protect the salmon without the acceptance from the Indigenous Sámi community was seen as "encroachment made under the veil of conservation; theft in the name of sustainability; colonialism under the mask of science" (p. 140; see also Holmberg, 2017; 2018).

In addition to the outcome of the agreement, the negotiation process itself was experienced as unjust and disrespectful of the rights of the locals – the Sámi and non-Sámi Finns alike. One of our interviewees, a Sámi fisher and a board member of a water cooperative, described that they were literally driven out of the negotiation rooms:

> The states, well, they acted so that when the time came to actually make decisions, the local negotiators were told to leave. So, the locals had no real position at the negotiation table. It was disrespectful of the rights of the locals, it was disrespectful of Sámi cultural autonomy, and in Norway, it was disrespectful of the Tana Fiskeförvaltning [Deatnu River Fish Management], and everything.
>
> *(Interview 4)*

In the spring and summer of 2017, resisting the agreement took an extraordinary turn when the Sámi activist group Ellos Deatnu! declared a moratorium on the Čearretsuolu island of the Deatnu River. The group announced that the moratorium suspending the implementation of the new fishing regulations would be in effect until the fishing regulations "are to be negotiated in a proper and fair way, and all discussions are to be led by local Saami people". During the moratorium in this region, "our traditional concepts of justice and fishing methods will be applied" (The Ellos Deatnu! Homepage, n.d.). Around the time of declaring the moratorium, the movement organised a large-scale – from the perspective of the small municipality of Ohcejohka – benefit concert to raise awareness of the controversial issue at both the local and national levels (Mäki, 2021). The young Sámi activists stayed on the Čearretsuolu island throughout the summer of 2017 in lávvus. They drafted press releases and letters for decision-makers, launched campaigns on social media, gave interviews to the traditional media, and produced art that delivered their message further (e.g. Holmberg & Gaup, 2017).

Declaring a moratorium and living on an island were modes of action that took shape gradually and in the course of time. As one of the interviewees states, the idea of the operational model was one that someone "once came upon and thought that it may become useful someday". A moratorium was considered suitable regarding the group's objectives because as a form of resistance, it was new and surprising and transferable to other locations or contexts within Sápmi.

The choice of the site for the moratorium was an important part of protesting and, for its part, determined the means and goals of protesting. First, the movement wanted to select a state-owned island. Second, the members of the movement saw it as important to negotiate with representatives of the Sámi family that was considered the main users of the island. Moreover, before declaring the moratorium, the Ellos Deatnu! activists had visited the island and "entered into dialogue with it", asking permission for the visit. The descriptions of the process show the particular kind of picture the members of the group wanted to convey of the Sámi community and the Sámi nature relationship. The community plays a central role, and within it, there are significant, well-known families whose traditional areas are respected. The Sámi nature relationship as it was articulated by activists is characterised by the idea that humans are not superior to nature but should be thought of as either visitors to nature, as an integral part of nature, or as beings living with nature in a relationship of equality.

Moratorium as a form of resistance clearly falls within classic civil disobedience. The actions involved in it are peaceful and nonviolent, but they openly challenge laws or provisions and deny their legitimacy. However, according to the moratorium rules published on the website of the Ellos Deatnu! the objective of the movement was perhaps more radical compared to an action that aims primarily to change, say, a single law. Ultimately, the movement sought not only to change fishing provisions but also to expand the Sámi right to self-determination clearly beyond its current scope:

> Our purpose on the Čearretsuolu island is to cherish and restore the legacy of our ancestors and nature. Our objective is to restore the rights of nature and those of ourselves to their former strength, and to lay a foundation for the right to self-determination in Sápmi by nonviolent means. It is our goal, our duty and our responsibility.
>
> *(Ellos Deatnu! Homepage (n.d.).*
> *The Rules of the Čearretsuolu island moratorium area)*

Nevertheless, despite of seemingly radical goals, the moratorium was in practice a rather "mild" instance of disobedience in that it did not interfere with people's everyday life or provoke strong legal or social counterreactions. In the public eye, the moratorium was largely received as an artistic protest – although an exceptional one with a strong message. The moratorium may, thus, also be interpreted as an instance of symbolic resistance aimed at producing representations of the local Sámi culture and the nature of the Sámi right to self-determination – quite similar to the Sámi symbols in Oslo 40 years earlier. The impression of symbolic resistance was enhanced by the fact that the participants included artists who contributed to the moratorium by delivering musical performances, for example. In addition, the moratorium participants launched an online "Moratorium Office" – an endeavour the participants themselves referred to as "a community artistic self-determination project" (Alajärvi, 2018).

Discussions with the members of the movement show that although the moratorium may be considered an instance of civil disobedience, the activists themselves did *not* perceive their activity as such. Above all, this conception seemed to be related to the idea that the members of the group did not ascribe sovereign authority over the land and waters to the state, and thus, the concept of civil disobedience did not seem suitable for describing their acts of resistance. This, at least partially, seemed to be associated with the Finnish translation of the term *civil disobedience*. Finnish word *kansalaistottelemattomuus* translates literally to "disobedience of citizens", and the members of Ellos Deatnu! were critical on what sense they are "citizens" of the states:

> [I]f the Sámi see that the lands belong to the Sámi and we use those lands the way we see fit, and we have the permission of the people whom we acknowledge as having authority over these lands, then who exactly are we being disobedient against?
>
> *(Interview 1)*

As in Áltá, also the activists at Deatnu were networked with other political activists and inspired by their struggles. For Ellos Deatnu! members, clearly the most meaningful examples for the action were drawn from the struggles of Indigenous peoples around the world. One of the major paragons was the struggle of the North Dakota Standing Rock Sioux tribe against an oil pipeline planned to run across their lands. It was mentioned in the interviews clearly more often than, for example, the Áltá dispute, although the significance of the latter was also acknowledged.

> Any Sámi activist has looked up to the 1970s and 1980s for inspiration, but I would say that what influenced us the most was the Standing Rock case, because there were several people in Ellos Deatnu who had visited Standing Rock as a group and it was there that they had experienced an awakening of sorts, to pursue direct action. We all were activists to start with, but in Standing Rock, people had learned how to maintain such micro-communities, what tools and equipment are needed when staying somewhere to exercise resistance and so on. So, what we learned from them was in particular related to the mindset and practical preparation.
>
> *(Interview 1)*

Civil disobedience and artistic protests **57**

Likewise, several well-known Indigenous activists followed and showed their solidarity to the struggles of Ellos Deatnu in social media. Among them were Clayton Thomas-Müller of the Cree Nation, who also visited the Čearretsuolu island, and Nina Gualinga from the Ecuadorian Amazon.

Fishing without a licence and judicial review

In addition to the Ellos Deatnu! activists in moratorium, another group exercising open resistance was active in the Deatnu River area. A group of five Sámi fishers publicly announced having fished without a licence with a rod and line in their home river Veahcejohka to have themselves sued, and another fisher announced having cast a net to catch salmon in the upper course of the river Ohcejohka after the official fishing season had ended (Lakkala, 2017). The fishers declared that they fished without a licence in order to go to the court, and through the court proceedings, they sought to change the Fishing Act that they considered unjust, by appealing to the right of the Sámi to use the Deatnu River watercourse "from time immemorial" (Rasmus, 2017). The case of the fishers proceeded to the consideration of charges in September 2017, and court proceedings took place during the winter of 2019. The charges against the Sámi fishers were dropped in March 2019 because the court ruled that they had practised fishing in accordance with their family traditions and thus did not commit a fishing offence. The district court ruled that the agreement restricting fishing violated the Constitution of Finland, which accords the Sámi the right to maintain and develop their own language and culture. In addition, according to the district court, the agreement violated the human rights conventions safeguarding the rights of the Sámi as an Indigenous people (Leisti, 2019).

The prosecutor appealed the decision of the district court directly to the Supreme Court in order to create a precedent to address the interpretational problem inherent in the fishing agreement. The Supreme Court dropped all the charges in April 2022, appealing to the constitutional rights of the Sámi people (KKO:2022:25, n.d.; KKO:2022:26, n.d.). According to the court, the restrictions were not "proportionate" to the benefits, considering the cultural rights of the Sámi. The court reasoned as follows:

> The Supreme Court noted that the constitutionally protected fishing rights of the Sámi people was not absolute, but that also these rights could be restricted in order to protect migratory fish stock. The sustainable and ecologically sound use of natural resources and the protection of fish stock serve also the interests of the Sámi people. In other words, the pursuit of traditional cultural fishing rights required in the first place that the fish stock of the Tenojoki river was at a sustainable level. Hence, the fishing rights could be restricted as a matter of principle, but it remained to be assessed whether the restrictions were proportionate to the benefits sought.
>
> *(KKO:2022:25, n.d.)*

The Supreme Court's decision was a precedent, and one can estimate that it will have a strong effect to the legislation and administrative decisions relating to the cultural rights of Sámi people in the future. However, by time of writing this chapter, it is unclear what the precise effects will be. According to the decision, the fishing rights of Sámi can be restricted in a "proportionate" way, if the protection of the fish stock requires this. It remains to be seen how this is understood in the future. Nevertheless, the decision was a clear victory for the fishers, and it showed that the cultural rights of the Sámi are not void of meaning in a legal respect.

Although the case of the fishers was, strictly speaking, not an instance of civil disobedience but, rather, can be regarded as an instance of testing laws against the Constitution ("judicial review"), the events are nevertheless closely linked to the tradition of civil disobedience. The fishers intentionally violated the provision on fishing, taking the risk or legal consequences, and made the case public. Their objective was to act towards changing the provision they saw as unjust, and, by extension, improve the legal status of the Sámi in a more general sense. The resistance was nonviolent and could be described as "courteous" or "civilised": The individuals were simply fishing and documented the event in pictures that can be seen as beautiful. A sign with the text "Valtion vesialue" (Government Owned Water Area) appears in the pictures, but the pictures also show the verdure of the river valley and smiling people (Rasmus, 2017).

What makes the case interesting is the way the Sámi fishers conceived of themselves as part of the nation state. The fishers identified themselves as subject to state power and often described themselves as law-abiding people. They also sought a solution to the problem precisely through the state legal system – by appealing to the Constitution of Finland and international conventions. On the other hand, a fisher we interviewed found the Finnish concept of civil disobedience ("disobedience of citizens") alien, and especially the idea of having acted in the situation primarily in the role of a *citizen* of Finland was alien to them. Rather, the interviewee identified as a Sámi person whose rights were not entirely linked to the state but also to membership of an Indigenous people. They also stated that "the thing is that we haven't done anything we haven't been doing before or anything to which, in our view, we have no right". A kind of double identification is reflected in the setting: on the one hand, the fishers feel connected to the state and view its legal system at least to some extent legitimate, but on the other hand, they clearly identify with Indigenous people and the local traditional rights (see also Nykänen & Valkeapää, 2019).

What was the wider impact of the protests of the Ellos Deatnu! movement and the case of the Sámi fishers? The precedent of the Supreme Court is clearly the single most important step forward. The case is expected to have a considerable impact from the perspective of the cultural rights of the Sámi. The Ellos Deatnu! movement, for its part, generated public debate regarding the significance of the traditional livelihoods of the Sámi to the culture and its continuity. In addition to the nationwide impact of the movement, the activists involved in the movement believed that their activities have a considerable impact at the local level and within the community. One activist we interviewed sees that the activities of the movement bear the imprint of the tradition that started in Áltá and are now further imbued with new meanings from the Deatnu events.

> Maybe time will tell if there has been a wider impact. And those I mentioned, [the people] who were [active] in the 1970s, they will see the impact of their struggles when they see us now. It brings a sense of kind of relief that the work has not been in vain, even though 30 years and 50 years have passed, and it feels like nothing has been gained. Personally, I think that it may well be that I don't get to see the successes this year, next year or even in ten years. But somehow I am convinced that something useful will come out of it.
>
> *(Interview 8)*

Civil disobedience and artistic protesting

What is noteworthy about both the Áltá and Deatnu disputes is that, in both cases, those engaging in acts of resistance primarily sought to defend everyday life as they lived it: their homes, livelihoods, the very foundations of their way of life. States, for their part, sought to interfere with people's everyday lives by extracting resources and by taking over areas of land to harness them for their own purposes or by denying people their way of life as they have led it thus far. In such situations, simple things such as continuing an activity – say, fishing – becomes civil disobedience or some other kind of activism.

On the other hand, the resistance soon assumed a constructive character (Vinthangen & Johansen, in this volume). Its purpose was not only to put an end to certain developments but to also build novel institutional and discursive structures that would enable the dispute at hand to continue and, at the same time, build a strong foundation and prepare for future disputes. In the case of Áltá, the constructiveness was of very practical nature. The Áltá events led to, or at least accelerated, the inauguration of Sametinget (the Sámi Parliament of Norway) as well as several legislative measures affecting the status of the Sámi. The Deatnu activists also engaged in acts of construction: They consciously promoted the idea of the Sámi culture being intertwined with the surrounding nature – in a way clearly different from Western mainstream culture.

It is worth noting that although the activists in Áltá and Deatnu opposed the aims and means of the states, they did not view state laws as *meaningless*. Even the radical hunger strikers of Oslo demanded that the issue regarding the rights of the Sámi be addressed in court (*Charta79*, p. 2). The activists on the Čearretsuolu island and those fishing without an official licence wanted to test laws against the constitution because they felt that the agreement restricting fishing violated the constitution. It is not entirely clear why seeking solutions through the legal system was important to them – after all, especially activists in Deatnu seemed to be not sure in what regard they held themselves even as citizens of the state. It might be that, as members of a relatively small minority, they considered challenging the entire legal system

60 Tapio Nykänen et al.

strategically ineffective. Then again, one possible interpretation is that the actors yet had a positive mindset towards the legal system or were at least hopeful about it.

It is striking but not surprising how important a role art and established and educated artists had in both Áltá and Deatnu. The prominent role of educated individuals in the resistance is natural in that civil disobedience and the related non-violent resistance are often "civilized" (*civil*) forms of resistance. Their power rests on convincing arguments, impressive performances and appealing impressions – exactly what artists and also researchers and political activists have been educated to produce. In this respect, Áltá and Deatnu may be quite typical events in the context of nonviolent resistance in general (see e.g. Gupto, in this volume; Pokharel et al., in this volume). Moreover, one should note that Sámi people have used art as a form of political resistance also before Áltá and Deatnu (see Autti & Lehtola, 2019; Gaski, 1987, 2004). It has offered a relatively safe but visible way to resist the stronger opponent. Hence, political art has its own traditions in Sámi history, and using it in Áltá and Deatnu is not surprising in this regard either.

One observation that can be made about the events is that civil disobedience at one location gives rise to civil disobedience action elsewhere. The Ellos Deatnu movement was born because, before that, people stood up for themselves in Standing Rock, at the Áltá River, in Oslo, and elsewhere. This is one of the indisputable effects of civil disobedience. Even losing a battle may leave a strong cultural imprint through the actions of those who resisted – sometimes with dramatic, or even tragic, results. It will not necessarily lead to a repetition of the same event, but it will create a cultural, political and social possibility for such an event.

Notes

1 The Sámi people are the Indigenous people of the northern part of the Scandinavian Peninsula and Finland and large parts of the Kola Peninsula. In terms of states, they live in Sweden, Norway, Finland, and Russia. In the Northern Sámi language, the region is called Sápmi. Sámi number in total between 50,000 and 100,000. See, for example, Sámediggi: Sámi in Finland (n.d.); IWGIA: Indigenous Peoples in Sápmi (n.d.).

2 The third visible organisation in the Sámi field was SLF (Samenes Landsforbund – Sámi Country Alliance), which was founded to support the measures taken by the Norwegian state. Although the members of the SLF were dismissed as "traitors" among the protesters and the organisation also had local non-Sámi members, the very fact that such an organisation was established in the first place and attracted membership is reflective of contradictory attitudes among the Sámi.

3 The protests in Oslo were not supported by all Sámi. According to Somby, although the hunger strike received also support, "most people called us [the demonstrators] the greatest shame to the matters concerning Sápmi (*stuorámus boalgan Sápmái*)". Somby (2016) recalls that a word was sent to the demonstrators from the meeting of the Saami Council – the representative body of the Sámi of the Nordic countries – telling them to stop staining the name of the Sámi, go home and be ashamed of what they had done. Somby was disappointed to find out that "all" Sámi people did not agree with the demonstrators' objectives, but rather, many Sámi people in the Homeland frowned on such visible forms of engagement. As Somby put it, "the Sámi were accustomed to submitting to others and tended to adjust" (p. 42).

4 In 1982, Somby tried to detonate a small bomb under a bridge on the road leading to the Alta power plant construction site near Fállijohka. The idea was to create a "performance" depicting the severity of the situation. Previously he and his acquaintances had even planned to sink the ship *Janina*, which served as the base of the police officers during the Stilla events. The group intended to follow through the plan while the police officers were at Stilla and to avoid damage to humans. At Tverrelvdalen, the activists noticed that the timer of the bomb was not working. When Somby was changing the timer battery, the bomb exploded in his face, and Somby lost his left arm and an eye. Somby was arrested and kept in custody suspected of terrorism offences and, after his release, escaped to Canada to stay with the local Indians. John Reier Martinsen, the other activist who had been arrested at the same time, was years later sentenced to prison for six months. The terrorism charges had been dropped. As the Canadian authorities found out in 1986 that Somby was residing in the country without a permit, he returned to Norway and was sentenced to prison for five months – a sentence he had already served. People's attitudes had still not calmed down. Somby tells about having faced hostility from Norwegians and having been called "a damn bridge exploder". Martinsen died after having been run over by car, and Somby and Synnøve Persen, among others, thought the act might have been intentional. For the process, see Persen (2020); Somby (2016, pp. 126–127).
5 The name Ellos Deatnu! is a wordplay: it reminds the catchphrase Ellos eatnu (Let the river live), used by protesters of Áltá (see Garcia-Antón et al., 2020).

Research material

Agreement between Finland and Norway relative to fishing in the Tana river fishing area. (2016, September 30). FAOLEX Database, Food and Agriculture Organization of the United Nations, Rome, Italy. www.fao.org/faolex/results/details/en/c/LEX-FAOC179992/

Alajärvi, M. (2018, July 8). Tenon kalastussäännön vastustamisesta lähtenyt kapina laajentui Saamenmaan laajuiseksi kansanliikkeeksi – nyt itsemääräämisoikeutta puolustetaan jo useiden paikallisyhteisöjen voimin. [The rebellion that started from the protesting of Deatnu Fishing Rule expanded to the civil movement of the whole Sápmi – right for self-determination is defended by several local communities]. Yle Uutiset. yle.fi/uutiset/3-10294937

Alattiojoen puolustajat documentary. (2011). Director Per Kristian Olsen. NRK. [Original title Vendepunktet – miljøkampen som ble en urfolksak] tv.nrk.no/program/DNPR64001010

ALVA – Sámi Human Rights Association. (2018). Homepage. www.samihumanrights.org/

Centre for Economic Development, Transport and the Environment 2020. (2020). *Kalastus Tenojoella – Paikkakuntalaisten ja kiintiölupalaisten kalastus vuonna 2020.* [Fishing in Deatnu – Fishing permits for 2020] www.ely-keskus.fi/documents/10191/23117928/Paikallis-+ja+kiinti%C3%B6lupalaisten+s%C3%A4%C3%A4nt%C3%B6j%C3%A4%202019/3e43f7e0-415f-456b-bb0d-50291506c2eb

Charta79. (1979). Huuto oikeuksien puolesta [Charta79. A cry for the rights] Assembled by Gaup, A., Somby, A., Sara, M., Idinvuoma, L., Utsi, E., & Johansen, H. Transl. from Norwegian to Finnish:, Tunset, M., Huotari, U., Oraviita, I. & Bogevedt. Ed.: in Finnish Valkeapää, N.-A.

Ellos Deatnu! Homepage (n.d.). ellosdeatnu.wordpress.com/

Finnish Federation for Recreational Fishing Suomen vapaa-ajankalastajat [Suomen vapaa-ajankalastajat]. (2020). *Lausunto maa- ja metsätalousministeriön asetuksesta Tenon kalastuslupien hinnoista vuodelle 2020, 25.3.2020.* https://www.vapaa-ajankalastaja.fi/tenonluvat250320/

62 Tapio Nykänen et al.

Holmberg, A. (2017, March 11). Indigenous salmon-fishing Saami criminalized by Finland and Norway [Video]. YouTube. www.youtube.com/watch?v=H8ObcQnncf8&feature=youtu.be

Holmberg, N. & Gaup, S. M. (2017). Ellos Deatnu. [Music video.] Youtube.

Interviews 1–8. (2020). (anon.) Interviewer Birgitta Vinkka.

IWGIA – International Work Group for Indigenous Affairs. (n.d.). Indigenous Peoples in Sápmi. www.iwgia.org/en/sapmi.html

KKO:2022:25. (n.d.). Fishing restriction imposed on the Sámi Indigenous people and its relationship to their fundamental rights (fishing offence). https://korkeinoikeus.fi/en/index/ennakkopaatokset/shortsummariesofselectedprecedentsinenglish/2022_1/kko202225.html

KKO:2022:26. (n.d.). Fishing restriction imposed on the Sámi Indigenous people and its relationship to their fundamental rights (game offence). https://korkeinoikeus.fi/en/index/ennakkopaatokset/shortsummariesofselectedprecedentsinenglish/2022_1/kko202226.html

Lakkala, A. (2017, August 2). Tenon kalastuskiista kuumenee: Neljä paikallista kalastajaa ilmoittaa tietoisesti rikkoneensa kalastuslakia. [Deatnu fishing dispute intensifies: Four local fishers announce that they've broken the Fishing Act intentionally] Yle Uutiset. yle.fi/uutiset/3-9752811

Leisti, T. (2019, March 6). Lapin käräjäoikeus on hylännyt kaikki Utsjoen saamelaisten syytteet luvattomasta kalastuksesta Vetsijoella ja Utsjoella. [The District Court of Lapland has dismissed all the charges on unauthorized fishing of Sámi in Veahcejohka and Ohcejohka] Yle uutiset. yle.fi/uutiset/3-10675382

Mäki, M. (2021, July 25). "Toisen omaa ei voi viedä" – Ellos Deatnun tukikonsertti keräsi 400 ihmistä Utsjoen Onnelantörmälle [One cannot take what's not yours – the support concert of Ellos Deatnu gathered 400 at Onnelantörmä in Ohcjejohka] *Lapin Kansa*. www.lapinkansa.fi/toisen-omaa-ei-voi-vieda-ellos-deatnun-tukikonsert/89125

Rasmus, L. (2017, September 4). Utsjoen luvattomat kalastajat pääsevät käräjöimään: "Asia menee suoraan syyteharkintaan". [Unauthorized fishers of Utsjoki allowed to go to court: "The consideration of charges starts right away"] Yle Uutiset. yle.fi/uutiset/3-9813917

Sámediggi, Homepage. Sámi in Finland (n.d.). www.samediggi.fi/sami-info/?lang=en

Somby, N. A. Personal communication, October 10, 2004. Interviewer Veli-Pekka Lehtola, Oulu.

Somby, N. A. (2016). *Gumppe diimmus*. ABC-Company E-skuvla AS.

Valkeapää, N.-A. (1972). *Terveisiä Lapista*. [Greetings From Lapland.] Otava.

Valtiosopimukset. (2017). Valtioneuvoston asetus kalastuksesta Tenojoen vesistössä Norjan kanssa tehdyn sopimuksen voimaansaattamisesta sekä sopimuksen lainsäädännön alaan kuuluvien määräysten voimaansaattamisesta ja soveltamisesta annetun lain voimaantulosta. 42/2017. *Finlex*.

Yle. (2019, March 6). Lapland's indigenous Sámi score victory in fishing dispute. Yle News. yle.fi/uutiset/osasto/news/laplands_indigenous_sami_score_victory_in_fishing_dispute/10676003

References

Arendt, H. (1972). *Crisis of the republic. Civil disobedience*. Harcourt.

Autti, O. & Lehtola, V.-P. (Ed.). (2019). *Hiljainen vastarinta*. [Silent Resistance.] Tampere University Press.

Bjørklund, I. (2020). The Álta action as a Sámi conflict. Forty years later. In K. Garcia-Antón, H. Gaski & G. Guttorm (Eds.), *Let the river flow. An indigenous uprising and its legacy in art, ecology and politics* (pp. 39–50). Valiz.

Delmas, C. & Brownlee, K. (2021). *Civil Disobedience. The Stanford Encyclopedia of Philosophy* (Winter 2021 Edition), Edward N. Zalta (Ed.). https://plato.stanford.edu/archives/win2021/entries/civil-disobedience/

García-Antón, K., Gaski, H. & Guttorm, G. (2020). *Let the river flow: An indigenous uprising and its legacy in art, ecology and politics.* Valiz.

Gaski, H. (1987). *Med ord skal tyvene fordrives. Om samenes episk poetiske diktning.* Davvi Media.

Gaski, H. (2004). When the thieves became masters in the land of the shamans. *Nordlit: Special Issue on Northern Minorities 15*, 45–60. University of Tromsø.

Hiedanpää, J., Saijets, J., Jounela, P., Jokinen, M., & Sarkki, S. (2020). Beliefs in conflict: The management of Teno Atlantic salmon in the Sámi homeland in Finland. *Environmental Management 66*, 1039–1058. link.springer.com/article/10.1007/s00267-020-01374-6#Sec2

Hjorthol, L. M. (2006). *Alta – kraftkampen som utfordret statens makt.* Glydendal akademisk.

Holmberg, A. (2018). *Bivdit Luosa – To ask for salmon. Saami traditional knowledge on salmon and the River Deatnu: In research and decision-making* [Doctoral Dissertation, The University of Tromsø]. UiT Munin. https://hdl.handle.net/10037/12868

Holmberg, A. (2020). Ellos Deatnu! – Long live the River Deatnu! Indigenous Sámi people's struggle for self-determination. In K. Garcia-Antón, H. Gaski & G. Guttorm, (Eds.), *Let the River Flow. An Indigenous Uprising and its Legacy in Art, Ecology and Politics* (pp. 139–152). Valiz.

Joks, S., & Law, J. (2017). Sámi salmon, state salmon: LEK, Technoscience and Care. *The Sociological Review, 65*(2), 150–171. https://doi.org/10.1177/0081176917710428

Kuokkanen, R. (2020). The Deatnu agreement: A contemporary wall of settler colonialism. *Settler Colonial Studies, 10*(4), 508–528. https://doi.org/10.1080/2201473X.2020.1794211

Lehtola, V.-P. (2015). *Saamelaiset. Historia, yhteiskunta, taide.* [The Sámi. History, society, art.]. Kustannus-Puntsi.

Nykänen, T. (2019). "I'll show you the tundra". The Sámi as an indigenous people in the political thought of Nils-Aslak Valkeapää. In J. Valkonen, S. Valkonen & T. H. Eriksen (Eds.), *Knowing from the indigenous North* (pp. 123–141). Routledge.

Nykänen, T. & Valkeapää, L. (2019). Ethnic reindeer herders. Groupness among reindeer-herding Sámi in Northwest Finnish Lapland. *Ethnicities, 19*(6), 1181–1201. https://doi.org/10.1177/1468796818810237

Persen, Synnøve (2020). The dream of Sápmi and the dream of nothing. In K. Garcia-Antón, H. Gaski & G. Guttorm (Eds.), *Let the river flow. An indigenous uprising and its legacy in art, ecology and politics* (pp. 51–56). Valiz.

Somby, N. A. (2020). The hunger strike. Recollections of a participant. In K. Garcia-Antón, H. Gaski & G. Guttorm (Eds.), *Let the river flow. An indigenous uprising and its legacy in art, ecology and politics* (pp. 29–37). Office for Contemporary Art.

Turunen, J-P., Peltonen, L. & Karjalainen, T. (2020). *Tenon kalastussopimuksen vaikutukset – sopimuksen toimivuuden arviointi eri osapuolten näkökulmasta.* [Effects of the Deatnu Fishing Agreement – the evaluation of the functionality of the Agreement from the perspectives of different stakeholders] [online]. Maa- ja metsätalousministeriön julkaisuja 2020:2. http://urn.fi/URN:ISBN:978-952-366-021-2

Vinthagen, S. (2015). *A theory of nonviolent action. How civil resistance works.* Zed Books.

5

DRUGS, DISOBEDIENCE, AND DEMOCRACY

Civil disobedience and drug policy

Mika Luoma-Aho

Seeds of civil disobedience

I first heard someone talk about civil disobedience in a drug policy context in the spring of 2019. I was doing fieldwork among Finnish cannabis activists in Turku and attended their most important annual event Hamppumarssi, a Finnish leg in the annual Global Marijuana March organised around the world on the first Saturday of May. There was a posse of 100 to 200 people, and the plan was to march through the city centre carrying signs and singing songs protesting the drug war and cannabis prohibition. Right as we were about to depart from the Puolala Park and head downtown, one of the activists opened a plastic bag and began sowing hempseed around the park, hoping that some of the "seeds of civil disobedience" become full-grown plants over the summer.

Even though cannabis has been prohibited in Finland since 1966, it is used and cultivated today more than ever before. When in 1992, less than 6 per cent of Finns had experimented with cannabis; in 2014, the number stood at nearly 20 per cent (THL, 2019). But does marching for marijuana have anything to do with civil disobedience? This question is much bigger than cannabis in Finland, because we currently live under a global drug prohibition regime (see Nadelmann, 1990), where all "drugs" are categorically banned (with some recent local exceptions). There are other forms and instances of wilful disobedience against this regime – I review some of them in this chapter – which led us to a more general question on whether activism in matters of drug policy can sometimes be identified in terms of civil disobedience. Activists themselves certainly seem to think so, as civil disobedience (hence CDO) has often and universally been cited, called on, and made use of in anti-drug-war politics.

The purpose of this chapter is to think about whether these claims are justified. Claims of civil disobedience are generally, perhaps always, normative claims to a

DOI: 10.4324/9781003320494-6

special standing that may be entitled to a more tolerant response before the law than other crimes. Can activities like guerilla growing of hemp or underground needle exchanges have such *locus standi*? Is there room for justified disobedience of drug laws in a democratic political system? Or is there something about the nature of drugs as a problem or drug policy as its solution that rules out attempts at lawbreaking committed with the intention of communicating a political message?

Harm reduction and public health civil disobedience

Contemporary drug policy is, broadly and figuratively, a structure of two policy paradigms, which may seem to contradict in their fundamental principles, but can exist side by side in a single jurisdiction (Neill, 2014). Law and order is the dominant policy paradigm. It is principled on the understanding that drugs are a dangerous threat to the individual and society, and must therefore be banned. Drugs are criminalised in order to reduce supply, making them unavailable or too expensive for people to abuse. This is the "war on drugs" declared by Richard Nixon in 1971, institutionalised in the United Nations, and enforced nearly universally today.

There is wide agreement in drug policy literature that this war has been and is an expensive failure (see e.g. Baum, 1997; Johns, 1992; Gray, 2012; Pryce, 2012). Rather than reducing drug use and related crime, alleviating the drug problem, law-and-order policies exacerbate it and actually contribute towards making illegal drugs the massive international criminal enterprise in operation today. Reducing drug policies to the denominators of prohibition and punishment, law and order has made not drugs but their users its enemy proper. Some commentators have observed that the drug war should more accurately be called what it has truly become: a war on drug users (Buchanan & Young, 2000).

In recent decades, law and order has been challenged by a public health drug policy model that views drug addiction not as a crime deserving punishment but as a disease to be prevented and treated. Within this policy paradigm, there are various approaches, and the example I discuss here is the harm-reduction approach, which is "a set of practical strategies and ideas aimed at reducing negative consequences associated with drug use" (HRI, 2021). It proceeds from the assumption that there will always be a demand for drugs in this world and humanity, and the aim of repressively eradicating it with law and order is not attainable, maybe not even desirable. Instead of attempting to free humanity of drugs altogether, harm reduction aims to minimise the negative health, social and legal impacts associated with drug use, drug policies, and drug laws.

One of the ideas and practices of harm reduction is offering healthcare and social services to people who use drugs (henceforth PWUDs). The pioneering effort in this regard took place in Vancouver, Canada, in the 1990s. Downtown Eastside is one of the most impoverished urban neighbourhoods in the country and has a history of overdose deaths and other health complications due to drug use since the 1970s. In 1997, a rapidly spreading HIV/AIDS epidemic among its population of injection drug users prompted local health authorities to declare a public health emergency. Following the announcement, locals and other activists took action and formed what in time became known as Vancouver Area Drug Users Network, VANDU for short, a non-profit society to address the ongoing health crisis. VANDU focused on political activism and advocacy, and identified marginalisation, "the distance that addicts are from society", as the biggest obstacle in the way of improving the life of PWUDs (Kerr et al., 2006, p. 64). It wanted to bring the voice of users into mainstream drug policy discourse and get across the point often overlooked in law and order drug policing: that "addicts" are people too and have every right to be treated and heard as such.

Today VANDU is an internationally renowned example of harm reduction as a pragmatic approach, as well as a political principle (Jozaghi & Yake, 2020). Over the past two decades, it has grown substantially in membership and made a direct impact on the legalities, politics, and health of PWUDs. "Through acts of public health civil disobedience", write Ehsan Jozaghi and Kevin Yake (2020),

> such as unsanctioned syringe distribution, illegal peer-run injection sites, illegal peer-run inhalation rooms, peer-based education, demonstrations, grassroots activism, and ground-breaking research, VANDU's members not only risked arrest and imprisonment, they have also eliminated barriers to many pioneering harm reduction initiatives.
>
> *(pp. 143–144)*

VANDUs initiatives have helped make a significant difference in averting bloodborne infections and overdose deaths in Downtown Eastside. They have also proved that, compared to law-and-order drug policing, harm reduction carries numerous public health benefits: decreased risky injection behaviour, decreased fatal overdoses, increased probability of initiating and maintaining addiction treatment, and cost-effectiveness (Andersen & Jozaghi, 2012; Jozaghi et al., 2018; see also DeBeck et al., 2006).

One of the most successful of these initiatives is supervised drug consumption rooms (DCRs; also called safer injection sites or facilities, safer consumption services, and drug consumption facilities). First, legally sanctioned DCRs were established in Switzerland in the mid-1980s, and in the 1990s, similar sites opened also in the Netherlands and Germany (Hedrich et al., 2012). These sites provide a safe, non-judgemental environment for injecting pre-obtained drugs while under observation of trained staff, as well as appropriate guidance, equipment, and on-site links to medical care and social services.

In the late 1990s, an Australian parliamentary inquiry recommended opening a DCR (called a Medically Supervised Injecting Center or MSIC) at King's Cross, Sydney, an urban area known for its large demographic of injection drug users and public health issues related to drug use. Despite an evidence-based recommendation, the government voted against opening the site. This led to "a group of concerned citizens" establishing an unsanctioned, illegal site, because "public health practitioners wishing to improve appalling outcomes from drug policies sometimes have to resort to civil disobedience in order to achieve their goals" (Wodak et al., 2003, p. 609). It was christened the Tolerance Room, or "T-Room", and it was

> a symbol of civil disobedience – that is, action taken by a diverse group of concerned citizens contravening the law to accelerate a decision on the establishment of a trial MSIC when all other options had either been explored unsuccessfully or outright denied.
>
> *(Wodak et al., 2003, p. 609)*

The purpose of the illegal operation was to highlight the need for a publicly sanctioned and funded DCR in King's Cross and force the government to reconsider its decision. This turned out to be a successful strategy in the end, as the government reconsidered and opened a trial facility in 2001, which remains open today.

Houborg and Frank (2014) report similar cases of public health CDO from Copenhagen, Denmark, where several non-governmental organisations established an illegal DCR on their premises in the 1990s. These experiences were used to advocate for a sanctioned site, first of which opened in 2012 in Vesterbro, Copenhagen, as soon as an amendment in Danish drug laws made it possible for municipalities to establish safe injection sites with authorisation from the government.

According to Kral and Davidson (2017), the United States has now seen the "beginning phases of similar civil disobedience" regarding supervised DCRs. In September 2014, after a year of planning and preparation, a social service agency opened an unsanctioned site in an undisclosed urban area in the United States. Just like the Australian T-Room and other initially illegal DCRs, the American facility has not worked as effectively as it could have for the reason of it being unsanctioned, but it has attenuated the medical and public health fallout of the opioid epidemic.

These case studies tell us that since the 1990s, CDO has been identified as the mode or motive of political action against law-and-order drug policies in different localities around the world. This opposition identifies itself today as harm reduction, which is widely recognised not only as an effective set of practical strategies and ideas to reduce negative consequences of drug use but also a global "movement for social justice built on a belief in, and respect for, the rights of people who use drugs" (NHRC, 2020). Harm reduction opposes, in practical as well as ideological terms, the harm-producing policies and ideals of the drug war: abstinence, zero tolerance, drug-free nation, and the like (Pauly, 2008; see also Keane, 2003).

But is harm reduction against law-and-order drug policies CDO properly speaking? To answer this question we must first define the acronym, which is the subject of the following section.

Justifiable civil disobedience in a democracy

Defining civil disobedience it has become customary to begin at John Rawls's *A Theory of Justice* (1971, hence *TOJ*) and orienteering from there. Here I am looking at a different map but following a familiar looking route by going with a conceptualisation published a year before Rawls's *TOJ* in *Ethics* by the American legal and political theorist Rex Martin. There is not a lot separating Rawls's and Martin's definitions: both make an attempt to capture essentially the same political practice taking place in similar political circumstances and provide a largely shared set of criteria for using the concept in an argument.

Whereas Rawls (1971, p. 319) develops a *constitutional* theory of civil disobedience for the needs of "a more or less just democratic state", Martin (1970, p. 123) offers a philosophical analysis of the *political* form of civil disobedience and shows how it is justifiable in a democracy, making it a very useful tool for my undertaking in this chapter. Martin also uses civil disobedience against the laws prohibiting alcohol, cannabis, and LSD as examples in his text: I am here extending them to test empirical claims of CDO made in actual opposition to drug policies. In this section, I outline Martin's definition and consider whether the "public health civil disobedience" (discussed in the previous section) of harm reduction is justified. I similarly consider the case of cannabis activism in the following section.

Martin (1970) defines *CDO* as

> the deliberate and public violation of the *command* of an authorized and accepted political superior on the ground that this decree is unjust, immoral, unconstitional [*sic*], contrary to good public policy, etc. Sometimes the objection is lodged not against a specific command (law, decree) but against some *policy* of the government with which the law is connected. And sometimes the connection between the law violated and the policy protested is remote, and the act of protest or defiance becomes largely symbolic. In any case, the law is broken as a way of "getting at" the policy – to somehow frustrate the government through disobedience in order to get it to modify its policies. We should be able to count such acts of lawbreaking as civil disobedience so long as the ground of action is the claim that the government's policy is unwise, unjust, immoral, or unconstitutional. And, in either case, there is a claim, explicit or implicit, that the act of disobedience is justifiable.
>
> *(p. 126, emphasis in original)*

When is civil disobedience justifiable? Martin begins by noting that as long as immoral, unjust, impolitic laws are possible in a democracy, we implicitly recognise standards of justice external or above the democratic political process. These standards may provide moral grounds for breaking the law, but such violations are necessarily not acts of bad citizenship or attempts to subvert democratic authority.

Martin argues that civil disobedience is not conceptually incompatible with demands of democratic citizenship as long as the citizen follows principles of allowable civil disobedience in a democracy, which he finds six. I next list Martin's principles in his numerical order and measure the justifiability of (public health) civil disobedience of harm reduction in their light:

Drugs, disobedience, and democracy **69**

1. The citizen does not violate the law on the ground that he opposes the governmental authority behind the law, or that he denies the fundamental legitimacy of the law, that is, its general process of formulation and decree. Here, as is required, civil disobedience is directed against a specific law, not against the whole system of authority or the process of enactment of law in that system.

(Martin, 1970, p. 131)

Harm reductionists clear the first of Martin's conditions by remaining politically agnostic about forms and processes of government in principle, but they do make a moral demand for socially just drug policy in practice. Harm reduction is interested and invested in the health and benefit of a certain minority of subjects within the body politic, whose legal standing and political existence are encroached on by law-and-order drug policies. Violating repressive laws for humanitarian reasons highlights the worth and dignity of all people *including* those who use drugs, which stands in sharp contrast to the disrespect often associated when drug use is considered a crime and users criminals.

2. The citizen perceives the decree in question to be democratically derived. It is a law, in the sense that it is not defective from the point of view of legality. The decree or command is regarded as part of the "law of the land".

(Martin, 1970, p. 131)

Reading the case studies, it seems that harm reductionists have no problem accepting the general legality of prohibitive drug laws: they are considered democratically derived legislation further legitimised by international agreements such as the Single Convention of 1961 and institutions such as the United Nations. Having said that, they tend to think these laws are socially unjust and counterproductive for public health, and also that they infringe on human rights, but the message is not that they are not part of the law of the land but that they are bad and harmful laws for its people as they stand. So harm reduction abides by the second principle, but how about the third:

3. The citizen does not intend that his action cause the replacement of democratic political procedures with nondemocratic ones. Nor does he intend that the authorized and existing governmental system and mode of enacting laws be substantially altered in structure as a direct result of actions in defiance of law. And it is reasonable to suppose that these intentions will be sustained by events. I will summarize this principle by calling it the condition of nonrevolutionary intent and consequence.

(Martin, 1970, p. 131)

There is a historic tension between those who see the practice of harm reduction today as primarily a medical means of promoting health and mitigating harm to

70 Mika Luoma-Aho

individuals and a more activist group that sees it or at least used to see it as a plat-form for broader and more structural social change (Roe, 2005). Prior to being institutionalised as public health policy following the HIV/AIDS epidemic – stories of which we recounted in the previous section – harm reduction was as an illegal, clandestine activity that took place either outside or in defiant opposition to state and legal authority. The original, early harm reductionists of the 1960s and 1970s were united not only by their willingness to defy the letter of prohibitive and punitive drug laws but also by political opposition of the scourge itself: the state and authorities attempting to suppress drug use and turn against their drug-using citizens. As a social movement harm reduction contained outsider groups with radical ideas, and still does, but ideology is deployed more selectively now that it has become institutionalised as part of governmental policies and practices. Steering away from directly challenging prevailing drug laws and policy may be to get more harm reduction done, but Gordon Roe thinks this "new", "official", "mature", or "mainstreamed" harm reduction is

> characterized by a dangerous acceptance of the present situation of drug users, fatalism towards the prospect of larger change, failure to challenge the contradictions of licit and illicit drug use, and a continuation of the assump-tions of addiction and morality that underlie abstinence and enforcement.
>
> *(2005, p. 248)*

According to Christopher B. R. Smith, the founding philosophy and spirit of harm reduction share a number of unique parallels with the political philosophy of anar-chism. It was guided by its principles: anti-authoritarianism, distrust of hierarchy, and mutual aid. Although the adoption of harm reduction by public health authori-ties since the 1990s has diluted the originary anarchist substratum of the movement, discourses of harm reduction can still be seen as "a disguised language developed to describe an emergent anarchist model of care for capitalism's most oppressed, yet symptomatic victims" (Smith, 2012, p. 212; see also Stoller, 1998).

Having said that, there is nothing in the case studies indicating that harm reduction-ists had any revolutionary intent to replace democratic powers that be. In all the cases reported, breaking the law had "the more modest goal of frustrating specific laws of existing governments rather than of replacing one system of government with another" (Martin, 1970, p. 125). Disobeying prohibitive laws on humanitarian and public health grounds is not (yet) a demand to substantially alter structures of government, how democratic they may be. The fact that harm reductionists identify their actions in terms of CDO clearly indicates an attempt to operate within the democratic ruleset.

4. The citizen in disobeying the law does not act merely out of self-interest or merely out of some conception of what he personally should do as a moral agent; rather his action is done from some conception of polit-ical justice, the public good, social utility, or human rights. This is not to say that he cannot also act out of self-interest or the deliverances of conscience – moral or religious. It is specified merely that these are not

enough; he must include some civic-regarding principle, some conception of civil good, among his reasons for action.

(Martin, 1970, p. 131)

Even though the case studies do not really discuss the issue, I would be surprised to learn that none of the people involved in acts of CDO in harm reduction's name had personal reasons for their activism or that nobody had moral problems with the outcomes of repressive drug laws and policies. Actually, I am certain that most practitioners of harm reduction believe they were and are doing what is good and right, but there is more than deliverances of individual moral conscience to draw on here. The international harm reduction movement has articulated its political ethos since the early 1990s, when it first rose to challenge prevailing drug policy. According to Tammi and Hurme (2007), the early programmatic texts of the movement outline four political theses or principles on how to view drug use and drug users:

I. Drug use as such should be viewed neutrally, not moralistically.
II. A drug user is a sovereign citizen and member of a community, not a deviant individual or only an object of measures.
III. Drug policy should be based on practice and science, not on ideologies and dogmatism.
IV. Drug policy should respect human rights and support justice, not trample on them in the name of a "war on drugs" or the goal of a drug-free society.

(Tammi & Hurme 2007, p. 85; see also HRI, 2021)

These principles have been formulated in opposition to the political principles presupposed in the war on drugs, which threaten freedom and rights, health, and well-being among drug users and make them outlaws within the body politic. Ideologically, the international harm reduction movement looks up to, represents, and argues for the civic goods of human rights and social justice for all citizens, whether or not they use illicit substances. But Tammi and Hurme (2007) note that while harm reduction is ideologically committed to individual freedom and human rights for PWUDs, its most important public service is the promotion of public health for the benefit of the whole body politic – sometimes even to the point of breaking the law, as reported in the case studies. This is achieved by practices that "allow drug users to be free and responsible citizens who are themselves able to control their actions in the right direction from the point of view of the public interest" (p. 86). So the ethos of human rights, social justice, and public health should be more than enough reasons to satisfy Martin's fourth condition.

How about the fifth principle?

5. In disobeying the law, the citizen does not intend nor does he bring about, in a way that could be reasonably foreseen, physical harm to other persons or their property. This principle might be called the condition of Nonviolence.

(Martin, 1970, p. 132)

None of the case studies reported violent behaviour on behalf of the harm reductionists. As the name implies, harm reduction aims to "minimise negative health, social and legal impacts associated with drug use, drug policies and drug laws" (HRI, 2021). It is ideologically committed to bringing about the *opposite* of harm to people who use drugs, but not only that: it also attempts to minimise the negative consequences of drug use to society.

Martin's (1970) sixth principle has two conditions:

> 6. Finally, the citizen should disobey the law publicly and on the condition that he is willing to take the consequences as regards punishment.
>
> *(Martin, 1970, p. 132)*

All reported cases of harm reduction since the 1990s' HIV/AIDS epidemic tell a similar story: citizens involved deliberately violate drug laws not only to help individual PWUDs but also to oppose the harm-producing laws and policies of the drug war in the public sphere. For example, in Copenhagen several non-governmental organisations (NGOs) got frustrated at drug policy inertia and committed "acts of civil disobedience" in establishing illegal DCRs at their premises (Houborg & Frank, 2014, p. 4). One of the sites was a mobile unit opened in an old ambulance to widespread media attention. The Danish government publicly challenged the legality of these operations but made no attempt to close them down and make arrests.

In the Sydney case, all members of the "group of concerned citizens," who ran the illegal DCR at King's Cross, signed a document accepting joint responsibility for the project in order to ensure collective legal responsibility for their actions (Wodak et al., 2003). Their harm-reduction interventions were obstructed despite strong evidence of effectiveness, while new law enforcement interventions were often accepted without much argument. Arguments for implementing a trial MSIC had been presented in several appropriate forums, but political resistance appeared to be the only barrier to a scientific trial of this intervention. Therefore, "this group of concerned citizens turned to civil disobedience in a last resort attempt to change public policy on this issue" (p. 609).

In all the case studies reviewed earlier, the law was broken publicly, at least in the sense that authorities were aware of what was going on, likely because effective harm reduction will not stay long in hiding. Also harm reductionists violating drug laws were themselves aware of personal legal exposure and took precautions to this end (e.g. Sydney MISC). From what we can gather from these cases is that practising harm reduction among PWUDs sometimes involves publicly violating the drug policy commands of an authorised and accepted political superior on the grounds these decrees are unjust, inhuman, and contrary to public health. This satisfies both conditions of the sixth principle in Martin's definition of justifiable CDO in a democracy: that law is broken publicly and punishment accepted willingly.

We are now ready to answer the following question: Is public health civil disobedience in harm reduction's name justifiable? It certainly seems that way, as the reviewed cases satisfy all of Martin's six principles of justifiable CDO in a democracy.

The only principle that could be called into question in this case is the third: the condition of nonrevolutionary intent and consequence. One could make an argument that harm reduction is essentially a revolutionary type of CDO, because its political origins are in the anarchism and paganism of 1980s' San Francisco (see Stoller, 1998, ch. 5; see also Szalavitz, 2022). According to Martin (1970),

> a person whose acts are of the revolutionary type intends political revolution. Moreover, we can assume that he is motivated by opposition to the existing governmental system and, hence, that he would be inclined to deny the fundamental legitimacy of the law in that society.
>
> *(p. 134)*

Is the public health CDO reported in the case studies part of a scheme to overthrow the government and replace democratic institutions and principles with something else – or nothing at all? While it seems plausible in the light of the case studies that some harm reductionists may share a degree of ideological opposition towards the powers that be and their drug policies especially, the harm reduction movement itself shows zero intent towards committing a political revolution of society. In fact, it has been criticised for neutralising and depoliticising its oppositional origins since becoming institutionalised as a public health policy of the state during the HIV/ AIDS epidemic (see Roe, 2005; Smith, 2012).

Harm reduction is vintage 1970s' CDO. It suits Martin's definition but fits just as snugly in Rawls's (1971) "public, nonviolent, conscientious yet political act contrary to law usually done with the aim of bringing about a change in the law or policies of the government" (p. 320).

Marching against the war on cannabis (users)

With an estimated 192 million users worldwide, cannabis (or marijuana) is the most consumed, produced, and trafficked psychoactive substance prohibited by the global drug prohibition regime (UNODC, 2020). In recent years, Canada, Uruguay, and 11 jurisdictions in the United States have allowed the manufacture and sale of cannabis products for non-medical use. However, cannabis remains the main drug that brings people into contact with the criminal justice system, accounting for more than half of drug law offences cases, based on data from 69 countries covering the five-year period, from 2014 to 2018.

In this section, I explicate a claim of CDO made globally by a movement opposing the criminalisation of cannabis: the Global Marijuana March (GMM; or Million Marijuana March, MMM). The event takes place on the first Saturday of May in different localities and under different names, like Los Angeles Million Marijuana March, NYC Cannabis Parade in New York, Marcha da Maconha in Brazil, Marche Mondiale pour le Cannabis in France, and Hamppumarssi in Finland, to name a few. Unfortunately, there are no published case studies of these marches, like we had about the harm-reduction movement. Previous studies make brief mentions

74 Mika Luoma-Aho

of cannabis activists identifying themselves or their actions as CDO, but these are little more than empirical observations without much conceptual consideration, whether or not they qualify as such according to any proper definition of CDO. For example, Hakkarainen and Perälä (2011, p. 83) report that Finnish small-scale cannabis growers like to regard their hobby as harmless CDO rather than criminal conduct. For another, Capler et al. (2017, p. 1) report that in Canada illegal cannabis dispensaries for those in the certified medical cannabis program identify their business as conscientious CDO.

In this section, I measure the case of Hamppumarssi against Rex Martin's definition of CDO and consider the justifiability of this kind of activism in a democracy. In these tasks, I use empirical data collected through ethnographic fieldwork in 2018 and 2019 Hamppumarssi's and interviews of activists taking part in these marches. Disobedience to law is key to Rex Martin's conception of CDO, so any cannabis activists claiming it must also be breaking the law to be eligible. Even so, Martin (1970) reminds that "there are many cases of disobedience to law which are not cases of civil disobedience" and that CDO "is to be distinguished from 'demonstrations' or confrontations in which laws are not violated" (pp. 123, 126). Since I want to assess whether marching in protest for the legalisation of cannabis is a case of CDO, the first thing we have to do is go back to the beginning of this chapter – to Finland, Turku, and the Puolala Park – and look for violations of Finnish law on Hamppumarssi.

Let's begin from the "seeds of civil disobedience": is it illegal to plant hempseed in a public park? The 50th chapter of the Finnish Criminal Code criminalises the growing of cannabis to be used as narcotics or manufacture of narcotics, but establishing who is growing and what is their intention would be challenging in this case (Finlex, 2015). This is a form of guerrilla gardening: cultivating on someone else's patch of land without their prior permission. If any of these seeds grow into full plants, they would not be owned by anybody really but might get noticed by people using the park, who might report them to the police, who might then come to destroy them. Such plants are likely not grown to provide raw material for narcotics, medicine, fibre, or seed but rather function as political symbols.

Signs and banners erect Hamppumarssi departs the Puolala Park and begins a slow and steady march towards the Market Square. Just a few hundred marchers manage to get plenty of attention with their message, costumes, singing, and carnivalesque. Marching is not an illegal act, but if it came to pass that a participant in the march chose to openly consume cannabis for anything else than a certified medical purpose, this would be disobedience to Finnish law. There is nothing surprising or atypical for such lawbreaking to take place in these rallies. Thomas Heddleston (2012) does well to capture the vibe in his ethnography of the American drug policy reform movement:

> I attended a "hemp rally" in Lafayette Park in Washington, D.C. on the fourth of July, and was introduced to a loosely organized group of activists and speakers who had set up tables at the event. Activists were distributing

literature, compiling mailing lists and talking to attendees. I was shocked that attendees were openly smoking cannabis within view of the Whitehouse. I was also shocked that somewhat formal looking organizations (with folding tables and everything!) were in attendance. This small act of civil disobedience was remarkable to me for several reasons, it was collective, it was fun and I felt like I was part of something bigger than myself (as many participants in movements do). The police did not arrest anyone, despite the rampant law breaking that was going on. During the event, attendees transformed cannabis smoking from a private act of criminality to a public statement of defiance. This experience opened my eyes to the political dimensions of drug use and to the existence of a collective challenge to drug policy.

(p. 27)

So if someone were to openly consume cannabis on Hamppumarssi, would that qualify as CDO? Defining the term as "deliberate and public violation of the *command* of an authorized and accepted political superior on the ground that this decree is unjust, immoral, unconstitional [*sic*], [or] contrary to good public policy", Rex Martin (1970, p. 126) emphasises the term *command*. What *command* is violated by lighting up? It would be §2a in chapter 50 of the Criminal Code (FINLEX, 2015):

[a] person who unlawfully uses or for personal use possesses or attempts to obtain a small amount of a narcotic substance shall be sentenced for unlawful use of narcotics to a fine or to imprisonment for at most six months.

Martin (1970) also emphasises that "sometimes the objection is lodged not against a specific command (law, decree), but against some *policy* of the government with which the law is connected" (p. 126, emphasis in original). Does the Hamppumarssi identify a government policy at the receiving end of its objections? I photographed all the signs and banners carried in the march while we were still in the Puolala Park. Out of a total of thirty signs, seven made a specific demand:

- Antaa kaikkien kukkien kukkia (Let all the flowers bloom)
- Loppu huumesodalle (End the drug war)
- Stop the war
- Kannabis irti huumeista (Dissociate cannabis from drugs)
- Myöntäkää jo virhe: kieltolaki epäonnistui taas (Admit it: prohibition failed again)
- Vapaa Suomi (Free Finland)
- Keep calm and legalize it

Hamppumarssi declares diametrical opposition to the prohibition of cannabis and the law-and-order drug policy in force in Finland today. Law is broken, joints lit to "get at" this policy, frustrate the government and pressure it to modify the *status*

76 Mika Luoma-Aho

quo through public disobedience of its drug laws at peak of spring in Turku Center. Such acts of lawbreaking count as CDO, Martin (1970, p. 126) argues, "so long as the ground of action is the claim that the government's policy is unwise, unjust, immoral, or unconstitutional".

So what qualms do the activists have with the government's law and order drug policy? Two signs question the wisdom of prohibiting growing of cannabis at home. "Kotikasvattaja torjuu rikollisuutta" (Home-grower tackles crime) and "Kotikasvatus torjuu terrorismia" (Home-growing tackles terrorism) both point out the fact that in attempting to weed out small home-grows for personal use, the government is actively pushing Finnish cannabis consumers to the illegal drug market and profiting drug cartels. One of the signs, "Olemme kunnon kansalaisia, miksi lain edessä rikollisia?" (We are good citizens, why criminals before the law?), points at the injustice of prohibitionist policy: that the act of cultivation and/or use of a plant transforms otherwise law-abiding citizens into criminals. Another sign that reads "4000 vuotta lääke, 50 vuotta rikos" (4000 years a medicine, 50 years a crime) and points at the inherent immorality of the war on drugs, which has accomplished, among many other things, in politically redefining a natural remedy used by human beings all over the world for thousands of years into a dangerous controlled substance. Finally, "Omistaako valtio kehoni ja mieleni" (Does the state own my mind and body?) questions the constitutionality of prohibition. In its section seven, the Constitution of Finland guarantees personal liberty for all citizens, but this right is routinely set aside if it turns out its subject is using cannabis.

But is marching against cannabis prohibition a justifiable form of CDO in a democracy? To answer this question it must pass the litmus test of Martin's six principles of allowable CDO in a democracy laid out in the previous section. I now apply these principles to the movement opposing the criminalisation of cannabis focusing especially on my ethnographic research on Hamppumarssi.

First, three principles pass without much to argue about. According to the first one (1), CDO should not be used to oppose the governmental authority behind the law or deny its fundamental legitimacy. There is virtually nothing in my research material indicating that Hamppumarssi opposes anything beyond the drug policy *status quo* in Finland. This opposition is articulated as support of drug policy reform, which to some activists means ending the prohibition of cannabis in Finland, while others look towards a more comprehensive decriminalisation or legalisation including not only cannabis but also most or all currently illegal psychoactive substances. The second principle decrees that the law or policy opposed with CDO is nevertheless perceived as democratically derived "law of the land". This is, by and large, accepted by the activists as a matter of fact, although they often like to add that the decision to criminalise personal drug use in the 1972 Narcotics Act passed a tied vote in the parliaments Grand Committee only after drawing a random ballot (see Hakkarainen, 1992). Martin called his third principle the condition of nonrevolutionary intent and consequence: that the citizen does not intend that his CDO causes the replacement of democratic political procedures with nondemocratic ones. Again, there is nothing in my materials betraying political motives beyond drug policy reform. It is of course possible that individual activists may harbour more far-reaching views and oppose principles of political and/or legal authority in Finland, but they are not on display in Hamppumarssi.

According to the fourth principle, the disobedient citizen does not act out of mere self-interest but rather acts "from some conception of political justice, the public good, social utility, or human rights" (Martin, 1970, p. 131). With this principle in mind, one may be tempted to argue that marching to end the prohibition of cannabis activists merely want to reserve their personal right to grow and consume the plant for themselves, and no sincere altruistic motives for disobedience actually exist. For example, Martin himself thinks that widespread breaking of laws prohibiting alcohol a century ago was not CDO properly speaking, because people doing so were not motivated by politics as much as "they liked gin" (Martin, 1970, pp. 123–124). It may be valid to infer that if you are ready to break laws prohibiting cannabis in broad daylight of spring in downtown Turku, then it is also plausible you like weed, but is there anything else motivating activists in this case? Martin reminds us that self-interest or deliverances of individual conscience are not enough to justify CDO in a democracy, as "some civic-regarding principle, some conception of civil good" must also be included as reasons for action (Martin, 1970, p. 131).

So the question is this: Is Hamppumarssi a demonstration of the personal moral considerations of cannabis activists taking part in the march, or a collective act of political objection aimed outside, above or beyond itself and its immediate participants? Looking for answers to this question from the signs carried at the march, they do make explicit and starkly oppose at least two types of "civil bad" caused by the prevailing law and order drug policy:

I. Prohibition has failed. Its outcomes are ineffective and unfair, and it is not achieving its goal of reducing harm caused by the drug to individuals and society. It is actually doing the opposite by sustaining a repressive policy in an environment where the use of cannabis is ever-increasing and has arguably become more or less normalised over the last few decades. Criminalisation of its users is no longer a good use of taxpayer euros (indeed if it has ever been), but has become "a wolf in sheep's clothing", as one of the signs carried in the protest proclaims.
II. Prohibition means war. It is not, however, a war on cannabis (or any other psychoactive substance) as such, but a kind of civil war on a minority of Finnish citizens using and cultivating the plant. This minority has been lawfully persecuted now for at least half a century and the legal, political, and social forms this persecution takes seem highly resistant to reform. Cannabis activism is essentially an anti-war movement and Hamppumarssi its most public statement of defiance in this country. "No more drug war", the signs protest, because "Huumesota tappaa" (Drug war kills).

Martin (1970) calls his fifth principle (5) the condition of nonviolence: that in disobedient acts of lawbreaking the "citizen does not intend nor does he bring about,

78 Mika Luoma-Aho

in a way that could be reasonably foreseen, physical harm to other persons or their property" (p. 132). It is not easy to foresee a plausible scenario where someone's consumption of cannabis would be a cause of direct harm to another person or their property. Of course, it may be disturbing or distracting to suddenly witness while shopping the Turku market square, but this hardly crosses the threshold of violence set by the condition. The sixth principle (6) decrees that the citizen "should disobey the law publicly and on the condition that he is willing to take the consequences as regards punishment" (p. 132). Breaking the law while demonstrating in Turku centre at noon on a spring Saturday is public disobedience without question. My interviewees recalled the police being present and making some arrests for narcotics offences in the early years of the march, the consequences of which were more or less willingly accepted. Since then, the police have given little to no attention to the event. I did not spot a single uniform or patrol vehicle during either 2018 or 2019 Hamppumarssi's.

So cannabis activism sometimes involves publicly violating the drug policy commands of an authorised and accepted political superior on the grounds these decrees are unwise and dehumanising. Taking part is to protest the law and order of the drug war.

Conclusion

The purpose of Rex Martin's philosophical analysis of the concept of CDO is to find a place for the political type of CDO in democratic political philosophy: In what sense and under what conditions can lawbreaking for political reasons be justifiable under a government ruled by law? Martin does not exclude any possible ground of disobedience to law or policy as democratically unjustifiable in his analysis, so basically any command made by any government we identify as "democratic" can be resisted with CDO – even the command not to do drugs.

Both harm reductionists and cannabis activists break laws and make claims about CDO while doing so. It seems they have the *locus standi* granted by the political form of CDO, at least in Martin's philosophical schema, but what do they want? The answer given as justification by both of our cases is human rights and social justice to PWUDs, which have been denied by governments fighting the war on drugs. This demand has been made by disobedient harm reductionists and cannabis activists around the world ever since the war was declared.

But law and order prevails, and the war continues. How can this be explained? How can democratic systems of government built on ideals of social justice and human rights for all continue to deny these rights from PWUDs? How, in defiance of global movements of CDO discussed in this chapter, can democracies around the world justify half a century of civil war against their drug-using citizens?

There are at least three objections democracies raise against the claims of drug policy reform made by both harm reductionists and cannabis activists. The first and most categorical objection is that CDO should not be permitted in drug policy contexts, because it is *in itself* an unjustifiable vehicle for changing policy in *any* context in a democratic system. Let me give an example. A Finnish law professor, Jukka Kekkonen, recently argued that CDO is incompatible in a "functioning democracy", where there is no longer reason to break the law to reform government policy. This is to say that in a democratic state governed by the rule of law, presumably a state like Finland, CDO should not be permitted even in principle (Kekkonen, 2020). In *TOJ*, Rawls (1971) states that his theory is "designed only for the special case of a nearly just society, one that is well-ordered for the most part but in which some serious violations of justice nevertheless do occur" (p. 363; see also Jubb, 2019). What Kekkonen seems to imply is that there can be democratic systems which have developed "just enough" that they can be considered beyond nearly just. In these (just or fully just?) societies, CDO is always unjustified and breaking the law for political reasons is either simply criminal behaviour or possibly revolutionary political action, and there is no legitimate justification for CDO in between.

Another objection lodged against drug policy CDO is that drugs are an existential threat to society which lie partly or fully outside the sphere of democratic principles and participation. Ever since the beginning of the war on drugs, drug production, use, and supply have all been presented as threats to human, national, or international security (see Crick, 2012). The first international drug control convention concerned itself with preventing the "social and economic danger to mankind" brought about by addiction (United Nations, 1961). After the Cold War, the focus of international drug policy was associated less with humankind's well-being than the security of the state (United Nations, 1988). In security's ambiguous logic, dangerous drugs are enemies of society and containing them one simply cannot afford to follow normal democratic rules or respect equal rights. In about 50 years, the war on drugs has gradually blurred the line between policing controlled substances and waging a low-intensity civil war. With these conventions and over decades political violence against PWUDs has become legitimate protection for people who *do not* use drugs.

The third objection to the CDO of both harm reductionists and cannabis activists is that there is something about using drugs that makes PWUDs lesser human beings and forfeits all or some of the rights of (fully) human beings, people who do not use drugs. This objection is difficult to understandably explain – how can dabbling in a man-made category of substances demote one's species of being? – but clearly recognisable in drug policy discourse, where it operates to legitimise law and order drug policing and keeping PWUDs at a distance from the rest of society. Ever since the 1990s (if not before that, see Szalavitz, 2022), drug policy CDO has played a key role in forcing policymakers to consider the broader implications of such a political anthropology and making dehumanising talk and policy more difficult to sustain. Harm reduction and cannabis activism are political forms of *rehumanising* how we see drug use and PWUDs and bringing about a reform: a sustainable policy that accepts that there is a minority (if not a majority) of people in every society who use drugs and will continue to do so, and there will never be enough of law and order to make it go away.

80 Mika Luoma-Aho

References

Andersen, M. A., & Jozaghi, E. (2012). The point of diminishing returns: An examination of expanding Vancouver's Insite. *Urban Studies*, *49*(16), 3531–3544. https://doi.org/10.1177%2F0042098012443865

Baum, D. (1997). *Smoke and mirrors: The war on drugs and the politics of failure*. Back Bay Books.

Buchanan, J., & Young, L. (2000). The war on drugs – A war on drug users. *Drugs: Education, Prevention, Policy*, *7*(4), 409–422. https://doi.org/10.1080/dep.7.4.409.422

Capler, R., Walsh, Z., Crosby, K., Belle-Isle, L., Holtzman, S., Lucas, P., & Callaway, R. (2017). Are dispensaries indispensable? Patient experiences of access to cannabis from medical cannabis dispensaries in Canada. *International Journal of Drug Policy*, *47*, 1–8. https://doi.org/10.1016/j.drugpo.2017.05.046

Crick, E. (2012). Drugs as an existential threat: An analysis of the international securitization of drugs. *International Journal of Drug Policy*, *23*(5), 407–414. https://doi.org/10.1016/j.drugpo.2012.03.004

DeBeck, K., Wood, E., Montaner, J., & Kerr, T. (2006). Canada's 2003 renewed drug strategy – An evidence-based review. *HIV/AIDS Policy & Law Review*, *11*(2–3), 1–5.

Finlex. (2015). *The Criminal Code of Finland 39/1889, amendments up to 766/2015 included*. https://www.finlex.fi/fi/laki/kaannokset/1889/en18890039.pdf

Gray, J. P. (2012). *Why our drug laws have failed and what we can do about it: A judicial indictment of the war on drugs*. Temple University Press.

Hakkarainen, P. (1992). *Suomalainen huumekysymys: huumausaineiden yhteiskunnallinen paikka Suomessa toisen maailmansodan jälkeen*. Alkoholitutkimussäätiö.

Hakkarainen, P., & Perälä, J. (2011). With a little help from my friends – Justifications of small-scale cannabis growers. In T. Decorte, G. Potter & M. Bouchard (Eds.), *World wide weed: Global trends in cannabis cultivation and its control* (pp. 75–90). Ashgate.

Heddleston, T. (2012). *From the frontlines to the bottom line: Medical marijuana, the war on drugs, and the drug policy reform movement* [Doctoral Dissertation, University of California, Santa Cruz]. eScholarship, Open Access Publications from the University of California. https://escholarship.org/uc/item/1t7220hj#main

Hedrich, D., Kerr, T., & Dubois-Arber, F. (2012). Drug consumption facilities in Europe and beyond. In T. Rhodes & D. Hedrich (Eds.), *Harm reduction: Evidence, impacts and challenges* (pp. 305–329). EMCDDA Monograph.

Houborg, E., & Frank, V. A. (2014). Drug consumption rooms and the role of politics and governance in policy processes. *International Journal of Drug Policy*, *25*(5), 972–977. https://doi.org/10.1016/j.drugpo.2014.01.008

HRI. (2021). *What is harm reduction?* Harm Reduction International. https://www.hri.global/what-is-harm-reduction

Johns, C. J. (1992). *Power, ideology, and the war on drugs: Nothing succeeds like failure*. Praeger.

Jozaghi, E., Greer, A. M., Lampkin, H., & Buxton, J. A. (2018). Activism and scientific research: 20 years of community action by the Vancouver area network of drug users. *Substance Abuse Treatment, Prevention, and Policy*, *13*. https://doi.org/10.1186/s13011-018-0158-1

Jozaghi, E., & Yake, K. (2020). Two decades of activism, social justice, and public health civil disobedience: VANDU. *Canadian Journal of Public Health*, *111*, 143–144. https://doi.org/10.17269/s41997-019-00287-0

Jubb, R. (2019). Disaggregating political authority: What's wrong with Rawlsian civil disobedience? *Political Studies*, *67*(4), 955–971. https://doi.org/10.1177/0032321718816208

Keane, H. (2003). Critiques of harm reduction, morality and the promise of human rights. *International Journal of Drug Policy*, *14*(3), 227–232. https://doi.org/10.1016/s0955-3959(02)00151-2

Kekkonen, J. (2020, Jan 18). Lukijalta: Kansalaistottelemattomuus ei kuulu demokraattiseen oikeusvaltioon. *Turun Sanomat.* https://www.ts.fi/lukijoilta/4830979

Kerr, T., Small, W., Peeace, W., Douglas, D., Pierre, A., & Wood, E. (2006). Harm reduction by a "user-run" organization: A case study of the Vancouver Area Network of Drug Users (VANDU). *International Journal of Drug Policy, 17*(2), 61–69. https://doi.org/10.1016/j.drugpo.2006.01.003

Kral, A. H., & Davidson, P. J. (2017). Addressing the nation's opioid epidemic: Lessons from an unsanctioned supervised injection site in the US. *American Journal of Preventive Medicine, 53*(6), 919–922. https://doi.org/10.1016/j.amepre.2017.06.010

Martin, R. (1970). Civil disobedience. *Ethics, 80*(2), 123–139. https://doi.org/10.1086/291760

Nadelmann, E. (1990). Global prohibition regimes: The evolution of norms in international society. *International Organization, 44*(4), 479–526. https://doi.org/10.1017/S0020818300035384

Neill, K. A. (2014). Tough on drugs: Law and order dominance and the neglect of public health in U.S. drug policy. *World Medical & Health Policy, 6*(4), 375–394. https://doi.org/10.1002/wmh3.123

NHRC. (2020). *Principles of harm reduction.* National Harm Reduction Coalition. https://harmreduction.org/about-us/principles-of-harm-reduction/

Pauly, B. (2008). Harm reduction through a social justice lens. *International Journal of Drug Policy, 19*(1), 4–10. https://doi.org/10.1016/j.drugpo.2007.11.005

Pryce, S. (2012). *Fixing drugs the politics of drug prohibition.* Palgrave Macmillan.

Rawls, J. (1971). *A theory of justice.* Belknap Press of Harvard University Press.

Roe, G. (2005). Harm reduction as paradigm: Is better than bad good enough? The origins of harm reduction. *Critical Public Health, 15*(3), 243–250. https://doi.org/10.1080/09581590500372188

Smith, C. B. R. (2012). Harm reduction as anarchist practice: A user's guide to capitalism and addiction in North America. *Critical Public Health, 22*(2), 209–221. https://doi.org/10.1080/09581596.2011.611487

Stoller, N. E. (1998). *Lessons from the damned: Queers, whores, and junkies respond to AIDS.* Routledge.

Szalavitz, M. (2022). *Undoing drugs: The untold story of harm reduction and the future of addiction.* Hachette GO.

Tammi, T., & Hurme, T. (2007). How the harm reduction movement contrasts itself against punitive prohibition. *International Journal of Drug Policy, 18*(2), 84–87. https://doi.org/10.1016/j.drugpo.2006.11.003

THL. (2019). *Alkoholi, tupakka ja riippuvuudet: Kannabiksen käyttö Suomessa.* Terveyden ja hyvinvoinnin laitos. https://thl.fi/fi/web/alkoholi-tupakka-ja-riippuvuudet/huumeet/kannabis/kannabiksen-kaytto-suomessa

United Nations. (1961). *Single convention on narcotic drugs.* https://www.unodc.org/unodc/en/treaties/single-convention.html?ref=menuside

United Nations. (1988). *Convention against illicit trafficking of narcotic drugs and psychotropic substances.* https://www.unodc.org/unodc/en/treaties/illicit-trafficking.html?ref=menuside

UNODC. (2020). *UNODC World Drug Report 2020: Global drug use rising; while COVID-19 has far reaching impact on global drug markets.* United Nations Office on Drugs and Crime. https://www.unodc.org/unodc/press/releases/2020/June/media-advisory---global-launch-of-the-2020-world-drug-report.html

Wodak, A., Symonds, A., & Richmond, R. (2003). The role of civil disobedience in drug policy reform: How an illegal safer injection room led to a sanctioned, Medically Supervised Injection Center. *Journal of Drug Issues, 33*(3), 609–623. https://doi.org/10.1177/002204260303300304

PART II

Alternative insights and extensions of civil disobedience

6

OPEN-SOURCE DISOBEDIENCE

Rise of civic hacktivism in Taiwan

Sami Kotiranta

Introduction

Taiwan has in recent years gone through a civil society driven shift towards a more participatory system of governance. The social unrest that grew out of widespread frustration towards the secretive elitist political culture led to weeks-long mass protests and the occupation of the parliament in 2014. The so-called Sunflower Movement was a watershed moment in Taiwanese politics that made the transformative agenda of hacktivist communities a key component of the ongoing public governance reform. I look into the use of digital civil disobedience to understand what factors contributed to a positive societal impact, which in Taiwan can be seen as a transformative process that moves through stages of civic action, from empowerment to engagement to establishment.

Research question and the concept of civil disobedience

Digital transformation has been a characteristic of many civic movements throughout the ongoing century. New media, new cultures, and globally networked societies are enabling new forms of protest. In Taiwan, civic hacktivists were able to combine the use of technology with other more traditional forms of civil disobedience and achieve a peaceful transformation in the Taiwanese political culture and system of governance. As many less successful movements around the world have applied some of the same methods, this raises the question, What factors contributed to the successful use of digital civil disobedience in Taiwan for a positive societal impact?

I approach this question by looking into the methods applied by key actors in the Taiwanese transition and to the interplay between civil society and formal power. There are a number of available sources that offer a detailed historical record of

DOI: 10.4324/9781003320494-8

the Taiwanese transition. This being said, as transparency has been long extending requisitions of the Taiwanese civil movements, they have made a conscious effort to document their work and the amount of available data sets constraints to the level of depth that can be reached in a short article. For the g0v network, the most important sources are websites and web-based tools hosted by the collective. For the Sunflower Movement, the best sources are the Daybreak Project (2021) archive and the Democracy at 4am (2014) timeline. As for the following work done within the cabinet, the best source is the transcription archive published by the digital minister Audrey Tang in SayIt (2021). Traditional news media is also used as a source throughout this study.

The amount and heterogeneity of the available data set constraints for a suitable research method. I use deductive thematic analysis to recognise key components that relate especially to the successful civil society–driven transition towards a participatory system of governance. These components include, but are not limited to, the use of civic technology. My understanding is that the success of the Taiwanese civic movements is based on the successful combination of online and offline activism and narrowly focusing on only one of these is counterintuitive, even though the use of civic technology is in focus. Outlining a metanarrative of the transition process and highlighting the most important aspects relating to the unobstructed flow of the process helps to draw some generalisable lessons from the Taiwanese example.

The concept of civil disobedience in this chapter builds on William Smith's (2013) deliberative theory of civil disobedience. This theory brings together elements of liberal and democratic concepts of civil disobedience which, according to Smith, both encounter problems with majoritarian decision-making. The liberal approach highlighted by John Rawls, Ronald Dworkin, and Gerald Cohen, is most concerned over infringements of personal freedom and sees the role of civil disobedience as ensuring the results of democratic process enact the liberal theory of justice. The democratic approach, associated with Hannah Arendt, Jürgen Habermas, and Daniel Markovits, on the other hand, highlights the justification of civil disobedience for its role in ensuring the democratic process enacts requirements set by the normative theory of democracy (Smith, 2013, pp. 8–9). Both liberal and democratic approaches have played a part in the Taiwanese transition at different times. Smith's deliberative theory of civil disobedience is, however, a particularly suitable approach when looking at the whole process of transformation as participatory governance and deliberative democracy are recurring themes that were carried over throughout the transitions.

The use of digital innovation and, more broadly, the effect of internet cultures can be seen as major contributing factors to the Taiwanese transition and the calls for a more personal and real-time interaction between the citizenry and the government mirrors the way services are designed and provided online. Even very early on in the Taiwanese transition, increasing the active civic participation in decision-making was an implicit aim of the activists. Initially, this encountered opposition from the government as powerholders are understandably hesitant to share power and to go over the process of creating a closer-knit working relationship with citizens. This conflict between demands for a more inclusive system of governance and the will to uphold the status quo is an important source of dissonance that relates to the justification of civil disobedience in the deliberative system.

As William Smith (2013, p. 60) points out, deliberative democracy and civil disobedience have a conflicted relationship, as placidity is often regarded as a precursor of a successful deliberation process. There is however only a thin line between an acceptable and a non-acceptable level of conflict. Some level of civil disobedience should be understood as an integral part of a functional deliberative system as it serves an important role in all democracies. Civil disobedience in deliberative democracy, according to W. Smith (2013, pp. 60–61), "contributes to the re-establishment of a deliberative environment in the event of inertial breakdowns and as a form of political communication that is a constitutive feature of that environment". Ideally, deliberation is always conducted in a respectful manner, but as the interaction in a deliberative setting inevitably cannot live up to this idea, breakaways are often regarded as useful when they contribute to reinstating of the environment (Smith, 2013, p. 12). In the Taiwanese example, deliberative civil disobedience has been a component throughout the transition, but as I aim to illustrate, civil disobedience has been justified differently at different times.

History

For understanding present-day Taiwanese society and politics, it is important to first look into the history of the Republic of China. In the fall of the Quin dynasty in the 1920s, the Chinese Nationalist Party, Kuomintang, led by Chiang Kai-shek and the Chinese Communist Party, took over the warlord ruled Chinese Mainland. This Northern Expedition campaign from 1926 onwards led to the forming of the Republic of China (Paltemaa, 2018, pp. 215–222). Despite having an alliance with the communists and being armed and trained by the Soviet Union, Chiang Kai-shek launched a purge against the Chinese Communist Party on April 12, 1927, igniting the Chinese Civil War of 1927–1949 (Paltemaa, 2018, pp. 222–225). During the civil war, which on its own claimed millions of lives, Imperial Japan was colonising parts of China, and this finally escalated to the devastating Second Sino-Japanese War of 1937–1945 (Paltemaa, 2018, pp. 225–228). War against Japan forged an uneasy alliance between the competing Chinese parties, but after the Japanese surrender in 1945 Kuomintang suffered a decisive defeat to the communists and more than 2 million people retreated to the island of Taiwan (Paltemaa, 2018, pp. 228–234).

In 1947, following a native Taiwanese uprising against the relocating Kuomintang regime, KMT soldiers massacred some 20,000 people around Taiwan and martial law was consequently declared in 1949. The martial law was enforced for 38 years and ended only in 1987. This period of systematic oppression of political dissidents is often referred to as White Terror. Democratic history of Taiwan begins after the end of martial law, when the formation of new political parties was allowed (Morris, 2019). The authoritarian era has a deep imprint on Taiwanese political culture as Kuomintang remained in office until 2016. Even though the KMT party is not the same it once was, Kuomintang has never truly had to reconcile with the era of White Terror, and even though modern Taiwan can be regarded as an open and democratic society (Lin et al., 2005, pp. 92–96), for many Taiwanese people the memories of the authoritarian rule are still vivid.

The relationship between the Republic of China (ROC) relationship and the People's Republic of China (PRC) is also an open wound. No formal truce was ever signed between ROC and PRC, and following the exile, as the president of the ROC, Chiang Kai-shek, continued to voice claims over the rightful rule over the entire Chinese mainland. Kuomintang continued to seek unification through conquest throughout the early Cold War era, but following the death of Chiang Kai-shek in 1975, this stance shifted towards a deepening cross-strait economic cooperation. Kuomintang has since all but given up on the anti-communist ideology following decades of close-knit economic cooperation with the PRC (Chen et al., 2020; Paltemaa, 2018, pp. 223–224). However, as PRC has over time become much stronger, both economically and militarily, and unequivocally regards the island of Taiwan as part of itself, all Taiwanese politics is overshadowed by this issue.

Relationship with the PRC remains the single biggest issue of Taiwanese politics. Present-day Taiwan can be seen divided over this issue into two camps, with one claiming de facto independence since 1949 or actively seeking legally recognised independence and the other seeking unification with the PRC by either accepting PRC rule over Taiwan or still pertaining to Chiang Kai-shek's claims of the ROC's rule over the entire Chinese mainland. Kuomintang and a few other right-wing parties belong to the latter "one China" encampment, whereas the left-leaning Democratic Progressive Party (DPP) and a few others are more vocal about Taiwanese independence. Within these encampments there is also a division over the need for a constitutional reform that would move the situation forward one way or the other, with some favouring the solution to the long-standing issue and some favouring the status quo. So far, the status quo has prevailed as any solution beyond the annexation of Taiwan to the PRC could potentially trigger the PRC invasion. These fears are reflected in public opinion as recent polls suggest that while a vast majority of the Taiwanese people (71.1%) support the DPP's stance of de facto independence since 1949, they would for now maintain the status quo (53.9%) Chen et al., 2020).

Despite the bloody history, prolonged authoritarian rule, and growing uncertainty over the future, Taiwan has advanced tremendously as a society. It is one of the economic and technological powerhouses of the region. Combining the well-performing national tech sector with the introduction of the commercial internet from 1989 onwards, Taiwanese democratic history has been characterised by rapid technological advancement and a high internet penetration rate. A generational gap exists between those who have witnessed poverty and the era of authoritarian rule and the younger generations, who have grown up with the internet in a free, stable, safe, and wealthy society, and this is reflected also in attitudes towards China. Younger cohorts and especially the DPP supporters favour closer economic and political ties with the United States over the PRC. Mere 24% of DPP supporters wish for closer economic ties with the PRC, with Kuomintang supporters hailing this with 83% support (Devlin & Huang, 2020). The political turmoil in Taiwan and the end of the Kuomintang rule can therefore be regarded also as a geopolitical shift towards the West, even though the pro-US or anti-PRC attitudes may not be explicit in the rhetoric, and for many activists, different themes may be more important.

g0v (gov-zero)

g0v (2021a) is a self-proclaimed hacktivist community that was established in 2012. The community is one of the key actors that paved the way for the 2014 Sunflower Movement protests. Although the Sunflower Movement was a joint action of several non-governmental organisations and activist groups, g0v contributed heavily to framing the issues before the protests, it played a key role in the facilitation of the occupation of the parliament building (Legislative Yuan), and after the protests, it achieved an established collaborative role with the government. One of the most active members of g0v, Audrey Tang, was even made the first digital minister of Taiwan in 2016.

g0v started out as a loose network of like-minded techies who drew inspiration not only from a shared sense of frustration towards the Taiwanese government due to its lack of transparency but also from a feeling that social media, despite its established role in Taiwanese society, had failed to act as a platform for civic engagement. In 2012, internet activist T. H. Schee (2012) outlined some issues with the present state of Taiwanese civil society (g0v, 2014a):

1. Nonprofit organisations' media exposure was ineffective and not proactive.
2. Individuals felt powerless to influence policies and politics.
3. Online participation could not translate into offline action or collaboration.
4. Open-source communities cared little for social issues.
5. A generation gap prevented offline and online activists from collaborating.

These themes and the issue of transparency in the Taiwanese political culture relate closely to the justification of civil disobedience. Bad government communication, outdated work practices, inaccessibility of information, and political culture that shunned the internet public hampered the Taiwanese civil society from taking part in decision-making, and all of this can be seen as a part of an exclusionary and elitist political culture. The lack of transparency and the accessibility of information are issues that relate to a broader question of freedom of information, which can be understood as a fundamental right (De Marneffe, 2014) as it is a key component to freedom of thought and freedom of expression (UN General Assembly, 1948). Arguably, g0v was positioning itself and seeking justification for its work from the liberal tradition of civil disobedience in which the justice aspect can override the formal power held even by a democratically elected parliament. At this stage

Taiwanese government was clearly not overstepping its prerogative, which would legitimise the civil disobedience from the point of view of the normative theory of democracy, but the infringement of fundamental rights can be argued to justify defiance based on the liberal theory of justice, especially if these issues are long-standing (Delmas & Brownlee, 2021).

The emergence of g0v in 2012 came with a backdrop of two embarrassing government failures, which offered an opportunity for civil society actors to challenge the political culture of Taiwan. Recently re-elected president Ma Ying-jeou had made the issues of transparency in real estate transactions a key component in his presidential campaign. In October 2012, the Taiwanese Ministry of Interior launched an online platform (內政部地政司, 2021) which allowed people to search for the transaction records of real estate based on street address. However, as the government website quickly became inaccessible due to heavy traffic, a small team of engineers from google.tw built a custom-made internet crawler for the website and lighter Google Maps based Real-Price Maps. This alternative website was well received by the public and initially also by the government, but the juxtaposition of these projects in the Taiwanese media quickly ruined any changes for possible collaboration, as the government was made into a laughing stock. The legality of crawling government websites was called into question, as this adds to the server downtime, and this was claimed to be one of the reasons why the official website was inaccessible. Eventually in November 2012, changes were made to the original website, making crawling more difficult. Real-Price Map was shut down due to these changes, but the bad press would not end there (g0v, 2014a).

Around this time, the government of Taiwan produced a short public relations video: "What's the Economy Power-Up Plan?" which was ridiculed for its lack of tangible content. Meanwhile, some members of the sprouting g0v hacktivist community took part in the Yahoo Open Hack Day 2012 hackathon and drew inspiration from the then ongoing scandal. The Hacker #15 team won the hackathon with a bird's-eye-view presentation of the government budget, which allowed the user to see the proportional spending of different government institutions. The tool challenged the widely ridiculed, public communication tactics applied by the Taiwanese government and offered a distinctly different approach to dealing with complicated public relations issues. Furthermore, team member CL Kao came up with a domain name g0v.tw mimicking the official government gov.tw domain. Budget visualisation (g0v, 2021b) was made publicly available after the hackathon (g0v, 2014a).

The g0v community was gaining momentum and decided to keep making civic remixes of government content and use the prize money from the Yahoo hackathon to start a new series of hackathon events supporting this cause (g0v, 2014a). These events quickly became a hub for like-minded people, the community grew, and many successful civic remixes followed (g0v, 2014a). The initial reluctance of the government to support or even to allow forking of government content gradually shifted towards an uneasy collaboration (g0v, 2014a). The government was simply unable to disagree with the claims of fair use as the community-driven efforts were strictly not-for-profit (g0v, 2014a). Audrey Tang depicts this dynamic between the g0v movement and the government as she first came across it on the MoeDict project.

Audrey Tang is a Taiwanese developer who had dropped out of high school with the blessing of the school's principal to pursue an international career as a developer at a very young age. She had worked or been associated with a number of US tech companies, notably SocialText and Apple (Azhar, 2020). Tang joined g0v soon after its origin and first started working on an online dictionary called MoeDict, which was a remake and an extension to an existing online dictionary hosted by the Ministry of Education (Tang, 2016a). The underlying dictionary has been updated since 1945 and was considered one of the best sources for traditional Chinese, but the official website was very old, dating back to 1996. Even though the site was still operational, it was needlessly difficult to access and use, as it predated the http protocol. Tang had previously had to use the content of the legacy website in a teaching role and had built a more accessible version of it. This could not however be made publicly available as it violated the copyrights. Encouraged by fellow g0v activists, Tang (2016b) used the g0v movement not only to crowdsource the work involved to perfect the remake but also to legitimise the copyright infringement:

> we used a loophole in the Taiwan copyright law. It says a government publication, if it's used in a non-profiting fair use doctrine, part of it may be reused without criminal penalties. But the problem fair use is of course the question: 'How much is too much?' We are using 100% of the data so we had to relinquish 100% of the copyright. We are not doing derived work, we're technically just converting formats for the government. So a complete reuse warrants a complete abandonment of copyright. We then argue under the Taiwan fair-use doctrine that this is fair-use. We are hundreds of people. This is really civil disobedience.
>
> *(Tang, 2016b)*

As the interaction between the Taiwanese government and the hacktivist community was becoming more familiar, g0v adopted a supportive role. Instead of merely criticising the work done by the government, g0v aimed to demonstrate how, in its view, things could be done differently. Changes within the public sector could be forwarded by building contesting and complementing models. The g0v community drew inspiration from examples of new approaches to policymaking worldwide. As g0v was forwarding an inclusive, transparent, and decentralised system of governance, the community made a conscious choice to start developing new systems for online participatory policy formation and drawing lessons from the open-source community's decades-long work of contesting the strictly for-profit business culture. When the Sunflower Movement took off in 2014, g0v was already an established network with a shared vision of an alternative way of engaging with the public. It had recognised fault lines in the Taiwanese administrative and political cultures and sought to find workable solutions. g0v highlighted many of the themes

92 Sami Kotiranta

that acted as a catalyst of the Sunflower Movement, but g0v was also able to use the momentum of the mass protests to bring about a more permanent paradigm shift in Taiwanese politics.

Sunflower Movement

The Sunflower Movement was a three-week-long mass demonstration and occupation of the Taiwanese parliament building, the Legislative Yuan. The protests were a collaborative effort of several civic rights organisations, and at its height, some 500,000 people took to the streets of Taipei. Where the work of g0v can be depicted as an ongoing battle for fundamental rights (freedom of information, freedom of expression, inclusion in decision-making), the justification of the Sunflower Movement comes closer to the normative democratic theory. Confining the Sunflower Movement to a narrow concept of civil disobedience is, however, counterintuitive, and it can be understood as a step in a larger mass movement for a more inclusive, open, and democratic system of governance and resisting the Chinese influence within Taiwan.

The Sunflower Movement grew out of a sense of disgruntlement voiced by g0v and other activist groups. The protests were a backlash against the handling of a proposed free-trade policy, which was perceived as a breach of democratic principles, although forwarded by a democratically elected majority government operating within its powers. This is a presentable case where a democratic authority is viewed to lose its prerogative as the forwarded policy seemed to infringe on citizens' preferences and the initial public outcry did not make the government reconsider this choice. As Daniel Markovits (2005, pp. 1933–1934) outlines, the justification of democratic civil disobedience comes from upholding democratic principles, even when this may contest the democratically elected parliament. A justification for civil disobedience does not automatically derive from disagreement with the elected parliament but from a widely supported idea that a policy goes against the citizen preferences or the institutional continuity. A particularly important component in the Taiwanese case is the perceived loss of Taiwanese sovereignty and that the government was thereby overstepping its republican democratic authority by enabling a system for possible external control.

The Sunflower Movement follows a plan of action that is somewhat characteristic of Taiwanese activism. Despite the long authoritarian past, Taiwan has now a fairly active civil society and there have also been several large-scale mass protests throughout the Taiwanese democratic history. These include the Wild Lily's movement in 1990 (Daybreak, 2017a) and the Wild Strawberries in 2008 (Daybreak, 2017b). Many pre-existing activist networks besides the g0v also played a vital role for the Sunflower Movement. All in all, some 53 activist groups (Daybreak, 2017c) took part in the protests and this alliance was called the Democratic Front (Daybreak, 2017d). It is arguable that despite many shared themes, such as opposing the lack of transparency in Taiwanese politics or free trade, or mere disenfranchisement with the ruling Kuomintang party and a left-leaning tendency among the activists

(Daybreak, 2017e), the true common ground shared by the participants may have been the resentment towards deepening Chinese influence in Taiwan. Even though this issue is not often explicitly voiced in the public communication around the movement (Daybreak, 2017f), resisting Chinese authoritarianism is often regarded as the most important factor of the Sunflower Movement (Daybreak, 2016).

Nevertheless, the Sunflower Movement was a backlash against the Cross-Strait Service Trade Agreement (CSSTA) (4am.tw, 2014). CSSTA was passed on June 21, 2013, as a part of the 2010 free trade agreement between Taiwan and the PRC. The secretive way that the ruling Kuomintang party seemed to rush forward the ratification of the CSSTA pact without properly addressing the concerns voiced about the impacts on national security led to brawls breaking out in the March 2014 deliberation sittings (4am.tw, 2014). Although the Kuomintang-led government did agree to deliberation so that the public can voice their concerns, it failed to address any of the raised issues and the dismissive way this was conducted nullified the use of democratic deliberation (Daybreak, 2017g). This can be seen as a violation of the idea of democratic principles, and it served as a loud signal for the Taiwanese public about the state of democracy in the country.

In the advent of the mass protests, it was most important for the civic activists to engage with the Taiwanese publics to ensure the people could make up their minds about the gravity of the CSSTA. According to Reporters Without Borders (2021), Taiwanese media has issues with press freedom and is focused mainly on entertainment and sensationalism, while the online sphere, on the other hand, is riddled with disinformation campaigns orchestrated by the PRC. Therefore, Taiwanese people could not simply rely on the media for balanced opinion formation. Grassroots activist organisations and networks stepped in to fill this gap. Their focus turned to social media and various self-governed new media platforms (Daybreak, 2017h). Perhaps the most notable of these outlets during the actual Sunflower Movement was a Facebook page NewseForum (Daybreak, 2017i) run by a group of journalism students. This became an outlet for real-time reporting from the site of protest and an important source for traditional media organisations.

As the NewseForum shows, social media acted as an important enabler for the Sunflower Movement. At the time Taiwan had the highest Facebook penetration rate in the world (Taipei Times, 2014) and it became the most important communications platform for the movement. While relying on Facebook made online participation effortless and accessible, the overall usability of the platform was hampered by the lack of privacy. Facebook was not however the only social media the protesters used (Daybreak, 2017j). A number of other platforms were important, and some were used for specific purposes. Perhaps most notably, bulletin board systems (BBSs) dating back to the 1980s are still widely used in Taiwan and the most popular "Professional Technology Temple" (PTT), was the most important platform for relatively secure communication during the protests (Daybreak, 2017k). PTT has for a long time been an incubation chamber for outrage and civic action in Taiwan and it was an important factor in the forging of civic rights groups such as Citizen1985 and Watchout. During the Sunflower Movement, PTT offered a venue for anonymous communication and QR codes could be used to link to these threads on the site of protest.

Some specific platforms were also built to target specific audiences and to increase awareness around the CSSTA. Here g0v again had an important role, as they created a website tisa.g0v.tw (g0v, 2014b) which allowed people to search for company names and see how the CSSTA would personally affect them. The website aimed to give Taiwanese people a better understanding of the issue, but the website is also named a component of the international outreach of the movement (Daybreak, 2017l). This was important also because Taiwanese media was regarded to hold a partisan standing (Daybreak, 2017m), and the need for direct, real-time communication on-site, on a national and an international level quickly became some of the most important forms of action during the movement.

The Sunflower Movement began as a public demonstration "Defend Democracy Tonight" held on March 18, 2014, next to the Legislative Yuan building escalated and some 200 student protesters broke through the police blockade to storm the national legislature and quickly managed to take hold of the building. (Daybreak, 2017d). Politicians from the opposition parties immediately sided with the protesters and blocked the doorways to the congress chamber (4am.tw, 2014). As legislators cannot be arrested in Taiwan, the police were forced to retreat – this created a deadlock (4am.tw, 2014).

The Sunflower Movement gave the Taiwanese civic hackers a chance to design situational applications and work on them during the occupation of the Legislative Yuan (Tang, 2016c). Situational application is software that is designed for a specific social group, has a short life span, iterative design cycle and is often built by the end users (Masnik, 2004; McNeill & Meacham, 2016). While many civic movements around the same time as the Sunflower Movement benefited from the use of technology, the systems used were often not designed but merely repurposed for the protests. g0v went further and started to provide original web content for the use of the movement and, perhaps even more important, designed a hardware architecture for the site of protest and set up a network service from scratch (g0v, 2014c). This included setting up Wi-Fi and fibre-optic networks, creating an intranet for the occupation, and maintaining several web-facing platforms and applications that made international participation possible (g0v, 2014c).

The protesters also started livestreaming the occupation. This was an important aspect as offering live feed from the site helped to combat the spread of malicious rumours as anyone could see in real time that the protesters conducted the occupation peacefully. Having cameras on-site also made it more difficult for the police to use force against the protesters, as unprovoked violence would only play in favour of the movement. Furthermore, the livestream from within the parliament was accompanied by numerous others from around the site, as anyone could use their phone to start livestreaming on YouTube (Daybreak, 2017n). These initial improvised feeds would later be accompanied with a properly set up broadcasting system within and around the parliament. g0v placed cameras around the area and set up a website g0v. today that brought all the live feeds together (奕之華, 2014; Rowen, 2015, p. 15).

This feed was accessible through the internet, but to further improve transparency, g0v also projected the feed to the wall of the parliament (Tang, 2016c).

As the occupation went on, the student organisations appealed to the congress asking for the ruling party Kuomintang to properly review the CSSTA (Daybreak, 2017o). The Head of the cabinet, Executive Yuan, premier Jiang Yi-huah came to the Legislative Yuan building to talk with the protesters but refused the prerequisites set by the movement. These included rejecting the CSSTA, forming a monitoring mechanism for agreements with China, allowing legislators to act without restrictions from their parties and the establishment of a citizens' constitutional assembly (4am.tw, 2014). Dismissal angered the protesters who on the evening of March 23 raided the Executive Yuan building (Daybreak, 2017p). This led to a night of violent clashes not seen after the end of the martial law as the police cleared out the building of some 1,000 student protesters (Daybreak, 2017p). Livestreaming (Daybreak, 2017n) these clashes would become important as on the next morning, Premier Jiang went on to deny the violence perpetrated by the police, despite viral videos depicting the crackdown (4am.tw, 2014).

The deadlock continued and the movement gained international visibility as the crowdfunding campaign supporting the Sunflower Movement raised NT$6.7 million in just three hours, and this funding was used to run front-page ad campaigns in the Hong Kong–based tabloid Apple Daily and the *New York Times* (Daybreak, 2017l). Initially, the protesters used an existing crowdfunding platform FlyingV, but as this infringed the terms of service (Atticus, 2014), the movement build a custom website vdemocracy.tw (2014), with help from g0v (Daybreak, 2017l; Rowen, 2015 p. 15). Around the same time g0v also set up a website 123. g0v.today (g0v, 2014d) that compiled phone numbers of Taiwanese legislators and made it easy for the protesters to find a representative from their own electoral districts (Lin, 2014). The site also gave information, even ready to use scripts, on how to argue for the establishment of a review mechanism and for the revision of the CSSTA. The aim of this crowdsourcing was not to sway the opinion of the legislators but to keep pressure on the issue and let other activist groups and the opposition use this momentum to better control the dialogue with the Kuomintang.

Relentless and multifaceted pressuring started to bear fruit, as after gradually expressing willingness to start the negotiations with the protesters, President Ma finally agreed on March 27 to meet the representatives of the movement without preconditions. The tide was turning, and on March 30 somewhere between 350,000 to 500,000 people took to the streets voicing their support for the Sunflower Movement (Daybreak, 2017p). On the next day, the Kuomintang legislator Chang Ching-chung, who had rushed forward the CSSTA in the joint committee, issued a public apology accompanied by the KTM party whip Lin Hung-chih, who also issued his resignation (4am.tw, 2014). On April 3, the cabinet unveiled a bill creating an oversight mechanism for cross-strait agreements. This mechanism would have exempted the CSSTA and was therefore quickly rejected by the protesters (Daybreak, 2017q). By this time, several polls had shown that a

96   Sami Kotiranta

majority of Taiwanese people approved of the occupation, and 17 workers' unions made their own call for action (Daybreak, 2017q; 4am.tw, 2014).

While the deadlock went on, the student movement organised three people's council deliberations and produced a report reviewing the CSSTA and the monitoring act proposed by the cabinet (Daybreak, 2017r). These deliberation processes were taken part by more than 1,000 citizens, and they aimed to work as a model for the future to address the flaws in the representative system. The protesters demanded an official response to the report produced by the People's Council (4am.tw, 2014). One enabling factor of these assemblies was that g0v had linked the sites of protest together and made the system accessible online. CSSTA could therefore be debated, both on-site and online. A report of the people's assembly deliberations was released after the occupation had ended (Daybreak, 2017r).

Coming back to William Smith's concept of deliberative civil disobedience, it can be seen that the Sunflower Movement was at this stage focusing on clearing the deliberative inertia around the cross-strait relations. Furthermore, the methods applied by the movement were consciously chosen to challenge the political culture in Taiwan so that the disobedience was not solely focused on the policy issue but also on the way the public is included in decision-making. These demands also included calls for direct democratic participation (Daybreak, 2017r).

The Sunflower Movement finally came to an end as on April 6 legislative speaker Wang Jin-pyng and a number of other high-ranking Kuomintang legislators publicly agreed with the protesters that the monitoring law should be enacted before the review of the CSSTA (Daybreak, 2017q). This was welcomed by the protesters, who regarded it as their main demand (4am.tw, 2014). On April 7, the movement released a statement outlining the end of the occupation (Daybreak, 2017s). The protesters finally left the Legislative Yuan on April 10 after holding congress for three weeks, wowing to continue the fight as a grassroots organisation (Daybreak, 2017q).

Digital Minister

The Sunflower Movement followed a wave of mass protests that shook the world in the early 2010s, which had inspired people to take civic action to a level of direct disobedience, but failed to create a positive change in the society and, in some cases, leading to prolonged societal unrest. Many of these movements faced the same problem of how to utilise the anti-establishmentarianist momentum while adapting to a new role closer to the establishment. What was done differently in Taiwan?

Coming back to the concept of civil disobedience, I have argued that the justification of the demonstrations has shifted through the process. g0v was more focused on the rights-based legitimacy that comes close to the liberal theory of justice, whereas the Sunflower Movement can be seen to draw its justification more from the normative democratic theory. The whole process, however, combines elements from these two and aims to work towards an inclusive system of governance founded on the idea of democratic deliberation. Deliberative civil disobedience as a way of clearing obstruction for debate is a core element in the ongoing work to foster a cultural change within the adjacent institutions to incorporate this as a permanent component of government functions. The concept of deliberative disobedience became the most important justification for disobedience, when the fight continued in a role closer to the establishment. This new role enabled the use of new methods while also bringing great responsibility and required finding compromises on a much broader forum. The use of technology became again an important factor as the activists were able to forward the idea of inclusive governance and deliberative democracy, by forwarding government digitalisation.

During the Sunflower Movement protests, many in the government recognised the need for reform. Soon after the protests ended, the new premier, Mao Chi-kuo, invited members of the civil society to facilitate this process (White, 2016). Crowdsourcing, both digital and physical, was in particular focus and in order to achieve this, a lot had to change within the Taiwanese public administration (Executive Yuan, 2014). Work practices were outdated, and the system still relied on paper documents. Before starting the construction of crowdsourcing platforms, civil servants had to be trained to be able to shift to an internet-based logic. Kuomintang commenced a reverse mentorship program as a part of this effort. Members of the Taiwanese civil society aged younger than 35 were brought in to mentor cabinet ministers (Azhar, 2020). While many activists were part of this effort, g0v member Audrey Tang's inclusion was arguably the most important. Building on her extensive career as a developer, Tang was teamed with the minister without portfolio Jaclyn Tsai, who was at the time working on issues relating to cyber regulatory reform (Azhar, 2020). The two started to innovate how to use technology to build a more inclusive system of governance. During the 2014–2015 period, Tang and other members of the Sunflower Movement organised training for more than 1,000 civil servants (White, 2016). Tang also spearheaded a design of a media literacy curriculum for Taiwanese elementary schools to help combat the threat imposed by the spread of fake news, especially in social media (Smith, 2017).

It is important to note that although Audrey Tang's work is now often associated with the DPP-led government that took office after the 2016 elections, the preceding regime, led by Kuomintang also supported these civil society driven reforms, and the ongoing process should not be interpreted as a solely partisan initiative. Tang herself says that her work in these two administrations was similar and the difference is mainly in the way that the latter DPP led government was willing to make open governance a stable agenda (White, 2016).

In the January 2016 elections, Kuomintang lost both the presidency and the legislature. Many strongholds of the Kuomintang swayed to the centre-left DPP, which secured its first majority (Tiezzi, 2016). After the elections, Audrey Tang was made digital minister without a portfolio. This allowed her to assume a fluid role, acting as an activist within the cabinet, instead of a traditional minister. Tang continued working with the g0v community and building a broad-based cooperation between public and private sectors, as well as the civil society. An important aspect of Tang's work was to rethink the role of the public service. Tang borrowed the methodology of the g0v and started using Public Digital Innovation and Service

(2021) spaces (Tang, 2018a). This is a leaderless network of public servants from across Taiwanese ministries that work out loud in the same spaces so that others can follow and contribute to their work. Public servants are encouraged to innovate and experiment without the fear of the head of the department taking credit for the successful trials and blaming the staff for the failures (Tang, 2018a). Work is done in a transparent environment with Tang leading by example and publishing verbatim transcripts (SayIt, 2021) of her meetings. This simple technique, building on the concept of radical transparency, and enabled by speech recognition systems, acts as a tool of historical accountability. Tang views that private conversations enable short-term thinking, whereas publishing the transcripts brings in an element of intergenerational solidarity (Risberg, 2021) while also shedding light on not only what is being decided but to why and how this is conducted. Meetings, and especially deliberation hearings, are also routinely livestreamed.

Many pioneering trials have followed with highlights such as the vTaiwan deliberation process (Hsiao et al., 2018) attracting international attention. This thoroughly transparent deliberation process continues the spirit of the civic assemblies held during the Sunflower Movement and combines both online and offline participation. Sandboxing has also been introduced to let social innovation steer regulatory innovation. Allowing companies that do not fit into the existing legal framework to apply for temporary permission to act beyond the law allows the regulators to closely monitor the trials and regulate the whole industry, based on first-hand information, thereby combining open innovation with informed decision-making. Sandboxing was first tried out only on fintech start-up companies (Executive Yuan, 2018; Green, 2018), but the system is being expanded to other walks of life (Tang, 2018b; Tang, 2018c). These trials are however just some components of a broader strategy of digital governance, which builds on the idea of bottom-up transparency, which enables the citizenry to use the open systems to participate more actively in decision-making. This contests the model of top-down transparency forwarded in surveillance states and surveillance capitalism (Newcomb, 2021).

Tang is also making some headway in forwarding this model of technology-empowered civic action in the international arena. Due to its widely unrecognised status as a state, Taiwan cannot be formally part of most international organisations (Newcomb, 2021). Tang has however started overriding these obstacles by working a technical bypass. Tang has for instance used her digital avatar when attending the United Nations Internet Governance Forum (Strong, 2017). Even though she is not allowed to attend the meeting, being introduced by the Paraguayan permanent representative and appearing on a video with a small lag technically made it a pre-recorded presentation of a stakeholder. By using digital spaces to overcome restrictions in real-life settings and blurring the outlines of exclusion, she is using multistakeholder cooperation as a way to hack the multilateralist norm:

> While Taiwan has no seat in the Westphalian arrangement in many organizations, those same organizations are becoming hybrid, like also multistakeholder. When I enter the UN Geneva building, my robot entered without

requiring a passport, bypassing the multilateral norm, but once they're in the Internet Governance Forum, that works on the multi-stakeholder norm, and of course, we are a stakeholder to the Internet.

(Tang, 2020)

Bypassing the restrictions enforced by the multilateral norm, Tang is forwarding the idea of transcultural inclusion forwarded by g0v and the Sunflower Movement on the international stage. Coming back to Smith's idea of civil disobedience in a deliberative setting as a way of clearing obstruction for debate, it can be seen that Tang's conscious refusal to abide by the norms of the international forums fits literally within this definition. Tang's disobedience on an international stage is based on a subtle form of polylateral coexistence (Tang, 2021) which clears the obstruction derived from the unrecognised statehood. As the stalemate between Taiwan and the People's Republic of China obstructs the multilateral deliberation that would be required for a peaceful and sustainable resolution of this dispute, Tang aims to gradually broaden the inclusion of the relevant international bodies so that the issue can be addressed in a more open and transparent fashion.

Audrey Tang has incorporated the roles of an activist and a minister. Her approach is deeply influenced by the Daoist tradition, and she upholds a guiding principle of conservative anarchism (Tang, 2019) which combines anarchic ideals of freedom and self-determination with a conservative respect of different cultures and traditions. She does not aim to force the Taiwanese people, public service, political system, or the international community to adopt a new model but to offer a better way of doing things and to let the change happen at its own pace. She rejects progressive anarchism, which can include the use of violence, and strives towards a transcultural republic of citizens. These principles are carried over to her work as she carries on the fight of the Taiwanese civic hacktivists.

Conclusion

The aim of this study, as outlined in the beginning of this chapter, was to look into what factors contributed to the successful use of digital disobedience in Taiwan for a positive societal change. Although the use of digital tools and web-based platforms has been characteristic of most mass movements of the 2010s, in Taiwan, the agility and persistence of the hacktivist communities in using open-source software and work practices, matured into an open-source mass movement, and eventually into open-source governance. Scattered communities forged their unity during the fight for accessible information and greater transparency, and by the time the Sunflower Movement posed the political opportunity to take this effort to the streets, these networks were ready to deal with the possible issues that they might encounter, such as police violence, harassment, the spread of misinformation, internet blackouts, and so on. Activists were able to out-innovate the political resistance and turn the actual site of protest as a living lab for democratic deliberation. While the use of specific software and technology is fascinating, what g0v and the Sunflower Movement were

100 Sami Kotiranta

really able to do was democratise the use of it and bring together societal needs with civic innovation. By the time the Sunflower Movement ended, even the ruling party was ready to commence the modernisation effort of the Taiwanese public administration with the help of the activists. As Audrey Tang stayed committed to the ideals of the g0v and Sunflower Movement and continued the effort in a ministerial role, this conservative anarchist continues the transformative climb towards a transparent, open, inclusive, and adaptive system of governance.

References

4am.tw. (2014). *Democracy at 4am: Timeline.* https://4am.tw/timeline/

內政部地政司. (2021). 不動產交易實價查詢服務網. http://lvr.land.moi.gov.tw/

奕之華. (2014). 太陽花資訊端最重要的一環，能夠讓你看到第一手現場的直播，來聊聊 *Skywatch.* Cool3C. https://www.cool3c.com/article/78457

Atticus. (2014). 原來 短時間我們如此強悍:太陽花運動科技應用創新總整理. Cool3C. https://www.cool3c.com/article/78266

Azhar, A. (2020). How Taiwan is using technology to foster democracy. *Harvard Business Review.* https://hbr.org/podcast/2020/10/how-taiwan-is-using-technology-to-foster-democracy-with-digital-minister-audrey-tang

Chen, F.-Y., Wang, A., Wu, C. K.S., & Yeh, Y.-Y. (2020, May 29). What do Taiwan's people think about their relationship to china? *The Diplomat.* https://thediplomat.com/2020/05/what-do-taiwans-people-think-about-their-relationship-to-china/

Daybreak. (2021). What is the Daybreak Project? *New Bloom Magazine.* https://daybreak.newbloommag.net/

Daybreak. (2016, December 7). Interview: Billy Zhe-Wei Lin. *New Bloom Magazine.* https://daybreak.newbloommag.net/2016/12/07/interview-billy-lin/

Daybreak. (2017a, July 24). Relation to history in the sunflower movement. *New Bloom Magazine.* https://daybreak.newbloommag.net/2017/07/24/sunflower-history-past-movements/#

Daybreak. (2017b, July 25). The wild strawberry movement: The most direct predecessor of the Sunflower Movement? *New Bloom Magazine.* https://daybreak.newbloommag.net/2017/07/25/wild-strawberry-movement/

Daybreak. (2017c, July 21). Declaration of "120 hours to protect democracy". *New Bloom Magazine.* https://daybreak.newbloommag.net/2017/07/21/120-hours-democracy-declaration/

Daybreak. (2017d, July 26). 317 to 322: The birth of an occupation. *New Bloom Magazine.* https://daybreak.newbloommag.net/2017/07/26/timeline-317-to-322/

Daybreak. (2017e, July 26). The left political vision of the Sunflower Movement? *New Bloom Magazine.* https://daybreak.newbloommag.net/2017/07/26/progressive-politics/

Daybreak. (2017f, November 13). Was the Sunflower Movement a taiwanese independence movement? *New Bloom Magazine.* https://daybreak.newbloommag.net/2017/11/13/taiwanese-independence-movement/

Daybreak. (2017g, July 20). What was the "black box" and why were occupiers opposed to it? *New Bloom Magazine.* https://daybreak.newbloommag.net/2017/07/20/what-was-the-black-box/

Daybreak. (2017h, June 17). New media and the Sunflower Movement. *New Bloom Magazine.* https://daybreak.newbloommag.net/2017/06/17/new-media/

Daybreak. (2017i, July 22). NewseForum. *New Bloom Magazine.* https://daybreak.newbloommag.net/2017/07/22/newseforum/

Daybreak. (2017j, June 17). Social media and the Sunflower Movement. *New Bloom Magazine.* https://daybreak.newbloommag.net/2017/06/17/social-media/

Daybreak. (2017k, July 20). PTT. *New Bloom Magazine.* https://daybreak.newbloommag.net/2017/07/20/ptt/

Daybreak. (2017l, July 20). Attempts at international outreach during the movement. *New Bloom Magazine.* https://daybreak.newbloommag.net/2017/07/20/international-outreach/

Daybreak. (2017m, July 24). The need to overcome traditional media in the movement. *New Bloom Magazine.* https://daybreak.newbloommag.net/2017/07/24/overcome-traditional-media/

Daybreak. (2017n, July 16). Livestreaming during the movement. *New Bloom Magazine.* https://daybreak.newbloommag.net/2017/07/16/livestreaming/

Daybreak. (2017o, July 24). The Cross Straits Oversight Bill and the civil society version of The Cross Straits Oversight Bill. *New Bloom Magazine.* https://daybreak.newbloommag.net/2017/07/24/civil-society-oversight-bill/

Daybreak. (2017p, July 26). 323 to 330: From crisis to resurgence. *New Bloom Magazine.* https://daybreak.newbloommag.net/2017/07/26/timeline-323-to-330/

Daybreak. (2017q, July 26). 331 to 411: Falling action. *New Bloom Magazine.* https://daybreak.newbloommag.net/2017/07/26/timeline-331-to-411/

Daybreak. (2017r, July 21). Report on the people's assembly. *New Bloom Magazine.* https://daybreak.newbloommag.net/2017/07/21/report-on-the-peoples-assembly/

Daybreak. (2017s, July 21). Statement on withdrawing from the legislative Yuan. *New Bloom Magazine.* https://daybreak.newbloommag.net/2017/07/21/legislative-yuan-withdrawal/

De Marneffe, P. (2014). Basic liberties. In J. Mandle & D. Reidy (Eds.), *The Cambridge Rawls Lexicon* (pp. 47–49). Cambridge University Press. https://doi.org/10.1017/CBO9781139026741.017

Delmas, C. & Brownlee, K. (2021). Civil disobedience: 3.2 justificatory conditions. *Stanford Encyclopedia of Philosophy.* https://plato.stanford.edu/entries/civil-disobedience/#JusCon

Devlin, K. & Huang, C. (2020). *In Taiwan, views of mainland China mostly negative.* Pew Research Centre. https://www.pewresearch.org/global/2020/05/12/in-taiwan-views-of-mainland-china-mostly-negative/

Executive Yuan. (2014). *Crowdsourcing to be used to gather youths' opinions on housing.* Department of Information Services. https://english.ey.gov.tw/Page/61BF20C3E89B856/d4db063c-73c7-4ac6-9a04-cd8e13a86ad5

Executive Yuan. (2018). *New fintech law to promote innovation, enhance competitiveness of financial sector.* Department of Information Services. https://english.ey.gov.tw/News3/9E5540D592A5FECD/9ff42f66-d4bb-45ae-bc69-bb6c973386ad

Green, D. (2018). Taiwan shines a light in the darkness with fintech sandbox. *The News Lens.* https://international.thenewslens.com/article/87071

g0v. (2014a). *First year of g0v.tw.* https://g0v.asia/tw/

g0v. (2014b). 你被服貿了嗎. http://tisa.g0v.tw/

g0v. (2014c). 太陽花學運:科技創新應用總整理. https://g0v.hackpad.tw/IuhVXDtMmWS

g0v. (2014d). 「打。道。掛。」 三動作護台灣. https://web.archive.org/web/20140416220832/http://123.g0v.today/

g0v. (2021a). *g0v.* https://g0v.asia/

g0v. (2021b). 中央政府總預算. http://budget.g0v.tw/budget

Hsiao, Y. T., Lin, S.-H., Tang, A., Narayanan, D., & Sarahe, C. (2018). *Vtaiwan: An empirical study of open consultation process in Taiwan.* SocArXiv. https://doi.org/10.31235/osf.io/xyhft

Lin, I-F. (2014, April 20). How technology and citizen media shaped Taiwan's Sunflower Movement. *Global Voices.* https://globalvoices.org/2014/04/20/how-technology-and-citizen-media-shaped-taiwans-sunflower-movement/

Lin, T.-C., Liao, J., & Fields, A. (2005). *An assessment of civil society in Taiwan.* CIVICUS: World Alliance for Citizen Participation. http://www.civicus.org/media/CSI_Taiwan_Report.pdf

Markovits, D. (2005). Democratic disobedience. *The Yale Law Journal, 114,* 1897–1952.

Masnik, M. (2004, March 30). Situational software: Who says software needs to scale? *Techdirt.* https://www.techdirt.com/articles/20040330/2243248.shtml

McNeill, K., & Meacham, S. (2016). *Situational application usage: A framework for success in enterprises. BCS SQM/Inspire Conference 2016 at Bournemouth University.* https://www.researchgate.net/publication/309385284_Situational_Application_Usage_A_Framework_for_Success_in_Enterprises

Morris, J. (2019, February 27). The 228 incident still haunts Taiwan. *The Diplomat.* https://thediplomat.com/2019/02/the-228-incident-still-haunts-taiwan/

Newcomb, M. (2021, July 5). Can Taiwan provide the alternative to digital authoritarianism? *The Diplomat.* https://thediplomat.com/2021/07/can-taiwan-provide-the-alternative-to-digital-authoritarianism/

Paltemaa, L. (2018). *Lyhyt johdatus Kiinan historiaan.* Turun yliopisto.

Public Digital Innovation and Service. (2021). *What do we do?* https://pdis.nat.gov.tw/en/

Reporters Without Borders. (2021). Taiwan. https://rsf.org/en/taiwan

Risberg, J. (2021). *Audrey Tang, Taiwan digital minister: Tools for openness: Asia & beyond.* Foresight Institute. https://foresight.org/salon/audrey-tang-taiwan-digital-minister-tools-for-openness-asia-beyond/#

Rowen, I. (2015). Inside Taiwan's Sunflower Movement: Twenty-four days in a student-occupied parliament, and the future of the region. *The Journal of Asian Studies, 74*(1), 5–21. https://doi.org/10.1017/S0021911814002174

SayIt. (2021). Audrey Tang. https://sayit.pdis.nat.gov.tw/speaker/audrey-tang-2

Schee, T.H. (2012, April 2). 總路動員的窘境. *Blog.schee.info.* https://blog.schee.info/2012/04/02/mobilization/

Smith, N. (2017, April 7). Schoolkids in Taiwan will now be taught how to identify fake news. *Time.* https://time.com/4730440/taiwan-fake-news-education/

Smith, W. (2013). *Civil disobedience and deliberative democracy* (1st ed.). Routledge. https://doi.org/10.4324/9780203758502

Strong, M. (2017). China protests against Taiwanese minister addressing UN meet. *Taiwan News.* https://www.taiwannews.com.tw/en/news/3326879

Taipei Times. (2014, February 28). Taiwan likes Facebook, has highest penetration. http://www.taipeitimes.com/News/biz/archives/2014/02/28/2003584495

Tang, A. (2016a, March 2). Conference at SuperPublic. *SayIt.* https://sayit.pdis.nat.gov.tw/2016-03-02-conference-at-superpublic#s156456

Tang, A. (2016b, March 2). Conference at SuperPublic. *SayIt.* https://sayit.pdis.nat.gov.tw/2016-03-02-conference-at-superpublic#s156462

Tang, A. (2016c, January 25). ARTE.tv Tous les internets. *SayIt.* https://sayit.pdis.nat.gov.tw/2016-01-25-artetv-tous-les-internets#s4232

Tang, A. (2018a, June 16). Interview with Nathan Storey. *SayIt.* https://sayit.pdis.nat.gov.tw/2018-06-16-interview-with-nathan-storey#s222143

Tang, A. (2018b, May 2). Conversation with Andrew Silver. *SayIt.* https://sayit.pdis.nat.gov.tw/2018-05-02-conversation-with-andrew-silver#s165856

Tang, A. (2018c, June 6). Interview with Erica Liu. *SayIt.* https://sayit.pdis.nat.gov.tw/2018-06-06-interview-with-erica-liu#s183992

Tang, A. (2019, December 27). Interview with Adrien Simorre. *SayIt*. https://sayit.pdis.nat. gov.tw/2019-12-27-interview-with-adrien-simorre#s357718

Tang, A. (2020, November 2). Zsuzsa Anna Ferenczy visit. *SayIt*. https://sayit.pdis.nat.gov. tw/2020-11-02-zsuzsa-anna-ferenczy-visit#s440817

Tang, A. (2021, September 14). Interview with Ryan Heath POLITICO. *SayIt*. https:// sayit.pdis.nat.gov.tw/2021-09-14-interview-with-ryan-heath-politico#s481187

Tiezzi, S. (2016, January 16). It's official: DPP's Tsai Ing-wen is Taiwan's next President. *The Diplomat*. https://thediplomat.com/2016/01/its-official-dpps-tsai-ing-wen-is-taiwans-next-president/

UN General Assembly. (1948). *Universal Declaration of Human Rights*. https://www.un.org/ en/about-us/universal-declaration-of-human-rights

VDemocracy. (2014). *VDemocracy*. https://web.archive.org/web/20140506235325/http:// www.vdemocracy.tw/

White, E. (2016, November 3). INTERVIEW: Taiwan's 'Digital' Minister, Audrey Tang (Part 2). *The News Lens*. https://international.thenewslens.com/article/53160

7

MASKED STRUGGLE

Uncivil disobedience on the streets of Finland

Johan-Eerik Kukko

Introduction: Soldiers of Odin and Loldiers of Odin

In this chapter, I examine the messages communicated by wearing masks and using other symbols in the history of the anti-immigration street patrol group known as the Soldiers of Odin (SOO). Moreover, I compare the messages to the ways another Finnish activist group, the Loldiers of Odin, uses masks and symbols. The SOO started its activity in Finland in 2015. Dressed in black bomber jackets with the Odin insignia in the back, the group's purpose was to keep Finnish cities safe from the alleged threat of asylum seekers. The SOO's activity started in response to the arrival of thousands of asylum seekers in Finland during the so-called European "refugee crisis",[1] and the anti-immigration group's activity spread to the Nordic and other European countries. In recent years, the SOO has received media attention about the members' backgrounds and far-right ties. In early 2016, the activist group Loldiers of Odin appeared in the Finnish streets to oppose the actions of the SOO. Using colourful make-up and dressing as clowns, the Loldiers of Odin represented an opposing force to the SOO and its vigilantism: the Loldiers of Odin aim was to ridicule the activity of the SOO and to call into question their self-appointed status as "safeguards" of Finnish people.

The Loldiers of Odin were mostly active in 2016, and its actions have been viewed through the lens of carnivalesque political performance and anti-fascist activism (Nummela, 2019; Paavolainen, 2018). The group's activities also have similarities with those of the Clandestine Insurgent Rebel Clown Army (CIRCA) founded in 2003 (Routledge, 2012, p. 429). The Loldiers of Odin may depoliticise its messages and actions,[2] but here my focus is on the situations in which they attracted publicity for disobeying police orders. Through doing so, they used civil disobedience tactics against the police and consciously crossed the line to attract public attention.

DOI: 10.4324/9781003320494-9

The groups examined here have used masks to both hide and reveal something. Wearing masks allowed the activists to hide not only their identity but also their real purposes, and in so doing, they were able to frame their actions as something other than they were. Recently, there has been a great deal of academic debate about civil disobedience and the eagerness of various groups to use it as a justification for violence and destruction of property.[3] Through the concept of uncivil disobedience, it becomes possible to analyse the masked resistance of far-right and far-left movements from a broader perspective and expose activist groups' political motives and moral grounds.

The actions of both groups have also been described using the term *vigilantism* (see Aharoni & Féron, 2020; Bjørgo & Mareš, 2019). Some theorists, such as Candice Delmas (2018, pp. 95–98), see vigilantism as part of uncivil disobedience, suggesting that not every form of vigilantism is justified. Regina Bateson has stated that vigilantism – where someone takes the law into their own hands – and nonviolent civil disobedience are fundamentally different concepts (Bateson, 2021, p. 932). Still, in political science terms, "vigilantism" has been associated with concepts such as "uncivil disobedience" (Kirkpatrick, 2008), "terrorism" (de la Calle & Sánchez-Cuenca, 2011), and "establishment violence" (Bateson, 2021, p. 925; Rosenbaum & Sederberg, 1976).

With a focus on the two previously mentioned activist groups, my research asks in what kinds of situations the members of the groups are wearing masks and examines their reasons for wearing them. I am interested in whether the SOO's vigilante activities or the Loldiers of Odin's street performances can be seen as acts of uncivil disobedience, and explain the activism of both groups using the theory of uncivil disobedience. My definition of *uncivil disobedience* is similar to Candice Delmas's definition of a subcategory of *principled disobedience* where acts could include covertness, violence, evasiveness, or anonymity unlike in civil disobedience, which includes non-evasiveness, nonviolence, decorum, and publicity acts (Delmas, 2018, pp. 17, 42–44).[4] In the end, I conclude by showing that the actions of only one of the two activist groups analysed here are morally justified in the context of uncivil disobedience, and those actions still have the element of civility even if the activists' actions include covertness and anonymity. The motives of the Loldiers of Odin's masked resistance are not against minorities, and they try not to undermine or destroy democratic institutions.

I focus on the cases where the members of the SOO wear masks – especially Guy Fawkes masks – to boost their public messages and statements. In these situations, the messages are mainly published in social media, and they flirt with the possibility of violence. These political messages are also targeted at their political opponents and the government. I analyse the statements published on the SOO's website and social media pages, previously on Facebook and now on VKontakte, as well as news articles on the group. In my analysis of the Loldiers of Odin, I discuss situations in which the police have arrested the "clown" activists, and I approach the subject through the Loldiers of Odin's own texts, video materials, and photographs, as well as news articles about them.

106 Johan-Eerik Kukko

First, I examine how vigilantism could be interpreted as uncivil disobedience but not civil disobedience, and after that, I elaborate on the masked actions of the SOO and the Loldiers of Odin. At the end of the chapter, I discuss the significance of masked disobedience and the real intentions of the masked activists' context of uncivil disobedience, building on the theoretical discussion by Kirkpatrick (2008), Brownlee (2012), Delmas (2018), and Scheuerman (2018, 2019).

Vigilantism is not civil but uncivil disobedience

People who take the law into their own hands are called *vigilantes*. The etymology of the word can be traced back to ancient Rome and the Latin word *vigil*, which means "watchful" or "alert", as well as from the Spanish word *vigilante*, meaning "watchman" or "guard" (Bjørgo & Mareš, 2019, p. 3). Bjørgo and Mareš based their definition of vigilantism on Les Johnston's (1996) work on vigilantism, with some changes. Bjørgo and Mareš (2019) understand vigilantism as "organized civilians acting in a policing role without any legal authorization, using or displaying a capacity for violence, claiming that the police (or other homeland security agencies) are either unable or unwilling to handle a perceived crime problem" (p. 5).

Professor Pertti Rannikko (2015) argues that taking the law into one's own hands is different from civil disobedience, and thus, vigilantism is not a form of civil disobedience. Civil disobedience also involves lawbreaking, although the actors engaged are ready to take responsibility for their actions (p. 150). Civil disobedience is something that is done openly and publicly (p. 150). It looks like vigilantism is far removed and something distant from the late John Rawls's liberal views on civil disobedience. To Rawls, civil disobedience is akin to political speech, and it should always be nonviolent and public. He defines civil disobedience as a "[p]ublic, nonviolent, conscientious yet political act contrary to law usually done with the aim of bringing about a change in the law" (Rawls, 1971, p. 364; see also Scheuerman, 2018, p. 117).

Civil disobedience in Rawlsian thought is also something that helps not only maintain and strengthen institutions but also make them fairer (Rawls, 1971, p. 383). Rawls believes in the power of institutions, although we must ask: What if these institutions oppress their citizens? In these kinds of situations, Rawls (pp. 365–367) sees civil disobedience as the last option, and therefore, it should be nonviolent and public. It is a violation of the law with the intent to change the law itself or the operation of the government, and if we receive punishment, we should accept it because we respect the law (Rawls, 1971, pp. 365–367).

Civil disobedience in a democratic society is only a narrow point in Rawls's book *A Theory of Justice* (1971), yet it is perhaps the best-known liberal view of civil disobedience. As the following quote suggests, William E. Scheuerman argues (2018, p. 117) that even if the Rawlsian definition of civil disobedience seems irrelevant now, it is also legitimate:

> What then do these broad structural shifts suggest about Rawls' liberal model? The story is messy. To be sure, the Rawlsian framework can occasionally help

us make sense of challenges faced today by those contemplating civil disobedience. However, shifts in state/society/relations tend to stretch his model to the limits. In some ways, it no longer seems relevant.

(Scheuerman, 2018, p. 111)

It is important that when lawbreaking follows religious, liberal and democratic models we have to respect these views even if we disagree with the activists and their actions. Scheuerman (2018, pp. 158–159) warns that this does not mean that we have to tolerate neo-fascists, racists, or xenophobic acts even if they sometimes mimic civil disobedience. Destroying migrants' housing or mob attacks on refugee buses is not civil disobedience, and these kinds of actions are direct assaults on the values of civil disobedience (Scheuerman, 2018, pp. 158–159).

According to Kimberley Brownlee, civil disobedience does not have to meet the requirements of publicity, nonviolence and acceptance of punishment: "In contrast with Rawls, I hold that the civility of civil disobedience lies not in non-violence, publicity, or willingness to accept punishment, but in the conscientious, communicative motivations of civil disobedients" (Brownlee, 2012, p. 23). Thus, justified civil disobedience could involve covert planning and rejection of punishments (Lai, 2020, pp. 44–45). Brownlee tries to push the boundaries of the concept of civil disobedience and, in her definition, even masked lawbreaking could be interpreted as civil disobedience. These views have been criticised by Candice Delmas (2018, pp. 35–37). In Delmas's view, Brownlee defends suffragist tactics as civil disobedience and sees Snowden's whistleblowing as an example of a civilly disobedient action (pp. 35–37). Robin Celikates's idea of civil disobedience as radically democratic is also criticised by Delmas (pp. 35–37). To Celikates, civil disobedience could challenge publicity of actions and include some damage of properties (Delmas, 2018, p. 37; see also Lai, 2020, p. 10).

Delmas is trying to show that some types of "uncivil disobedience", including vigilante self-defence, whistleblowing, and political riots, are legitimate in liberal democratic states (Delmas, 2018, p. 48), yet she sees two problems in Brownlee's and Celikates's views on civil disobedience. First, both of them stretch the concept of civil disobedience beyond recognition, encompassing in it some features previously deemed to be incompatible (p. 39). According to Delmas (2018), for instance, sabotage and violence can be civilly disobedient in Brownlee's view (p. 39). A second problem with inclusive accounts is that they miss the point of many disobedient actions, which is to refuse to follow the standard script of civil disobedience (Delmas, 2018, p. 39).

Delmas points out that the Rawlsian view of civil disobedience is too narrow for contemporary society. What about people who are wearing masks in political protests or doing graffiti or people who are whistleblowers or part of vigilante groups? These kinds of actions are hard to put under the rubric of civil disobedience, but uncivil disobedience is not trying to expand the definition of civil disobedience. In Delmas's view, civil disobedience is its own sub-category of *principled disobedience*. Even if Delmas (2018) sympathises with theorists like Brownlee and Celikates, she highlights that principled disobedience is more useful politically (p. 37).

Principled disobedience includes two sub-categories: *civil* and *uncivil*. When civil disobedience's characteristics are non-evasiveness, nonviolence, decorum, and publicity, uncivil disobedience can be conceived of as a cluster concept in which evasiveness, violence, covertness, and offensiveness are sufficient (Delmas, 2018, pp. 42–44). In this view, wounding or killing a member of the Ku Klux Klan and preventing lynching are justified, but violent acts a year later against clansmen are not (p. 96). Revenge is not tolerable but the capacity to respond to violence with violence could be justified in some situations (p. 96).

There are certain situations in which vigilantism could be justified, but it is important to notice that Delmas also mentions that not all vigilantism is justified (Delmas, 2018, pp. 48, 95). Using tactics of uncivil disobedience depends on four moral grounds: *the natural duty of justice, the principle of fairness, the Samaritan duty,* and *political association*. Delmas has chosen these moral grounds because these are "well established in ordinary and critical morality" (pp. 8–10). She uses sanctuary workers and their help to unauthorised migrants as an example of covert disobedience because the Samaritan agent must operate and break the law covertly because helping could put the migrants in risk of getting arrested (pp. 59, 142–143).

In Delmas's (2018) view, the left and other movements should reclaim the term *vigilance* and defend vigilance's attentiveness and alertness, not distrust (p. 211). She emphasises the importance of vigilante groups' possibility to disguise their actions: "Neighborhood watches and other vigilante groups identify their raison d'être in vigilance against criminals and illegal immigrants, often smokescreens for racism and xenophobia" (p. 211). There can be two kinds of masks: one to wear and one with which to cover one's true actions and motives.

Even if the concept of uncivil disobedience includes different acts of lawbreaking from sanctuary assistance to borderline vigilantism still some acts of uncivil disobedience can be justified. To Delmas (Çıdam et al., 2020, p. 528), uncivil acts could be justified if they realise better "the norms at the basis of the duty to obey the law" or acts could be justified "by [the] same rationales used to justify civil disobedience". There is also a possibility that the uncivil form of disobedience could express something valuable that civil disobedience could not (p. 528).

According to Delmas (2018), the concept of uncivil disobedience is something that theoreticians, with the exception of Jennet Kirkpatrick, have not really dealt with (p. 17).[5] Kirkpatrick (2008, p. 15) views uncivil disobedience as something that lies between civil disobedience and revolution even if uncivil disobedients are not common criminals, pirates, bandits, or revolutionaries. An important difference between civil disobedience and its uncivil form is the acceptance of punishment (p. 15). Vigilantes have been described by many scholars as engaging in "lawless lawfulness", and Kirkpatrick (2008) argues that when vigilantes and lynch mobs are taking the law into their own hands, they are doing something legal and something illegal: Uncivil disobedients seem thus to be both "inside" and "outside" the law (p. 115).

Scheuerman (2019) maintains that uncivil disobedient participants see "people" as a homogeneous collective (pp. 13–15). He criticises Delmas's and Brownlee's ideas, especially those that leave the door open to lawbreaking. This means that "the stakes are high" when violent resistance and vigilantism are on the table, because these uncivil political phenomena can do harm. He points out that we should treat these things carefully (p. 2). Scheuerman's view on uncivil disobedience is critical in that he sees its problems, in particular from the perspective of pluralism and modern law (p. 14).

As Ten-Herng Lai (2020) notes, "anonymous publicity" leaves the moral judgement to the viewer. Even if hiding one's identity indicates uncivility, "anonymous publicity" highlights actions, and people could target their moral judgement to the consequences of actions done by masked actors and the identities of individuals would be irrelevant (pp. 42–43). To Delmas (2018), vigilante actions could be uncivil disobedience, but its justifiability depends on what the activists' purposes are. Far-right organisations and neo-Nazi movements could mimic acts of civil disobedience (Scheuerman, 2018, pp. 158–159), but ultimately, violent attacks against migrants and minorities are not tolerable in civil disobedience or even in the forms of uncivil disobedience. Delmas (2018) highlights that uncivil disobedience is part of principled disobedience, but even if covertness or violence is tolerable, in the end, ulterior motives are decisive, and masked vigilantism against migrants is not justified (pp. 42–44, 95–98).

In popular culture, vigilantes may be heroes; however, real-life opinions about groups who are seeking justice have been mostly negative, and the legality of groups such as the SOO has provoked controversy. Mikko Kärnä, a member of the Parliament of Finland, has twice urged the police and Finnish government to investigate the legality of actions by the SOO (Lampi, 2020; Suomenmaa, 2019).

Next, I explore cases in which the SOO have used masks on social media and flirted with using extra-legal force against criminals and political opponents and how these situations differ from their street activity during which they patrol wearing Viking symbols on their jackets.

SOO and the threat of violence

In October 2015, the SOO appeared on the streets of several Finnish cities. The vigilante group, which used an image depicting the Norse god Odin wearing a mask as their insignia, was founded to "safeguard" Finnish cities from the alleged threat of asylum seekers. Since then, the movement has expanded to several countries around the world. Between 2015 and 2016, the street patrol activity spread to other Nordic countries, European cities, and North America. The members of the SOO dress in a rather uniform way in all countries: black bomber jackets emblazoned with the Odin insignia and hoods, with the exception that Odin's beard is coloured differently depending on the country. According to them (Soldiers of Odin, 2021a), the SOO is an anti-immigrant movement that opposes multiculturalism, the European Union, and globalisation. Its alleged goal is to form "an independent welfare society". During the last five years, it has operated in a grey zone; it has done things that are not illegal but have been deemed "bad behavior" (Kotonen, 2019a, p. 241).

The SOO claims to patrol the streets to keep them safe for Finnish women and children. In recent years, there has also been a lot of discussion about the members' backgrounds and their close connections to far-right organisations and neo-Nazi movements (Jansson et al., 2018). Mika Ranta, the founder of the SOO, was a former supporting member of the neo-Nazi movement Nordic Resistance. Ranta has told the media that he describes himself as "a national socialist, not a nazi" (Rigatelli, 2016). The Finnish broadcasting company Yle published a long article in March 2016 about some group members' openly racist private Facebook messages. Yle also discovered pictures of some members posing with masks and guns (Viljamaa, 2016).

Tommi Kotonen (2019a) has stated that the political climate contributed to the growth of the SOO. When the "refugee crisis" was in the headlines, it created a political opportunity. The SOO's growth was also advanced by the media, counter-movements and interaction with local authorities (p. 247). Kotonen also states that loyalty is a central theme in the communication of the SOO, which they repeat in their visual elements. One commonly shared ideological theme of the SOO leaders is white nationalism. This becomes clear in the memes they use on social media. Kotonen analysed 26 SOO leaders' Facebook profiles, and they show that the leaders use violent rhetoric on social media, but they are not part of violent subcultures like skinhead culture (p. 243). In its public statements, the SOO has underlined that members should only use violence in self-defence and not engage in any illegal activities (pp. 251–252).

In February 2019, the SOO published a video titled "The pedophile hunting season has been opened" (Ranta, 2019; see also *Uusi Suomi*, 2019). In the video, masked men armed with clubs and chains walk towards the camera. One of them claims that since politicians and authorities "do nothing", they have to take justice into their own hands. They are hunting "rapists and pedophiles of all colors" by creating fake accounts on social media. When the video was released, police officer Pekka Hätönen said in an interview that masked men have been in contact with the police and they regret what they have said in the video (Helakoski, 2019). After that, Mika Ranta released a message in social media claiming that this story is not true at all (Soldiers of Odin, 2019c). Ranta said to MTV3 news (Forsman, 2019), "I don't really care what they [the police] investigate in our dealings. If people are so nervous that they take the law into their own hands, then at that point the alarm bells should ring."[6]

According to the Ministry of the Interior report from 2020, the SOO has not been involved in violent acts on the streets, but the video it released in February 2019 could be an incentive for racist hate crimes or create and maintain an atmosphere that justifies violence (Ministry of the Interior, 2020, p. 17). The 2019 video seems to be a watershed moment in the group's rhetoric. Prior to this, the SOO was using harsh language and made clear that it is capable of violence if its members find themselves in a situation where they have to use force. This video makes clear that its members will not call the police when they arrange "memorable dates" for sex criminals. This message is contradictory to their earlier messages in the

Masked struggle **111**

news where the SOO members seem to have a desire to be authorities' "eyes and ears" on the streets (Voanews, 2016). What is even more remarkable is that, in this video, all members of the SOO are wearing Guy Fawkes masks. A month earlier, the SOO published in its VKontakte pages (Soldiers of Odin, 2019b) a picture in which a person is wearing a Guy Fawkes mask and the SOO membership hood. The accompanying text reads: "let's show to whom Finland belongs and what is the traitors reward".[7]

The SOO's using a Guy Fawkes mask in their social media posts is an example of appropriating a well-known anti-globalisation protest symbol for their own use. In a since-deleted message from January 2017 by Mika Ranta which shows that he urged people to use Guy Fawkes masks, Ranta invited people to a happening called *Suomen itsenäisyyden julistus* (Ranta, 2017).[8] In this message, he expressed his idea that revolution is the only option if the government does not pursue the interests of its own people and declared that it was time to act. The happening was open to everyone who felt disappointed by the government and wanted to shut it down.[9]

The Guy Fawkes mask was one of the most iconic masks of the 2010s, during which time it became a symbol of the Anonymous group (Coleman, 2013, p. 4). According to Andreas Beer (2018) the mask is well known from a comic book series *V for Vendetta* by Alan Moore and David Lloyd, and in 2005, it appeared in a Hollywood adaptation. Guy Fawkes was a revolutionary who lived in England in the 1600s and attempted a bomb attack on the Houses of Parliament, but in the comic book, the story takes place in a future Great Britain which is ruled by a fascist party called Norsefire. The mysterious V fights back, combining his personal vendetta with revolutionary acts against fascists. V sends his message to the public by hijacking mass media broadcasts and the citizens follow his lead and rise against the government (p. 6).

The videos and pictures released on VKontakte in 2019 were the only occasions during which the SOO members have been wearing Guy Fawkes masks. Before that, they have mainly used scarves to cover their faces on posts where they make threats of violence, or there have been pictures of Viking symbols. The VKontakte post was connected to an event during which a person wearing an SOO supporter's hoodie tried to hit a Finnish politician and the then foreign minister Timo Soini (Jauhiainen, 2019; Nyqvist, 2019). According to Tommi Kotonen (2019b), the SOO stated to the media that the person who engaged in this attack had nothing to do with the SOO, because the attacker was wearing a supporter's hoodie, not a membership hoodie. The SOO washed its hands of this violent strike, but it sold its supporter hoodies exploiting the fame of this violent act: The supporter hoodies were offered for sale under the name "Soini beater hoodie"[10] (2019b).

Over the six years of street patrol activity, the SOO also burned an Antifa flag in January 2019 (Soldiers of Odin, 2019a) and a pride flag in March 2020 (Soldiers of Odin, 2020). In the video of the burning pride flag, only one of the SOO members is not wearing a mask. The member is holding the burning flag, and on the other side, there are masked members also holding the flag. This situation is symbolic and shows two sides of the SOO's politics. In the released video, its members accept the

112 Johan-Eerik Kukko

burning of the flag – while wearing and not wearing masks. This is a very powerful example of the fact that the SOO is not defending democratic institutions, with the act also having the marks of a hate crime.

Loldiers of Odin and crossing the lines

Paul Routledge has studied the activities of CIRCA, an activist group founded in 2003 in response to President George Bush's visit to the United Kingdom (Routledge, 2012, p. 429). The common thing to all CIRCA activists was that they were all disguised by personal clown face make-up, and their military uniforms were decorated according to their personal style (Routledge, 2012, p. 435). According to Routledge, masks have several functions. They hide identities and protect the wearer from the police, but they also exaggerate absurdity. Wearing a mask is protection from everyday routines and etiquettes (Routledge, 2012, p. 436). Routledge (2004) interviewed an activist called "General Unrest", who stated that CIRCA's point is making clowning dangerous again. The point is to give back the social functions clowning used to have and "reclaim its disobedience" (p. 114).

The CIRCA clowns oppose war using nonviolent civil disobedience tactics, and the Loldiers of Odin's street performances could be seen as an act of "protestival" where traditional political rituals meet creativity and are inspired by carnivalism (St John, 2008, p. 168). Masks are an important part of "protestival", where the traditional way of protests meets carnivalism, but the CIRCA clowns were developing new forms of civil disobedience where binary and oppositional thinking were breaking down. They claimed it as "rebel clowning" (p. 181). CIRCA wanted to combine clowning and non-violent direct action into a new form of political activism and carnival as a form of resistance, thus providing a tool for the global anti-capitalist movement (Routledge, 2004, pp. 113–114).

The Loldiers of Odin made their first public appearance on 16 January 2016 (Rimpiläinen, 2017). Researcher and historian Jussi Jalonen told the *New York Times* (Martyn-Hemphill, 2016) that the Loldiers of Odin use the art of parody to make the SOO's vigilante patrolling look ridiculous. The *New York Times* interviewed a member of the SOO who said that the clown activists are not causing trouble for the SOO, rather the clowns are making trouble only for themselves. The clowns received a lot of attention in the international media. *The Washington Post*, *The Independent*, and the BBC featured articles about the activists and their performances (Nummela, 2019, p. 6).

On its webpage, the Loldiers of Odin has answered the question about using masks and funny names. "A clown is anyone and no-one – everyone can join!" (Loldiers of Odin, 2016). This message seems similar to that of the CIRCA clowns and even to the Zapatista's message about identity.[11] Using a mask blurs the boundaries and gives an opportunity to be everywhere and nowhere at the same time. It also allows one to be no one and anyone; masks blur the boundaries between activists and people who are near them.

The Loldiers of Odin knows how to make headlines, because by breaking police orders they cause situations where the police have to use force against the clown activists. These kinds of situations occurred in Rovaniemi and Tampere in 2016. I followed one of these situations in April 2016 in Rovaniemi on Lordi's Square, when there was a "Close the Borders!" demonstration organised by Suomen Sisu, a movement associated with the far right. Members of the SOO also participated in the demonstration, and the police arrested one Loldiers of Odin activist, because the activist did not obey police orders (Ruokangas, 2016). According to Yle news, the police stated that the activist was "apprehended to protect public order and security "(Ruokangas, 2016). (See Figure 7.1)

Yle (see Yle Areena, 2016)[12] tried to interview a couple of Loldiers of Odin activists during its live broadcast, but it was not actually an interview at all because the activists did not answer the questions. The reporters tried to ask questions about the group's connections to the far left and wanted to know why the group uses the Norse God Odin as a symbol. At the end of the discussion, the masked clowns turned the interview situation upside down and asked questions from the reporters. The activists asked about the role of the media in the rise of the far right and why the reporters did not ask difficult questions from politicians but only easy ones, as well as why the media did not describe Finnish people using words like "flood", "wave", "flow", "problem" or "crisis" like the media talks about asylum seekers (Yle Areena, 2016).

FIGURE 7.1 Police arresting a clown in "Close the Borders" demonstration on Lordi's Square, Rovaniemi, Finland, 9 April 2016. Photo: Tapio Nykänen (2016).

The Finnish newspaper *Aamulehti* reporter Tuomas Rimpiläinen (2017) wrote that the newspaper knows the identity of two clowns and that those activists have a criminal record. They were sentenced to fines, and neither of them had previous violent acts on their account. Rimpiläinen thinks that this is an important point because nonviolent acts are at the core of civil disobedience. He also mentions that the members of Loldiers of Odin know how to get media attention because they understand how to utilise the Assembly Act; they create situations in which police action seems exaggerated.

Teemu Paavolainen (2018) considers the situations where police are arresting an activist dressed as a clown to be an example of L. M. Bogad's principle called "irresistible image".[13] This refers to a situation where ideological opponents have to reproduce the image even if it could highlight the narrative. When cameras are connected to the internet, there is always an audience to whom one can perform (p. 233; see also Bogad, 2016, p. 32). Paavolainen (2018) sees three parts in the life of the photos where police are arresting the activists. The first one is that the Loldiers will always edit pictures before publication because they want to make sure that the audience sees the world as they want them to see it. The second point is that the antagonist storyline remains in the background when the image receives more media attention from a "more hostile wing of media". The nonviolent message will emerge even if the media focuses on patrols or police. The third point underlines that the image could become more powerful when the actual happening fades away from cultural memory. It comes closer to the situation where the Anonymous mask could represent a symbol anyone can relate to. This somewhat resembles Jonathan Bachman's photograph of Ieshia Evans and the iconic photo of *Tank Man* in June 1989 (p. 233).

Masks of disobedience

Masks are the ultimate tool of politics and the role of the mask is not only to hide identity, as masks will also give a face to resistance (Riisgaard & Thomassen, 2016, pp. 76, 88; see also Vinthagen, 2006). Riisgaard and Thomassen (2016) view masks as connected to social representations of power, and they could be seen as an effective vehicle for symbolic expression. Protests where people wear masks bring up notions of modern emancipatory politics and issues such as free speech and representative democracy (p. 94). The same kind of mask could give a different meaning in different contexts, and in some countries, wearing a mask is prohibited in demonstrations. An idea about a mask as an ultimate political tool always needs a time and place. These two things together will create a context and tell us what the political message communicated by the mask is.

Scheuerman (2018) notes that civil disobedience is not only for "good guys" (p. 158) but there are still some rules that must be adhered to if we are to say that something is called civil disobedience. Delmas (2018) has stated that sometimes vigilantism could be a tolerable option in an act of uncivil disobedience, although to Delmas, acts of uncivil disobedience must be based on four moral grounds. For example, vigilantism is justified in the case of self-defence situations but not in the case of revenge. Wearing masks is problematic in the case of civil disobedience, because – if we look at John Rawls's definition of civil disobedience – action should always be public and openly done. This view highlights transparency, and therefore, if activists are wearing masks, it is hard to maintain civil disobedience, even if some theorists like Brownlee and Celikates have tried to broaden the definition of civil disobedience.

Delmas points out that vigilante groups could smokescreen and hide their real purposes. This leads to a situation where there are two kinds of masks: one to hide the real purposes and another to cover identity. Using masks could protect the activists' identity from police and political enemies, but SOO members have used masks to threaten by use of force and in situations where they have targeted their messages at their political enemies (anarchists, Antifa, Loldiers of Odin, rapists, paedophiles, political traitors), mainly on social media and on their own websites. In the case of the Loldiers of Odin, its carnival resistance has been encountered against the far right; without their masks and make-up, there would be no such thing as the Loldiers of Odin. Their actions have similarities with the left-wing CIRCA clowns on the streets, and their colourful carnivalesque style seems an opposing force to the SOO. Their actions include nonviolent approaches, but besides that, it is interesting to observe that, in 2019, one of the former Loldiers of Odin activists engaged in an attack against SOO members in Tampere. When committing this violent act, the attacker was not wearing clown make-up and costume (Rimpiläinen, 2020).

The Rawlsian view of civil disobedience states that lawbreaking will strengthen institutions and encourage them to do their job better. However, it should be done openly and without violence against persons and property. In Brownlee's (2012) view of civil disobedience, "civility" is connected to conscientious and communicative motivations (p. 23). In the case of uncivil disobedience, lawbreaking could be anonymous, and activists can still be "good guys" only attempting to protect themselves with masks against political enemies or state agents. Whether the activists' actions are justified depends on their purposes, because after all, vigilante lawbreaking or violent strikes against criminals could be covert action for a hate crime, as Delmas has stated.

In the end, it looks like both groups use uncivil tactics but only the Loldiers of Odin's actions are justified. Even if activists hide their identities, through their actions they want to highlight nonviolent objectives and it looks like a mix of Rawlsian view and Brownlee's vision of civil disobedience; even if activists use covertness and anonymity, they want to apply pressure for making democratic institutions work better and fairer in the treatment of refugees, and therefore, it can be interpreted that there is civility behind the masks. Clown activists have an important role in diversifying the idea of anti-fascist activism and turning their activism into humorous street theatre (Nummela, 2019, p. 34). The SOO wants to be presentable on the streets and protect Finnish citizens, yet their activity on the internet tells something else. They have made clear many times through their social media posts that they are capable of violence with and without masks. This recalls the old tale of a wolf in sheep's clothing.[14]

116 Johan-Eerik Kukko

Concerning uncivil disobedience, activists' actions matter more than their identity, although using a mask emphasises the context of lawbreaking. The mask is a powerful political tool and there is always a reason why to wear and not to wear a mask. The Guy Fawkes mask and the clown mask are powerful political symbols, and both of them can be seen as symbols of resistance all over the world. The SOO members are using Guy Fawkes masks as a well-known political symbol of their own anti-governmental purposes, although in doing so they will not put themselves in a position of anti-governmental movements like Anonymous or Occupy Wall Street. Utilising the fame of the popular mask does not cover for the fact that under the surface of Viking symbolism, there is considerable hate directed at politicians and the left wing, as well as sexual minorities as the video of burning the pride flag clearly indicates.

The Loldiers of Odin's street performances have not prevented the street patrol activities of the SOO. In recent years, there have been no more actions by the Loldiers of Odin, yet the SOO continues to operate and is trying to focus more on putting pressure on politics and politicians in Finland. The Ministry of the Interior's (2020) report about violent extremism in Finland claimed that, in 2018, the SOO resumed its activities (p. 17) and presently, the SOO is the largest street patrol association in Finland which wants to secure the streets. In May 2021, it stated on its webpage that Finland is no longer an independent state, but its struggle to restore an independent Finland has only just begun (Soldiers of Odin, 2021c). Just over a week earlier, the SOO posted that "The greatest race, is the white race!" (Soldiers of Odin, 2021b) Few Finnish politicians have been talking about banning the association, yet the vigilante group continues to recruit new members, and unsurprisingly, there is a picture of a masked member in one of their recruitment flyers (Soldiers of Odin, 2021d).

Conclusion

The activists of Loldiers of Odin wore clown makeup and used funny names, but the true identities of the activists could be ascertained if necessary. Unlike the members of the SOO, all Loldiers of Odin activists used covertness and anonymity, given the fact that their resistance is dependent on masks. They hide their true identities, but more important, they wear make-up whenever they want to be seen. Their appearances and tactics have similarities with the left-wing CIRCA clowns and "rebel clowning" invented by CIRCA. Using anonymity made their actions an uncivilly disobedient form of resistance even if their tactics were closer to nonviolent civil disobedience. In doing so, the activists wanted to get public attention to their actions more than their identities. Their arguments for using anonymities are also similar to those of CIRCA and even to those of the Zapatistas. The message of the Loldiers of Odin is that it does not matter who is behind the clown make-up because everyone is welcome to their nonviolent carnival against the far-right but they also welcome people to ridicule the views of anti-immigrant streets patrols and their way of using the Norse god Odin as an insignia.

The SOO wants to represent the Finnish people's hate against illegal immigrants, the European Union, and globalisation, but, in recent years, members of the SOO have made news headlines in connection with illegal activities and their far-right ties. This means that its Viking logo has been seen in negative contexts in news articles, and in the media, its logo has been connected to political attacks and violence. The SOO has used masks mainly for intimidation, and an example of this is the way the group has used a Guy Fawkes mask in its online communication. Behind the mask, there has been a desire to do violence against "traitors" and "sex tourists who have invaded our country" even if the SOO has stated that it will use violence only in self-defence situations. Using the Guy Fawkes mask revealed something about the street patrol group's true nature: revolutionary desires to take down governmental institutions and take a leading role as the machinery of state violence. These kinds of actions are not justified in the Rawlsian view of civil disobedience or in Delmas's theory of the moral grounds of uncivil disobedience. For both groups, using a mask is an invitation to action. Hence, clown make-up and costume are an invitation to everyone to join nonviolent disobedience against the far right; behind the Guy Fawkes masks, the SOO invites people to join vigilante acts against criminals and traitors.

Even if the theory of uncivil disobedience has been criticised for leaving the door open to lawbreaking and harmful phenomena such as vigilantism (Scheuerman, 2019, p. 2), academic debate around the theory has been fruitful with a focus on how the Rawlsian view of civil disobedience should be redefined in contemporary society. The theory of uncivil disobedience gives a good viewpoint on masked resistance and helps identify activists' purposes if they try to mimic civil disobedience but their actual motives are something else. To Delmas, uncivil disobedience is a sub-category for principled disobedience and this definition does not try to push the boundaries of civil disobedience. Delmas (2018) has criticised Brownlee's and Celikates's views about civil disobedience because both of them include possibilities of violence and anonymity (p. 37).

To Delmas (2018), an uncivil form of disobedience could sometimes preserve more options for democracy and justice than civil disobedience. Duty to obey and disobey are strongly connected to the four moral grounds (pp. 8–10) and vigilante self-defence or giving shelter to illegal immigrants are both acts that could be described as uncivil disobedience in contrast to civil disobedience. Still if we seek justifications for lawbreaking, the focus should be on actions "civility" and to Brownlee (2012) civility lies in communication and conscientiousness more than publicity (p. 23). Sometimes it could be hard to tell if the actions are justified, and thus, it is important to consider the various dimensions of the context. If the purposes behind the mask are against minorities or display revolutionary desires to strike down democratic institutions, they are not morally acceptable and justified.

118 Johan-Eerik Kukko

Like Alan Moore's mysterious creation V said, "Beneath this mask there is more than flesh. Beneath this mask there is an idea, Mr. Creedy, and ideas are bullet-proof!" (V for Vendetta, 2005). This quote from V not only highlights that an idea is more important than the individual behind the mask, but it also emphasises the power of masks. While masks give resistance a face, they also give a face for activists' real purposes. After all, masks hide identities, and acts of covertness could be vengeful or communicative but breaking the law wearing a mask highlights not only the actions but also activists' moral grounds.

Acknowledgements

This chapter is based on the longer article of the same name published earlier in the *Journal of Resistance Studies*, 7(2) and republished in this book with the permission of the *JRS*.

Notes

1 For more details on the so-called refugee crisis, see Seppälä in this volume.
2 This means that they are using silly and colourful language talking about political issues such as their ideology and women's rights (see Loldiers of Odin, 2016).
3 William E. Scheuerman (2019) and Candice Delmas (Çıdam et.al., 2020) have argued recently about differences between civil disobedience and its uncivil form. In this volume, Manohar Kumar writes about whistleblowing, asking whether it is civil disobedience or uncivil action.
4 This definition of uncivil disobedience is different from Jennet Kirkpatrick's. Kirkpatrick (2008) has called uncivil disobedience "a homegrown version of terrorism" (p. 6).
5 Delmas (2018) mentions Kirkpatrick as a notable exception in "Duty to resist", but in Delmas's interpretation, Kirkpatrick uses the term "uncivil disobedience" in connection with violence and terrorism (p. 258).
6 Own translation.
7 The picture is still available on the SOO's VK pages (uploaded 11 January 2019). Own translation.
8 Ranta's message was titled "Declaration of Finnish Independence".
9 The message is still available on forums such as *Punk in Finland* and *Jatko-aika*. It is also visible at the "Wherevent" site.
10 Own translation from the word *soininhakkaushuppari*.
11 In the longer version of this article published by the *Journal of Resistance Studies*, I examine masks and their connections to political resistance in more detail (Kukko, 2021). The CIRCA clowns have made a similar statement about using masks as the Zapatistas saying "we are you". To CIRCA, rebel clowning includes the vision of "you are me" (Klepto, 2004, p. 411).
12 The interview was removed from Yle Areena, but it can still be found on YouTube, uploaded by different user profiles like *Finnish Immigration* and *Petozzi. Loldiers of Odin YLE Aamu tv 21-1-2016*. 2016. *YouTube* (original video Yle Areena deleted).
13 Bogad (Contemporary theatre review, 2015) has explained that a perfect example of an irresistible image is the picture where a CIRCA clown is kissing a police officer's riot shield during a protest in Scotland. "The image of disobedient clowning was an eloquent gesture that was both disarming but fearless."
14 Tore Bjørgo and Ingvild Magnæs Gjelsvik (2019) have used the same metaphor in their article "Sheep in wolf's clothing": The taming of the Soldiers of Odin in Norway' in *Vigilantism against migrants and minorities* (p. 257) to describe the Soldiers of Odin Norway as clearly less militant and less extremist than the SOO Finland.

References

Aharoni, S. B., & Féron, É. (2020). National populism and gendered vigilantism: The case of the Soldiers of Odin in Finland. *Cooperation and Conflict*, *55*(1), 86–106. https://doi.org/10.1177/0010836719850207

Bateson, R. (2021). The politics of vigilantism. *Comparative Political Studies*, *54*(6), 923–955. https://doi.org/10.1177/0010414020957692

Beer, A. (2018). Just(ice) smiling? Masks and masking in the occupy-Wall Street protests. *European Journal of American Studies, Special Issue: Envisioning Justice: Mediating the Question of Rights in American Visual Culture*, *13*(13–4), 1–14. https://doi.org/10.4000/ejas.13982

Bjørgo, T., & Gjelsvik, M. (2019). Sheep in wolf's clothing?: The taming of the Soldiers of Odin in Norway. In T. Bjørgo & M. Mareš (Eds.), *Vigilantism against migrants and minorities* (pp. 257–271). Routledge.

Bjørgo, T., & Mareš, M. (2019). Vigilantism against migrants and minorities. Concepts and goals of current research. In T. Bjørgo & M. Mareš (Eds.), *Vigilantism against migrants and minorities* (pp. 1–30). Routledge. https://doi.org/10.4324/9780429485619

Bogad, L. M. (2016). *Tactical performance: The theory and practice of serious play*. Routledge.

Brownlee, K. (2012). *Conscience and conviction: The case for civil disobedience*. Oxford University Press.

Çıdam, Ç., Scheuerman, W. E., Delmas, C., Pineda, E. R., Celikates, R., & Livingston, A. (2020). Theorizing the politics of protest: Contemporary debates on civil disobedience. *Contemporary Political Theory*, *19*(3), 513–546. https://doi.org/10.1057/s41296-020-00392-7

Coleman, G. (2013, September 23). Anonymous in context: The politics and power behind the mask. *Internet governance papers*, Paper no. 3.

Contemporary theatre review. (2015). Irresistible images. https://www.contemporarytheatrereview.org/2015/irresistible-images/

de la Calle, L., & Sánchez-Cuenca, I. (2011). The quantity and quality of terrorism: The DTV dataset. *Journal of Peace Research*, *48*(1), 49–58. https://doi.org/10.1177/0022343310392890

Delmas, C. (2018). *A duty to resist: When disobedience should be uncivil*. Oxford University Press.

Forsman, T. (2019, February 2). Soldiers of Odin julisti "pedofiilien metsästyskauden alkaneen" – näin järjestön perustaja kommentoi poliisia huolestuttanutta videota MTV Uutisille. *MTV Uutiset*. https://www.mtvuutiset.fi/artikkeli/soldiers-of-odin-julisti-pedofiilien-metsastyskauden-alkaneen-nain-jarjeston-perustaja-kommentoi-poliisia-huolestuttanutta-videota-mtv-uutisille/7278566#gs.vq1xxv

Helakoski, J. (2019, February 13). Seksuaalirikoksia tehneille uhonnut Soldiers of Odin katumapäällä: Videon julkaisijat vetäytyivät uhkauksistaan ja aloittivat keskustelun poliisin kanssa. *MTV Uutiset*. https://www.mtvuutiset.fi/artikkeli/seksuaalirikoksia-tehneille-uhonnut-soldiers-of-odin-katumapaalla-videon-julkaisijat-vetaytyivat-uh-kauksistaan-ja-aloittivat-keskustelun-poliisin-kanssa/7280776#gs.vj669l

Jansson, K., Roslund R., & Rissanen J. (2018, December 3). Ylen selvitys paljastaa: Jopa kahdella kolmesta natsijärjestö PVL:n ja Soldiers of Odinin näkyvimmistä suomalais-jäsenistä on rikostaustaa. *Yle*. https://yle.fi/uutiset/3-10534206

Jauhiainen, I. (2019, March 25). Soldiers of Odinin sivuilla kehotettiin ryhtymään toimeen. *Tivi*. https://www.tivi.fi/uutiset/soldiers-of-odinin-sivuilla-kehotettiin-ryhtymaan-toimeen/07e84a22-3d18-35c4-bd9d-2f96dec2d4d0

Johnston, L. (1996). What is vigilantism? *The British Journal of Criminology*, *36*(2), 220–236. https://doi.org/10.1093/oxfordjournals.bjc.a014083

Kirkpatrick, J. (2008). *Uncivil disobedience: Studies in violence and democratic politics*. Princeton University Press.

120 Johan-Eerik Kukko

Klepto, K. (2004). Making war with love: The Clandestine Insurgent Rebel Clown Army. *City*, *8*(3), 403–411. https://doi.org/10.1080/1360481042000313536

Kotonen, T. (2019a). The Soldiers of Odin Finland: From a local movement to an international franchise. In T. Bjørgo & M. Mareš (Eds.), *Vigilantism against migrants and minorities* (pp. 241–256). Routledge. https://doi.org/10.4324/9780429485619-15

Kotonen, T. (2019b, March 26). Soininhakkaushuppari. *Uralehti*. https://uralehti.fi/blogit/soininhakkaushuppari/

Kukko, J-E. (2021). Masked struggle: Uncivil disobedience on the streets of Finland. *Journal of Resistance Studies*, *7*(2), 55–84.

Lai, T-H. (2020). *Uncivil disobedience: Beyond the orthodox view of resistance and counter-resistance*. [Doctoral dissertation, the Australian National University]. Open research repository, Australian National University. https://openresearch-repository.anu.edu.au/bitstream/1885/205504/1/THL%20Uncivil%20Disobedience%20Thesis%202020.pdf

Lampi, S. (2020, September, 12). Kärnältä aloite Soldiers of Odinin lakkauttamiseksi – "murhayritys osoittaa, millaiseen toimintaan ovat valmiita". *Suomenmaa*. https://www.suomenmaa.fi/uutiset/karnalta-aloite-soldiers-of-odinin-lakkauttamiseksi-murhayritys-osoittaa-millaiseen-toimintaan-ovat-valmiita/

Loldiers of Odin. (2016). "FAQ". https://loldiersofodin.wordpress.com/faq/

Martyn-Hemphill, R. (2016, February 2). A three-ring circus in Finland: Soldiers, "loldiers" and asylum seekers. *The New York Times*. https://www.nytimes.com/2016/02/10/world/europe/a-three-ring-circus-in-finland-soldiers-loldiers-and-asylum-seekers.html

Ministry of the Interior. (2020). Violent extremism in Finland – situation overview 2020 assessment on the status and trends of violent extremism in Finland in 2019. *Sisäministeriön julkaisuja*, *2020*(8). Valtioneuvosto. https://julkaisut.valtioneuvosto.fi/bitstream/handle/10024/162174/SM__2020_08.pdf?sequence=1&isAllowed=y

Nummela, J. (2019). *Loldiers of Odin and clowns against fascism: Powers of performative failure in grassroots anti-fascist activism*. [Master's thesis, University of Helsinki]. University of Helsinki Helda Repository. https://helda.helsinki.fi/bitstream/handle/10138/312366/Nummela_Jonna_Pro_gradu_2019.pdf?sequence=2&isAllowed=y

Nykänen, T. (2016, April 9). Police arresting a clown (photograph).

Nyqvist, P. (2019, March 24). Ohje "pettureiden palkasta" löytyy Soldiers of Odinin somesivulta. *Uusi Suomi*. https://puheenvuoro.uusisuomi.fi/petranyqvist/272449-ohje-pettureiden-palkasta-loytyy-soldiers-of-odinin-somesivulta/

Paavolainen, T. (2018). *Theatricality and performativity writings on texture from Plato's cave to urban activism*. Palgrave Macmillan.

Rannikko, P. (2015). Omankädenoikeutta valtiottomassa tilassa. In J. Hiedanpää & O. Ratamäki (Eds.), *Suden kanssa* (pp. 147–174). Lapland University Press.

Ranta, M. (2017, January 1). *Suomen itsenäisyydenjulistus*. Facebook. Original message deleted. https://www.punkinfinland.net/forum/viewtopic.php?f=2&t=265041&start=8520

Ranta, M. (2019, February 15). We started to hunt pedophiles and grooming gangs who are chasing Finnish girls. [Video]. YouTube. https://www.youtube.com/watch?v=124Yx-43S4s

Rawls, J. (1971). *A theory of justice*. Harvard University Press.

Rigatelli, S. (2016, May 7). Henkilökuva: Kemin katujen pikkukingi – kuinka Mika Ranta tuli perustaneeksi Soldiers of Odinin. *Yle*. https://yle.fi/uutiset/3-8822027

Riisgaard, L. & Thomassen, B. (2016). Powers of the mask: Political subjectivation and rites of participation in local-global protest. *Theory, Culture & Society*, *33*(6), 75–98. https://doi.org/10.1177/0263276416651685

Rimpiläinen, T. (2017, March 14). Analyysi: Näin Loldiers-klovnit pyörittävät mediaa – osalla on lievää rikostaustaa. *Aamulehti*. https://www.aamulehti.fi/a/23489669

Rimpiläinen, T. (2020, June 4). Kolme miestä vastusti Tampereella äärioikeistolaista Soldiers of Odinia ja sai syytteet väkivaltaisesta mellakasta – joukossa Loldiers of Odin -klovniryhmän jäsen. *Aamulehti.* https://www.aamulehti.fi/a/056566b1-9b7b-42a1-ab94-86e92bc25a81

Rosenbaum, J., & Sederberg, P. (1976). Vigilantism: An analysis of establishment violence. *Comparative Politics, 6*(4), 541–570. https://doi.org/10.2307/421337

Routledge, P. (2004). Reflections on the G8 protests: An interview with general unrest of the Clandestine Insurgent Rebel Clown Army (CIRCA). *ACME: An International Journal for Critical Geographies, 3*(2), 112–120.

Routledge, P. (2012). Sensuous solidarities: Emotion, politics and performance in the Clandestine Insurgent Rebel Clown Army. *Antipode, 44*(2), 428–452. https://doi.org/10.1111/j.1467-8330.2010.00862.x

Ruokangas, P. (2016, April 9). Rovaniemellä vaadittiin rajoja kiinni. *Yle.* https://yle.fi/uutiset/3-8800286

Scheuerman, W. E. (2018). *Civil disobedience.* Polity Press.

Scheuerman, W. E. (2019). Why not uncivil disobedience? *Critical Review of International Social and Political Philosophy,* 1–20. https://doi.org/10.1080/13698230.2019.1693158

Soldiers of Odin. (2019a, January 1). "Hyvää uutta vuotta! Fck antifa". https://soldiersofodin.fi/hyvaa-uutta-vuotta-fck-antifa/

Soldiers of Odin. (2019b, January 11). Nöyristelyn ja hyssyttelyn aika on ohi. *VKontakte.* https://vk.com/public156729173?z=photo-156729173_456239096%2Falbum-156729173_00%2Frev

Soldiers of Odin. (2019c, February 13). Poliisi väittää että olisimme olleet yhteydessä… *VKontakte.* https://vk.com/public156729173?w=wall-156729173_330

Soldiers of Odin. (2020, March 18). Video Jyväskylästä 7.3.2020. https://soldiersofodin.fi/video-jyvaskylasta-7-3-2020/

Soldiers of Odin. (2021a). Tietoa meistä. https://soldiersofodin.fi/tietoa-meista/

Soldiers of Odin. (2021b, May 8). Happy white lives matter day!. https://soldiersofodin.fi/happy-white-lives-matter-day/

Soldiers of Odin. (2021c, May 19). Lepää rauhassa itsenäinen Suomi!. https://soldiersofodin.fi/lepaa-rauhassa-itsenainen-suomi/

Soldiers of Odin. (2021d). Turvallinen Suomi Takaisin! https://soldiersofodin.fi/materiaalia/

St John, G. (2008). Protestival: Global days of action and carnivalized politics in the present. *Social Movement Studies, 7*(2), 167–190. https://doi.org/10.1080/14742830802283550

Suomenmaa. (2019, October 22). Kärnä vaatii poliisia selvittämään Soldiers of Odinin toiminnan laillisuuden. https://www.suomenmaa.fi/uutiset/karna-vaatii-poliisia-selvittamaan-soldiers-of-odinin-toiminnan-laillisuuden/

V for Vendetta. 2005. Directed by James McTeigue. Warner Bros. DVD.

Viljamaa, A. (2016, March 16). Yle paljasti Soldiers of Odinin suljetun Facebook-ryhmän kuvia ja viestejä – Supo: "Aineisto puhuu puolestaan". *Helsingin Sanomat.* https://www.hs.fi/kotimaa/art-2000002891598.html

Vinthagen, S. (2006.) *"Political undergrounds – Can raging riots and everyday theft become politics of normality?"* Unpublished working paper.

Voanews. (2016, January 13). Anti-immigrant "Soldiers of Odin" Raise Concern in Finland. https://www.voanews.com/a/finland-anti-immigrant-soldiers-of-odin/3144705.html

Uusi Suomi. (2019, February 11). "Raiskaajien ja pedofiilien metsästys on alkanut" – Poliisi puuttuu Soldiers of Odinin videoon. https://www.uusisuomi.fi/uutiset/raiskaajien-ja-pedofiilien-metsastys-on-alkanut-poliisi-puuttuu-soldiers-of-odinin-videoon/f7c66a05-c7b6-32e2-895a-e9a57a0dd3ee

Yle Areena. (2016, January 21). Loldiers of Odin YLE Aamu tv 21-1-2016. (Video). YouTube. https://www.youtube.com/watch?v=lxMg-b9bJY8

8

IS THERE AN ALTERNATIVE TRADITION OF CIVIL DISOBEDIENCE IN EUROPE?

Taru Haapala

Introduction

Hannah Arendt (1972) famously defined civil disobedience as an American phenomenon. She argued that nowhere else the political language was better suited for dealing with the phenomenon than in the country that was built on a tradition of voluntary associations (p. 83). According to Arendt, the "spirit of American laws", in the sense of Montesquieu, is based on a "mutually binding contract" originating from the country's pre-revolutionary period that first established the individual colonies and then the federal union (p. 94). In this sense, Arendt's concept of civil disobedience departs from the idea that civil disobedience is a democratic phenomenon that came into existence in the political context of the United States, and thus, it should be understood in political terms, not legal, positioning it against the Rawlsian legalistic notion.

While the current scholarship on civil disobedience has encountered a so-called critical turn (Delmas & Brownlee, 2021), the Rawlsian legalistic account of civil disobedience remains dominant, defining it as a public, non-violent, and conscientious breach of law with the aim of changing the law or government policy. The suggestion is that those who use civil disobedience to bring about change are respectful of the regime and willing to accept the legal consequences of their actions (Rawls, 1971). The scholarly influence of the Rawlsian model is further attested by the fact that it has become the "definitional launching pad" (Scheuerman, 2020, p. 517) of attempts to redefine the liberal model of civil disobedience in the field of political theory. Radical political theorists have further criticised Rawlsian "ideal theory" as dissociated from the daily practices of civil disobedience and ignoring the "available alternative accounts" (Celikates, 2014, p. 218). They have proposed, instead, to focus on civil disobedience as an expression of constituent power (e.g. Balibar, 2014; Celikates, 2014) which has been viewed by some scholars as distorting its "core features" (see esp. Scheuerman, 2019).

DOI: 10.4324/9781003320494-10

Here, I reflect on the theoretical debates on civil disobedience in the light of recent examples in which civil disobedience has been used rhetorically as a political device in the European context. First, I introduce debates on the political significance of civil disobedience in the Western history of political thought and discuss some current critiques of the liberal definitions of civil disobedience. Recently, Scheuerman (2020) has referred to civil disobedience as an "essentially contested concept", following the idea by W. B. Gallie (1956). He maintains that approaching civil disobedience in this way helps to "do justice" to its conceptual and historical complexities, as well as to navigate the different "conceptual renditions" (Scheuerman, 2020, p. 517). Developing the conceptual approach still further, however, I suggest approaching civil disobedience as an argumentative tool for politicising, or raising issues on the political agenda (Wiesner et al., 2017). Second, I provide two recent cases where civil disobedience has been used as a political tool to define European democracy. I, first, discuss the case of Catalonian separatist leaders who organised the 2017 referendum of independence with acts of "mass civil disobedience" and attempted to justify their actions in front of the Spanish Supreme Court with the argument that they had a right to civil disobedience. Then, I introduce the case in which the French MEP Manon Aubry argued for her right to freedom of expression and civil disobedience after having been threatened with a sanction for inviting the Extinction Rebellion protest movement to occupy the plenary of the European Parliament in October 2019. Third, I discuss a historical case of voluntary association from post-war Europe to provide analytical distance to the understanding of contemporary political phenomena (cf. Vaarakallio & Haapala, 2013, p. 5). The Union of European Federalists (UEF) was a post-war association inspired by the ideas of resistance, autonomy, and personalism stemming from the crisis of democracy in the 1930s. I illustrate how their political activism in the name of "integral federalism", stemming from the French interwar debates (see e.g. Marhold, 2019; Ruge, 2015), had also features of anti-liberal civil disobedience as a political tool for mobilisation. Finally, in the conclusion of the chapter, I reflect on the findings with the Arendtian definition of the concept and her claim that there is a need to theorise civil disobedience as a political act in modern democracies.

Civil disobedience as a political tool in Western political thought

The classic understanding of civil disobedience in Western political thought takes its cue from resistance to civil government *à la* Henry David Thoreau (1817–1862). Thoreau's famous essay on civil disobedience was first published in 1849, originally under the title "Resistance to civil government" (Glick, 1952, p. 35). Although Thoreau is commonly considered the author who coined the term (see Delmas & Brownlee, 2021), his essay was renamed "Civil Disobedience" only after it was reprinted posthumously (Walls, 2018, p. 220; see also Glick, 1952). In fact, Thoreau's essay was part of a wider scholarly discussion on civil disobedience,[1] and it has been shown that Thoreau's political activism was heavily influenced by the terms and the historical context of his time (Leon, 1990).

124 Taru Haapala

Thoreau's "civil disobedience" was directed against the idea of the English philosopher William Paley, whose texts Thoreau had read as a student at Harvard (Adams, 1945, p. 651) claiming that allegiance to the government of the state, for example, by public servants and soldiers, was something comparable to obeying the word of God. Thoreau was provoked by the relativism of Paley and his contemporaries. In his view, not abiding by absolute moral truths would restrict "the 'free exercise' of the 'moral sense'" (Glick, 1952, p. 37). In his essay, Thoreau's aim was to promote the definition based on a moral principle rather than on political expediency or the changing circumstances in which a law was interpreted. He was interested in reasoning to determine "what was right by absolute moral standards" rather than obeying the law which was arbitrary and based on decisions by potentially corrupt governments (Glick, 1952, p. 40).

As a response to Thoreau's definition, Hannah Arendt (1972) directed the idea and practice of civil disobedience towards democratic, political challenges. In her definition, Arendt separated moral conscience and legalistic responses of civil disobedience from the one of democratic politics. Civil disobedience was primarily an American phenomenon "in origin and in substance" (p. 83). Following Tocqueville, she located civil disobedience in the American tradition of voluntary associations and argued that it was the main reason why the US government was best equipped to cope with the phenomenon.

> Consent and the right to dissent became the inspiring and organizing principles of action that taught the inhabitants of this continent the "art of associating together," from which sprang those voluntary associations whose role Tocqueville was the first to notice, with amazement, admiration, and some misgiving; he thought them the peculiar strength of the American political system.
> *(Arendt, 1972, p. 94)*

In this way, Arendt placed the origins of civil disobedience on the American tradition of voluntary associations. They were not political parties but rather ad hoc movements that became dispersed once their goals were met.

Arendt (1972) distinguishes between (private) thinking and (public) political action, and for her, acts of civil disobedience require political, not legal, responses. In her view, lawyers are not equipped to deal with the phenomenon: "Whenever the jurists attempt to justify the civil disobedient on moral and legal grounds, they construe his case in the image of either the conscientious objector or the man who tests the constitutionality of a statute" (p. 55). She considered it especially problematic to accuse an individual of civil disobedience. For civil disobedience to be seen as politically justified, according to her, is not to see it performed by an individual but a group. In sum, Arendt formulated civil disobedience in terms of a "non-institutionalised political instrument" to express disagreement by "organised minorities, bound together by common opinion" (p. 56).

By now, it has become a rather common argument that the Rawlsian legalistic definition misses the complexities of the phenomenon (Cooke & Petherbridge, 2016, p. 954). It has been claimed that these liberal interpretations of what civil disobedience is (and can be) have produced a "sanitised" way of understanding the phenomenon (Celikates, 2016). This critique of the liberal tradition is addressed especially against the Rawlsian notion. Celikates (2014) maintains that the Rawlsian definition of civil disobedience does not incorporate instances of non-public and violent acts as well as those founded on motives that are not conscientious considerations, which do not appeal to any common sense of justice and can become revolutionary (p. 217). In this sense, he calls for a "less normatively demanding and therefore less restrictive" (p. 218) way of understanding civil disobedience focusing on "actually existing" civil disobedience and its justifications (p. 226). Celikates (2016) redefines the concept of civil disobedience as "political disobedience" that emphasises the practice of contestation.

In her essay on the political idea of civil disobedience, Arendt (1972) argued that the phenomenon was not fully theorised which was one of the main causes of the problems in grasping the political realities of American mass movements in the 1960s and 1970s:

> Whatever the actual causes of the period of turmoil – and they are of course factual and political ones – the present confusion, polarization, and growing bitterness of our debates are also caused by a theoretical failure to come to terms with and to understand the true character of the phenomenon.
>
> *(p. 55)*

Her message was that, approached merely in legalistic and moralistic terms, the concept did not correspond with the politics of the day.

Compared to Celikates' "political disobedience", the Arendtian notion makes a clear distinction between the activity of citizens in the political realm and revolutionary, violent activity. According to Arendt, civil disobedience derives from non-violent practices of pressure groups and voluntary associations. While also Celikates (2016) seems to place civil disobedience beyond the sphere of liberal institutions and party politics, he underlines that civil disobedience is an act of citizens "reclaiming" their "political capacities" (p. 43) which can be violent and revolutionary. Against his view, Scheuerman (2019) argues that radical political theorists such as Celikates are risking while introducing such a notion as constituent power to theorise beyond the "core features" of civil disobedience, which involves, for example, non-violence and fidelity to law. For him, constituent power is an "open-ended" concept as "it simply does not get us far enough in making sense of civil disobedience as a specific type of political illegality" (p. 55).

In the following section, I examine recent cases in Europe where civil disobedience has been used as a political tool to make claims about democracy challenging the liberal democratic institutions. More specifically, I discuss the case of the Catalonian independence referendum that took place in 2017 and the French MEP Manon Aubry, who incited the Extinction Rebellion protest group to occupy the European Parliament in 2019. In both cases civil disobedience was framed as a justification for democratic activities.

Civil disobedience as a political tool in Europe

In recent years, European political movements have resorted to using civil disobedience as a rhetorical tool to promote their political agendas in the name of democracy. The approach I use to analyse them here has as its starting point that, as one acts in the name of civil disobedience for democracy, by marking it as such, one also creates room for new interpretations about what democracy "really" is for one's own political purposes (cf. Dunn, 2005; Skinner, 1973). At the same time, however, the activity challenges the boundaries of what is considered justified in a democracy, thereby politicising the situation (Wiesner et al., 2017).

Currently, a major strand of EU studies refers to the politicisation of the EU. In recent interventions, the phenomenon has been approached as embedded in European integration from the very beginning (Haapala & Oleart, 2022; Kauppi et al., 2016). The act of politicising, more generally, becomes visible whenever a new interpretation or definition is proposed to allow new horizons or spaces of action (Wiesner et al., 2017, p. 11). In the context of Europe, making claims about civil disobedience also frames the debate and positions of the actor(s) in the debate in which they make their interventions. As the public debates, in which scholars, activists and politicians alike participate, assume that European democracy requires reformulation, there are efforts by political actors to frame the debate for their own purposes. From this perspective, the uses of civil disobedience described here can be considered as a form of political activity, as actors clearly aim at extending the conceptual boundaries of democracy.

In 2017, the independence referendum in Catalonia was justified by the leaders of the separatist movement, who were mostly MPs of the regional parliament, in the name of civil disobedience. The Catalonian independence referendum took place on 1 October 2017. The argument of the leaders for organising the referendum was to exercise the "right to decide" (*derecho de decidir*), and thus it was claimed that the Spanish government should respect the results irrespective of the constitutional settlement of 1978 which legally binds the autonomous community of Catalonia to Spain. It was argued that civil disobedience allowed the freedom of rights. The referendum created a major political crisis in the country. The leaders refused to acknowledge their trial in the Spanish Supreme Court (*Tribunal Supremo*) and fled to other EU countries.[2] In this sense, the (liberal) Rawlsian interpretation of civil disobedience was not met in practice, as the independentists did not show fidelity to the law.

In the Supreme Court's final sentence, delivered on 14 October 2019, it was directly expressed that, what the referendum had caused was a redefinition of constituent power (*Tribunal Supremo*, 2019), coming very close to a case of "political disobedience" argued by Celikates. However, the leading actors of disobedience in the Catalonian referendum were democratically elected representatives in the regional parliament. The Court declared that this act, which was claimed to be a form of civil disobedience by the leaders, was, in fact, against the constitution of the democratic Spanish state of 1978, as it had laid down the constituent powers of a democratic regime which were inviolable.

From the point of view of the Court, however, the politics related to the independence referendum, that is, the political ideas expressed, should not be tried in a courtroom in the first place (*Tribunal Supremo*, 2019, pp. 217–218). In this way, the Court recognised that the referendum was a political project. However, the act of civil disobedience was not seen as justifiable. Since the defendants were elected representatives of a democratic system, they could not be acting in the name of civil disobedience in a political sense: "Models of civil disobedience do not include legislative production as a mechanism for the expression of dissent. It is prevented by constitutional distribution of powers, one of the pillars for the validity of the democratic system"[3] (*Tribunal Supremo*, 2019, p. 240). In other words, the Court did not recognise the interpretation of civil disobedience, which was based on a re-interpretation of constituent power, by the independentist leaders. From the viewpoint of the Court, the accused had no case of civil disobedience, as a mere reference to having no "organic links with the political power" cannot justify any kind of citizen mobilisation led by them which is "protected by the legitimate exercise of the right to civil disobedience"[4] (*Tribunal Supremo*, 2019, p. 241).

The Court argued its case by following the definition of civil disobedience in Rawlsian terms, noting that the "proper" way of conducting civil disobedience included the "acceptance of the punitive and/or penal consequences" (*Tribunal Supremo*, 2019, p. 241):[5] "In fact, this gesture of acceptance of punishment has been seen by some as a moral example for the community" (Ibid.).[6] Rawls is not mentioned here explicitly, but his concept of civil disobedience is used in the sentence implicitly.

In sum, the Court did not recognise the Catalan independentist leaders' actions as civil disobedience, as they were political leaders holding public office against the Spanish constitutional system from which their own legitimacy as political representatives derived. The Court argued that the separatist claims about civil disobedience were not based on the rightful principles of civil disobedience (for a discussion, see also Toscano, 2019).

Another recent case in Europe of a democratically elected political representative who has used civil disobedience as a justification for promoting their own political agenda while reframing the concept of democracy is the French MEP Manon Aubry. After the EU elections in 2019, in which Manon Aubry was elected to represent the extreme leftist *La France Insoumise* (France Unbowed), she was named as the vice-chair of the GUE/NGE party in the European Parliament (EP). On the website of *La France Insoumise*, Aubry presents herself as "activist deputy" (*La France Insoumise*, 2021). Her political career only started when she became a candidate for the EU elections. Previously, she was a spokesperson for Oxfam France. Aubry is a "new face" and known for not being afraid of conflict (Laïreche, 2018).

Led by Jean-Luc Mélenchon, the party was reformed as a political movement in 2017, as he was running for the French presidency. With the aim of creating a bottom-up organisation, it was inspired by Syriza in Greece and Unidas Podemos in Spain (Marlière, 2018, p. 10). In 2018, Aubry was appointed by the electoral committee of *La France Insoumise* to lead the list of the movement in the EU elections in May 2019. She was elected as MEP along with five other candidates of the movement.

128 Taru Haapala

In late 2019, Aubry (2019a) posted a YouTube video on her Twitter account where she addressed her followers. While posting the video, she tweeted with an emoji smiling and winking: "We have a little suggestion for #ExtinctionRebellion."[7] Broadcasting from the lobby of the EP, the video shows Aubry inside the building inviting the international activist group known for acts of civil disobedience to organise a protest in the plenary.

In the video (Aubry, 2019a), she applauds the Extinction Rebellion for their activism and civil disobedience. Arguing that civil disobedience is a tool that should be used for political purposes, and especially in the case of climate change, she maintains that the EP is the key stage for accomplishing them. According to her, the use of civil disobedience is called for because not all member states in the EU recognise the urgency of the climate situation.

The tweet was reacted to by the EP president David Sassoli. Aubry received a letter from Sassoli warning her of a sanction (Sánchez-Nicolás, 2019). She reacted to this by posting the letter to her Twitter account. In her tweet, Aubry (2019b) accused Sassoli of undermining the freedom of expression of MEPs: "This letter threatening me with sanctions for a tweet constitutes a serious questioning of the freedom of expression of MEPs!"[8] Aubry's claim about being a victim of institutional infringement of liberties was accompanied with the following (rhetorical) questions: "Are NGOs practising non-violent civil disobedience now banned from staying in Parliament? Should MEPs who support their actions now worry about the censorship that might be exercised against them?"[9] In other words, Aubry claimed that civil disobedience means the freedom of rights.

From the point of view of EP's rules of procedure (Rules of Procedure of the European Parliament, VII, Ch. 4, Rule 175), the threat of sanction is a standard policy in any such case of disorderly behaviour. The EP's rules of procedure dictate that if the president must intervene more than two times and in case a member continues to behave in a disruptive manner despite repeated reprimands, the member "may be denied the right to speak". From this angle, Aubry's claim that Sassoli's threat of sanction undermined MEPs rights to freedom of expression was not any such attempt, at least, not according to the parliamentary rules. Reprimanding the member in question is, according to the rules, within the powers of the EP president, and only in the case the MEP in question offends the EP repeatedly will there be some form of action to deny the MEP from speaking.

Aubry was interpreting the situation for her own political purposes. With her tweet, she politicised the letter to be able to make a claim about civil disobedience. By politicising the status quo, actors can bring issues into a new light, for example, by challenging traditional institutions, boundaries, or ways of acting (Wiesner et al., 2017, pp. 10–11). Contrary to Celikates's (2016) definition of "political disobedience", it does not necessarily mean that citizens are reclaiming their political capacities. In both cases discussed earlier, civil disobedience is resorted to as an argument by democratically elected representatives, not by citizens who engage in "reclaiming" their "political capacities" (Celikates, 2016, p. 43).

Is there an alternative tradition of civil disobedience in Europe? **129**

In the two examples described earlier, the controversiality can be seen in efforts to use civil disobedience to reinterpret democratic settings. In the Catalan case, the Spanish Supreme Court refused to recognise the separatist leaders' claim for civil disobedience due to their positions as public servants. And, in the case of Manon Aubry, the president of the EP threatened to sanction the MEP but did not discipline her for civil disobedience.

In fact, the two cases discussed can be seen as interconnected. Since Aubry's claim that what had happened as a result of civil disobedience was a case of an attempt at limiting her rights, she has also been vocal about the lifting of parliamentary immunity from Catalan separatist leaders some of whom were also elected to the European Parliament in 2019. As a member of the committee who decided about lifting immunity, Aubry declared that she did not share the committee's decision. According to Aubry, it was a serious threat to democracy in Europe that allowed the national judicial systems to persecute democratically elected representatives (Barnils, 2021).

In the next section, my aim is to investigate the historical background of the recent cases of civil disobedience in European debates as a "right" in efforts to promote political agendas. The idea is to add analytical distance to the political phenomena and to discuss a chance of an alternative tradition of civil disobedience by highlighting the movement of "integral federalism" which is also behind ideas of regionalism advocated in the EU.

Integral federalism and civil disobedience in European political thought

The main federalist argument in the creation of the post–Second World War European polity was that wars between nation states were embedded in the international system of sovereign states (Burgess, 2012). The European federalist post-war movement relying on "integral federalism" demanded autonomy for persons instead of the sovereignty of nation states. Deriving their ideas from Proudhonian theory of federative principle, the movement had its origins in interwar French anti-liberalism (Ruge, 2015). The movement was successful in launching the idea of the "Europe of the Regions". According to Loughlin (1996), both federalism and regionalism have been interpreted as political movements with long traditions in Europe. They incorporate conservative reactions towards the liberal nation state which is viewed with hostility as it is seen as creating a "levelling" of "natural hierarchies" (Loughlin, 1996, p. 141). Despite its anti-liberal and anti-democratic origins, the "Europe of the Regions" is still present in the EU. The Committee of the Regions was established by the Maastricht Treaty in 1993 "ensuring a stronger integration of regional actors into the policy-making process" (Crepaz, 2016, p. 28).

During the Second World War, the European federalists had collaborated on ending the war and reconstructing the continent. The movement advocated for "a kind of Proudhonian federation" with occupational groups, while it also promoted the limitation of a centralised state, first in France and later in Europe as a whole (Delzell, 1960, p. 243). Pierre-Joseph Proudhon's (1809–1865) *Du principe fédéraliste*, first published in 1863, was a central work for European federalists. For Proudhon, politics is constituted by two opposing poles, or contradictory regimes: authority and liberty. Authority is represented by absolute monarchy and liberty by democracy. However, the dualism of authority and liberty is always seen in movement.

> [T]he political problem, reduced to its simplest expression, is that of finding an equilibrium between two contrary elements, authority and liberty. Any error in balancing the two leads at once to the disorder and ruin of the state and the oppression and distress of the people. In other words, the anomalies and disturbances of society arise from contradictions between its principles and will vanish when its principles are harmonized in such a manner that they can damage one another no longer.
>
> *(Proudhon, 1863/2018)*

The Proudhonian theory of federation is construed as a balance between the contradicting principles of authority and liberty, which is founded on a voluntary pact or agreement between persons. In this voluntary pact, persons must see as much gain as sacrifice for it, while retaining all their liberties.

Inspired by these ideas, postwar integral federalists based their ideas on the principle of autonomy, of persons and states, which is the foundation of regionalism in their thought. One of the key figures of the movement was Alexandre Marc,[10] the inventor of integral federalism. He was a staunch opponent of institutionalised politics, especially in terms of political parties. Marc's mistrust of institutionalised politics was shown in his federal thinking. He conceptualised integral federalism as a project of mobilisation instead of political activity (Vayssière, 2002, p. 123). Compared to more recent politics in Europe, a similar suspicion against political parties seems to have inspired movements such as La France Insoumise in France, Syriza in Greece, and Unidas Podemos in Spain, for example.

The European federalist movement was created as a form of organisation which did not originate in intergovernmental agreements, or pacts negotiated between governments. The movement itself was started with a gathering of representatives of federalist groups from different Western European countries, who themselves signed a "draft of an alliance", the aim of which was "to unify the principles and co-ordinate the actions of the participating movements" (Lipgens, 1982, p. 300). This new departure was designed to give the federalists credibility on the world stage, as they were not being led by various governmental interests.

The UEF was founded in Paris in December 1946. The UEF organised the first postwar meeting of which the aim was to constitute a new supranational regime for Europe. The meeting was held at the Congress of Montreux on 27–31 August 1947. It was also the first time after the war that German and Austrian delegates were invited to join in an international congress formed democratically on an equal footing with other participants (Gouzy, 1968, p. 43). In the Congress, the UEF managed to form postwar cooperation between federalist groups by creating a new space that was declared to be "democratic".

The chief innovator of the European federalist project was Alexandre Marc. For Marc, integral federalism was not to be reduced to verbal explanations because action was considered an essential part of its definition. Integral federalism recognised the autonomy of ethnic groups and of functional units, such as enterprises and professional organisations. European federalism was only seen as a step forward in a larger scheme. In its founding statute, the aim of the organisation was laid out as follows: "To work towards the creation of a European federation, which will be a constitutive element of a world confederation, in order to secure durable peace respecting human rights, fundamental liberties to all, and social justice" (*Union européenne des fédéralistes*, 1947; transl. by TH). Here, the Proudhonian idea of balancing authority and liberty with a voluntary pact can be detected.

The first president of the UEF was Henri Brugmans,[11] who had a background in the resistance movement during the Second World War. In February 1947, Brugmans (1947a) published a text in the French federalist group's journal *Fédération*, outlining the scope of action for the newly created federalist movement: "Federalism is, on the one hand, a collective perception of the common interest and, on the other, concern for 'higher' authorities. It is a respect for freedoms and an instrument for their realisation. It is, in fact, the doctrine of balanced autonomies" (p. 2). The "higher authorities" were a reference to nation states and governments that, he claimed, were incapable of seeing the real problems of the continent. What was needed, was a balance in the Proudhonian sense.

The UEF proposed "mobilisation of the peoples of the world" to form pressure on their governments and representative assemblies (*Union européenne des fédéralistes*, 1947). The overall emphasis of the UEF being on voluntary associations of persons and regions accentuated that collective collaboration was ideal compared to political institutions in the framework of liberal representative democracy. According to Brugmans, federalists were not politicians nor technocrats, but "institutionalists" who were prepared to reconstruct and fight against "the European chaos to prepare for a more viable global unity and to work towards the birth of global security bodies for the sake of European prosperity" (Brugmans, 1947b, p. 3).

The UEF considered politics in a nation state in terms of potential abuse of power and corruption. To stay outside of conventional politics was to retain control of choosing one's side in the Proudhonian sense. Vayssière (2008) has noted, however, that the roots of many of the UEF's constituent federal groups were connected to national party politics. For example, the groups that were founded during the war were categorically leftist, taking their inspiration from the resistance movement. One of the most important among them was *Movimento federalista europeo*, which was founded in August 1943 in Milan, and was responsible for publishing the Ventotene Manifesto. Some groups established at the end of the war were more militant than others, for example, the Dutch group, *Europeesche Actie*, and *La Fédération*, which was the most organised French movement with clear right-wing leanings (pp. 74–75). Even though the UEF, and Brugmans at its helm, renounced conventional politics, the role of a federalist was not to stay out of the realm of politics altogether. Brugmans (1947b) highlighted that, to propose a new world order, was about posing questions about the political order, and thus to turn the movement into a political force (pp. 3–4). These ideas resemble those of the more recent European political movements, such as *La France Insoumise*, who claim that political parties are redundant.

Integral federalism's background lay in the French *Ordre Nouveau* movement that was founded in December 1930. During the interwar period, this group of nonconformist intellectuals was among the critics of liberal, especially parliamentary institutions. Marc was one of the key figures of the interwar movement. Its members belonged to a generation that had lived through the Great War and was not willing to "yield to party pigeon-holing" (Vayssière, 2002, p. 125). During the Second World War, Marc was enlisted in the Alpine infantry, but he was discharged in 1940 and spent the rest of the war in Switzerland. According to Vayssiére, he became inspired by Proudhon's theories and managed to get his work published in wartime (p. 126).

Both Marc and Brugmans, UEF's leading figures, were influenced by the idea of personalism. Personalism meant taking "the spiritual first and foremost, then the economic, with politics at the service of both of them" (Vayssière, 2002, p. 125). The combination of the idea of "person" and "spirituality" was put in contrast with so-called holistic philosophies, such as nationalism. It meant liberation from state monism (along with capitalism and parliamentarism) and the "natural" movement towards non-nationalised economic organisations. Integral federalism was portrayed as a "third way", not in the right and not in the left side of the political spectrum. It was considered as a revolutionary movement whose aim was to obliterate nation states and liberate persons to form communal entities, or regions. In other words, the UEF's agenda was to use political tools to liberate persons from institutions that served nation states.

Integral federalism was a strand of political thought developed in the historical context of interwar Europe when many movements and groups were formed in the political climate of extreme ideological cleavages (Marhold, 2019). As discussed earlier, integral federalism equates civil disobedience to voluntary association. However, it has anti-liberal and anti-democratic roots (Ruge, 2015). The ideal imagined by Brugmans was a voluntary, democratic movement outside the liberal democratic institutions. This vision of a political space was rhetorically created in opposition to totalitarianism which could be re-created in liberal democratic institutions.

Is there an alternative tradition of civil disobedience in Europe?

I have examined earlier the possibility of an alternative tradition of civil disobedience in Europe, thereby engaging in critical reflection of Hannah Arendt's (1972) definition. I proposed to approach civil disobedience as an argumentative tool for politicising, or raising issues on the political agenda (cf. Wiesner et al., 2017). Applying and going slightly further on Scheuerman's (2020) suggestion to investigate various "renditions of the concept", I examined political arguments for using "civil disobedience" in the European context. I discussed recent cases in which civil disobedience was used for justifying political acts which could be considered extra-legal, namely the independence referendum in Catalonia in 2017, and the tweet posted by MEP Manon Aubry in October 2019 to incite a protest group to occupy the European Parliament. In this way, I approached the uses of civil disobedience in terms of political tools while reflecting their connection to current scholarship on political thought.

Since the Second World War and the creation of international law organisations based on democratic values, civil disobedience has become used in a variety of contexts in different corners of the world related to fights for the values of freedom, human rights, and self-determination. In liberal democracies, profound tensions have been created, for example, between normative values of universal human rights and democratic self-determination (Benhabib, 2004). In this context, the liberal tradition has become challenged by the recent radical political theories on civil disobedience as it is seen as too restrictive in normative terms. To theorise civil disobedience in political terms, some theorists have resorted to the notion of constituent power. As Scheuerman (2019) has noted, however, these theories derive their notion of civil disobedience in a somewhat extended way and do not always adhere to the core features of the concept such as non-violence and fidelity to the law.

Even though there are differences of opinion among scholars on several aspects of civil disobedience, the current literature commonly approaches it as a deliberate act (principledness) appealing to reconsideration (communicative) of established order in a non-coercive manner (non-violence) (Delmas & Brownlee, 2021). All these features can be seen also in integral federalism that attempted to replace nation states and liberal democracy with a world federation based on voluntary pacts and political movements. The principledness can be seen in the Proudhonian federative principle that guarantees the liberties of citizens. The communicative aspect was realised in the mobilisation of persons through which governments were meant to be put under pressure to realise the federalists' aims. And, finally, the non-coercive aspects can be seen in the voluntary character of the agreement or the pact.

For Proudhon, federalism is, essentially, a free pact or a voluntary act of agreement:

> The contract of federation, whose essence is always to reserve more powers for the citizen than for the state, and for municipal and provincial authorities than for the central power, is the only thing that can set us on the right path. In a free society, the role of the state or government is essentially that of legislating, instituting, creating, beginning, establishing; as little as possible should it be executive.
>
> *(1863/2018)*

In the Proudhonian theory, the federative principle guarantees the higher powers to the citizen over political institutions to exercise their rights as well as more powers to regions than to any central power.

134 Taru Haapala

In a similar way, the Catalan independentist leaders and Manon Aubry have attempted to justify their claims for exercising their rights through civil disobedience in the recent EU context. Their actions in the name of civil disobedience seem to resemble the Proudhonian federative principle. The voluntary aspect of mobilisation guaranteed liberties which, under established order and institutions, are susceptible to corruption. According to Proudhon (1863/2018), the "privileged classes" used "the flag of liberty" to "disguise despotism" by using "liberal and egalitarian institutions" for their own political benefit. For the sake of being corruptible, institutions could not be trusted to uphold "faith" and "civic spirit". As with integral federalism, the Proudhonian suspicion against liberal institutions is present also in more recent arguments that denounce political parties and institutions. In both European cases discussed earlier, civil disobedience was utilised in attempts to redefine democracy. The underlying assumption seems to be that civil disobedience offers better chances to exercise rights and freedoms than liberal institutions which can succumb to corruption.

The post-war integral federalists and more recent European political movements shared the idea of a voluntary pact that is embedded in the preference for mobilisation over established political institutions. The idea of voluntary associations was also a key aspect of civil disobedience for Hannah Arendt. However, she connected it to the American tradition (Arendt, 1972). According to Arendt (1977/2006), the sovereignty of nation states was the antithesis of freedom. For her, sovereignty contradicts the principle of plurality, which is the key aspect of free political association. In essence, Arendt comes very close to the arguments of the UEF with the claim that

> [t]he famous sovereignty of political bodies has always been an illusion, which, moreover, can be maintained only by the instrument of violence, that is, with essentially nonpolitical means. ... If men wish to be free, it is precisely sovereignty they must renounce.
>
> *(p. 163)*

Through federalism, it was possible to abolish sovereignty. Some scholars have claimed that Arendt can be viewed as a political thinker who advocated for integral federalism (e.g. Guérot, 2017). It seems unlikely, however, that she was a participant in the postwar movement.[12]

While taking into consideration the concept's historical complexity, I also aimed to show that there could be an alternative tradition of civil disobedience in the European political thought that derives from Proudhonian federative principle. This tradition can be traced back to postwar integral federalism and Hannah Arendt's definition of civil disobedience, challenging the Arendtian argument that civil disobedience is primarily an American phenomenon as there is not a political language for it elsewhere. Arendt argued (1972) that, while there was a political language for civil disobedience only found in America, it was based in the tradition of voluntary association that the problems of civil disobedience could be best solved. Arendt also maintained that the theorising of civil disobedience was needed to handle the problems that modern democracies were faced with mobilisations of citizens and the legal frameworks of the phenomenon posed. In other words, as she argued for political theorising of civil disobedience, Arendt pointed out that mere legal or moral handling of the phenomenon was not enough.

Arendt (1972) argued that theorising on civil disobedience is essential for democracies. The need for theorising in the democratic framework is further testified in the European cases discussed earlier. It seems that in the two cases civil disobedience was used as an argument but in a way that has not been previously theorised. For example, the notion of constituent power was used by Catalan separatists who are also holders of public offices as they attempted to justify their civil disobedience. The Spanish Supreme Court refused to recognise their version of civil disobedience as it considered it primarily a political enterprise. Also, the case of MEP Manon Aubry illustrates that civil disobedience was used as a political tool to promote a specific version of democracy. These were not examples of just any citizens reclaiming their political rights but of democratically elected representatives who derive their authority from the political system and who do not accept the punishments for breaking the law and rules of conduct in liberal democracies.

The examples discussed here illustrate that there is further study required to uncover the alternative tradition of civil disobedience in Europe. In the tradition, political activity that tests the boundaries of the established order is closely related to redefinitions of democracy. This "testing" derives from hostility towards and an idea of potential failure of political institutions, first articulated by Proudhon and then revived in the deep democratic crises of interwar and post-war Europe. Although the post-war integral federalists did not use the term as such, they used what could be called as the "core features" of civil disobedience (Scheuerman, 2019) for democratic reform. Recently, scholars have attempted to revive the basic tenets of integral federalism aiming for protecting European democracy from "hollowing out" (Guérot, 2017) and from the nation states' resorting to violent "destruction of civil society" (Balibar, 2017). In the light of not only scholarly but also wider public debates, some of which remain oblivious to the anti-liberal and anti-democratic roots of the European integration, it seems to me that Arendt's suggestion to theorise civil disobedience in a democracy is more relevant than ever.

Acknowledgements

The author acknowledges the funding received from InterTalentum-Marie Curie MSCA-COFUND programme which was financed by the European Union's Horizon 2020 research and innovation programme under grant agreement No. 713366.

Notes

1 Thoreau's definition of civil disobedience was an attack on moral relativism addressed in works such as the English philosopher William Paley's (1743–1805) *Of the duty of civil disobedience*. For further details, see for example Glick, 1952.

2 In March 2021, the European Parliament decided that it will not harbour the separatists and, in effect, will assist Spain to deport them to be tried in the country.

3 *"Los modelos de desobediencia civil no incluyen la producción legislativa como mecanismo de expresión de la disidencia. Lo impide la distribución constitucional de competencias, uno de los pilares para la vigencia del sistema democrático."* Translations from Spanish to English are done by the author.

4 *"Y es que no basta con carecer de explícitos vínculos orgánicos con el poder político para concluir que toda movilización ciudadana por ellos liderada puede estar amparada en el ejercicio legítimo del derecho a la desobediencia civil."*

5 *"[l]a propia doctrina de la desobedencia civil ... incluye entre sus postulados la aceptación de las consecuencias sancionadoras y/o penales ..."*

6 *"De hecho, en ese gesto de aceptación de la pena se ha visto por algunos un ejemplo moral para la comunidad."*

7 *"On a une petite suggestion pour #ExtinctionRebellion."* Translations from French to English are done by the author.

8 *"Cette lettre me menaçant de sanctions pour un tweet constitue une grave remise en cause de la liberté d'expression des eurodéputés!"*

9 *"Les ONG pratiquant la désobéissance civique non violente sont-elles désormais interdites de séjour au Parlement? Les députés qui soutiennent leurs actions doivent-ils désormais s'inquiéter de la censure qui pourrait être exercée à leur encontre?"*

10 A. Marc (1904–2000), born in Odessa as Alexandr Markovitch Lipiansky, was a Russian *émigré*.

11 H. Brugmans (1906–1997), born in the Netherlands, was an intellectual of the European Movement, co-founder and first president of the UEF, and the rector of Collège de l'Europe in Bruges 1950–1972.

12 I'm grateful to Tuija Parvikko for pointing this out.

References

Adams, R. (1945). Thoreau's sources for "Resistance to civil government". *Studies in Philology, 42*(3), 640–653.

Arendt, H. (1972). Civil disobedience. In H. Arendt (Ed.), *Crises of the republic* (pp. 49–102). Harcourt Brace Jovanovich.

Arendt, H. (1977/2006). What is freedom? In H. Arendt (Ed.), *Between past and future. Eight exercises in political thought*. Viking Press. (Original work published 1961).

Aubry, M. [@ManonAubryFr]. (2019a, October 17). *On a une petite suggestion pour #ExtinctionRebellion ;) L'intégralité de l'Aubry qui court* → https://youtube.com/watch?v=13dGNL [Tweet]. Twitter. https://twitter.com/ManonAubryFr/status/1184705598824181761

Aubry, M. [@ManonAubryFr]. (2019b, November 5). *A-t-on encore le droit d'exprimer son soutien aux actions de désobéissance civique non violente? Pour le @EP_President, la réponse est* [Tweet]. Twitter. https://twitter.com/ManonAubryFr/status/1191653005696876549

Balibar, E. (2014). *Equaliberty: Political essays* (J. Ingram, Trans.). Duke University Press. (Original work published 2010).

Balibar, E. (2017). Our European incapacity. In D. Büllesbach, M. Cillero & L. Stolz (Eds.), *Shifting baselines of Europe: New perspectives beyond neoliberalism and nationalism* (pp. 18–25). Transcript Verlag. (Original work published 2011) https://www.transcript-open.de/isbn/3954

Barnils, A. (2021, February 2). Manon Aubry: "We are facing a threat to democracy". *VilaWeb.* https://english.vilaweb.cat/noticies/manon-aubry-we-are-facing-a-threat-to-democracy/

Benhabib, S. (2004). *The rights of others: Aliens, residents and citizens*. Cambridge University Press.

Brugmans, H. (1947a). Europe, an open society. *Fédération. Revue de l'ordre vivant* 25, 5p. Paris. (Trans. from French by cvce.eu.) http://www.cvce.eu/obj/europe_an_open_society_from_federation_february_1947-en-0c6d2230-ad82-4a13-84f8-1e12c7415e46.html

Brugmans, H. (1947b). L'unité de l'Europe. *Cahiers du Monde nouveau. Revue mensuelle* n° 6; 3e année. Paris. (Trans. from French by cvce.eu.) http://www.cvce.eu/obj/"henri_brugmans_l_unite_de_l_europe"_dans_cahiers_du_monde_nouveau_juin_1947-fr-bc106aea-c1a9-4dee-a6e7-7e4f2b977bed.html

Burgess, M. (2012). Federate or perish. The continuity and persistence of the federal idea in Europe, 1917–1957. In M. Hewitson & M. D'Auria (Eds.), *Europe in crisis: Intellectuals and the European idea, 1917–1957* (pp. 305–322). Berghahn.

Celikates, R. (2014). Civil disobedience as a practice of civic freedom. In J. Tully (Ed.), *On global citizenship: James Tully in dialogue* (pp. 207–228). Bloomsbury Academic.

Celikates, R. (2016). Rethinking civil disobedience as a practice of contestation – beyond the liberal paradigm. *Constellations, 23*(1), 37–45. https://doi.org/10.1111/1467-8675.12216

Cooke, M., & Petherbridge, D. (2016). Civil disobedience and conscientious objection. *Philosophy and Social Criticism, 42*(10), 953–957. https://doi.org/10.1177/0191453716659522

Crepaz, K. (2016). 'Europe of the regions': An approach to counter separatist tendencies? *L'Europe en formation, 379*(1), 24–39. https://doi.org/10.3917/eufor.379.0024

Delmas, C., & Brownlee, K. (2021). Civil disobedience. In E. N. Zalta (Ed.), *The Stanford encyclopedia of philosophy* (Summer 2021 Edition). https://plato.stanford.edu/archives/sum2021/entries/civil-disobedience

Delzell, C. F. (1960). The European federalist movement in Italy: First phase, 1918–1947. *The Journal of Modern History, 32*(3), 241–250. https://doi.org/10.1086/238542

Dunn, J. (2005). *Setting the people free: The story of democracy*. Atlantic Books.

La France Insoumise. (2021). *Manon Aubry*. Official website. https://lafranceinsoumise.fr/les-parlementaires-de-la-france-insoumise/manon-aubry/

Gallie, W. B. (1956). Essentially contested concepts. *Proceedings of the Aristotelian Society, 56*(1), 167–198. http://www.jstor.org/stable/4544562

Glick, W. (1952). "Civil disobedience": Thoreau's attack upon relativism. *Western Humanities Review, 7*(1), 35–42.

Gouzy, J.-P. (1968). *Les pionniers de l'Europe communautaire*. Centre de recherches européennes.

Guérot, U. (2017). Our European capacity. Which Europe do we want? Rediscovering Hannah Arendt's concept of integral federalism. In D. Büllesbach, M. Cillero & L. Stolz (Eds.), *Shifting baselines of Europe: New perspectives beyond neoliberalism and nationalism* (pp. 26–32). Transcript Verlag. https://doi.org/10.14361/9783839439548-004

Haapala, T., & Oleart, Á. (Eds). (2022). *Tracing the politicisation of the EU. The future of Europe debates before and after the 2019 elections*. Palgrave Macmillan.

Kauppi, N., Palonen, K., & Wiesner, C. (2016). The politification and politicisation of the EU. *Redescriptions: Political Thought, Conceptual History & Feminist Theory, 19*(1), 72–90. https://journal-redescriptions.org/articles/abstract/10.7227/R.19.1.5/

Laïreche, R. (2018, December 9). Manon Aubry, dans le bain politique jusqu'à la tête de liste. *Libération*. https://www.liberation.fr/france/2018/12/09/manon-aubry-dans-le-bain-politique-jusqu-a-la-tete-de-liste_1696941/

Leon, L. (1990). *The historical and literary context of Henry David Thoreau's "Civil disobedience"*. [Doctoral Dissertation, Middle Tennessee State University]. James E. Walker Digital Repository, Middle Tennessee State University. http://jewlscholar.mtsu.edu/handle/mtsu/3966

Lipgens, W. (1982). *A history of European integration. Volume 1: 1945–1947. The Formation of the European Unity Movement*, with contributions by W. Loth and A. Milward. (Trans. P. S. Falla & A. J. Ryder). Clarendon Press.

Loughlin, J. (1996). "Europe of the regions" and the federalization of Europe. *Publius: The Journal of Federalism, 26*(4), 141–162. https://doi.org/10.2307/3330775

Marhold, H. (2019). Integral federalism. In S. S. Krause (Ed.), *Theories of modern federalism* (pp. 253–282). Nomos.

Marlière, P. (2018). Jean-Luc Mélenchon and France insoumise: The manufacturing of populism. In G. Katsambekis, & A. Kioupkiolis (Eds.), *The Populist Radical Left in Europe*. Routledge. https://discovery.ucl.ac.uk/id/eprint/10053910/1/P.%20Marliere-France%20Insoumise.pdf

Proudhon, P.-J. (1863/2018). *The federative principle, and the need to reconstitute the party of revolution*. (Trans. Richard Vernon). https://theanarchistlibrary.org/library/pierre-joseph-proudhon-the-principle-of-federation

Rawls, J. (1971). *A theory of justice*. Harvard University Press.

Ruge, U. (2015). The call for a new European order. Origins and variants of the anti-liberal concept of the "Europe of the regions". In D. Gosewinkel (Ed.), *Anti-liberal Europe: A neglected story of Europeanization* (pp. 90–101). Berghahn.

Rules of procedure of the European Parliament, 8th Parliament term, March 2019. European Parliament. https://www.europarl.europa.eu/doceo/document/RULES-8-2019-03-25_EN.pdf

Sánchez-Nicolás, E. (2019, November 5). EP president threatens MEP with sanctions over a tweet. *EUObserver*. https://euobserver.com/environment/146526

Scheuerman, W. E. (2019). Constituent power and civil disobedience: Beyond the nation-state? *Journal of International Political Theory, 15*(1), 49–66. https://doi.org/10.1177/1755088218806642

Scheuerman, W. E. (2020). Civil disobedience as an essentially contested concept. In Ç. Çıdam (Ed.), Critical exchange: Theorizing the politics of protest: Contemporary debates on civil disobedience. *Contemporary Political Theory, 19*, 517–522.

Skinner, Q. (1973). The empirical theorists of democracy and their critics: A plague on both their houses. *Political Theory, 1*(3), 287–306.

Toscano, M. (2019, October 21). "No tiene razón la defensa": Notas sobre la desobediencia civil y la sentencia del procés. *Letras libres*. https://letraslibres.com/politica/no-tiene-razon-la-defensa-notas-sobre-la-desobediencia-civil-y-la-sentencia-del-proces/

Tribunal Supremo (de España). (2019, October 14). Sala de lo Penal, Sentencia núm. 459/2019.

Union européenne des fédéralistes. (1947). *Rapport du premier congrès annuel de l'UEF 27-31 août 1947, Montreux (Suisse)*. 141 p.

Vaarakallio, T. & Haapala, T. (2013). Introduction. In T. Vaarakallio & T. Haapala (Eds.), The Distant Present (pp. 4–11). *SoPhi, University of Jyväskylä*. http://urn.fi/URN:ISBN:978-951-39-5102-3

Vayssière, B. (2002). Alexandre Marc. Personalism at the service of Europe. *Il federalista, XLIV*(2), 123–135.

Vayssière, B. (2008). La recherche face à un militantisme « supranational »: le cas de l'union européenne des fédéralistes. *Les cahiers Irice, 1*(1), 63–79. https://doi.org/10.3917/lci.001.0063

Walls, L. D. (2018). [Review of the book *Civil disobedience. Early American literature*, by H. D. Thoreau, ed. by B. P. Taylor]. *Early American Literature, 53*(1), 220–222. https://www.jstor.org/stable/90019143

Wiesner, C., Haapala, T., & Palonen, K. (2017). *Debates, rhetoric and political action: Practices of textual interpretation and analysis*. Palgrave Macmillan.

9

DIFFERENT FORMS OF DISSENT IN ANTI-DEPORTATION ACTIVISM IN FINLAND

From refugee protests to civil disobedience

Tiina Seppälä

Introduction

This chapter explores the rise and different phases of anti-deportation activism in Finland since the beginning of the so-called European refugee crisis in 2015. There have been several movements which have used different types of strategies in their dissent, for example, public protests and campaigns against forced deportations, providing asylum seekers under the threat of deportation with legal help, as well as shielding them by hiding them from the police, an act that can be considered a form of covert civil disobedience. There have also been a few cases of explicit civil disobedience. So far they have, however, remained isolated incidents. As such, this invites the question of why civil disobedience has not featured as a more attractive form of dissent in Finnish anti-deportation activism, given that it is more commonly used in some other European countries and by certain other social movements in Finland.

Hence, the objective of this chapter is two-fold – first, to offer a holistic view of different forms of dissent used in Finnish anti-deportation activism in recent years, including the "Right to live" protest, "No one is illegal" campaign, protests against deportation flights at the Helsinki–Vantaa airport, and civil disobedience conducted on commercial flights in an effort to stop a deportation. The activities have mainly been conducted by citizen subjects (activists and solidarity actors) to protect non-citizen subjects (asylum seekers with negative decisions) from being deported. Yet, asylum seekers have also participated in some protests and activities.[1] Second, the chapter seeks to construct a better understanding of the factors behind the limited utilisation of civil disobedience in the context of Finnish anti-deportation activism.

The research material consists of several types of data, including news; social media and website posts; public statements; and interviews published by the "No one

DOI: 10.4324/9781003320494-11

140 Tiina Seppälä

is illegal" campaign and "Stop Deportations" network during the time when anti-deportation activism peaked in Finland, that is, in 2017–2018. Additionally, three semi-structured thematic interviews were conducted in the autumn of 2021 with activists/solidarity actors intimately involved in organising and coordinating the previously mentioned campaigns, protests, and networks. The interviews lasted from 50 minutes to 1 hour 25 minutes. The material was analysed through quali-tative text analysis.

Producing illegality and deportability

The rise of refugee solidarity movements and anti-deportation activism in Finland is intimately related to the so-called European refugee crisis in 2015. The large number of refugees arriving in Europe was characterised as a serious "crisis", even a state of "emergency" requiring exceptional measures (Crawley et al., 2017; Krzyżanowski et al., 2018; Triandafyllidou, 2017; see also Nykänen et al., 2018; Seppälä et al., 2020).[2] While many other EU and Scandinavian countries received over 100,000 asylum seekers in 2015, in Finland the number was about 32,000 (Finnish Immigration Service, 2019). Yet, in the Finnish context this was unprecedented as, for example, in 2014 only 3,000 asylum seekers had arrived in the country.

After 2015, governments all over Europe not only used strong rhetoric but also introduced a broad range of restrictive measures, including tighter asylum controls, stricter requirements for permanent residency, and lower social benefits for asylum seekers. In Finland, this took place through the tightening of The Aliens Act, the national immigration law in 2016. The process was led by the conservative gov-ernment consisting of the Centre Party, National Coalition Party, and nationalist Finns Party. The category of humanitarian protection from international protection in The Aliens Act was removed as a reason for granting a residence permit, which had been used in cases in which the grounds for asylum or subsidiary protection were not fulfilled, but it was impossible to deport a person due to war, conflict, or natural disaster in the country of origin (Finnish Immigration Service, 2016a), and temporary residence permits to asylum seekers with a negative decision to their sec-ond asylum application were no longer granted. Moreover, their right to legal help was restricted (Laki ulkomaalaislain muuttamisesta, 2016), and the requirements for providing evidence of personal persecution were made stricter (Laki oikeusapulain muuttamisesta, 2016).

These changes were implemented by the Finnish Immigration Service, which additionally tightened some of its own interpretations and policies. For example, it redefined its country information on three countries (Iraq, Afghanistan, Somalia) from where Finland was receiving most arrivals, considering certain areas safe for return (Finnish Immigration Service, 2016a, 2016b, 2016c), which enabled nega-tive asylum decisions. The number of cases in which fear of violence was accepted as a justification for asylum also declined remarkably (Saarikkomäki et al., 2018). Together, the changes resulted in a rapidly growing number of negative asylum decisions and paperless people who were considered illegal in the eyes of the state.

Different forms of dissent in anti-deportation activism in Finland **141**

This made their situation very difficult (Nieminen, 2016), also resulting in "deportations at a level never seen before" (Horsti & Pirkkalainen 2021, p. 183). As Näre argues (2020, p. 987), "[a]fter these legal changes, asylum-seekers were no longer equal before the law".

The changes were justified on the basis that it was necessary to manage incoming migration, reduce its costs (Government proposal HE 43/2016 vp., 2016), and streamline asylum policies with other European countries, especially with Sweden (Ministry of the Interior, 2018; Mäntymaa, 2018). Other Scandinavian countries, too, argued for more equitable sharing of the "refugee burden" (Hagelund, 2020; Hernes, 2018). While Finland sought to ensure that it "does not appear as a particularly attractive country for asylum seeking" (Government proposal HE 43/2016 vp., 2016), Sweden argued that it "could not offer better conditions and prospects than other countries", and Norway that it should not "appear as economically attractive in relation to comparable European countries" (Hagelund, 2020, pp. 9, 13).

In Finland, the government's new restrictions and their justifications also started to influence the broader public discourse. As the number of paperless rapidly grew due to the tightened provisions of The Aliens Act, the concept of "paperlessness" was obscured in the public debate – it became equalled with illegality. Although it does not refer to any criminal activity but a lack of administrative status of legal residence and staying in the country without permission, in the state discourse paperlessness was increasingly often connected to illegality. In documents by the Ministry of the Interior (2016, n.d.-a., n.d.-b.), it was explicitly recommended to avoid using the term *paperless* – instead, it should be evaluated whether a person resides in the country "legally or illegally". This recommendation was strongly criticised by the Project for Undocumented Migrants, Finnish Refugee Advice Centre, and other refugee associations – they argued that people should not be categorised based on their residence status and that the basic human rights of any group cannot be restricted (Paperittomat.fi, 2016).

The terminology of illegality is linked with unwanted phenomena such as criminal activities and security risks (Hirvonen, 2019), and it creates strong connotations of the need to protect the security of the state and maintain its internal order (Nieminen, 2016), thus legitimising measures of surveillance, control, and punishment (Hirvonen, 2017). As argued by critical migration scholars, stigmatising or criminalising paperlessness can be understood as "technologies of citizenship" which are constitutive of state/nationhood, serve to maintain structural inequality, and reinforce racialised social hierarchies based on the logic of socio-political exclusion/inclusion embedded in state-centric modern sovereignty (e.g. Cruikshank, 1999; Khosravi, 2018; Walters, 2002). The entanglement of the state's illegality discourse and its concrete policies and practices is also closely connected to *deportability*. Horsti and Pirkkalainen (2021, p. 182) define it as "a condition in which a person might be deported at any time", which involves *slow violence*, "a cruelty that does not appear to be violence in the conventional sense". As I argue elsewhere (Seppälä, 2022), producing deportability, that is, making deportation easier and increasing its public acceptability, is the main goal in the construction of state discourse in which

142 Tiina Seppälä

asylum seekers are illegalised (see also Anderson et al., 2011; De Genova, 2002; Hasselberg, 2016; Jansen et al., 2014; Peutz & De Genova, 2010).

Anti-deportation activism in Finland

There are tens of (in)formal institutions, associations, and networks working with refugee issues in Finland. Many are connected to international initiatives, such as the "Stop Deportations" and "No one is illegal" networks, which bring together various groups working with non-resident immigrants and refugees staying in a country without permission and thus under risk of deportation. These solidarity groups support people in obtaining work, medical care, education, training, and accommodation regardless of their immigration status and actively utilise their national and international networks in organising awareness campaigns and demonstrations. So far, the most visible and longest large-scale protest in Finland has been the "Right to live" demonstration, which started in February 2017 in Helsinki and lasted for over six months. It was initiated by Iraqi and Afghani asylum seekers who arrived in Finland in autumn 2015 (Näre, 2020) and implemented through the "Stop Deportations" network they established, receiving support from solidarity actors (Interview 3). These protests are argued to have generated "the 'we' of political subjects between refugees and citizens" (Hirvonen, 2019) that binds them "together in a relationship of political reciprocity" (Oudejans, 2014, p. 14).[3]

The "Right to live" protests have been interpreted as a way for the asylum seekers to visibilise the structural and bureaucratic violence of the asylum/migration regime that violates their human rights by rendering "them illegal from one day to the next – thereafter denying them access to basic services" (Näre, 2020, pp. 279, 990). Based on her ethnographic research, Näre (2020, p. 979) regards these non-citizen protests as an involvement "in the politics of human rights". As also Hirvonen (2019) explains, the "Right to live" protest camp represented the politics of human rights, because for the activists, "human rights were not depoliticized rights but weapons for promoting equality, advancing emancipation and protecting human beings from alienating state power". They sought to make visible the fact that the rights of the asylum seekers had been "deprived by means of policy-making, legislative, normative, judicial and administrative practices" (Hirvonen, 2019).

The "Right to live" activists strongly critiqued the Finnish Immigration Service's asylum decisions, arguing that they were faulty, unjustified, and leading to life-threatening forced deportations (Hirvonen, 2019). The violent treatment of the detained and deported, as well as the evictions of asylum seekers from reception centres after receiving negative decisions, were also criticised. The protesters demanded that all deportations to unsafe countries should be stopped as the right to life, the most fundamental of all human rights, is uncompromisable and belongs to everybody. In their activism, they ued many different forms of dissent – ranging from a long-term protest camp to small-scale strikes, petitions, legal initiatives, and artistic performances (Interview 3).[4] In ideating and implementing these, solidarity actors, many of whom were academics and cultural field representatives,

Different forms of dissent in anti-deportation activism in Finland **143**

collaborated closely with diaspora and refugee communities, as well as human rights activists, lawyers, and professionals from many other fields.

In 2017, several demonstrations against forced deportations in which the "Stop Deportations" network played an important role, were organised at the Helsinki–Vantaa airport. In April 2017, the protesters gathered in the departure hall to demonstrate (STT–Ilta-Sanomat, 2017).[5] Prior to the protest, it was reported that a pregnant woman would be deported but the police postponed the deportation (Jaulimo, 2017). The police argued that the media and activists misrepresented many important details of the deportation case (Koskinen, 2017a, 2017b; Leinonen, 2017a), an argument echoed by state authorities in the Ministry of the Interior (Lakka, 2017). Later, the police were criticised for not being able to correct the information it had argued to have been faulty (Humalamäki, 2017; Myllymäki, 2017; Turkki & Myllymäki, 2017).

On 26 June 2017, the "Stop Deportations" network gathered about 50 people to protest at the airport (Blencowe & Grünn, 2017). On that day, the authorities had to stop the deportation of a 24-year-old Iraqi woman who was shouting on the plane. One passenger also stood up to support her. On 4 July 2017, about 200 people demonstrated against forced deportations, some of them at the Helsinki–Vantaa airport. The police arrested two persons, but overall, the demonstration was peaceful (Mäkinen & Harmanen, 2017; Yle–STT, 2017). Again, in August 2017, the "Stop Demonstrations" network organised a protest at the airport; this time the aim was to show support to activists in Tampere demonstrating against the deportation of an Iraqi asylum seeker, Karrar (Leinonen, 2017b, 2017c).

According to the activists, from the autumn of 2017 onwards, it became difficult to protest at the Helsinki–Vantaa airport due to tightened control and increased police presence and security measures, and the epicentre of protesting was moved back to the city centre:

> The protests … had been so big … and the police told us that we could not come to the airport anymore. The airport security personnel and the police … started to obstruct us, they moved the flight departures to the cargo terminal … they started fining people … The protests were just removed from there … It became practically impossible … to get anywhere close to those to be deported … So, protesting at the airport, was only one phase for us … Then, we started to protest at the Kansalaistori, Narikkatori, and in front of the Ministry of the Interior … Few times we tried to block police cars leaving from Pasila to pick up people to be deported from Metsälä … Some people gathered around the exit points … We tried something like this … but it did not work very well.
>
> *(Interview 3)*

In February 2018, a new campaign, "No one is illegal", was launched. It continued a similar line of protests. The main difference was that while the "Right to live" protest was initiated and implemented by asylum seekers themselves, in the "No one is

144 Tiina Seppälä

illegal" campaign, solidarity actors played a more central role. It was also connected to parliamentary politics, as it was organised by the youth association of the national Left Party, one of the opposition parties at the time. Thus, the campaign's criticism towards the conservative government must be, on one hand, understood also as a part of broader opposition politics. On the other hand, in 2017, the Left Youth of Finland had established a specific political profile area against the rise of fascism, in which migration- and refugee-related themes were central.

The stated aim of the "No one is illegal" campaign was to support asylum seekers and work against forced deportations. It straightforwardly argued that the government was ignoring the refugees' human rights. In a campaign interview, one organiser emphasised that "asylum seekers, refugees and paperless immigrants are entitled to legal rights" and that "the actions of the Finnish government do not bear critical examination" (Vasen Kaista, 2018). The government's asylum policy was considered unconstitutional, inhumane, and cruel, as it resulted in deportations to unsafe countries, thus jeopardising lives (Kansan Uutiset, 2018; Libero, 2018; Vasemmistonuoret, 2018a, 2018b, 2018c, 2018d, 2018e, 2018f; Vasen Kaista, 2018). The campaign critiqued the government's decision to no longer grant residence permits based on humanitarian protection when the requirements for granting asylum or providing subsidiary protection are not met, but the applicant could not return to their home country (or country of former habitual residence) because of an environmental catastrophe or a bad security situation due to an armed conflict or a poor human rights situation. Returning humanitarian protection as a reason for granting a residence permit was a key political demand in the campaign.

During 2018, the "No one is illegal" campaign organised action days in Helsinki, Tampere, Joensuu, Turku, Oulu, and Jyväskylä. The activists also participated in writing petitions and co-organising several anti-deportations protests, for example, the "Don't Send Afghans Back" protest, the "Lov is an asylum" protest in Loviisa to defend an Iraqi family under the threat of deportation, and demonstrations against the deportation of Kurdish activist Behdad and an Iraqi asylum seeker, Mostafa (Vasemmistonuoret, 2018b, 2018c). In the case of Mostafa, the activists noted that "Finland is bound by international law and its own constitution to not send anyone to mortal danger" and demanded the government to abide "by the non-refoulement law written in its constitution" and not to "send Mostafa to the mortal danger at the mercy of the militia in Iraq" (Kukaan ei ole laiton, 2018, June 11). The "No one is illegal" campaign also shared practical instructions produced by the "Stop Deportations" network on how to practice civil disobedience to protect asylum seekers against deportations (Kukaan ei ole laiton, 2018, July 23, 25 and 31).[6] The instructions were widely circulated in the last week of July 2018, a few days before the most widely reported case of civil disobedience in Finnish anti-deportation activism took place.

The Aino Pennanen case of civil disobedience

On 31 July 2018, Aino Pennanen, the legal secretary of the Green Party's parliamentary group, entered the Finnair flight AY1433 that was about to take off from

Different forms of dissent in anti-deportation activism in Finland   **145**

Helsinki to Berlin. Pennanen noticed a man in the last row of the aeroplane, sur-rounded by police officers, his head being pushed down (Hujanen, 2018b; Latvala et al., 2018). The man was moaning, and Pennanen realised she was witnessing a forced deportation. The person was an Iraqi asylum seeker, Ahmed, who was on the plane to be deported to Basra. Pennanen talked about the man's situation with the flight personnel (Latvala et al., 2018). She told them that she would not attend the flight if the deportation was not stopped. After that, she refused to sit down on her seat, also encouraging the other passengers to do the same. The captain told Pennanen that unless she agreed to sit down, she would be removed. She did not respond to the request. Consequently, she was escorted out of the plane by the police, and her mobile phone was confiscated. Pennanen had filmed a video of the incident and posted it on her Facebook wall (Hujanen, 2018a, 2018b; Latvala et al., 2018). A criminal case for disturbing air traffic was filed against her, an offence that was, however, considered minor (Hujanen, 2018a; Konttinen, 2018; Yle, 2018).

When interviewed by journalists (Hujanen, 2018b; Latvala et al., 2018), Pennanen was asked if she believed that her protest was the right way to effect change. She explained that normally juridical and political means offer the best way forward to push for the needed changes but that none of the previously tried out measures had been effective. Therefore, she had felt that in this kind of situation, it was necessary for her to stand up against the deportation and bring also broader attention to Finland's asylum policy (Hujanen, 2018a, 2018b). Pennanen referred to a 21-year-old Swedish woman, Elin Ersson, a social work student at the University of Gothenburg, who had only a few days earlier, on 23 July, refused to sit down on a Turkish Airlines flight until the deportation of a 52-year-old Afghan man from Gothenburg to Afghanistan was stopped (Latvala et al., 2018). Ersson, too, had livestreamed her action on her Facebook page.[7] The 14-minute video went viral, with millions of people across the world watching it (Shelton, 2018). Additionally, over 13 million people watched the short film *Grounded* which was produced about the event (Pham & Hakim, 2019). Ersson's action was commented upon in dozens of news articles, and she was described, for example, as a "hero" and "hope for humanity" (Shelton, 2018).

During her protest, Ersson was supported by a football team that stood up with her on the plane. When Ersson was indeed able to stop the deportation, the passen-gers applauded her (Crouch, 2018; Embury-Dennis, 2018; Saner, 2018; Shelton, 2018; Stop Deportations, 2018, July 23). In contrast, Pennanen's action did not manage to stop the deportation of Ahmed, and the flight itself was delayed only for 10 minutes. The incident, however, became a huge media spectacle and one of the most commented cases of civil disobedience in Finland, thus attracting a lot of attention to the issue that Pennanen sought to promote. Her action was discussed extensively in all major news outlets, discussion programs, and social media. Many newspapers took a stance in their editorials regarding Pennanen's action – most often a sceptical or critical one.

The key critiques concerned the issue of breaking the law, as taking issues in one's own hands was considered controversial. It was also stressed that Pennanen did not know at the time for what reason the man was deported; that he could be a convicted criminal, or even a terrorist.[8] However, Pennanen's civil courage was also embraced by many journalists, academics, politicians, and activists. For example, Touko Aalto, a member of parliament (MP) of the Green Party, praised Pennanen for conducting a peaceful protest in defence of human rights, calmly agreeing to be removed from the flight, and being ready to accept the legal consequences of her act of civil disobedience (Ukkonen, 2018; Vuorinen, 2018). Aalto used civil rights activist Rosa Parks and people who helped Anne Frank during the Holocaust as points of reference. He stated that a person is courageous and to be respected when she stands up to protect another person without any personal gain to herself. These views resonated with many of Aalto's party colleagues' perspectives. A survey conducted in 2017 found that many Green Party and Left Party MPs approved of the use of nonviolent civil disobedience in defence of paperless persons under the threat of deportation (Yle, 2017); however, not everyone shared these views (*Etelä-Suomen Sanomat*, 2018; Waris, 2018).

Aalto demanded that all forced deportations from Finland should be temporarily stopped until the problems in the asylum process were fixed (Parkkinen & Hakahuhta, 2018). The minister of the interior, Kai Mykkänen, did not support this view (Hakahuhta & Tolkki, 2018). Jussi Halla-aho, the leader of the nationalist Finns Party, also commented on Pennanen's civil disobedience and Aalto's views critically, stressing that it is unacceptable that some people place themselves above the law (Laurila, 2018). On the contrary, some other political groups and anti-deportation activists reacted in very positive terms to Pennanen's action. Some supported her indirectly, but many also explicitly and publicly (Interviews 1–3).

Some activists criticised Finnair, the national airline, for participating in forced deportations (Finér, 2018; Kukaan ei ole laiton, 2018, July 31). They also shared a satirical "From HEL to hell" image that imitated Finnair's own advertisement. Additionally, they recommended everyone to clearly demonstrate their views if they would be on the same flight with a person to be deported. When Finnair argued that it was merely following state authorities' instructions (Sullström, 2018), the "Stop Deportations" network noted that in Germany, more than 220 planned deportations had been classified to have "failed" due to pilot refusal between January and September 2018 (Stop Deportations, 2018, July 27; also Schumacher, 2017). Similar cases have occurred also elsewhere – for example, the Virgin Airlines stopped assisting British authorities in deporting undocumented migrants, and United Airlines and American Airlines requested the Trump administration to stop deporting migrant children separated from their parents at the border (Anderson & Karasz, 2018; BBC, 2018; Fausset, 2018; Gentleman, 2018).

One week after the Pennanen incident, the story of Ahmed was shared in a public post, reflecting on his difficult history and his bleak future in Iraq (Stop Deportations, 2018, August 6). It was mentioned that Ahmed had, indeed, seen Aino Pennanen on the plane. According to Ahmed, the police officers had used violence during his deportation. His hands and legs had been tied up, and on the plane, his head had been pushed down so that he had experienced difficulties in breathing.

He had been picked up by two police officers from the Metsälä detention centre. On the plane, he was accompanied by four police officers. Some parts of Ahmed's story were, however, later questioned in the media (e.g. Kärnä, 2018).

Pennanen was sentenced to a fine of 720 euros for her refusal to sit down on the plane (Kilpeläinen, 2019; STT–HS, 2019; *Uusi Suomi*, 2019).[9] She had pleaded the court to take into account the exceptional amount of public hate mail and harassment that she had received in different forms, including an unfounded child welfare notification, but the court refused to regard this as an extenuating circumstance (Kilpeläinen, 2019).

The overall significance of the Pennanen case in anti-deportation activism in Finland is somewhat controversial and includes several interesting aspects. From the perspective of the "what and how", it comes very close to classical civil disobedience in the sense of the Rawlsian standards: (prior) publicity, nonviolent nature of the action, and willingness to accept the legal consequences (Rawls, 1971). Her justifications were also very clear from the beginning – trying to stop a person's deportation to an unsafe country when such an opportunity emerged – and as a legal secretary of a parliamentary group, she was well aware of the legal aspects related to her action. However, the location can be considered extraordinary – although this was not the first time that civil disobedience was practised on an aeroplane in Finland, it is the only case that has received significant media attention.[10] In this regard, the evidence is clear that Pennanen was acting spontaneously and that she was mimicking a similar act conducted by Elin Ersson in Gothenburg earlier in July 2018. Unlike Ersson, Pennanen was not successful in her efforts. Yet, in terms of public and political debate, the action was effective in the sense that Finland's asylum/deportation policies were discussed extensively after the incident. It gained strong support from anti-deportation activists and refugee organisations, and Pennanen was highly praised for her civil courage, even though/because she was not an activist herself in a conventional sense. The case is remarkable also because civil disobedience is not a frequently used method in Finland generally, and even less so in the context of anti-deportation activism.

Then, why not more civil disobedience?

To gain a better understanding of why civil disobedience has not featured as a more common form of dissent in the context of anti-deportation activism in Finland, I conducted thematic interviews with activists and solidarity actors involved in the "No one is illegal" campaign, the "Stop Deportations" and related networks (for details, see the introduction). All interviewees stated that they/their networks do not perceive civil disobedience in negative terms but as one among dozens of potential methods that can be utilised in political activism (Interviews 1–3). The Pennanen case was characterised as a well-justified, timely, and important example of civil disobedience even though it failed to stop the deportation. Some interviewees considered it a manifestation of the kind of civil courage that is urgently needed in anti-deportation activism. Some others, however, pointed out that it was

148 Tiina Seppälä

a rare case in the sense that Pennanen had just happened to be on that flight and that generally activists cannot count on such exceptional circumstances to occur. When asylum seekers are facing life-threatening deportations to unsafe countries, activists cannot merely wait for such "windows of opportunities" to open unexpectedly. It was maintained that in anti-deportation activism, which primarily seeks to assist vulnerable persons in their individual circumstances, civil disobedience is not usually a very effective/realistic method of practising dissent. Moreover, it has become increasingly difficult for activists to enter actual deportation flights, as most deportations are no longer conducted through commercial but coordinated and centralised deportation flights.

> It requires that you ... know that the person will be deported on this flight ... I think it is a great form of activism ... but not always possible ... It requires young people without families ... [who] live very close to the airport and ... have sufficient financial resources ... It has been kind of self-entrepreneurship ... People have bought cheap flight tickets and distributed information on the gate ... that in this place, there will be ... possibly a person to be deported, and if you don't think that it is right, so here you have instructions on what you can do ... You cannot ... distribute the flyers for a long time ... you have to come out soon ... They have tried to pacify the airport for security reasons ... it is continuously more difficult ... more punishable.
>
> *(Interview 3)*

The type of mass civil disobedience practised by some other actors, such as Elokapina, the Finnish branch of Extinction Rebellion, which aims at influencing public opinion, was not considered well suited for anti-deportation activism due to imago related risks (Interviews 1–3). As a controversial method, civil disobedience was regarded as risky from the perspective of public opinion – it might turn the already critical public opinion of asylum seekers even more critical:

> We are afraid of ... that if we would block traffic from those who are irritated of whatever we do ... it would not advocate our cause, it would make it more difficult ... that they would tighten the asylum policies ... Elokapina has a climate strike in front of the Parliament and ... blocks [roads], so it is a narrative continuum ... but what we want is ... these people to get residence permits and have an opportunity to ordinary life ... So, if we acquire even more people who hate and oppose ... it will not take us towards our goal.
>
> *(Interview 3)*

> Although we support ideologically and sometimes also practically ... civil disobedience ... for human rights and such ... generally public opinion might be afraid... People are so obedient to law in this part of the world.
>
> *(Interview 2)*

Different forms of dissent in anti-deportation activism in Finland **149**

Even though civil disobedience has not been used, its potential has been discussed within the networks:

> Civil disobedience has belonged to our methods cavalcade, but I don't remember that we would have used it … I personally would have wanted us to chain ourselves somewhere … in the Migri lobby and do something startling … All methods were definitely considered … When … liberal democratic Finland … deports [someone] to Iran where that person would be taken into custody at the airport … and hanged soon, so Finland, according to its own laws, does not send anyone to mortal danger but under the pressure from *persut* [the Finns Party], they do it anyway. So, if the state violates these essential principles … why do we have to remain obedient to law.
>
> *(Interview 2)*

Some networks have participated also in activities that they have not talked publicly about:

> Some deportations on commercial flights have been successfully stopped by coaching … people who are going to be deported, let's say it in this way… This is something that social movements and private citizens have done, I will not comment more on this, but…it is possible to say this much publicly. This is international information … we do similar things than what is done in other European countries.
>
> *(Interview 3)*

Some activists mentioned that asylum seekers themselves cannot practice civil disobedience in Finland due to their legally marginalised position – they "cannot afford" to face any criminal charges.[11] The interviewees also believed that one reason behind the limited use of civil disobedience is that individuals may face an enormous amount of hate speech, which was characterised as a risk concerning especially female activists (Interviews 1–3). Some had experienced harassment themselves or knew people who had received death or rape threats due to having merely participated in "normal" anti-deportations protests or campaigns.

> I've been thinking about this a lot … why is it that in Finland civil disobedience is such a red cloth … I read an interesting article on the history of our civil war … that the white won the red, and that we still maintain this myth, and defend it. And that … a rebellious young … woman is such a red cloth in our society … It is a similar metaphor … where we have these dark men of Middle Eastern origin and then these *suvakkihuorat* [red whores].
>
> *(Interview 1)*

150 Tiina Seppälä

When explicitly asked whether they believed that civil disobedience would be practised in Finnish anti-deportation activism in future, all interviewees considered it
possible, depending on the situation:

> We don't know what will happen in the world … what kind of activism there
> might be, and what kind of an influence this Elokapina has on it.
>
> *(Interview 1)*

> If it is considered having a chance… If now, for example, with this Poland–
> Belarus border … any topical situation in the context of asylum or refugee
> policy … I think it would be possible.
>
> *(Interview 2)*

> Yes, [in some situations] it would be possible.
>
> *(Interview 3)*

Conclusion

This chapter's main objective has been to analyse different phases and forms
of dissent, including an explicit case of civil disobedience, in Finnish anti-
deportation activism since the beginning of the so-called refugee crisis in 2015.
The first section introduced the broader context by explaining how the Finnish
state "illegalised" asylum seekers, both discursively and through new restrictions
in law and policy, thus rendering them deportable "others". The second section
discussed diverse forms of collective action organised against forced deportations
by asylum seekers and solidarity actors, demonstrating that they have utilised a
wide variety of methods in different phases very creatively. In the third section,
the case of civil disobedience by Aino Pennanen was analysed in detail, showing
also that it was related to a similar case by Elin Ersson in Sweden. Indeed, they
were conducted within a period of a few weeks during the same summer (prox-
imity in time), using similar tactics (refusing to sit down on an aeroplane) and
justifications (to prevent a deportation to an unsafe country). Both disobedient
subjects were women who tried to stop deportations of men of Middle Eastern
origin. However, while Ersson was supported by other passengers and managed
to stop the deportation, Pennanen was not able to prevent the deportation, and
the flight was delayed only for 10 minutes. This invites some questions: Why did
Ersson gain support from other passengers, and Pennanen did not? What kind of
an impact the fact that the immigration/refugee contexts are quite different in
Finland and Sweden might have had? One can consider the differences, for example, in terms of the actual number of asylum seekers/refugees in general, history
of anti-deportation activism, and traditions of fidelity and civil disobedience in
these two countries.

As the Pennanen case stands almost alone as an example of civil disobedience
in Finnish anti-deportation activism,[12] in the fourth section, the potential reasons

behind the limited utilisation of civil disobedience were discussed, based on interviews with anti-deportation activists/solidarity actors. It was concluded that there are at least four reasons or explanations – civil disobedience is not necessarily considered an efficient form of dissent in anti-deportation activism as it is not always practically possible to utilise it in stopping deportations; civil disobedience may result in decreasing the already low public support for the anti-deportation cause through negative publicity; and, as a controversial method, it is considered risky also in terms of movement/organisational image and/or individual safety and well-being of the disobedient subject, especially if female.

When considering these factors, the fact that anti-deportation activists in Finland have not engaged in direct, public acts of civil disobedience and that only the case of Pennanen fulfils the publicity criteria of civil disobedience in the way outlined by Ralws (1971), becomes less surprising. It must be also understood in a broader context – there have been many cases in which activists/solidarity actors have engaged in non-public or covert forms of law- or norm-breaking,[13] for example, when hiding asylum seekers under the threat of deportation from the authorities, or when offering specific "training" for asylum seekers to be able to effectively resist their own deportation. These have happened out of the sight of the public eye for a very good reason – if they were made public, the asylum seekers, solidarity activists, their networks, and movements would be placed under even stricter measures of surveillance and control.

So far, any acts of mass civil disobedience have not occurred in the context of anti-deportation activism in Finland. The "Right to live", "No one is illegal", and protests at the Helsinki–Vantaa airport involved large numbers of participants but did not constitute civil disobedience in the Rawlsian sense. This is interesting considering the strategies adopted by Elokapina, the Finnish branch of Extinction Rebellion, which uses civil disobedience as one of its primary tools. The key difference is that its main object of resistance is much broader, and it is concerned with the whole planet and humankind – not only one individual to be deported. This invites the question of whether it can be that the tradition of fidelity and obeying law[14] is so strong in Finland that stopping deportations of foreigners is not considered legitimate enough a cause to engage in explicit acts of breaking the law. Is it regarded as easier to legitimate civil disobedience in relation to more "universal" issues, such as climate change and environmental destruction? Further studies on this topic are clearly needed.

Notes

1 On the relationship between citizenship and civil disobedience, see Koikkalainen et al. (in this volume) and Cabrera (2010, 2021). On "proxy resistance", see Baaz et al. (2017).
2 This "crisis" rhetoric has been strongly criticised, and many scholars argue that "refugee management crisis" would be a more suitable term as the situation demonstrated the inability of national reception/registration systems to keep up with the arrivals, casting doubt on the sustainability of the Common European Asylum System (Brekke & Staver, 2018; Crawley et al., 2017; Triandafyllidou, 2017).

152 Tiina Seppälä

3 Yet, as Näre (2020, p. 982) suggests, there are paradoxes in asylum seekers' activism and political claims based on shared humanity. In the "Right to live" protest, these become evident when they contested "the exclusiveness of citizenship as a means for inclusion in the political sphere, while being dependent on the same logic", as the demand for equal and inseparable human and basic rights can only be made to "the authority that ultimately guarantees these rights" – the nation state. This echoes the common interpretation of Arendt's (1968) take on human rights, which Näre (2020, p. 982) extends by suggesting that instead of "perceiving human rights in existential terms, as Arendt seems to suggest, human rights can be understood as strategic", which enables talking about the politicisation/politics of human rights (cf. Schaap, 2011).
4 Additionally, litigation, training, education, lobbying, and collaboration with certain political parties, parliamentary groups, and even some state officials/representatives were utilised (Interviews 1–3).
5 There have been similar protests elsewhere, for example, at the Berlin airport (*Deutsche Welle*, 2021) and in Glasgow where anti-deportation activists surrounded an immigration wan (BBC, 2021; Morrow, 2021; Westwater, 2021).
6 One interviewee noted that it is easy to find similar instructions online and that they "work everywhere" in Europe due to the joint European Aviation Law (Interview 3; see also Getting the Voice Out, n.d.).
7 Interestingly, Ersson (2018) referred to her action as something *legal*: "So all I want to do is to stop the deportation and then I will comply with the rules here. This is all perfectly legal and I have not committed a crime".
8 In Ersson's case, it was later revealed that the man she had wanted to help was not on that flight, and instead, she ended up helping a man convicted of abusing his wife and daughter (Crouch, 2018; *Deutsche Welle*, 2018; Hakim, 2018; Pham & Hakim, 2019; VanOpdorp, 2019).
9 The impacts for Ersson were quite similar. Originally, it was reported that she could even face prison (Crouch, 2018). The Gothenburg district court rejected her argument of not violating the law – the ruling stated that the situation did not classify as passenger distress. She was sentenced to a fine of 3000 Swedish kronor (about 290 euros). Although the prosecutors had demanded a six-month prison sentence, the court ruled that a fine was sufficient punishment (Anderson & Karasz, 2018; Pham & Hakim, 2019; Shelton, 2018; VanOpdorp, 2019).
10 In 2017, the "Stop Deportations" network shared a story about co-travellers who had stood up to oppose the forced deportation of an Iraqi asylum seeker on a Turkish Airlines flight from Helsinki – and succeeded in their effort (Stop Deportations, 2017, August 15). It is very difficult to gain information on this incident, as it did not attract any coverage in the news media, which invites many critical questions (for more details, see Kotilainen, forthcoming).
11 Despite similar risks, refugees in many other countries have engaged in civil disobedience. Scholars have interpreted these actions as *transnational* or *global* civil disobedience (e.g. Hidalgo, 2019).
12 As mentioned in previous section, it is debatable whether it should be considered the *only* case, as in August 2017, several people stood up to stop the deportation of an Iraqi asylum seeker on a Turkish Airlines flight from Helsinki (Stop Deportations, 2017, August 15; Kotilainen, forthcoming).
13 On covert civil disobedience in refugee solidarity movements, see for example Delmas (2018, pp. 59, 142–143); also Kukko (in this volume).
14 On traditions of fidelity and legalism, see Koikkalainen et al. (in this volume).

References

Anderson, B., Gibney, M. J., & Paoletti, E. (2011). Citizenship, deportation and the boundaries of belonging. *Citizenship Studies*, *15*(5), 547–563. https://doi.org/10.1080/13621 025.2011.583787

Anderson, C., & Karasz, P. (2018, July 25). Swedish student blocks Afghan's deportation by refusing to sit down on flight. *New York Times*. https://www.nytimes.com/2018/07/25/world/europe/elin-ersson-afghanistan.html

Arendt, H. (1968). *The Origins of Totalitarianism*. Harcourt.

Baaz, M., Lilja, M., & Vinthagen, S. (2017). *Researching resistance and social change: A critical approach to theory and practice*. Rowman & Littlefield.

BBC. (2018, June 30). Virgin Atlantic stops accepting forced deportations. https://www.bbc.com/news/uk-44665397

BBC. (2021, May 13). Police release men from immigration van blocking Glasgow street. https://www.bbc.com/news/uk-scotland-glasgow-west-57100259

Blencowe, A., & Grünn, E. (2017, June 27). Pakkopalautus keskeytyi eilen Helsinki-Vantaalla – "Hän oli huutanut niin kovaa koneessa". *Yle Uutiset*. https://yle.fi/uutiset/3-9691116

Brekke, J.-P., & Staver, A. (2018). The renationalisation of migration policies in times of crisis: The case of Norway. *Journal of Ethnic and Migration Studies*, 44(13), 2163–2181. https://doi.org/10.1080/1369183X.2018.1433026

Cabrera, L. (2010). *The practice of global citizenship*. Cambridge University Press.

Cabrera, L. (2021). Global citizenship, global civil disobedience and political vices. In W. E. Scheuerman (Ed.), *The Cambridge companion to civil disobedience* (pp. 313–337). Cambridge University Press.

Crawley, H., Düvell, F., Jones, K., McMahon, S., & Sigona, N. (2017). *Unravelling Europe's "migration crisis": Journeys over land and sea*. Polity Press.

Crouch, D. (2018, July 26). Swedish student's plane protest stops Afghan man's deportation "to hell". *The Guardian*. https://www.theguardian.com/world/2018/jul/25/swedish-student-plane-protest-stops-mans-deportation-afghanistan

Cruikshank, B. (1999). *The will to empower: Democratic citizens and other subjects*. Cornell University Press.

De Genova, N. P. (2002). Migrant "illegality" and deportability in everyday life. *Annual Review of Anthropology*, 31(1), 419–447. https://doi.org/10.1146/annurev.anthro.31.040402.085432

Delmas, C. (2018). *A duty to resist: When disobedience should be uncivil*. Oxford University Press.

Deutsche Welle. (2018, July 27). How Elin Ersson and other European activists derail deportations. https://www.dw.com/en/how-elin-ersson-and-other-european-activists-derail-deportations/a-44847381

Deutsche Welle. (2021, April 8). Demonstrators gather at Berlin airport to protest deportation flight to Afghanistan. https://www.dw.com/en/demonstrators-gather-at-berlin-airport-to-protest-deportation-flight-to-afghanistan/a-57127987

Embury-Dennis, T. (2018, July 25). Swedish student who stopped Afghan asylum seeker's deportation by refusing to sit down on plane could face prison. *The Independent*. https://www.independent.co.uk/news/world/europe/elin-ersson-flight-deportation-sweden-gothenberg-afghan-asylum-seeker-charges-prison-a8463881.html

Ersson, E. (2018, July 24). Deportation from Gothenburg to Afghanistan [Video]. Youtube. https://www.youtube.com/watch?v=DHz4ZGgO53U

Etelä-Suomen Sanomat. (2018, January 12). Kansalaistottelemattomuus jakaa presidenttiehdokkaat kahteen joukkoon. https://www.ess.fi/paikalliset/196549

Fausset, R. (2018, June 20). Airlines ask government not to use their flights to carry children separated at the border. *New York Times*. https://www.nytimes.com/2018/06/20/us/airlines-transport-immigrant-children.html

Finér, S. (2018, July 31). Illaksi kuolemaan? *Finnwatch*. https://finnwatch.org/fi/blogi/563-illaksi-kuolemaan

154 Tiina Seppälä

Finnish Immigration Service. (2016a, May 9). Humanitaarista suojelua ei myönnetä enää 16.5.2016 alkaen, jatkoluvalle oltava muu peruste. Asiakastiedote. https://migri.fi/-/humanitaarista-suojelua-ei-myonneta-enaa-16-5-2016-alkaen-jatkoluvalle-oltava-muu-peruste

Finnish Immigration Service. (2016b, December 22). Vastaanottopalvelujen lakkaaminen vastaanottolain 14 A §:n nojalla. MIGDno-2016-1144. http://www.paperittomat.fi/wp-content/uploads/2016/09/Maahanmuuttovirasto_-vastaanottopalveluiden_lakkaamisesta.pdf

Finnish Immigration Service. (2016c, May 17). Humanitaarista suojelua ei myönnetä enää, uudet maalinjaukset Afganistanista, Irakista ja Somaliasta. Lehdistötiedote. https://migri.fi/-/humanitaarista-suojelua-ei-myonneta-enaa-uudet-maalinjaukset-afganistanis-ta-irakista-ja-somaliasta

Finnish Immigration Service. (2019). Statistics: International Protection. https://tilastot.migri.fi/index.html#applications/23330?l=en&start=540&end=563

Gentleman, A. (2018, June 29). Virgin airlines says it will no longer help to deport immigrants. *The Guardian*. https://www.theguardian.com/uk-news/2018/jun/29/virgin-airlines-no-longer-help-deport-immigrants-lgbt-windrush

Getting the Voice Out. (n.d.). How to stop a deportation. https://www.gettingthevoiceout.org/how-to-stop-a-deportation/

Government proposal HE 43/2016 vp. (2016). Hallituksen esitys eduskunnalle laiksi ulkomaalaislain muuttamisesta. https://www.eduskunta.fi/FI/vaski/HallituksenEsitys/Sivut/HE_43+2016.aspx

Hagelund, A. (2020). After the refugee crisis: Public discourse and policy change in Denmark, Norway and Sweden. *Comparative Migration Studies, 8*(13). https://doi.org/10.1186/s40878-019-0169-8

Hakahuhta, A., & Tolkki, K. (2018, August 1). Sisäministeri Mykkänen pitää vihreiden Aallon vaatimusta suhteettomana: Ilman palautuksia koko turvapaikkajärjestelmä menettää merkityksensä. *Yle Uutiset.* https://yle.fi/uutiset/3-10332381

Hakim, A. B. (2018, July 26). The man whose deportation Elin Ersson tried to prevent. *Deutsche Welle.* https://www.dw.com/en/the-man-whose-deportation-elin-ersson-tried-to-prevent/a-44841129

Hasselberg, I. (2016). *Enduring uncertainty: Deportation, punishment and everyday life.* Berghahn.

Hernes, V. (2018). Cross-national convergence in times of crisis? Integration policies before, during and after the refugee crisis. *West European Politics, 41*(6), 1305–1329. https://doi.org/10.1080/01402382.2018.1429748

Hidalgo, J. S. (2019). *Unjust borders: Individuals and the ethics of immigration.* Routledge.

Hirvonen, A. (2017). Kukaan ei ole laiton. *Haaste, 3*/2017. https://www.haaste.om.fi/fi/index/lehtiarkisto/haaste32017/nakokulmakukaaneiolelaiton.html

Hirvonen, A. (2019, December 8). Refugee struggles: From Helsinki to Paris. *Critical Legal Thinking: Law and the Political.* https://criticallegalthinking.com/2019/12/08/refugee-struggles-from-helsinki-to-paris/

Horsti, K., & Pirkkalainen, P. (2021). The slow violence of deportability. In M. Husso, S. Karkulehto, T. Saresma, A. Laitila, J. Eilola, & H. Siltala (Eds.), *Violence, gender and affect: Interpersonal, institutional and ideological practices* (pp. 181–200). Palgrave McMillan.

Hujanen, M. (2018a, July 31). Poliisi tutkii vihreiden Pennasen toimintaa liikenteen häirintänä – mahdollinen rangaistus sakkoja tai vankeutta. *Ilta-Sanomat.* https://www.is.fi/kotimaa/art-2000005775474.html

Hujanen, M. (2018b, July 31). Vihreiden Aino Pennanen oli lähdössä lomalle, kun huomasi vaikertavan miehen – idea protestista syntyi hetkessä. *Ilta-Sanomat.* https://www.is.fi/kotimaa/art-2000005775585.html

Humalamäki, A. (2017, April 5). Miksi poliisilla kesti oikoa väärät huhut pakkopalautuksista? – "Ryhdyimme heti aamulla töihin". *Aamulehti.* https://www.aamulehti.fi/kotimaa/art-2000007409433.html

Interview 1, activist/solidarity actor, (2021, November 11). Online interview. Rovaniemi/Helsinki. 50 minutes.

Interview 2, activist/solidarity actor, (2021, November 11). Online interview. Rovaniemi/Helsinki. 55 minutes.

Interview 3, activist/solidarity actor, (2021, November 12). Online interview. Rovaniemi/Helsinki. 1 hour 25 minutes.

Jansen, Y., Celikates, R., & de Bloois, J. (Eds.) (2014). *The irregularization of migration in contemporary Europe: Detention, deportation, drowning.* Rowman & Littlefield.

Jaulimo, J. (2017, April 4). Raskaana olevan naisen perheineen piti olla maanantaina palautuslennolla – poliisi lykkäsi toimeenpanoa. *MTV Uutiset.* https://www.mtvuutiset.fi/artikkeli/raskaana-olevan-naisen-perheineen-piti-olla-maanantaina-palautuslennolla-poliisi-lykkasi-toimeenpanoa/6376760?mtv_ref=twb_uutiset_uusimmat#gs.4mo1fa

Kansan Uutiset. (2018, August 21). "Kukaan ei ole laiton" – Vasemmistonuoret avasi maahanmuuttokampanjan. https://www.kansanuutiset.fi/artikkeli/3856307-kukaan-ei-ole-laiton-vasemmistonuoret-avasi-maahanmuuttokampanjan

Kärnä, L. (2018, August 7). Harvinainen video: Kohulennolla pakkopalautettu Ahmed väittää asuvansa roskakatoksessa aavikolla – Migri: "Tilanne ei usein ole sellainen kuin annetaan ymmärtää". *MTV Uutiset.* https://www.mtvuutiset.fi/artikkeli/harvinainen-video-kohulennolla-pakkopalautettu-ahmed-vaittaa-asuvansa-roskakatoksessa-aavikolla-migri-tilanne-ei-usein-ole-sellainen-kuin-annetaan-ymmartaa/7020738?fbclid=IwAR3Zrdcxh-JiW79UOLeHquSJxDBDa8ujO1tjpSPSr6d0bdI_3WR5dWWtLyN4#gs.u8j5j0

Khosravi, S. (Ed.) (2018). *After deportations: Ethnographic perspectives.* Palgrave MacMillan.

Kilpeläinen, K. (2019, May 3). Aino Pennaselle tuomio lentokoneprotestista, pyysi alempaa tuomiota julkisuuden vuoksi – kohu poiki vihapostia ja perättömän lastensuojeluilmoituksen. *Iltalehti.* https://www.iltalehti.fi/kotimaa/a/77e6175f-b4dc-40f6-9e87-6b69bcae7037

Konttinen, M. (2018, August 23). Poliisi epäilee vihreiden Aino Pennasta ilmailurikkomuksesta ja haitanteosta virkamiehelle – kieltäytyi istumasta protestina ulkomaalaisen palautukselle. *Yle Uutiset.* https://yle.fi/uutiset/3-10366864

Koskinen, A. L. (2017a, April 4). Pakkopalautuksista liikkuu hurjia huhuja – Nyt puhuu poliisi: "Väärää tietoa liikkeellä". *Aamulehti.* https://www.aamulehti.fi/kotimaa/art-2000007409406.html

Koskinen, A. L. (2017b, April 4). Uutta tietoa palautuslennoista: Joka viikko sata ihmistä palaa tai palautetaan lähtömaahansa. *Aamulehti.* https://www.aamulehti.fi/kotimaa/art-2000007409451.html

Kotilainen, N. (forthcoming). Resisting deportation live: Affective witnessing and recognition of airplane deportation protests. *Nordic Journal of Migration Research.*

Krzyżanowski, M., Triandafyllidou, A., & Wodak, R. (2018). The mediatization and the politicization of the "refugee crisis" in Europe. *Journal of Immigrant & Refugee Studies, 16*(1–2), 1–14. https://doi.org/10.1080/15562948.2017.1353189

Kukaan ei ole laiton (2018, June 11, July 23, July 25, July 31). Facebook posts. https://www.facebook.com/kukaaneiolelaiton/

Laki oikeusapulain muuttamisesta. (2016). 650/2016. [Law to change the law on legal aid]. https://www.finlex.fi/fi/laki/alkup/2016/20160650

Laki ulkomaalaislain muuttamisesta. (2016). 332/2016. [Law to change The Aliens Act]. https://www.finlex.fi/fi/laki/alkup/2016/20160332

156 Tiina Seppälä

Lakka, P. (2017, April 4). Sisäministeriön Nerg: "Väärä tieto palautuslennosta lähti liikkeelle organisoidusti ja voimakkaasti". *Aamulehti.* https://www.aamulehti.fi/kotimaa/art-2000007409486.html

Latvala, J., Sieppi, J., & Leppänen, M. (2018, July 31). Vihreiden lainsäädäntösihteeri vastusti pakkopalautuksia lentokoneessa: kieltäytyi istumasta ja kuvasi tilanteen livenä somessa – poliisi poisti koneesta. *Yle Uutiset.* https://yle.fi/uutiset/3-10330803

Laurila, S. (2018, August 1). "Vihreiden puheenjohtaja Aalto lietsoo kapinaa" – Finnairin lennolla protestoineelle Pennaselle ja Touko Aallolle sataa tiukkaa kritiikkiä. *MTV Uutiset.* https://www.mtvuutiset.fi/artikkeli/vihreiden-puheenjohtaja-aalto-lietsoo-kapinaa-finnairin-lennolla-protestoineelle-pennaselle-ja-touko-aallolle-sataa-tiukkaa-kritiikkia/7014536

Leinonen, N. (2017a, April 4). Poliisi kiistää tiedot alaikäisestä tai raskaana olleesta pakkopalautetusta: "väärää tietoa liikkeellä". *Iltalehti.* https://www.iltalehti.fi/uutiset/a/201704042200096649

Leinonen, N. (2017b, August 8). Aktivistit vastustavat pakkopalautuksia – Mielenosoituksia Tampereella ja Helsinki-Vantaan lentoasemalla. *Iltalehti.* https://www.iltalehti.fi/kotimaa/a/201708082200313107

Leinonen, N. (2017c, August 8). Näkökulma: Turvapaikkapäätösten kokonaiskuva syytä ruotia. *Iltalehti.* https://www.iltalehti.fi/kotimaa/a/201708082200313449

Libero. (2018, February 20). Työpajoja turvapaikanhakijoille ja painetta poliitikoille – Vasemmistonuoret avasi maahanmuuttopoliittisen kampanjan. https://liberolehti.fi/tyopajoja-turvapaikanhakijoille-ja-painetta-poliitikoille-vasemmistonuoret-avasi-maahanmuuttopoliittisen-kampanjan/

Mäkinen, J., & Harmanen, S. (2017, July 4). Parisataa mielenosoittajaa vastusti pakkopalautuksia Pasilan poliisitalon edustalla ja Helsinki-Vantaan lentokentällä. *Helsingin Sanomat.* https://www.hs.fi/kotimaa/art-2000005278090.html

Mäntymaa, E. (2018, March 22). "Meiltä edellytettiin yhtenäistä linjaa Ruotsin kanssa" – Näin Maahanmuuttovirasto perustelee Suomen turvapaikkalinjan tiukennusta. *Yle Uutiset.* https://yle.fi/uutiset/3-10128229

Ministry of the Interior. (2016, December 16). Toimenpidesuunnitelma laittoman maassa oleskelun ehkäisyyn ja hallintaan. Press release 557/2016. https://valtioneuvosto.fi/-/10616/toimenpidesuunnitelma-laittoman-maassa-oleskelun-ehkaisyyn-ja-hallintaan-hyvaksyttiin

Ministry of the Interior. (2018, March 22). Turvapaikkakäytäntöjä on yhtenäistetty muiden EU-maiden kanssa. Press release 33/2018. https://intermin.fi/en/-/turvapaikkakaytantoja-on-yhtenaistetty-muiden-eu-maiden-kanssa

Ministry of the Interior. (n.d.-a). The fight against illegal immigration requires cooperation between authorities. https://intermin.fi/en/areas-of-expertise/migration/combating-illegal-immigration

Ministry of the Interior. (n.d.-b). Laitonta maahantuloa ehkäistään viranomaisyhteistyöllä. https://intermin.fi/maahanmuutto/laittoman-maahanmuuton-torjunta

Morrow, D. (2021, May 14). Anti-deportation groups' plea for mobile phone top up donations to help asylum seekers after Glasgow protest. *Daily Record.* https://www.dailyrecord.co.uk/news/scottish-news/anti-deportation-groups-plea-mobile-24108493

Myllymäki, L. (2017, April 4). Palautuslentoa Kabuliin valvonut yhdenvertaisuusvaltuutettu: Meillä on samat tiedot kuin poliisilla. *Aamulehti.* https://www.aamulehti.fi/kotimaa/art-2000007409455.html

Näre, L. (2020). "Finland kills with a pen" – asylum seekers' protest against bureaucratic violence as politics of human rights. *Citizenship Studies, 24*(8), 979–993. https://doi.org/10.1080/13621025.2020.1769559

Nieminen, E. (2016, February 23). Paperittomuuden määrittelystä. *Politiikasta.fi*. https://politiikasta.fi/paperittomuuden-maarittelysta/

Nykänen, T., Koikkalainen, S., Seppälä, T., Mikkonen, E., & Rainio, M. (2018). Poikkeusajan tilat: Vastaanottokeskukset pohjoisessa Suomessa. In E. Lyytinen (Ed.), *Turvapaikanhaku ja pakolaisuus Suomessa* (pp. 161–182). Siirtolaisuusinstituutti.

Oudejans, N. (2014). The right to have rights as the right to asylum. *Netherlands Journal of Legal Philosophy*, *43*(1), 7–26. https://www.elevenjournals.com/tijdschrift/rechtsfilosofieentheorie/2014/1/NJLP_2213-0713_2014_043_001_002

Paperittomat.fi. (2016, December 22). Oikeuksien rajoittaminen ja valvonnan lisääminen eivät ratkaise paperittomuutta. http://www.paperittomat.fi/?p=1850

Parkkinen, S., & Hakahuhta, A. (2018, August 1). Vihreiden Aalto: Pakkopalautukset keskeytettävä, kunnes turvapaikkaprosessin ongelmat on korjattu – "Ketään ei saa lähettää hengenvaaraan". *Yle Uutiset*. https://yle.fi/uutiset/3-10331907

Peutz, N., & De Genova, N. P. (2010). *The deportation regime*. Duke University Press.

Pham, K., & Hakim, A. B. (2019, February 31). Elin Ersson and Ismail K. – How an activist tried in vain to rescue an asylum-seeker. *Deutsche Welle*. https://www.dw.com/en/elin-ersson-and-ismail-k-how-an-activist-tried-in-vain-to-rescue-an-asylum-seeker/a-47295356

Rawls, J. (1971). *A theory of justice*. Harvard University Press.

Saarikkomäki, E., Oljakka, N., Vanto, J., Pirjatanniemi, E., Lavapuro, J., & Alvesalo-Kuusi, A. (2018). *Kansainvälistä suojelua koskevat päätökset Maahanmuuttovirastossa 2015–2017. Pilottitutkimus 18–34-vuotiaita Irakin kansalaisia koskevista myönteisistä ja kielteisistä päätöksistä*. Oikeustieteellisen tiedekunnan tutkimusraportteja ja katsauksia 1/2018. Turun yliopisto.

Saner, E. (2018, July 25). Swedish plane protester Elin Ersson: 'I knew I couldn't back down – I had to do what I could. *The Guardian*. https://www.theguardian.com/world/2018/jul/25/swedish-plane-protester-elin-ersson-interview-afghanistan

Schaap, A. (2011). Enacting the right to have rights: Jacques Rancière's critique of Hannah Arendt. *European Journal of Political Theory*, *10*(1), 22–45. https://journals.sagepub.com/doi/10.1177/1474885110386004

Schumacher, E. (2017, December 7). German pilots refuse to carry out deportations. *Deutsche Welle*. https://www.dw.com/en/german-pilots-refuse-to-carry-out-deportations/a-41638832

Seppälä, T. (2022). 'No one is illegal' as a reverse discourse against deportability. *Global Society*. https://doi.org/10.1080/13600826.2022.2052023

Seppälä, T., Nykänen, T., Koikkalainen, S., Mikkonen, E., & Rainio, M. (2020). In-between space/time: Affective exceptionality during the "refugee crisis" in Northern Finland. *Nordic Journal of Migration Research*, *10*(1), 87–105. https://doi.org/10.2478/njmr-2019-0029

Shelton, J. (2018, July 24). Swedish student Elin Ersson halts plane in anti-deportation protest. *Deutsche Welle*. https://www.dw.com/en/swedish-student-elin-ersson-halts-plane-in-anti-deportation-protest/a-44813432

Stop Deportations. (2017, August 15; 2018, July 23, July 27, August 6). Facebook posts. https://www.facebook.com/SeisKarkotuksille/

STT–HS. (2019, May 3). Vihreiden Aino Pennaselle sakkoja lentokoneprotestista. *HS.fi*. https://www.hs.fi/politiikka/art-2000006092707.html

STT–*Ilta-Sanomat*. (2017, April 3). Helsinki-Vantaan lähtöaula täyttyi mielenosoittajista, jotka vastustivat turvapaikanhakijoiden pakkopalautusta. *Ilta-Sanomat*. https://www.is.fi/kotimaa/art-2000005154966.html

158 Tiina Seppälä

Sullström, H. (2018, August 1). Finnair pakkopalautuksista: Viranomaisen päätökseen on voitava luottaa. *Yle Uutiset.* https://yle.fi/uutiset/3-10331962

Triandafyllidou, A. (2017). A "refugee crisis" unfolding: "real" events and their interpretation in media and political debates. *Journal of Immigrant & Refugee Studies, 16*(1–2), 198–216. https://doi.org/10.1080/15562948.2017.1309089

Turkki, K. & Myllymäki, L. (2017, April 4). Mitä turvapaikanhakijoiden palautuslennoilla tapahtuu? Näin valvojat kertovat matkoista. *Aamulehti.* https://www.aamulehti.fi/kotimaa/art-2000007409431.html

Ukkonen, E. (2018, January 31). Vihreiden poliitikko poistettiin lentokoneesta – Touko Aalto pitää Pennasen toimintaa perusteltuna: "Kunnioitettavaa rohkeutta". *MTV Uutiset.* https://www.mtvuutiset.fi/artikkeli/vihreiden-poliitkko-poistettiin-lentokoneesta-touko-aalto-pitaa-pennasen-toimintaa-perusteltuna-kunnioitettavaa-rohkeutta/7013918

Uusi Suomi. (2019, May 3). Kohuprotestista sakkotuomion saaneen Aino Pennasen ulostulo: "Kyse on aivan oikeusvaltiomme ytimestä – En olisi voinut toimia toisin". https://www.uusisuomi.fi/uutiset/kohuprotestista-sakkotuomion-saaneen-aino-pennasen-ulostulo-kyse-on-aivan-oikeusvaltiomme-ytimesta-en-olisi-voinut-toimia-toisin/1fec5268-ec04-3aa6-9f34-57004336d21c

VanOpdorp, D. (2019, February 18). Elin Ersson sentenced to fine for anti-deportation protest. *Deutsche Welle.* https://www.dw.com/en/elin-ersson-sentenced-to-fine-for-anti-deportation-protest/a-47560924

Vasemmistonuoret. (2018a, February 20). Kukaan ei ole laiton – Vasemmistonuorten kampanja alkoi. https://vasemmistonuoret.fi/fi/kampanjat/kukaan-ei-ole-laiton/uutiset/kukaan-ei-ole-laiton-vasemmistonuorten-kampanja-alkoi

Vasemmistonuoret. (2018b, February 27). Loviisalaista perhettä uhkaa palautus Suomesta Irakiin. https://vasemmistonuoret.fi/fi/kampanjat/kukaan-ei-ole-laiton/uutiset/loviisalaista-perhetta-uhkaa-palautus-suomesta-irakiin

Vasemmistonuoret. (2018c, March 1). Lov is an Asylum -mielenosoitus Loviisan torilla. https://vasemmistonuoret.fi/fi/kampanjat/kukaan-ei-ole-laiton/uutiset/lov-asylum-mielenosoitus-loviisan-torilla

Vasemmistonuoret. (2018d, March 5). Turvapaikanhakijoita ei saa asettaa keskenään eriarvoiseen asemaan. https://vasemmistonuoret.fi/fi/kampanjat/kukaan-ei-ole-laiton/uutiset/turvapaikanhakijoita-ei-saa-asettaa-keskenaan-eriarvoiseen

Vasemmistonuoret. (2018e, March 21). Maahanmuuttoviraston toiminnasta on tehtävä riippumaton selvitys. https://vasemmistonuoret.fi/fi/kampanjat/kukaan-ei-ole-laiton/uutiset/maahanmuuttoviraston-toiminnasta-tehtava-riippumaton-selvitys

Vasemmistonuoret. (2018f, October 1). Pakkopalautukset on keskeytettävä riippumattoman selvityksen tekemiseen asti! https://vasemmistonuoret.fi/fi/kampanjat/kukaan-ei-ole-laiton/uutiset/pakkopalautukset-keskeytettava-riippumattoman-selvityksen

Vasen Kaista. (2018, April 7). Kukaan ei ole laiton. https://vasenkaista.fi/2018/04/kukaan-ei-ole-laiton/

Vuorinen, T. (2018, July 31). Touko Aalto myöntää, ettei tunne lentokonekohun taustaa – "On mahdollista, että kyseessä oli oikea rikollinen". *Ilta-Sanomat.* https://www.is.fi/politiikka/art-2000005775661.html

Walters, W. (2002). Deportation, expulsion, and the international police of aliens. *Citizenship Studies, 6*(3), 265–292. https://doi.org/10.1080/1362102022000011612

Waris, O. (2018, November 3). Vihreiden uusi puheenjohtaja Pekka Haavisto Aino Pennasen kohutusta lentokoneprotestista: "Ei vihreiden politiikkaa". *Iltalehti.* https://www.iltalehti.fi/politiikka/a/500a0789-e15a-44db-8870-418b93c4f524

Westwater, H. (2021, May 13). Glasgow protestors surround immigration van to stop Home Office raids. *The Big Issue*. https://www.bigissue.com/latest/glasgow-protestors-surround-immigration-van-to-stop-home-office-raids/

Yle. (2017, September 10). Kansalaistottelemattomuus paperittomien auttamisessa saa hyväksyntää vihreiltä ja vasemmistoliitolta. https://yle.fi/uutiset/3-9824986

Yle. (2018, October 3). Vihreiden Aino Pennasen lentokoneprotesti siirtyy syyteharkintaan. https://yle.fi/uutiset/3-10436795

Yle–STT. (2017, July 4). Mielenosoitus Helsinki-Vantaan lentokentällä päättyi rauhallisesti. https://yle.fi/uutiset/3-9703597

10

DISSENTING CIVIL SOCIETY, HUNGER STRIKES, AND THE TRANSITIONAL JUSTICE PROCESS IN NEPAL

Neetu Pokharel, Som Prasad Niroula, and Tiina Seppälä

Introduction

Ten years of internal armed conflict in Nepal (1996–2006) that occurred between the Nepal Communist Party of Maoists (CPN-M) and the government of Nepal of that time took the lives of more than 13,000 people. It also resulted in many other forms of violence, torture, and abuse, as well as in over 1,300 enforced disappearances. Furthermore, a large number of people become internally displaced when being forced to leave their homes and move from rural areas to urban centres due to the civil war. During the past two decades, the conflict victims have been actively voicing their demands for justice. As the state has not responded positively to their claims, the conflict victims have formed loose networks and started working together with a broad spectrum of civil society organisations that advocate for their rights. Over the years, they have utilised many means and methods, such as public consultation and public hearings, documentation (generating evidence), and litigation in courts. They have also engaged in many different forms of dissent, including peaceful protests and civil disobedience in challenging laws they consider unjust.

Despite the continuous, active efforts of this Transitional Justice movement in Nepal, none of the numerous human rights violations has been seriously addressed by the state – it has failed to deliver justice to the victims of the conflict. Even though the situation has not significantly improved, the civil disobedience movement for Transitional Justice has, nevertheless, succeeded in bringing national and international public attention to the failure of the state of Nepal to address these issues. It has also articulated important legal and moral questions related to the state's accountability and the role and functioning of democratic institutions in the Transitional Justice process. From the perspective of the conflict victims, it is crucial that the state is committed to finding and punishing the perpetrators of the crimes and human rights violations conducted during the civil war.

DOI: 10.4324/9781003320494-12

In this chapter, our research question is, What kind of a role and impact has civil society in Nepal had in trying to make the state accountable? The objective is to explore different forms and phases of activism by the conflict victims, human rights activists, and civil society organisations. We discuss their key strategies and actions, including forms of dissent that can be considered civil disobedience and/or nonviolent resistance, such as non-cooperation and hunger strikes by individuals who demand justice for themselves, their family members, or other victims. The chapter is based on an analysis of relevant literature, one focus group discussion, and six semi-structured interviews with, altogether, four conflict victims, five activists, and civil society representatives, conducted in Kathmandu by the first and second authors. The focus group discussion was organised in October 2021. The interviews were conducted in April, September, and October 2021.

Next, we outline the broader context of our study, reflecting on the background and impacts of the civil war, as well as the history and traditions of nonviolence and civil disobedience in Nepal. We start our discussion with Gandhi and his empirical examples while also introducing some historical cases of civil disobedience in Nepal. Then, we explore different forms of dissent and disobedience practised by the conflict victims, activists, and civil society organisations as a part of the Transitional Justice movement, which include, for example, peaceful protests, the burning of the Putla (effigy), and the Chakka Jam (Stop Vehicle) movement. Thereafter, we analyse the nonviolent strategy of fast-onto-death hunger strike by Nanda Prasad and Ganga Maya Adhikari, whose son was kidnapped and murdered by the Maoists. Even though we mainly focus on different forms of dissent, we also pay some attention to the responses of the state to them. In the concluding section, we discuss the effects and the political meaning of the Transitional Justice movement in Nepal from a broader perspective.

Context: the background of the conflict

The armed conflict in Nepal started in 1996. One of the political parties of that time, the CPN-M submitted a 40-point demand charter to the government regarding livelihoods, gender and caste-based discrimination, poverty, regional disparity, and various other political issues (Thapa, 2003). As the government did not pay any attention to the demand, the CPN-M decided to formally declare a "People's war". This declaration was made on 13 February 1996 from far-western Nepal, a rural area where people felt discriminated against and excluded from the government's mainstream development priorities, including education, health care, infrastructure, and communication. At the beginning of the conflict, the Maoists targeted government offices and institutions, such as police posts, security offices, and agricultural banks with the aim of destroying them. The Maoists also targeted the political cadres and political parties, after which the government's security forces launched a counterattack on them.

The conflict between the Maoists and the government drove Nepal into a 10-year civil war, creating an atmosphere of fear, insecurity, and instability in the

162 Neetu Pokharel et al.

country. There have been several allegations made according to which the Maoists forcefully recruited children as soldiers, sexually harassed and abused women, forcefully abducted civilians and recruited them as cadres, looted public and private properties, killed and tortured civilians who they accused of espionage, and brutally killed also politicians to fuel fear within the government (OHCHR, 2012). Similarly, also the government military forces have been alleged to have conducted many kinds of cruelties, including rape and sexual abuse, as well as abducting and torturing civilians suspected of being Maoist or gathering intelligence information (spying) on their behalf. Caught in between these violent forces, the everyday life of ordinary people became very difficult (Human Rights Watch, 2004; OCHA, 2005). Many did not dare to speak publicly about their concerns and problems. In addition to more than 13,000 casualties and 1,300 missing persons, the conflict caused a lot of physical destruction. Moreover, the education and healthcare systems were severely affected, which caused long-term effects on people's lives and the development of the country. The indirect effects of the conflict are enormous, and it is impossible to evaluate the extent of its psychosocial impact.

The decade-long armed conflict ended in 2006 with the signing of the Comprehensive Peace Agreement (CPA) between the CPN-M and the government, supported by the Seven Party Alliance. With the CPA, the country entered into the peace process. Through the Seven Party Alliance, the 240-year-old regime and long-rooted monarchy also became overthrown in 2008. The Seven Party Alliance and the Maoists agreed to form a committee to draft an Interim Constitution, which was promulgated in January 2007 (International Crisis Group, 2007). The former rebellion party, the Maoists, became part of the government in 2008 through the elections of the constituent assembly. The CPA and the Interim Constitution were designed to transform grievances and address human rights violations conducted during the armed conflict through the Transitional Justice process, along with political and socio-economic transformation of the country (Comprehensive Peace Agreement, 2006). Both documents include provisions for the formation of commissions to investigate the atrocities, disappearances, and other human rights violations committed during the civil war. In addition, the Interim Constitution of Nepal (2007) promised "to provide relief to the families of the victims, on the basis of the report of the Investigation Commission constituted to investigate the cases of disappearances made during the course of the conflict". Both the government and the CPN-M agreed to expedite the processes of establishing mechanisms that provide support to the conflict-affected people. However, the CPA has been only partially implemented in terms of supporting the conflict victims.

After the promising beginning of the peace process, the government's plan to establish a mechanism of delivering justice to the conflict victims was significantly delayed. It took seven years for the state to initiate new laws and establish the Transitional Justice commissions. It started working on these issues only after the Supreme Court ordered, in its verdict on the Rajendra Dhakal's case, the government to form a commission to investigate the whereabouts of disappeared persons and formulate a law criminalising enforced disappearances. In 2014, the government promulgated the Enforced Disappearances Enquiry, Truth and Reconciliation Commission Act, on the basis of which two commissions were established – the Truth and Reconciliation Commission (TRC) and the Commission of Enforced Disappeared Persons (CIEDP). However, they involved several problems and challenges (OHCHR, 2014). The act itself was strongly criticised. The conflict victims, human rights activists, and civil society organisations pointed out that the act was prepared without proper consultation with them as the key stakeholders. Another major point of criticism was that the act included provisions for providing blanket amnesty to persons involved in serious human rights violations during the conflict. The conflict victims, activists, and civil society organisations expressed their dissatisfaction and their concerns through press releases and statements, and by protesting on the streets. Amidst the protests and harsh critique, the government established both commissions in February 2015. After that, the victims, together with civil society organisations and human rights lawyers, filed a writ to the Supreme Court with a demand to amend the act. The court gave its verdict in favour of the victims' demand and ordered the government to amend the act in line with international human rights principles with no amnesty in cases that concern grave human rights violations (Supreme Court of Nepal, 2015).

The TRC received more than 60,000 complaints. It started the preliminary investigation of the cases, but the process did not work properly. The victims and civil society organisations have closely monitored the work of both commissions – the TRC and CIEDP. According to them, the commissions have failed even in protecting the information of the victims who filed the complaints. The TRC has also identified its challenges: it has not been able to work as actively as originally planned because neither the government nor the parties of the conflict have cooperated (Truth and Reconciliation Commission, 2018). Hence, it has failed to win the confidence of the conflict victims. Human rights organisations, the United Nations, and the international community have not either recognised or collaborated with the commissions. While the commissions have provided some monetary relief to direct conflict victims and adopted some inclusion policies to bring the marginalised and vulnerable groups into the political process, they have not been able to accomplish their primary objectives.[1] Thus, the main promise of the CPA and the Interim Constitution – to bring justice to the victims of human rights violations that occurred during the armed conflict – has not been delivered.

In 2015, Nepal witnessed another political reform. The country adopted a new constitution that was regarded as significantly more progressive than the previous constitutions, with the provisions related to guaranteeing the fundamental rights to equality, justice, social justice, reparation, and relief. Nepal also started practising decentralised power devolution at the three tiers of the government after the local elections in 2017. This reform of the governance system created an opportunity for the political parties to build political consensus and a framework for the implementation of unaddressed agendas of the past. However, a key objective of the CPA, dealing with Transitional Justice, still was not addressed by the political parties. The state revised the act several times, however, there has not been proper consultation

164 Neetu Pokharel et al.

with the conflict victims or the civil society (Advocacy Forum-Nepal, 2020). The act has not been amended by the parliament, nor the revised version of the bill has been brought to the public or conflict victims for consultation. The state's inability to enable and ensure the ownership of the conflict victims and civil society actors in the law-drafting processes, establishing the TRC and the CIEDP commissions, and appointing their officials has created serious scepticism amongst the conflict victims. They are unsure of how long the process of delivering justice may take and how long the victims will need to raise their voices and protest for the sake of justice. So far, there has not been much progress; most of the victims' demands remain unaddressed at the time of writing. At the same time, there have been several cases in the context of the CPA in which the alleged perpetrators of the conflict era have been granted impunity between 2006 and 2021.

The conflict victims and civil society organisations have acted as a watchdog of the state and several different governments' work on the Transitional Justice process from the very beginning. In fact, the victims started organising the movement for Transitional Justice already before the CPA of 2006. When the conflict atrocities began and people were forcefully displaced, they collectively voiced their concern over their security and livelihoods. However, in the middle of the armed conflict, it was not safe or easy for them to demand justice for the killed, the disappeared, and the raped. When the armed conflict ended, it became to some extent safer for them to protest and express their demands and dissenting voices.

Civil disobedience and hunger strikes in Nepal

Civil disobedience has long traditions in South Asia where it has been utilised, for example, in efforts to dismantle undemocratic governments and in struggles against colonial forces (Rajopadhyaya, 2020; see also Koikkalainen et al. in this volume). The most prominent example is the independence movement in India, which was also connected to Nepal as the main Nepalese political parties – the Nepali Congress and the Nepal Communist Party – were formed in India. The Nepali leaders contributed to the Indian independence movement, and they were deeply impressed and influenced by the movement's strategies of nonviolence and civil disobedience.

The example set by Mohandas Karamchand Gandhi (1869–1948), a civil rights activist and lawyer who launched nonviolent resistance against British rule in India, was powerful. His ethical practice of civil disobedience inspired movements not only in Nepal but across the world as well. Gandhi started his public campaign in South Africa to where the British colonisers had transported Indian workers who were considered slaves and treated inhumanly (Zinkin, 1983). The colonisers represented Indians as unclean and dirty and did not allow them access to the first class in public trains. Gandhi was also forcibly removed from the first class and thrown off a train when travelling. After this incident, he started to organise Indian communities in South Africa, launching a series of nonviolent campaigns. Gandhi helped many Indians in South Africa by providing them with legal assistance, as well as moral and political support. When back in India, Gandhi launched several movements and actively challenged British rule through protests, such as the Salt March in 1930 (Diwakar, 1969, p. 106). He encouraged people to practise civil disobedience by refusing to pay the salt tax (a violation of the salt tax law) which was imposed by the British on salt produced in India. Gandhi was imprisoned several times both in South Africa and India for practising and initiating different forms of nonviolence and civil disobedience.

Inspired by their Indian fellows and Gandhi in particular, also the Nepalis started to utilise civil disobedience in the context of different social movements. Civil disobedience has been coined in the Nepali vernacular language as "*Bhadra Abhagya*" or "*Nagarik Abhagya*", which means to disobey an unjust law through different tactics. As explained by Rosenberg (2019),

> [a] person using *satyagraha* could resist injustice by refusing to follow an unjust law or putting up with physical assaults and/or confiscation of his property without anger. There would be no winners or losers; all would understand the "truth" and agree to rescind the unjust law.

Historically, marginalised and vulnerable communities in Nepal have used multiple strategies and methods in their civil resistance, varying from nonviolent protests to public strikes and non-cooperation with the authorities, among other means. The methods have greatly varied depending on the contexts and political situations. For example, Bishweshwar Psasad Koirala, who led Nepal's democratic struggle for socio-economic transformation and later became Nepal's first elected prime minister in 1959, resorted to hunger strike as a means of protest. He and his colleagues were on hunger strike for 21 days while in jail in 1948.[2] In the end, the people's movement led by Koirala managed to outcast the Ranas, the traditional rulers of the country, putting an end to the 104-year long autocratic regime. In initiating and encouraging civil disobedience to the law and order imposed by the state, this democratic movement of 1951 was utilising strategies adopted from the Indian independence movement, including the Gandhian legacies of nonviolence and nonviolent mass movements.

Traditional, community-based organisations have also played an important role in challenging unjust laws and policies, as well as in empowering communities in Nepal. For example, associations and societies such as the Guthi, Parma, Dhikur, and Paropakar Sansthans provided marginalised and disadvantaged communities with education and services based on voluntarism and philanthropy. The individuals engaged in these institutions were regarded as persons who were willing to sacrifice their lives in the service of the poor and the needy, and hence, they were respected by all. The founder of Shree Chandra Kamdhenu Charkha Pracharak Mahaguthi, an organisation established in 1927 to support poor and marginalised communities, was also deeply influenced by the Gandhian philosophy of nonviolence (Nepal Charkha Pracharak Gandhi-Tulshi Smarak Mahaguthi, n.d.). He was arrested several times and his weaving wheel was confiscated by the authorities;

166 Neetu Pokharel et al.

however, despite the harassment, the movement he initiated continued, and ultimately, contributed to the establishment of democracy in Nepal in 1951.

Similarly, the movements of 1990 and 2006 which demanded democratic rule and governance in Nepal were mainly based on the principles of nonviolent resistance (Bhatta, 2006). After the 1990s, also a broad spectrum of civil society organisations which work on advocacy and promotion of human rights have emerged in Nepal. Together, these organisations and social movements have engaged in many different forms of dissent. However, while the causes of the internal armed conflict and its impacts have been widely discussed in Nepal, the agency of civil society actors, whose role is vital in the Transitional Justice process, has not received enough attention. In the next section, we discuss this aspect in more detail, focusing especially on the ways in which the conflict victims have organised collectively and practised different forms of nonviolent resistance, including civil disobedience and non-participation.

Conflict victims and the Transitional Justice movement

Since the beginning of the internal armed conflict in 1996, there have been many informal ways for the conflict victims to organise. Around 2000, they started to organise more formally when they registered, for example, the Nepal Maobadi Pidit Sanstha (Maoist Victims' Association of Nepal, MVA), a society dedicated to supporting especially the victims of Maoist violence. The MVA was initiated by 250 conflict victims and their families who moved to Kathmandu from rural areas where their lives were under constant threat. In Kathmandu, the conflict-affected families urged the state to provide relief and support to them. While the state refused to deal with issues related to human rights violations, it agreed to provide some financial support to them. The amount was 300 Nepali rupees per month per family, which was not enough even to acquire food. However, when increasingly more families started to arrive in Kathmandu, the government stopped distributing relief. Later in 2008, also another association, the Conflict Victims' Society for Justice (CVSJ-Nepal) was established with the aim of supporting the survivors of violence and relatives of those killed and disappeared at the hands of *both* the state and the Maoist rebels (Conflict Victims' Society for Justice, n.d.; Advocacy Forum-Nepal, n.d.-a). The previously mentioned and other civil society organisations have helped the conflict victims in many different ways, for example, by registering their complaints and systematically documenting their cases which include crimes and human rights violations, such as physical and sexual violence, displacement, killings, disappearances, and unauthorised confiscation of property (Advocacy Forum-Nepal, n.d.-a). The civil society organisations have also provided them with legal, psychosocial, and medical assistance. Furthermore, they have actively encouraged the conflict victims to organise collectively to voice their demands for truth and justice.

For the conflict victims, peaceful means of protesting have been the most common tool in their efforts to pressurise the state and parties of the conflict. They have especially often utilised the tactics of non-cooperation, which Gandhi considered one of the most effective and peaceful means in the nonviolent approach for expressing dissent and struggling against injustices (Diwakar, 1969, pp. 161–162). In the conflict victims' case, non-cooperation has been manifested, for example, in the form of voluntary withdrawal of support to and participation in the Transitional Justice mechanism. At times, however, the conflict victims have engaged with the legal system (courts) and government agencies in their efforts to bring about change. Moreover, as already mentioned earlier, they have established many organisations and formed networks to advance their goals and mobilise collective action. The conflict victims have demonstrated a clear dissatisfaction with the Transitional Justice process, and especially the state's role in it, through multiple forms of dissent. In the following, we introduce and discuss a few of them in more detail.

In 2000, nine conflict victims led by Dilli Bahadur Khadka engaged in a nonviolent protest in Kathmandu which included a hunger strike that lasted for 14 days (Focus group discussion; Interviews 1–2). The protesters were demanding justice for persons killed by the Maoists, requesting the government to support the victims' family members by securing their livelihoods and ensuring them access to health care and education. They had also faced difficulties in finding a place to stay in Kathmandu due to the landlords being afraid of retaliation by the Maoists. More than 300 conflict victims demonstrated solidarity and support to the protesters. The government did not, however, respond to their claims or address their concerns. To strengthen their demands, the conflict victims established a protest camp in the Ratnapark (an open park located in the city centre) in 2001. They stayed and protested there for 11 months. The government did not provide them with shelter or any relief; instead, it forcefully evicted the camps.

In 2004, many conflict victims engaged in a protest organised by the Maoist Victims' Association, during which the effigy of Prachanda, the supreme commander of the Maoists during the conflict, was burned (Interview 1). After this, the conflict victims experienced a tragic incident. Their main leader Mr. Ganesh Chilwal, who was also the founder of the Maoist Victims' Association, was shot dead by the Maoists. This episode created an atmosphere of fear within the victims' movement; yet, at the same time it also fuelled more anger and stronger commitment towards their cause. The movement base grew broader, as an increasing number of conflict victims affected by either the Maoists or state violence from all 75 districts of Nepal became associated with the movement.

As the government did nothing to address the issues raised by the conflict victims, they continued to protest on the streets of Kathmandu. They also established a new protest camp in Gausal, a public transport hub near the Pashupati temple (Focus group discussion; Interview 6). More than 2,500 conflict victims gathered in Bankaali, a jungle area in Pashupati, and protested there for 14 months. During that period, the regime was undertaken by King Gyanendra Shah. The authorities of the king's regime arrested 17 conflict victims, an act which the victims' movement strongly protested. Finally, those who had been detained were released after ten days. After this incident, the victims started to utilise a more proactive strategy that also aimed at increasing their public visibility. They expanded their protest

168 Neetu Pokharel et al.

camps, for example, in Tinkune (one of the most open and busy public places in Kathmandu) where they protested continuously for four months. The police used to come and intimidate the protesters regularly. Sometimes, physical violence was also deployed. Moreover, 62 women were arrested for ten days; they were registered as political detainees. In detention, they started a hunger strike, demanding compensation for their arrest based on their engagement in a peaceful protest. The other conflict victims expressed their solidarity to the detained and their dissatisfaction with the government through civil disobedience. To draw the government's attention to their demands, they called on the Chakka Jam (Stop Vehicles, or No Vehicles) movement for a specific day, which caused serious disruptions in public traffic and transportation around the main junction in the Ratna Park, as well as in Tinkune and Ranipokhari. It also affected the mobility of government officials and thus, the availability of services. The government decided to impose a curfew, but the protesters actively breached it. They walked on the streets wearing red ribbons on their heads. According to the interviewees, the movement organised the Chakka Jam over 50 times within a period of two years, blocking the traffic continuously to express their dissatisfaction.

In 2007, the country entered into the CPA between the Seven Party Alliance and the Maoists, which put an end to the king's regime. There was a collation between the political parties and the Maoists who were involved in the conflict. After the CPA, the Interim Constitution, which provisioned a mechanism to address conflict-related issues, problems, and injustices, gave new hope that Transitional Justice issues would be addressed in line with constitutional principles and human rights. For the conflict victims, this offered new opportunities for organising and raising their claims and concerns more openly and fearlessly. New associations and organisations were formed, and novel initiatives were taken forward by various victim groups, including the families of the disappeared, families of the killed, female victims, victims of rape, victims of torture, and many more.

In 2014, the Conflict Victims Common Platform (CVCP) was formed in consultation with the conflict victims with the aim of putting pressure on the government to expedite the Transitional Justice process. The CVCP has continuously organised protests and different types of consultations, engaging with both civil society actors and political parties (Conflict Victim Common Platform, 2014; Himalayan News Service, 2020). As an umbrella organisation, the CVCP offers the conflict victims access to important resources through its network and supports them in public advocacy and capacity building. It has been successful in building consensus amongst the conflict victims, which has enabled them to demand justice and accountability more firmly. In mobilising its members, the CVCP has also encouraged them to disobey laws and policies related to the Transitional Justice process – as a result, the conflict victims chose not to cooperate with the Transitional Justice mechanisms that were formed in 2015. Besides registering dozens of associations and organisations at the national level, the conflict victims have also raised their concerns at the international level through various advocacy campaigns. These collective, long-term efforts have compelled

Dissenting civil society, hunger strikes **169**

the government to start consulting and negotiating with the conflict victims and their networks in the context of the Transitional Justice process.

Nonviolent resistance for justice and truth: the fast-unto-death hunger strike of Nanda Prasad Adhikari

As we have demonstrated earlier, the conflict victims have utilised a diverse selection of approaches, methods, and tools in their activism. In this section, we focus on hunger strike as a means of nonviolent protest in more detail, analysing the case of Mr. Nanda Prasad Adhikari who died at the age of 53 after staying in hunger strike for 11 months while demanding justice for his son, Krishna Prasad Adhikari, who was killed by the Maoist cadres in 2004. The information and analysis in this section are based on the focus group discussion, interviews (Interviews 3–5), the Krishna Prasad case report (Advocacy Forum-Nepal, n.d.-b), and the lived experiences of Nanda Prasad's wife Ganga Maya as described in her autobiography (Adhikari, 2018).

Nanda Prasad and Ganga Maya Adhikari were living a peaceful life in the village of Phujel in the district of Gorkha with their two sons, Noor Prasad and Krishna Prasad. On 6 June 2004, the youngest son, Krishna Prasad, 17, who had just finished his secondary school exam, left Phujel for the Chitwan district to meet his grandparents. On his way there, he was kidnapped and murdered by the Maoist cadres (Advocacy Forum-Nepal, n.d.-b). The kidnapping took place in Parsauni, Chitwan, by three Maoist rebels who were riding on motorcycles. The body of Krishna Prasad was found at 8 p.m. on the same day in Bakulahar Chowk, Chitwan. The Maoist cadres from Gorkha claimed responsibility for his murder.

Nanda Prasad was, however, first informed by some of his relatives who were affiliated with the Maoists that his son had died in an accident (Adhikari, 2018; Interview 3). He was taken to the hospital where his son's body had been brought. In observing the dead body of his son, Nanda Prasad discovered that his son's both legs were broken, there were several holes from being shot in his head, as well as wounds in his body. When he returned home, Nanda Prasad heard that his neighbour, one of the local leaders of the Maoist cadres, had given the instructions to kill his son (Adhikari, 2018; Advocacy Forum-Nepal, n.d.-b; Interview 3). In her autobiography, Ganga Maya describes how she and her husband heard the local leader of the Maoists admitting that their son was murdered as a revenge over a land dispute issue in which his parents were involved (Adhikari, 2018). In their view, this was supported by the fact that at the time of his murder, Krishna Prasad was a student and not involved in any political activities.

Nanda Prasad and Ganga Maya Adhikari started resenting the perpetrator and publicly calling him a "criminal" (Adhikari, 2018; Interview 3). Together with his supporters, the local Maoist leader threatened the couple several times, urging them to stop talking about the murder of their son. They did not, however, remain silent despite the risks and costs that this – continuing fearlessly to talk about the crime – entailed. At the time, the Phujel village was dominated by the Maoist cadres and rebels, and with their strong presence in the community, most people were

170 Neetu Pokharel et al.

afraid to ask critical questions about their actions, especially concerning crimes. To intimidate the Adhikari family, the Maoist rebels cut their pipeline to drinking water, forbade the local shopkeepers from selling any items to them, and threatened the villagers not to work on the lands owned by the Ahdikari family. Hence, they became deprived of water, electricity, food items, and other groceries. Their land was not cultivated as they were not able to hire any labourers from the village. They were not invited anywhere to work or to attend any communal meetings or cultural events. All this was meant to compel them to not talk about the killers of their son Krishna.

Despite the continuous threats they received, the Adhikari couple bravely continued to talk about the issue and make inquiries (Adhikari, 2018; Advocacy Forum-Nepal, n.d.-b; Interview 3). This resulted in them becoming physically abused by the local leader of the Maoists. When the Adhikari couple's elder son, Noor Prasad contacted the Gorkha district police and the District Administration Office about the violence his parents had experienced, the police tried to settle the case through reconciliation. However, Nanda Prasad and Ganga Maya Adhikari refused to reconcile and stated that they wanted to see the criminals who killed their son punished for their crimes. The case was not investigated further due to the dominance of the Maoists in the area. Fearing even more aggressive retaliation from the perpetrator and his supporters, the Adhikari couple was forced to leave their home village without being able to take their belongings with them. First, they stayed in the district headquarters for a few days, but the district government officials recommended they go to Singh Durbar, the prime minister's office, to seek justice for their cause.

Nanda Prasad and Ganga Maya Adhikari travelled to Kathmandu with empty hands and stomachs (Interviews 3–4). In Kathmandu, they continued their struggle for justice. They went to Singh Durbar to meet the prime minister, Girija Prasad Koirala, appealing for his support in their case. The prime minister asked them to come again after the elections. Next, they met with the minister of home affairs, Krishna Prasad Sitaula. His response was similar. After the elections, when Pushpa Kamal Dahal – Prachanda – was appointed as the prime minister, the Adhikari couple tried to arrange a meeting with him. For six days in a row, they went to the prime minister's office and waited there for the whole day to meet him, but without success. After Prachanda's term, Madha Kumar Nepal became the new prime minister. The Adhikari couple also went to meet him at his party office but were escorted out by his assistants. The couple stayed at an old orphanage as they did not have any money for food and accommodation. Despite this, they kept returning to Baluwatar, Hanuman Dhoka (the prime minister's residence).

Again later, when Dr. Baburam Bhattarai was the prime minister of the country in 2012, the Adhikari couple went to Baluwatar (Interviews 3–4). They waited for a whole day, standing in front of the gate, but could not meet with the prime minister. They tried again the next day, but the prime minister left the residence without meeting them. This made the couple angry, and they started to protest. Then suddenly, the police came and took them into custody without any warrant, preformation, or official charges. After they had been kept in custody for one week, the Adhikari couple refused to eat while in custody. They told the authorities that they were ready to die but would not bow their heads in front of injustice. They also wanted to know the reason for their arrest. The police told them that they had been arrested because they disturbed the prime minister daily in front of his residence. There is a provision in Article 15 of the Civil Rights Act that an alleged perpetrator cannot be kept in custody for more than 25 days without filing the case in court (Civil Rights Act, 1955). However, the Adhikari couple was kept in custody for several months (Interviews 3–4). The police also shifted them from one place to another several times, from Kathmandu to Gorkha, and again back to Kathmandu. During this period, the Adhikari couple continued their hunger strike, and their health condition started to deteriorate.

At some point, Ganga Maya could not even speak because of her bad health condition (Interviews 3–4). The police took them to the Bir hospital, where a doctor gave Ganga Maya four treatments of glucose saline. The police left the Adhikari couple in the hospital from where they went directly back to Baluwatar and continued their protest (Advocacy Forum-Nepal, n.d.-b; Interviews 3–4). The police took them, again, to the hospital. This cycle continued daily for several months. Time went on, and again, Nepal got a new prime minister, Khil Raj Regmi. The Adhikari couple considered this a novel opportunity, so they went to Baluwatar, once again, to demand justice for their son. This time, the police took them to a mental health hospital where they were injected with medicine without their explicit consent. At one point, Ganga Maya became unconscious for three days. The government kept them in the mental health hospital for 39 days. The couple was discharged from the hospital after their long struggle for justice surfaced in the media headlines, and civil society and human rights organisations started publicly commenting on the government's actions in highly negative terms (Advocacy Forum-Nepal, n.d.-b).

Again, the couple went to Baluwatar where they were standing in front of the prime minister's residence (Focus group discussion; Interviews 3–4). After one week, the prime minister sent someone to ask them about their demands. They said they wanted justice for their son, as well as their confiscated property returned to them. The prime minister promised them justice after they would first receive medical treatment. The Adhikari couple was taken to a hospital where the doctors forcefully fed them and used saline without their consent. Nanda Prasad and Ganga Maya were, however, determined not to break their fast-unto-death hunger strike until and unless they get justice. Finally, due to substantial national and international pressure, the government arrested two of the alleged perpetrators. Human rights activists and government representatives met with the Adhikari couple in the hospital and requested them to end their hunger strike with an assurance of providing them with justice. The government also made a written agreement with them. The Adhikari couple ended their hunger strike on 7 September 2013. After six months, on 18 March 2014, the government released the accused two perpetrators on bail. The Adhikari couple felt betrayed and resumed their hunger strike, continuing it for 11 months. The government did not respond to their demands, and their health kept deteriorating further. Ultimately, Nanda Prasad Adhikari died in the hospital in the presence of his wife, doctors, some police officers, and a few human rights activists. Even the death of her husband did not stop Ganga Maya from protesting – she has resumed her hunger strike several times and intends to continue her struggle until the murderers of her son Krishna are brought to justice.

Other conflict victims, together with activists and civil society organisations, have actively tried to save the life of Ganga Maya Adhikari by appealing to the government to give her a reason to end her fast-unto-death hunger strike. For example, in 2015 on Nepal's Democracy Day, 19 February, they arranged a peaceful protest in Tudikhel where they waited for the passing through of the president and prime minister (International Federation of Human Rights, 2016). According to the protesters, it was a peaceful and legal protest based on the constitution. However, the authorities regarded it as a breach of law, and 12 human rights activists were arrested.

The struggle of Nanda Prasad and Ganga Maya Adhikari is one of the emblematic cases in the conflict victims' enduring struggle for justice. The Adhikari couple tried out everything, all means at all possible levels – they appealed to the local police, the local government, the district government, and the country's political leadership, including several different prime ministers. The state ignored all their appeals, and there was never a proper investigation conducted. In fact, the state closed the case file of Krishna Prasad Adhikari already in 2006. Hunger strike was the Adhikari couple's ultimate, final resort. Nanda Prasad *literally* fasted unto death – he sacrificed his life while seeking truth and justice. Other conflict victims, human rights activists, journalists, and lawyers tried to save his life, and continuously expressed their solidarity to the Adhikari couple. They made several appeals to the state to investigate and address the case so that the Adhikari couple could discontinue their hunger strike. Together with civil society actors, the other conflict victims tried to pressurise the state through a variety of different means of nonviolent dissent and civil disobedience; their efforts were, however, unsuccessful.

Dissenting civil society as the backbone of democracy

Even though they have not succeeded in reaching their primary goals, it can be argued that the conflict victims, human rights activists, and civil society organisations co-constitute the backbone of Nepalese democracy. During the past decades, they have courageously and continuously challenged unjust laws and policies, such as the draconian Terrorist and Disruptive Activities Control and Punishment Ordinance which the state introduced in the middle of the internal conflict in 2000. Civil society actors protested it strongly, challenging it also in the court on the basis that granting security forces permission to arrest and detain a person for up to 90 days without a trial undermines the citizen's fundamental rights (Himalayan News Service, 2005). A substantial number of cases of human rights violations conducted during the conflict have been also systematically documented by civil society organisations. One of their key aims is to end the culture of impunity in Nepal. In addition to the Adhikari case described earlier, there have been several other emblematic cases which the civil society organisations have addressed, such as the case of Maina Sunuwar (for more details, see Advocacy Forum-Nepal, n.d.-c; Informal Sector Service Centre, 2011). They have strongly critiqued the state's inability and unwillingness to investigate the cases and prosecute the perpetrators of the conflict era, while protesting vigorously against the political decision to grant amnesty to perpetrators who have been found guilty of grave human rights violations, such as torture and sexual abuse (The Himalayan Times, 2016; see also Advocacy Forum-Nepal, n.d.-d).

In recent years, civil society organisations have also started launching international campaigns which aim at increasing broader awareness of pressing human rights issues in Nepal. Reaching out to the international community has helped them mainstream Transitional Justice issues and bring attention to the need to protect human rights activists who become targets of violence, threats, and intimidation (see e.g. Amnesty International, 2020a, 2020b). Many international human rights organisations have expressed their solidarity to the conflict victims and offered support to civil society actors who struggle against human rights violations, as well as unjust laws and policies in Nepal. The support that the activists have received from the international community has been significant in boosting their morale and strengthening their commitment to struggle for truth, peace, equality, and justice (OHCHR, 2014).

Conclusion

In this chapter, we have discussed different phases and forms of dissent in Nepal, focusing especially on the conflict victims' struggle for justice in the context of the Transitional Justice process. We have demonstrated that with support from human rights activists and civil society organisations, they have utilised a wide variety of different types of dissent, ranging from peaceful protests, sit-ins, and non-cooperation to intentional traffic jams and hunger strikes. While demanding just laws and policies, they have also disobeyed laws that they consider unjust. They have, for example, decided not to cooperate with the Transitional Justice mechanism formed under laws and policies they regard as flawed and discriminatory. Through these different forms of dissent, the conflict victims have effectively articulated their dissatisfaction in the public arena, receiving extensive media attention at both the national and the international level. In their activism, they have also been active in building alliances within the victims' network, as well as in seeking solidarity and support from those civil society actors, who share their perspectives and emphasis on the rule of law and justice. Their collaboration has resulted in the active exchange of ideas and the creation of new strategies for combatting the culture of impunity and challenging unjust laws and discriminatory policies.

174 Neetu Pokharel et al.

Despite their courageous and creative forms of activism, the conflict victims have not been able to compel the government to fulfil its responsibilities in making the perpetrators of the conflict era accountable and punishable for their crimes and human rights violations, as was clearly demonstrated in our discussion of the Adhikari case. Indeed, if evaluated from this perspective, the efforts of the conflict victims cannot be regarded as successful. Yet, the process itself has resulted in many productive outcomes that can be of great importance in the future. For example, after observing and supporting the Adhikari couple's resistance, the conflict victims are less inclined to make compromises for justice at any cost. The example the Adhikari couple set through their 11 months of hunger strike, with Nanda Prasad ultimately sacrificing his own life, was immensely powerful in manifesting courage, commitment, and dedication to the cause that the activists are fighting for.

The fact that Nanda Prasad and Ganga Maya Adhikari were themselves not aware of Gandhi's theory of nonviolence, invites interesting questions in terms of the connection between theory and practice. While they themselves did not base their hunger strike on any theoretical considerations, the Adhikari couple's fast-unto-death hunger strike can be interpreted as a clear example of Gandhian non-violent resistance. The decision to put their bodies and lives on the line emerged and originated from their own life experiences and the local context. By including this particular case in our analysis, we have sought to highlight the importance of contextual understanding of dissent and civil disobedience, as well as of local experiences and practises that create their own theory.

To conclude, we emphasise that it is remarkable that in a conflict-affected society that has been so strongly dominated by the legacy of violence, the civil society, activists, and conflict victims have continually chosen to pursue justice through the nonviolent approach.[3] The persistence of the conflict victims' efforts has been fuelled with passion, and their firm belief in nonviolence continues to be their prime armament.

Notes

1 The TRC's main aims are to investigate and publish the incidents/realities of gross violations of human rights violations; recommend processes to promote reconciliation; recommend processes to promote the reparation processes; recommend the rehabilitation and return of property to victims; and recommend amnesty (rare) to the perpetrators with conditions (Truth and Reconciliation Commission, n.d.). The CIEDP's main objectives are to investigate the enforced disappeared persons during the armed conflict and bring the real facts to the public by assimilating the spirit of the CPA and the Interim Constitution; provide compensation and relief after providing identity cards to the victims; recommend legal sanctions against the perpetrators; address issues related to the underlying causes of armed conflict; suggest measures for political, legal, institutional, administrative and practical reform to enhance sustainable peace; and protect the country from similar types of armed conflicts in the future (Commission of Investigation on Enforced Disappeared Persons Nepal, n.d.).
2 On hunger strikes in other kinds of contexts, see Nykänen et al. in this volume.
3 Interestingly, as Subedi and Bhattarai (2017) argue, also the major political parties in Nepal have often built on the nonviolent approach in seeking to transform the conflict and violent political processes into more peaceful, democratic ones.

References

Adhikari, G. M. (2018). *Nyayako awasan [Demise of Justice]*. Autobiography. Book Hill Publication.

Advocacy Forum-Nepal. (2020). *Fake transitional justice consultations: How long can the government fool victims?* Briefing paper. http://advocacyforum.org/downloads/pdf/publications/tj/briefing-paper-on-tj-consultation-february-2020.pdf

Advocacy Forum-Nepal. (n.d.-a). Transitional justice department – Conflict Victims' Society for Justice (CVSJ-Nepal). http://www.advocacyforum.org/what-we-do/transitional-justice-department/conflict-victims-society-for-justice-cvsj-nepal.php

Advocacy Forum-Nepal. (n.d.-b). Emblematic cases – Krishna Prasad Adhikari. http://www.advocacyforum.org/emblematic-cases/2013/09/krishna-adhikari.php

Advocacy Forum-Nepal. (n.d.-c). Emblematic cases – Maina Sunuwar. http://www.advocacyforum.org/emblematic-cases/2011/01/maina-sunuwar.php

Advocacy Forum-Nepal. (n.d.-d). Emblematic cases – Arjun Bahadur Lama. http://www.advocacyforum.org/emblematic-cases/2011/01/arjun-bahadur-lama.php

Amnesty International. (2020a, January 25). Nepal: Recent steps undermine transitional. https://www.amnesty.org/en/latest/news/2020/01/nepal-recent-steps-undermine-transitional-justice/

Amnesty International. (2020b, January 27). Amnesty International staff detained in Nepal. https://www.amnesty.org/en/latest/news/2020/01/nepal-release-human-rights-activists-immediately/?utm_source=TWITTER-IS&utm_medium=social&utm_content=3072199023&utm_campaign=Amnesty&utm_term=News

Bhatta, C. D. (2006, April 11). Civil disobedience and people power. *The Himalayan Times*. https://thehimalayantimes.com/opinion/topics-civil-disobedience-and-people-power

Civil Rights Act. (1955). Nepal Law Commission. www.lawcommission.gov.np

Commission of Investigation on Enforced Disappeared Persons Nepal. (n.d.). Home page. https://ciedp.gov.np/en/home/

Comprehensive Peace Agreement. (2006). Comprehensive peace agreement between the Government of Nepal and the Communist Party of Nepal (Maoist). English translation available at the United Nations Peacemaker website https://peacemaker.un.org/nepal-comprehensiveagreement2006

Conflict Victims Common Platform. (2014). Concept note on Conflict Victims Common Platform for national coordination and collective initiative to drive transitional justice process in Nepal. Unpublished Paper.

Conflict Victims' Society for Justice. (n.d.). Home page. Introduction. http://www.cvsjnepal.org/ (Accessed 24.9.2021).

Diwakar, R. R. (1969). *Saga of satyagraha*. Gandhi Peace Foundation.

Focus Group Discussion. (2021, October 1). Interviewers Neetu Pokharel and Som Niroula.

Himalayan News Service. (2005, November 19). TADO provision challenged in SC. https://thehimalayantimes.com/nepal/tado-provision-challenged-in-sc

Himalayan News Service. (2020, July 11). Conflict victims lament govt's apathy in their joint submission. https://thehimalayantimes.com/nepal/conflict-victims-lament-governments-apathy-in-their-joint-submission

Human Rights Watch. (2004). *Between a rock and a hard place: Civilians struggle to survive in Nepal's civil war*. Report, October 2004, Vol. 16 No. 12(C). https://www.hrw.org/reports/2004/nepal1004/nepal1004.pdf

Informal Sector Service Centre. (2011). *Extrajudicial killing of Maina Sunar: A case report*. https://www.insec.org.np/wp-content/uploads/2017/12/Extrajudicial-Killing-of-Maina-Sunar-A-Case-Report.pdf

Interim Constitution of Nepal. (2007). https://www.lawcommission.gov.np/np/wp-content/uploads/, if not accessible, alternatively http://www.ilo.org/wcmsp5/groups/public/---ed_protect/---protrav/---ilo_aids/documents/legaldocument/wcms_126113.pdf

International Crisis Group. (2007). *Nepal's Constitutional Process*. Asia Report No 128–26.

International Federation of Human Rights. (2016, March 4). Nepal: Arbitrary arrest of twelve human rights defenders and victims of human rights violations. https://www.fidh.org/en/issues/human-rights-defenders/nepal-arbitrary-arrest-of-twelve-human-rights-defenders-and-victims

Interview 1. (2021, April 2). Kathmandu. Interviewers Neetu Pokharel and Som Niroula.

Interview 2. (2021, April 2). Kathmandu. Interviewers Neetu Pokharel and Som Niroula.

Interview 3. (2021, September 19). Kathmandu. Interviewers Neetu Pokharel and Som Niroula.

Interview 4. (2021, September 19). Kathmandu. Interviewers Neetu Pokharel and Som Niroula.

Interview 5. (2021, September 21). Kathmandu. Interviewers Neetu Pokharel and Som Niroula.

Interview 6. (2021, October 1). Kathmandu. Interviewers Neetu Pokharel and Som Niroula.

Nepal Charkha Pracharak Gandhi-Tulshi Smarak Mahaguthi. (n.d.). Home page. About us. https://www.gandhitulasiashram.org/about/

OCHA. (2005, July 19). Refugee voices: Maoist victims association in Nepal. *ReliefWeb*, United Nations Office for the Coordination of Humanitarian Affairs. https://reliefweb.int/report/nepal/refugee-voices-maoist-victims-association-nepal

OHCHR. (2012). *Nepal Conflict Report 2012*. United Nations Office of the High Commissioner for Human Rights. https://www.ohchr.org/Documents/Countries/NP/OHCHR_Nepal_Conflict_Report2012.pdf

OHCHR. (2014, May 21). *The Nepal Act on the Commission on Investigation of Disappeared Persons, Truth and Reconciliation, 2071 (2014)*. OHCHR Technical Note–as Gazetted. United Nations Office of the High Commissioner for Human Rights. https://www.ohchr.org/Documents/Countries/NP/OHCHRTechnical_Note_Nepal_CIDP_TRC_Act2014.pdf

Rajopadhyaya, A. (2020, August 8). History of social movements in Nepal: From medieval period to democracy. *Online Khabar*. https://english.onlinekhabar.com/history-of-social-movements-in-nepal-i.html

Rosenberg, J. (2019, July 28). Biography of Mohandas Gandhi, Indian independence leader. *Thought.co*. https://www.thoughtco.com/mohandas-gandhi-1779849

Subedi, D. B. & Bhattarai, P. (2017). The April uprising: How a nonviolent struggle explains the transformation of armed conflict in Nepal. *Journal of Peacebuilding & Development*, *12*(3), 85–97. https://doi.org/10.1080/15423166.2017.1372795

Supreme Court of Nepal. (2015). Decision of the Supreme Court on the cases number 069-WS-0057 and 069-WS-0058. Translation to English by Trial. https://tbinternet.ohchr.org/Treaties/CCPR/Shared%20Documents/NPL/INT_CCPR_CSS_NPL_16473_E.pdf

Thapa, D. (Ed.) (2003). *Understanding the Maoist Movement of Nepal*. Martin Chautari/Centre for Social Research and Development.

The Himalayan Times. (2016, May 11). Conflict victims, rights activists stage protest in Baluwatar. https://thehimalayantimes.com/nepal/conflict-victims-rights-activists-stage-protest-against-nine-point-deal

Truth and Reconciliation Commission. (2018). *Interim report*. http://trc.gov.np/wp-content/uploads/2018/03/Interim-Report-Magh-22.pdf

Truth and Reconciliation Commission. (n.d.). Home page. https://trc.gov.np/

Zinkin, T. (1983). *Gandhi*. Methuen Publishing Ltd.

PART III

Defending civility in civil disobedience

11
ACADEMIC FREEDOM, RESISTING INTELLECTUALS, AND THE IDEA OF UNIVERSITY IN SOUTH ASIA

Arun Gupto

Introduction

Universities in South Asia are the most active spaces for resistance, dissent, dissensus, and resentment against government establishments. They have been both organised and spontaneous locations for widespread protests, and at times, normative spaces to define the course of political ideas at large. They have been mostly, not always, peaceful, legal, and civic in nature.

In Bangladesh, academics and students were instrumental in the Bangladesh language movement and later in the Shahbagh[1] protests which were related to crimes committed during the 1971 war. The Shahbagh protest began in 2013 around the premises of the Dhaka University and colleges in the area. In Nepal, during the Maoist insurgency in the late 1990s and early decades of the 21st century, universities and colleges reeled under suppression while resisting the dictatorial regime of the monarchy. Furthermore, at present, universities in many Indian metropolises are struggling to retain intellectual freedom regarding pedagogic contents, educational rights, as well as resistance against the suppression of the *dalits*,[2] the marginal Hindu groups in terms of caste and class hierarchy.

This chapter discusses the role of the university as a central location of South Asian resistance. The analysis is based on some key questions: What have been the major contesting issues for widespread dissent which define the South Asian idea of the university? and What are the features and dynamics of dissent in such universities? Through description and analysis of resistance, it is possible to understand how educational institutions define the idea of university in terms of their political functions both for heuristic goals and democratic ideals in general.

It is not a coincidence that South Asian universities have been important for cultural and political resistance. Instead, universities in general have been central locations for modern civil rights resistance at least from the 1960s onwards.

DOI: 10.4324/9781003320494-14

180 Arun Gupto

The University of Paris Nanterre as the sheet of the May 1968 Revolution in France, the New Left movement in the United States, the hippie era, the Beatles Revolution songs of 1968, the Vietnam War, Cuban politics, the space race, the third-world movement, and many events of the 1960s paved ways for academics to engage in mass protests, from the University of Michigan to Sorbonne in Paris. Indian scholar Rakesh Batabyal writes:

> The sixties were easily the point of entry into a new phase for institutions in the contemporary world. There were unmistakable signs that the older institutional frameworks in many fields of human existence were either questioned or were beginning to show cracks.
>
> *(Batabyal, 2014, p. 67)*

Furthermore, when describing the socio-political context of the 1960s in Europe and the United States, he says,

> In terms of discourse, institutions themselves became sites of contention. Intellectuals contested not only the existing institutional designs but also the legitimacy behind such designs. The students' sit-ins in the United States, strikes in Paris and students rallies in Hyde Park, London, all in 1968, were open demonstrations of a larger fatigue, if one may call it that, with the lack of dynamism of the institutions, academic and non-academic, to catch up with the political and social changes.
>
> *(Batabyal, 2014, p. 67)*

Student protests in Asia have a significant history in the last three to four decades of the 20th century; for example, the Tiananmen Square student protest in 1989, students in Indonesia fighting to oust Suharto, South Korean students fighting against military dictatorship in the 1980s, and the Burmese student revolt in 1988[3] have been remarkable and visible manifestations of dissent. In all, the modern history of the university is also a history of resistance. At the end of this chapter, I introduce views and perspectives of South Asian academics and students who have belonged to various university resistance movements or directly witnessed them and been influenced by them. I have conducted the interviews in person and later documented them also through emails.

Forms of resistance

Since the *resistance* is a key term in this chapter, it is important to define it. Resistance, in general, can range from simple denial to violent acts against any opposition while withstanding any form of power. When the terms *culture* and *politics* are used in conjunction with that of resistance, the former challenges and demands less from the authority than political resistance which is more forceful. Civil disobedience, in turn, seems a more defensive than an aggressive form of resistance. All these terms can be understood in a conceptual continuum, and for

Academic freedom, resisting intellectuals **181**

analytic use, it is necessary to seek their boundaries. Next, I elaborate on the ideas of Stephen Duncombe (2012), Alain Badiou (1989), Jacques Rancière (1999), and finally Henry David Thoreau (1849/2004) and M. K. Gandhi (1961/2012) to clarify my use of the terms.

Political activist and researcher Stephen Duncombe writes about two forms of dissensus, cultural resistance and political dissent:

> Equipped with new ideas, skills, confidence, and comrades, the step into the unknown terrain of political resistance may seem less frightening. And because cultural resistance often speaks in a more familiar and less demanding voice than political dissent, it makes this move even easier. In this way cultural resistance works as a sort of stepping stone into political activity.
>
> *(Duncombe, 2012, p. 6)*

Duncombe exemplifies the term cultural resistance with popular cultural styles and music and slave songs in America. Moreover, he sees Gandhi's concept of *swaraj*, or home rule for India against British colonialism, as cultural resistance. In this sense, also Gandhi's civil disobedience for *swaraj* was cultural resistance which became political dissent as time passed.

The boundary between cultural resistance and political dissent is not always clear. For instance, Jacques Rancière and Alain Badiou connect affirmative political agency, politics, and event to resistance and disobedience. For Rancière (1999), "politics comes about solely through interruption, the initial twist that institutes politics as the deployment of a wrong or of a fundamental dispute" (p. 13). For Badiou (1989), dissensus is an event: "Nothing has better attested the fact that an event is supernumerary, not only with the respect to its site but also the language available to it, than this discord between the opacity of intervention and the vain transparency of representation" (p. 85). The discord between what is fixed and hence, what can be intervened in the fixed ("opacity of intervention"), is Rancière's (1999) politics, or dissensus against *la police*, or *la partage du sensible* which are, for him, the rule of law (p. 13).

Henry David Thoreau (1849/2004), for his part, explained resistance: "All men recognize the right of revolution, that is, the right to refuse allegiance to, and to resist the government, when its tyranny or its insufficiency are great and unendurable" (p. 9). Thoreau saw resistance as a suspicion in the context of being ready to conform to the state laws. He takes a cautious stand regarding "civil disobedience":

> I do not wish to quarrel with any man or nation. I do not wish to split hairs, to make fine distinctions, or set myself up as better than my neighbors. I seek rather, I may say, even an excuse for conforming to the laws of the land. I am but too ready to conform to them. Indeed, I have reason to suspect myself on this head; and each year, as the tax-gatherer comes round, I find myself disposed to review the acts and position of the general and State governments, and the spirit of the people to discover a pretext for conformity.
>
> *(pp. 31–32)*

182 Arun Gupto

For Gandhi (1961/2012), resistance was more than a physical event; it was a "soul-force". According to him, non-violent resistance is based on man's capabilities to recognise the truth and one's limits to know the absolute truth:

> Satyagraha is literally holding on to Truth and it means, therefore, Truth-force. Truth is soul or spirit. It is, therefore, known as soul-force. It excludes the use of violence because man is not capable of knowing the absolute truth and, therefore, not competent to punish. The word was coined in South Africa to distinguish the non-violent resistance of the Indians of South Africa from the contemporary "passive resistance" of the suffragettes and others. It is not conceived as a weapon of the weak.
>
> *(p. 3)*

I use the term *resistance* as a cultural-political force that is also an event, or a series of events. My empirical examples of resistance are not sufficiently civil disobedience in a Gandhian way. Images of violence can be seen in university spaces. Evolving from university premises by students and teachers, resistance at times transforms into violence in terms of death and destruction. However, the resistance that I examine shares features with civil disobedience, the use of art is one good example (see also Nykänen et al. in this volume). Hence, I also discuss the boundaries of civil disobedience and forms of resistance that came close to it.

University protests in Bangladesh, Nepal, and India

The three spaces I focus on are in and around the university premises. The Shahbagh mass protest and the role of the Dhaka University in Bangladesh in it, student dissent against monarchy at the Tribhuvan University in Kathmandu, and protests for academic rights at the University of Hyderabad (Hyderabad), and the Jawaharlal Nehru University (JNU, New Delhi) in India, can explain the questions raised above regarding contesting issues about dissent, features of dissent, and the political function of the universities. The methodology for analysing the concept of university is based on my interactions with academics and students who belonged to and participated in protest movements as part of the academic community in these universities in Bangladesh, India, and Nepal.[4]

Dealing with three resisting spaces, the Shahbagh movement in Bangladesh, the Maoist movement at the Tribhuvan University in Kathmandu, and student agitation at the University of Hyderabad and the JNU in India, I demonstrate that they each have their exclusive characteristics, like the New Left in the United States and the May 1968 uprising in Paris had. Since my thesis is about contesting issues for widespread dissent, the poetics[5] and dynamics of dissent, and its political function around heuristic goals, I present these three incidents of dissent in their specific temporal and spatial contexts.

The Shahbagh uprising of 2013 manifested resistance toward the memory of the violence of the 1971 war of independence in Bangladesh.[6] Shahbagh is a neighbourhood close to the famous University of Dhaka, and national medical and engineering colleges. In their resistance, the protesters argued in favour of violence – they demanded the hanging of Abdul Quader Mulla based on the war crimes, like rape and murder, that he had committed. The protestors' demand was supported by the ruling party, the Bangladesh Awami League.[7] The dissent, I argue, was a demand for secularism through punishment; it was also a conflict between democratic forces and religious fundamentalism. The memory of the atrocities of the 1971 war became fresh in 2013 with the demands for a death sentence for Abdul Quader Mulla. In this sense, the uprising in Shahbagh functioned to heal the wounds of the past. Shahbagh was a sheet of memory, the pain and trauma of the past.

The Maoist revolution in the 1990s that spread from the jungles of mountainous Nepal to the Tribhuvan University in Kathmandu was essentially a war against the monarchy. In the beginning, it was mainly a student movement and only later turned into a revolutionary war of independence. The communist revolutionaries were and are associated with the ideology of the famous communist leader Mao Zedong of China – hence, the name the "Maoists".

The incidents at the Tribhuvan University were striking when considering the initial phases of the revolution. As the English department was the largest, many students based their revolutionary activities at the humanities department in general and the English department in particular. From the late 1990s onward, the heads of department, especially the English department where I taught for decades, opened up the floodgates as they started to admit increasingly more MA students. The number of admitted students increased from 200 to almost 700, and this upward trend continued year by year. In practice, this meant that the university was allowed to build a community of resistance; a kind of institutional conscience working at large. While outside the university walls, the army held its blockades, inside the university, it was possible to freely talk about the revolution and putting an end to the monarchy.

At the University of Hyderabad in India, Rohith Vemula, a 26-year-old *Dalit* PhD student committed suicide in 2016, allegedly raising caste and *Dalit* issues. The question of *Dalit* rights initiated subsequent protests in many Indian universities during the same year. In 2019, students and civil society members at JNU in New Delhi demanded a roll-back of hostel regulations due to rising residency prices. The regulations also reduced research funds provided by the University Grants Commission (UGC), which is a powerful funding body for Indian university research. Students opposed such measures taken by the Bharatiya Janta Party (BJP)[8] ruled government.

Dr. Nirmala from Hyderabad, who was a student then and is a teacher now, told me that social science, as a field of study and research, is targeted by the establishment, especially by the BJP-led governments in the Indian states. For instance, if a scientific researcher focuses on tea plantations, it is regarded as adding up to the developmental processes of governmentality but if social science students study the plight of tea plantation workers, the research is discouraged. Blocking scholarship

184 Arun Gupto

funding to humanities and social science research has become very common in India as well as in South Asia in general.[9]

Even though the causes of the uprisings in Bangladesh, Nepal, and India were different, the difference has conceptual variety. The idea of dissent has always its temporal and spatial characteristics. The Shahbagh protest began with a demand for a death sentence of an alleged war criminal. Mulla was initially given a life sentence by the International Crimes Tribunal of Bangladesh, which the movement regarded as too lenient a verdict. The demand was not less violent, as the movement asked for slaughtering the criminals and one of the famous war cries was "Ekta ekta Shibir dhor, dhoria, dhoria jobai kor", which translates as "catch hold of a Shibir member and slaughter them one by one." (Bangladesh Islami Chattrashibir, or Bangladesh Islamic Student organisation or Shibir, in short was a religiously oriented student organisation which opposed the Shahbagh movement). Shibir opposed the court proceedings as an extra-judicial killing[10] which had its origin at the Dhaka University Mosque in 1977. The death penalty is still given in Bangladesh.

The students who supported the Shahbagh uprising were from the colleges and universities like the University of Dhaka and other universities in Bangladesh, although there were participants also from other sections of society. There were two types of conflict. One was the clash between opposing student unions affiliated with the political parties in Bangladesh, the secular and the religious, and the other was between the state and the people who had committed crimes on the side of the Pakistani army during the freedom movement of the early 1970s.

There was critical solidarity, wrote academics like Azfar Hussein and Naeem Mohaiemen, and at the same time, there were activists like Faruk Wasif who wanted the Shahbagh movement to be free from the rhetoric of secularism, atheism and faith (Alal O Dulal, 2013). However, it was difficult for the protestors to completely separate the movement from these aspects because the war of 1971 had been so deeply religiously political in nature.

If trauma and memory shaped the Shahbagh violence, the Maoist movement, along with the multiparty movement in Nepal, was a class struggle in an essentially Marxist sense. There were two developments in the Maoist struggle: one was the romantic nostalgia toward the rise of the proletariat, and the second was the desire to participate in the democratic system. Both these traits were visible at the Tribhuvan University and colleges in Nepal.

Enzo Traverso (2016) writes that revolution brings melancholia: "Melancholy was always a hidden dimension of the left, even if it came to the surface only at the end of the twentieth century, with the failure of communism" (p. 38). Such melancholia was evident among many of the students I knew as a teacher; they went through depression during the late 1990s and early 21st century because of the failure of the revolution in gaining success in its war against the monarchy. Along with such sadness and depression, the students who had receded from the war and opted for education were honoured by the masses at the colleges. This is what Traverso refers to as heroism even in defeat. Defeat because there was nothing going right for the revolutionaries in the hills and forests of Nepal. The war kept on going without

Academic freedom, resisting intellectuals **185**

any substantial steps taken by the democratic government of the time while the king still was the head of state.

But there were songs, dance, performances, and sit-ins outside classes. The nostalgia for the utopian vision always worked with the students, and defeat or setbacks were not disavowed as failures. Ultimately, in late 2007 and in 2008, the Maoists went to the polls almost cutting across the conventional idea of a Marxist revolution as a timeless war against capitalist forces. Hisila Yami (2021), a leading member of the Maoist party writes:

> In the first CA[11] election held on 10 April, 2008, we won 229 out of 608 seats and became the single largest party to hold so many seats. The agenda of making Nepal a republic started becoming a reality. It was the last phase of our journey to end monarchy. This republic, however, did not come to us easily.
>
> *(p. 205)*

The student wings of various communist parties collaborated, at times with the force of their victory to the ousting of the then king Gyanendra Bir Bikram Shah. The protests throughout the previous decades were at times performances which included singing and dancing at the university and college premises. Performances used to be loud and continuous, and they disturbed the class routines. However, the changing atmosphere of the nation, after centuries of kingship, was more significant than the class disturbances.

Elements of memory worked both in the Shahbagh movement and the Nepali revolution, but they were of different natures: The Bangladeshi one was trying to erase the trauma of war, the memory of crimes by almost violent means as the modality of justice. The Nepali one illustrated nostalgia of the revolutionary times of the Bolshevik and Cultural Revolutions, the memory of heroism told through the literature and narratives forming the ideological make-up of students and youths. The glory of the past was evident in performances at the university premises. This very romanticism of the past, as Traverso would conceptualise, was also an acceptance of the revolution's failure. This arguably helped in moving out of nostalgia and worked for increasing participation in society.

These three dissenting times at and around university spaces in Bangladesh, India, and Nepal as the story of the last two to three decades manifest how universities were and still are antagonistic forces challenging the establishment. Like American university liberalism, the epistemic freedom that universities represent has been considered a threat to the American establishment from the Reagan era to the present, similar to how South Asia academic freedom is regarded as an intolerable risk by governments.

The space of university in such troubling times bears upon democratic values; the role of educational institutions bears responsibilities. Referring to Rabindranath Tagore's university Vishwabharati, Martha C. Nussbaum (2010) writes that the "their entire education nourished the ability to think for oneself and to become a

186 Arun Gupto

dynamic participant in the cultural and political choice, rather than simply a follower of tradition" (pp. 70–71).

A political choice is taken to oppose decisions made by states or authorities of any institution. When JNU students were agitating in New Delhi in 2018 against raised fee structures and tightening of study times in the library, I witnessed[12] incidents in which many students and academics were beaten by the police during *dharana* (a Nepali word for protest) or sit-ins. They were branded as "troublemakers" who did not wish to study. The popular opinion is that the Science students do not participate in politics as do the Humanities and Social Sciences students. The former is considered studious and responsible, focused, careerists, and "good" (whatever the term suggests). On the contrary, democratic sensibilities are the bedrocks of the humanities and social sciences, the concern for the margins is the implicational philosophy of the courses, and the corruption of the corporates, undoing of scholars, and violence and rapes conducted by security institutions on the *Dalits* are the tea talks of immense concerns inside the premises of the universities.

The following two instances are the result of resistance against the ruling party in India. They are not direct consequences of the university dissensus I have been writing about, but they certainly are a reflection of general disagreement with the ways in which rightist parties and organisations are suppressing the voices of students and academics and minorities in general. The universities in South Asia have been intellectual secular spaces in general. Along with broader resistance movements, there have been incidents of resistance to the suppression by university authorities when the administration has faced pressure from the ruling party in the centre to suppress the opposition. In 2016, an English department academic[13] at a north Indian university staged Mahasweta Devi's play *Draupadi*. She was a renowned literary figure in India who passed away in 2016. The play revealed atrocities conducted by the army; it revealed how security forces have raped and killed women in forest areas of an Indian state where communist insurgencies and resistance against the government are still rampant.[14] There was a huge uproar and shaming of the teachers in the department by people from inside and outside of the university. Some demanded sedition charges, some glorified the heroes of the war, some declared the teachers as anti-nationalists. The teachers wrote letters in desperation to an intellectual of Indian origin in the United States. I was forwarded the letter, along with scores of local newspapers which wanted the teachers thrown out of the university.

The paradox of literary expression depends on how a story does not create uproar, but dramatic presentation is intolerable for the audience. The visual immediacy of the atrocity on the stage became the bone of contention for the people of the province. The news and opinion website *The Wire* reported:

> Interestingly, many senior leaders of the BJP, to which ABVP[15] owes its allegiance, had expressed their condolences when Mahasweta Devi died in the last week of July this year. Among those who condoled her death were Prime Minister Narendra Modi, party president Amit Shah, and cabinet ministers Sushma Swaraj, Arun Jaitley and Rajnath Singh.
>
> *(Mahaprashasta, 2016)*

Academic freedom, resisting intellectuals **187**

What followed was an inquiry commission under the pressure of agitating political parties and their supporters. The very defence by the organisers of the play was shamed as anti-nationalism. The idea of academic exercise faltered against the nationalist veneration for sacred institutions, such as the army, which cannot commit wrong and even if they commit wrong, they are perceived as defenders of the country against its enemies. It is also significant to note that in many Indian universities, like the JNU and Jamia Millia Ismalia (JMI) in New Delhi, and the Indian Institute of Technology (IIT) in Kanpur, students and academics sang[16] a famous revolutionary song that was performed by Pakistani singer Iqbal Bano in 1985 as a form of resistance to then president Ziaul Haq, who had imposed the martial law. The military dictator had also imposed bans on wearing black saris. The singer defied the bans and sang to an electrifying response of the more than 50,000-person crowd in the Lahore stadium. The lyrics were written by the famous poet Faiz Ahmad Faiz who lived and died in Pakistan. The song sung by university students in India was criticised by the supporters of Hindu nationalist organisations because it deals with the atrocities of dictatorial regimes. Such university performances were organised with the aim of creating general resentment against the rightist government of India and its political and non-political allies which support Hindu nationalism. Such performances are marks of support and solidarity towards the university dissensus in general.

The name-of-the-leader

"The name-of-the-leader" is a metaphor of authority against which or whom resistance or disobedience is acted on. In this section, my purpose is to discuss the authorities who oppose and/or quell resistance. In short, I claim that the grip of authorities has gotten tighter and the space for university politics in South Asia has become narrower.

The name-of-the-leader is the rule of the law, the Freudian Name-of-the-father, who makes the system work by distribution, allocation and roles given to every individual in society. Jacques Rancière's (2010) idea of *la police* and politics is

> [t]he police is not a social function but a symbolic constitution of the social. The essence of the police lies neither in repression nor even in control over the living. Its essence lies in a certain way of dividing up the sensible. I call "distribution of the sensible" a generally implicit law that defines the forms of partaking by first defining the modes of perception in which they are inscribed.
>
> *(p. 36)*

He further writes: "The essence of politics is dissensus. Dissensus is not a confrontation between interests or opinions. It is the demonstration (manifestation) of a gap in the sensible itself" (p. 38). The police behave like the name-of-the-leader/ father to make the system sensible, *la partage du sensible* or the distribution of the sensible.

188 Arun Gupto

> The essence of the police lies in a partition of the sensible that is character-
> ized by the absence of void and of supplement: society here is made up of
> groups tied to specific modes of doing, to places in which these occupations
> are exercised, and to modes of being corresponding to these occupations and
> these places. In this matching of functions, places and ways of being, there is
> no place for any void.
>
> *(Rancière, 2010, p. 36)*

In the process of filling up the "void," any act of dissensus is politics. Dissensus
for the police comes from every nook and corner of society. The father (the symbolic *la police*) is worried about how and when the politics unbuilds again, from
the street, from the university, from the farms. South Asian policing behaviour is
concerned about such politics, and even more so when it arises from university
contexts.

Rancière's (1999) differentiation of the police and politics is most visible in
university spaces in South Asia, where the common term used for dissensus in educational institutions is student politics:

> I now propose to reserve the term politics for an extremely determined activ-
> ity antagonistic to policing: whatever breaks with the tangible configuration
> whereby parties and parts or lack of them are defined by a presupposition
> that, by definition, has no place in that configuration – that of the part of
> those who have no part.
>
> *(p. 29)*

Student politics is "antagonistic to policing" and its extreme form is unlawfulness
despite its nature as a peaceful protest for rights. Slavoj Žižek explains the extrem-
ities of categorising dissensus:

> When Donald Rumsfeld designated the imprisoned Taliban fighters "unlaw-
> ful combatants" (as opposed to "regular" prisoners of war), he did not simply
> mean that their criminal terrorist activity placed them outside the law: when
> an American citizen commits a crime, even one as serious as murder, he
> remains a "lawful criminal".
>
> *(Žižek, 2002)*

Every act of dissent is unlawful for the Police. When protests are intolerable to
the Police, the sensibility of democracy is annihilated with intolerance. Poetry
ceases to be. It is because the extent of atrocity reached heights of barbarism – if
even a single person dies while resisting atrocity, it is a mark of barbarism, hence
the sublime expression through the arts cannot encompass the inhumanity of
civilizations.

Resistance, dissensus, and civil disobedience are becoming ineffective in the
global era of revolutions from the Arab Spring to such university dissents. It is
as if teachers and students were sitting in a "philosophy steamer,"[17] being unable

Academic freedom, resisting intellectuals **189**

to act due to populist governments in South Asia. Resisting voices thus find themselves ideologically expelled.

Academic responses

In this section, I introduce some views, perspectives, and critical comments by students and teachers based on my interview material. In total, I have interviewed more than 40 students and academics but have selected only a few responses for the purposes of this chapter. They reflect on the general idea about the nature of university. The significance of these responses is due to the fact that all my interviewees have experience with university activism in the context of the cases that I have described earlier. Some of them were directly involved in these struggles, while others were not. They all come from an academic culture of active resistance and hence their ideas are academically important to comprehend the worldviews of educational locations on an individual basis.

During the interviews, I posed three main questions: How is the idea of the university primarily an epistemic one instead of a territory of political activism? What role does the university have in the era of populist governments which are on the rise? and What have been your experiences in protest activities?

The first three respondents are Nepalis. Dr. Tika Lamsal is an academic at the Department of Rhetoric and Language, University of San Francisco, the United States. He was a student at the Tribhuvan University during the heyday of the Maoist movement in Nepal. He responded to the three questions I asked:

How is the idea of the university primarily an epistemic one instead of a territory of political activism?

> The purpose of university as an epistemic platform should be to enhance learners' critical thinking and offer them options to evaluate the strength of any argument or academic deliberation. While some political issues may be of imminent significance for universities to address lest they pose threat to democratic values, they are less relevant compared to epistemic value that these non-political institutions are supposed to promote.
>
> *(2018)*

What role does the university have in the era of populist governments which are on the rise?

> Universities should inculcate in students democratic values and critical thinking skills in such a way that populist agendas could be challenged and questioned before being supported and followed. In this sense, universities can play a crucial role in conducting and promoting open-ended and fair discourses to address historical, cultural, and political inequalities in the society, whereby students could actively participate in the discussion and decide on their own whether such populist agendas bear any merit.
>
> *(2018)*

190 Arun Gupto

What have been your experiences in protest activities?

> When actively participating in democratic movements as a student activist, I found university as a safe haven to voice our concerns not only as students but also as concerned citizens of the country; to that extent, protest activities seemed to contribute to challenging unethical and undemocratic practices meted out by the regime to hold power. While such protests may be worth our sacrifices as students, they should not be made the primary agendas of any university at the cost of quality of education.
>
> *(2018)*

Dr. Komal Phuyal is a faculty member of the Central Department of English at Tribhuvan University. He also was a student during the last days of the Maoist revolution. Answering the question 1, he responded:

> To approach this question, I begin with rationalist intervention of human agency in society. Knowledge necessarily wants the people to give a new direction to the society. In this regard, the epistemic and the activism move simultaneously together. So far as the university as the location is concerned, it is primarily and pedagogically epistemic. Very radical universities can take up the challenges of political activism as well. For instance, Indian Universities have played a significantly powerful role in Indian Independence Movement. The question of activism is also related to [the] academic freedom that faculties enjoy in a particular university. Very honestly, the function of university is epistemic. Still, the political interest groups would attempt to divert the goal into the secondary one.
>
> *(2018)*

To the second question, he replied:

> Public universities are funded by the government. The populist governments want to legitimise their position through universities. The first target is the leadership of the university at the rise of populist government. The universities also begin to prepare political activists for the future leadership under the wave of the populist governments. However, the faculties and universities should continually make use of rationalist intervention by exposing the implications of the populist governments. The universities can bring knowledge to the service of the mass and show their power. The universities in [a] true sense can connect themselves to the needs of the people. The nexus between the people and the university is the key to genuinely serve the cause of the people.
>
> *(2018)*

To the third query, he sent the following response:

> Frankly speaking, I have taken epistemic protest as the form of activism in university. I have prepared people through research, debate, and writings to take up the challenges of the contemporary times. I find university as the best locale for protest.

(2018)

Dr. Subhasree Ghosh comes from Kolkata, one of the centres of the freedom movement in India. She was a doctoral student at the Jadavpur University (JU) in Kolkata, an institution with strong ties to political activism. JU was the centre of political activities when the then Indian government was quelling the communist insurgency in Bengal in the 1970s. The university has also been an active place in supporting human rights activities. The three questions are responded in the following passages, respectively:

> While epistemology remains the thrust, I do not see how political activism is not part of the broader educational project to which universities or institutions of higher education are committed. Unless theory and praxis go hand in hand, the whole purpose of education shall collapse. Political activism does not have to necessarily premise itself on aggression and violence (unless absolutely necessary). Universities are spaces that should allow students as well as teachers to engage in healthy political activism.
>
> Universities have always played a significant role in providing that dissenting space to students and at a time when populist governments are on the rise, it becomes even more necessary for universities to 1. design a syllabus that encourages students to identify flaws in political structures and come up with alternatives 2. to encourage discussions where students can engage in and interrogate the dangers of populist governments.
>
> I have witnessed the idealism and courage with which people participate in protest activities and that, to me, is the biggest testimonial of the indomitable human spirit. However, sometimes protest movements go out of hand and become statements without purpose. So, the participants should also train themselves and not let go of the purpose which propelled them in this direction in the first place.

(2018)

I have collected the responses to all the three questions posed to Dr. Dhruba Karki, an academic at the Central Department of English and Army Campus, both located in Kathmandu. His responses are documented in the three subsequent paragraphs:

> University primarily has an epistemic role than the political one. University students and professors could give right directions to the society rather than

be influenced by populist movements. Students could develop their leadership to command different institutions and communities in the future with their academic values they are inculcated in their university programs. They could still advocate for justice and righteousness to develop an ideally happy and prosperous society with noble values of the humanity. In recent years in Nepal, governments and politicians have departed from their specific goals and objectives to serve the people and accelerate the process of socio-economic transformation. The university should, therefore, solely champion the cause of the humanity with knowledge and scholarship.

University should be able to save core values of service to the humanity and transformation of consciousness in the times of rampant populist governments. Political leaders and architects of social transformation should be consulting the university communities, including professors and experts to get new ideas and execute viable strategies to resolve multiple problems in the nation. Properly guided by credible guidelines and executive orders, technocrats and representatives should launch missions to ameliorate problems, rescue people and alleviate them better social status. Ensuring security, public welfare and strengthening democratic institutions, governments and political leaders can best their nation with full supports from the university communities and subject experts.

Indeed, I do not have direct experience in protest activities during my college years. However, I have seen some strikes under the command of the college and university students in the past. During my college years in Prithivi Narayan Campus in the late 1980s, I had seen students protest the authoritarian Panchayati Regime. At times, policemen disrupted students' protests, interrupted cultural programs, and arrested student leaders. Other times, students launched hunger strikes with their demands to release the arrested students. Students not only protested the government security authorities but also called for campus shut down. Eventually, those strikes and protests in the campus interrupted our regular classes and postponed our final examinations. However, I did not see those protests in Tribhuvan University, Kirtipur during the early 1990s when I was pursuing Master's Degree in English. After that, I did not see such political protests in the US universities during the 2000s. At one point, I saw students protesting the Bush Administration's decision to wage war against Iraq in the University of Central Oklahoma in 2003. Moreover, I saw only a few election campaigns in University of Texas at Dallas during the presidential race from 2006 through 2008. In fact, I am not in favor of students unions in protests in the ideological line of their political parties. Precisely, unwanted political interferences in different private and public institutions have not only hindered smooth transition of peace process but also halted rapid socio-economic transformation in Nepal. So, the university communities

Academic freedom, resisting intellectuals **193**

and experts should be acting, considering their goals and missions higher than the party principles and ideological lines.

(2018)

Mr. Sadat Khan is the head of the Department of English Language and Literature at the Premier University, Chittagong, Bangladesh. His responses were significant for me because Chittagong has been a leading city of the Indian independence movement and later the Bangladesh freedom movement. Answering the first question, he responded:

> Now, the question whether political activism should burgeon in an area that is meant to be a place for academic venture [is important]. On the contrary, the current phenomenon as observed in the universities are noticeably politically active. Again, there are such activities in campus which the university itself does not endorse. If the politics ran around relevant issues that concerns the community, the society; in long run, the nation or the humanity, university space may accommodate the activities, as the spirit is benevolent.
>
> However, if the space is meant to showcase the contentious muscle power, racism, violence or any malicious intent, that, in plain terms, contrast standard values, humane feelings and act of benevolence, the territory, then, turns to be a non-academic-front. In such occasions, the political activism (not addressing the issues mentioned) in such territory, must not be encouraged.
>
> *(2018)*

He responded to the second question:

> University is a space promotes democracy, globalization, freedom of knowledge and scholarship, open-endedness to others whereas populism counters these dogma and appraisals. The university, being capacitated of certain empowerment through educating and civilizing young minds, should come forward to academically face the challenges of any communal, controversial and counter-productive machinery, in whatever form it appears. Educating minds is missionic. And the essence of the mission is ingrained in the seeds of tutoring the values benevolent and productive, and at length, humanitarian in nature. So, the university has a great role to play to fend of populism as the idea is restrictive, narrow and non-inclusive.
>
> *(2018)*

To the third question, Mr. Khan answered:

> I had not been involved with any protest activities as, in my circumstances, the phenomenon is yet to appear. In any such case, where populism aggravates

194 Arun Gupto

values. Long born, I would certainly protest and actively work for the cause of human emancipation.

(2018)

Most of the respondents whose answers I have not included here, also considered university space a place of resistance along with its core responsibility to impart education. Such views generally are not at par with Western notions of university at present. The interviews were conducted with the sole purpose to understand what the idea of university is in this part of the world. University has multiple roles to fulfil and one of the most significant roles is dissensus at times when democratic ideals are in danger. There is one striking trend at universities and colleges in the sub-continent. Activism begins mostly from the faculties of the humanities and social sciences. The pure Science departments generally do not initiate or take part in any activism. The Humanities generally have been, and continue to be, the vanguard of activism.

Pedagogy and political activism

The universities in South Asia have resisted oppressions of multiple kinds. The more dominant populist governments are in the world, the more intensive universities are as locations of resistance. Such resisting locations are pervasive in South Asia. There have been debates about how universities should function for pedagogic purposes only and not for political activism. However, universities in South Asia have always been locations of resistance, more so in the last quarter of the 20th century and in recent times. What should be the future of university as such a powerful intellectual space? Should it show leadership in struggles against all forms of oppression or ignore authoritarian oppression and focus only on studies? What then is the idea of "studies"? Do they only refer to classroom engagements and writing qualitative and quantitative papers or dissertations? Does "studies" mean ignoring social plights outside university premises? Does it indicate non-engagement with activism and producing only research documents?

Furthermore, many of the political leaders who hold ministerial positions originally were involved in university student organisations. Almost in every South Asian country, government ministers have been actively engaged in student organisations which belong to various political parties. Such university political parties, it is widely known, are the feeding grounds of national politics in this region. How do we study the relationship between university politics and national politics? The same leaders have resisted government atrocities while being students, but when they hold government positions, they work or have to work against university resistance. Do changes in roles determine ideologies, perspectives, and responsibilities? After analysing university protests and suppression of such protests, my chapter concludes by posing new critical questions which are crucial for broadening our understanding of universities in South Asia as central locations of resistance.

Notes

1 Shahbagh is an area near the Dhaka University where protests were held against those who were charged with committing crimes against Bangladeshi people during its war of independence against Pakistan.
2 *Dalits* are marginalised lowest castes in India. The term is used also to identify untouchables; however, not all *Dalits* are untouchables.
3 See Weiss and Aspinall (2012).
4 The interviews were conducted during my several visits to Bangladesh and India. My interview notes were mostly written after our informal conversations. Initially, the purpose behind such interviews was to compile research data on resistance movements in South Asia for my book project on *Rethinking South Asian Studies*.
5 By poetics, I mean the rule and method behind any idea or action concerning dissent. Poetics can also be understood as the rules of functioning.
6 Before 1971, Bangladesh was called East Pakistan. After a bloody revolution with the support of the Indian government, the country gained its independence. The violent events of the revolution constitute one of the most traumatic experiences in the country's history and remain strong in the collective memory.
7 There are three major political parties in Bangladesh. The Awami League (AL) is currently the ruling party. The prime minister, Sheikh Hasina, is the daughter of Sheikh Muzibur Rahman, the father of the nation who was assassinated by a faction of the army. The Bangladesh Nationalist Party (BNP) is arguably a rightist party. Begum Khaleda Zia is the party's chairperson. When the BNP was in power, Zia was the prime minister. Jamaat e Islami is a party based on Islamic ideologies. It initially opposed the independence of Bangladesh. Many of the leaders have been charged with atrocities and faced death sentences, especially during the AL rule.
8 BJP is a Hindu nationalist party, and JNU is mainly a left inclined educational institution. The cause of contention between the JNU students and the government is based on ideological lines. For a comprehensive review of the JNU history, see Batabyal, 2014.
9 Dr. Dhar talked to me in person in June and July 2018. Additionally, there were multiple exchanges and online debates during our interactions in 2020, which were related to the Rethinking South Asian studies for the South Asian Foundation for Academic Research (SAFAR) project.
10 On the contrary, judicial killing refers to capital punishment, that is the death penalty inflicted by the process of law.
11 CA refers to the Constituent Assembly which was given the responsibility to write a new constitution. It was a legislative body of 601 members who worked from 2008 to 2012 to draft the constitution. (Footnote by A. G.)
12 I was invited to New Delhi by my colleague to give a lecture on the Goddess tradition in South Asia.
13 The incident happened at the Central University of Haryana in Mahendragarh. The play was prepared by the English and Foreign Languages Department.
14 The Indian states where communist revolutionaries are visible are Andhra Pradesh, Chhattisgarh, Bihar, and Bengal.
15 Akhil Bharatiya Vidyarthi Parisad (ABVP) or All Indian Student Council is a Hindu rightwing student organisation, politically supported by BJP and other rightwing Hindu organisations. (Footnote by A. G.)
16 There are some videos available of the songs (e.g., see "Hum Dekhenge" by Faiz Ahmad Faiz [A Revolutionary Poet; 2019], "RJ Sayema Explains – and Sings – Faiz's Hum Dekhenge" [2020] and "Hum dekhenge" by Iqbal bano [2010]). The first few lines of the "Hum Dekhenge" can be translated in the following way: "We too shall see, it is inevitable that we will see the day that has been vowed, that is destined. We shall see!"

196 Arun Gupto

17 In 1922, the Soviet authorities evicted many of the country's famous thinkers, which is often referred to as a "philosophy steamer". For example, Platonovich Karsavin was exiled from Russia to Germany in a "philosophy steamer" (see Karsavin & Steinberg, 2010).

References

Alal O Dulal. (2013, Feb 22). Shahbagh: The forest of symbols. https://alalodulal.org/2013/02/22/shahbagh-symbols/

Badiou, A. (1989). *Manifesto for philosophy*. New York Press.

Batabyal, R. (2014). *JNU: The making of a university, 1964–89*. Harper Collins.

Dhar, Dhiksa. Personal communication June–July 2018. Interviewer Arun Gupto.

Duncombe, S. (2012). *Cultural resistance: A reader*. Adarsh.

Gandhi, M. K. (2012). *Non-violent resistance (Satyagraha)*. Dover. (Originally published in 1961).

Ghosh, Subhasree. Personal communication June–July 2018. Interviewer Arun Gupto.

Hum Dekhenge by Faiz Ahmad Faiz. (A Revolutionary Poet). (2019, December 30). [Video]. YouTube. https://www.youtube.com/watch?v=jyBi0zlAxO0

Hum Dekhenge by Iqbal Bano. (2010, October 29). [Video]. YouTube. https://www.youtube.com/watch?v=dxtgsq5oVy4

Karki, Dhruba. Personal communication June–July 2018. Interviewer Arun Gupto.

Karsavin, L., & Steinberg, A. (2010). Russia and Israel symphonically intertwined. In D. Rubin (Ed.), *Holy Russia, Sacred Israel: Jewish-Christian encounters in Russian religious thought* (pp. 335–444). Academic Studies Press. https://www.jstor.org/stable/j.ctt1zxsj24.8?seq=1#metadata_info_tab_contents

Khan, Sadaat. Personal communication June–July 2018. Interviewer Arun Gupto.

Lamsal, Tika. Personal communication June–July 2018. Interviewer Arun Gupto.

Mahaprashasta, A. A. (2016, September 27). Threat of sedition charges looms as ABVP objects to Mahasweta Devi Play on campus. *The Wire*. https://thewire.in/politics/abvp-central-university-haryana-draupadi

Nussbaum, M. C. (2010). *Not for profit: Why democracy needs the humanities?* Princeton University Press.

Phuyal, Komal. Personal communication June–July 2018. Interviewer Arun Gupto.

Rancière, J. (1999). *Dis-agreement: Politics and philosophy* (J. Rose, Trans.). University of Minnesota Press.

Rancière, J. (2010). *Dissensus: on politics and aesthetics*. (S. Corcoran, Trans.). Continuum.

RJ Sayema Explains – and Sings – Faiz's Hum Dekhenge. (2020, January 3). [Video]. YouTube. https://www.youtube.com/watch?v=ianWNZGP9Rk

Thoreau, H. D. (2004). *On the duty of civil disobedience*. Project Gutenberg. (Original work published 1849) https://www.gutenberg.org/ebooks/71

Traverso, E. (2016). *Left-wing melancholia. Marxism, history, and memory*. Columbia University Press.

Weiss, M. L., & Aspinall, E. (Eds.) (2012). *Student activism in Asia: Between protest and powerlessness*. University of Minnesota Press.

Yami, H. (2021). *Hisila Yami: from revolutionary to first lady*. Penguin Books.

Žižek, S. (2002, May 23). Are we in a war? Do we have an enemy? *London Review of Books*, *24*(10). https://www.lrb.co.uk/the-paper/v24/n10/slavoj-zizek/are-we-in-a-war-do-we-have-an-enemy

12

UNDERSTANDING WHISTLEBLOWING

Civil disobedience or uncivil action?

Manohar Kumar

Introduction

The 2013 disclosures by Edward Snowden split political opinion. Critics of Snowden were worried that his disclosures encourage a culture of leaking that can undermine national security, collaborative security efforts between nations and put sources of intelligence information at risk. Whistleblowing, in their opinion, disrupts the culture of mutual accountability and benefits the enemy by providing important and classified information. Finally, critics argued whistleblowing undermines trust in democratic institutions by enabling individual deviant actions. On the other hand, civil liberty groups supported the disclosures by highlighting its impact on individual rights and structures of democratic accountability. For them, these covert acts of mass surveillance by the National Security Agency (NSA), run without proper due process, and violated the privacy rights of millions of individuals worldwide. Classified information is only justified to the extent that it does not violate the fundamental rights of citizens and aliens living within a national territory. Whistleblowing, for them, is a new form of democratic engagement, a form of disobedience that challenges the legitimacy of state secrecy and discloses the information that is of public interest.

Political whistleblowing[1] represents a rather new form of democratic engagement that has brought in new styles and modes of articulation that betrays easy classification within vocabularies of dissent. The debate on how to understand new modes of protest throws up two contrasting conclusions. On one hand, we notice that old terminologies like *civil disobedience* have been used by activists and scholars to categorise new forms of dissent,[2] including whistleblowing. On the other hand, we notice that there are scholars and activists who see civil disobedience as a restrictive category that does not capture the nature of protest by ordinary actors, which even though they do not conform to the standards of civil disobedience might not be

DOI: 10.4324/9781003320494-15

198 Manohar Kumar

less conscientious (Delmas, 2018). The concept is considered to be too elitist and too demanding to serve the interest of various marginal groups. The demands of civility and the fidelity to the law that the dominant conception demands might be too restrictive and demanding for certain groups and pose unfair unburdens on them. The connection of civil disobedience with certain idealised cases like that of Gandhi, Thoreau, and King puts increasing demands on dissenting actions; courts evaluate civil disobedience cases against these idealised ones. Against a revision of the concept of civil disobedience these theorists advocate for the concept of uncivil disobedience that includes incivility, and forms of everyday resistance that visualises the civil as both limiting alternate forms of expressions and excluding outside voices.

In this chapter, I analyse whether civil disobedience is a relevant category to understand whistleblowing. The case of whistleblowing is particularly interesting because it has emerged as a particularly salient mode of protest in recent times[3] even though its antecedents can be traced to Daniel Ellseberg. Despite the crucial Pentagon Paper disclosures, that had an important impact on the public perception of the Vietnam War,[4] whistleblowing never entered the repertoire of civil disobedience as understood in the work of Gandhi, King, or Thoreau. Contrary to this, by focusing on the "civil" aspect of whistleblowing (that has been neglected in the debate), I argue that whistleblowing is a form of civil disobedience. I argue against the sceptical claim that forms of whistleblowing should be read in their own right as making legitimate claims for attention towards purported wrongs and that civil disobedience is not an appropriate category for it. Contrary to the sceptical point of view, I argue that new forms of dissent do represent forms of civil disobedience on a different reading of the concept. The confusion I believe arises due to a notion of civil disobedience (the Rawlsian, that is also the dominant) that is quite demanding for forms of dissent that, although democracy-enhancing, need not demonstrate features similar to classic forms of civil disobedience. The gap in accepting whistleblowing as civil disobedience is particularly surprising because it not only highlights limitations and blind spots in "conventional" (Rawlsian) theories of civil disobedience but also challenges us to reconsider our understandings of different forms of disobedient political behaviour and their political justifiability. In contemporary times, whistleblowing as a dissenting activity challenges us to reconsider the shifting lines between civil and uncivil forms of disobedience, and also the fact that any theory of civil disobedience needs to be sensitive to the changing historical contexts of political action and the conditions of justifiability of those actions may often be dependent on the context. The deviance of whistleblowing from standard models is no testimony to a lack of sincerity and seriousness (as defendants of Rawls would have us believe) but rather represents a response to the demands of the specific situation, the changing nature and forms of political engagement and governance, and a personal regard for individual circumstances.

This chapter contributes to the volume in two ways. It contributes at a broadly theoretical level by formulating an understanding of civility that is relatively under-examined in discussions of civil disobedience. The major contestation in discussions of civil disobedience happens over what constitutes civility. It is a proper formulation of civility that enables us to separate a civil act from an uncivil act of disobedience. Yet it is quite surprising that barring a few theorists not many have paid sufficient attention to it. A failure to define or engage with a proper conception of civility is also behind the recent movement towards defining new forms of disobedience as uncivil. It is thus an urgent task that any serious work on civil disobedience needs to undertake.

The chapter also captures the transnational nature of the problem of civil disobedience. From Nepal to Norway is not merely a geographical landscape but represents the transnational dimension of civil disobedience. Civil disobedience does not merely respond to domestic forms of injustice but is often undertaken in response to concerns shared by national audiences with their global counterparts. The issue of government whistleblowing and the concern of justice and wrongdoing that it represents is not merely restricted to geographical boundaries but also represents the concerns of outsiders. The revelations by Edward Snowden and Chelsea Manning are a case in point, so are the revelations around the Paris, Panama, and Paradise Papers. This chapter does not aim to conceptualise whistleblowing and civil disobedience as a transnational problem. It has a rather modest aim. By capturing the transnational dimension of the problem, the chapter argues that even when the aims of disobedience are limited in their repercussions, their impact can be wide and varied.

The chapter has the following sequence: in the first part of the chapter, I present the current state of the art on understanding whistleblowing as an act of disobedience. I offer the communicative and rule-of-law justification for reading whistleblowing as a civil disobedience. This reading of whistleblowing is counterposed against the sceptical reading of whistleblowing that considers it as either a form of uncivil disobedience or as an act of civil dissent. In the next part, I argue that the reading of whistleblowing as civil disobedience or not is based on different interpretations of what constitutes civility. In this part, I explicate the reading of civility that different interpretations hold and make a case for a minimal reading of civility. I conclude by arguing that if my reading of civility is correct then whistleblowing too qualifies as an act of civil disobedience.

Whistleblowing as civil disobedience?

Political whistleblowing is the disclosure of government information that is in the public interest with the purpose of making it available to the public (Kumar & Santoro, 2017; Santoro & Kumar, 2018). Whistleblowing arises in a context of governmental practices of secrecy. Governments tend to over classify information: sometimes to hide acts of wrongdoing, sometimes just as a manifestation of power (Gowder, 2005), to be cautious in protecting even seemingly harmless bits of information, or as a logic of the bureaucracy that does not have sufficient information (Arendt, 1972) and seeks to err on the side of caution. Whistleblowers, who are generally insiders,[5] reveal information considered to be in the public interest. Contrary to some readings,[6] whistleblowing does not challenge the legitimacy of the government to keep secrets (Santoro & Kumar, 2018). They do not disagree with the law or the policy on classified information[7] but rather with the application of the policy in a given instance and the impact it has on democratic structures of accountability and the system of justice. It is this act of disclosure that raises questions about the legitimacy, justification, and nature of dissenting acts. In what follows, we explore those arguments that specifically read whistleblowing within the tradition of civil disobedience and those opposed to such formulation.

Rule-of-law justification

William Scheuerman (2014) argues that Edward Snowden is a civil disobedient in the classic understanding of the term. His disclosures, although unauthorised, do comply with the civility, conscientiousness, and the last-resort feature of civil disobedience. Although he sidesteps the Rawlsian requirement of fidelity to the law, his actions are consistent and supportive of the ideal of a rule of law. Scheuerman argues that what demands our compliance and obedience is the rule of the law and not the law of the land per se. He claims that citizens are bound to the rule of the law and not the laws instituted by the state which may, sometimes, deviate from the rule of the law. He argues that the situation of whistleblowers is quite precarious as the law regarding their treatment is uncertain, vague and poorly defined (pp. 619–620). This impairs the possibility of a fair trial (p. 619) and that citizens who use their judgement on complex constitutional matters ought to be encouraged (when it can be done with less damage to other policies), and tolerated in the name of conscience (p. 621).

Any reliance on the rule of law justification raises crucial questions on its effectiveness in protecting whistleblowers. The rule-of-law justification, argues Brownlee (2016), can protect individuals against unjust state actions that are arbitrary and unpredictable and non-proportional, but may not "protect against substantive injustices, such as those to be visited upon whistle-blowers who are charged and convicted under the US Espionage Act 1917" (p. 4).

In other words, Scheuerman's kind of justification is open to interpretation on the correct understanding of the rule of law; it is thus left unclear whether such interpretation would always have beneficial consequences for the whistleblower.

Communicative justification

Against a rule of law reading of Scheurman, Kimberley Brownlee (2016) offers a communicative defence of Edward Snowden. She argues that "Snowden's actions constitute an act of civil disobedience in a broader reading of the concept as "a constrained, conscientious and communicative breach of law that demonstrates one's opposition to a law or policy and one's desire for lasting change" (p. 968). Under this conception, a disobedient is not required to adhere strictly to the publicity and fidelity to law conditions of civil disobedience as demanded by Rawls. The publicity condition of civil disobedience is rather contingent upon an assessment of the

Understanding whistleblowing **201**

context. Following Raz (1979), Brownlee (2016) argues that where prior publicity inhibits the realisability of the dissenting action it should be discarded in favour of ex post publicity of the motivation and the reasons governing the disclosure (p. 966). For her, the fidelity to law should also be read broadly. Any unwillingness to submit to the law does not by itself constitute a lack of respect for the law "because the punishment for an offense may be the very thing that the disobedient opposes and which she seeks to highlight by breaching the law in question" (p. 966). Under this reading, Snowden's unauthorised disclosure is a form of civil disobedience as it "satisfies a more modest and more plausible condition for civil disobedience, which is non-evasiveness broadly construed." By making his identity public Snowden demonstrated "that he was willing to bear the risk of being punished as well as to endure the substantial losses of his citizenship rights and residence rights in the USA" (p. 966). Thus, these are the features of his action that make it an act of civil disobedience.

Whistleblowing as uncivil disobedience

In Brownlee, we see a level of permissiveness that is troubling for Candice Delmas. In her recent book *A Duty to Disobey. When Disobedience Should Be Uncivil*, Candice Delmas (2018) argues that emerging forms of protest need to be seen in their own light and be true to the self-conception of protestors. She argues that the concept of civil disobedience as propounded by liberal political philosophy is elitist. It leaves less scope for many forms of dissent which, though justified, may not conform to the civil aspect of civil disobedience. Arguing with Harcourt (2012), she sees the demands of civility as constraining genuine voices of dissent. Contrary to what she calls the ameliorative account of disobedience presented by Celikates (2014) and Brownlee (2012) that are (for her) too inclusive of emancipatory struggles, too stretched to the extent of becoming incompatible with an understanding of civil disobedience (Delmas 2018, p. 37) and thus less useful as a convincing tool for the public, she offers a principled account of disobedience calling it uncivil disobedience. Uncivil disobedience is "a cluster concept" that displays any one of the four features: covertness, evasiveness, violence, and offensiveness (p. 44).

Whistleblowing, under this reading, is a form of uncivil disobedience. By usurping the power to determine the proper scope of secrecy, and through its anonymity, and evasion of law, whistleblowing "usually fails to adhere to the norms of civility (especially publicity and non-evasiveness) and poses threats to national security" (Delmas, 2018, p. 55). For Delmas (2018), it is a form of vigilantism that usurps the monopoly of the state as a legitimate source of violence and thus manifests "disrespect for democratic institutions and is likely to scare and antagonize the majority, erode the civic bonds, and compromise future social cooperation". Unauthorised disclosures also undermine the duty to support just institutions (p. 103). She argues that whistleblowing, even when not civil, shares the democratic function of civil disobedience due to its stabilising function that enables the overcoming of "deliberative ignorance" and cognitive deficits that may result from secrecy. By revealing information it upholds the democratic value of transparency and fair procedures in decision-making (Delmas, 2017, pp. 210–211).

Santoro and Kumar (2018) also argue that whistleblowing is not civil disobedience. For them, whistleblowing "is a form of civil dissent, distinctive in its aim and character. It shares features of civil disobedience but stands alone as a theoretical category" (p. 164). Whistleblowing disclosures are less disruptive and non-partisan than disobedience. The circumstances of whistleblowing are privy to only the whistleblower or those having access to the information. There is thus an "informational asymmetry between the whistleblower and the public, the informational privilege that it entails, and the dangers that it involves". This contextual difference "impose communicative and prudential constraints that distinguish whistleblowing from other kinds of civil Action". In civil disobedience, they may be a shared epistemic basis on the circumstances of injustice (p. 165–168). Whistleblowing is thus an "indirect manifestation of a wrong or injustice" with a narrow scope, while civil disobedience is a "reaction to the injustice of the law" (p. 166) and thus has a broad aim.

In the preceding discussion, it is clear that at least three accounts rely on the Rawlsian account of civil disobedience to interpret whistleblowing. Scheuerman (2014) and Santoro and Kumar (2018) directly interpret whistleblowing within the Rawlsian framework,[8] while Candice Delmas in offering an alternative account accepts it as the dominant understanding of civil disobedience and civility. Scheuerman offers a rule of law reading of Rawls under which a failure to abide by existing laws is justified. Whether the Rawlsian scheme allows for that interpretation is Brownlee's contention in offering a communicative defence of whistleblowing. For her, the primary purpose of civil disobedience is the communication of the injustice of the law which captures the non-ideal circumstances of disobedience.

The Rawlsian view is too optimistic about the set of background conditions, the political order being opposed to, and the sense of justice of the majority that is being appealed to (Aitchison, 2018), that the conceptualisation of civil disobedience in a nearly just society does not offer us any clues regarding actual cases of dissent in societies that are far from just leaves ample room for interpretation regarding the act and justification of disobedience itself. As Koikkalainen et al. rightly point out in this volume, interpretations regarding the shared sense of justice, the "basic structures" that one wishes to defend, or whether one lives in a "well-ordered society" may vary. It is these conflicts over interpretations that is behind the discussion on what constitutes an essential component of civil disobedience and what are those features that are contingent on the justness of a society. What has really followed, is an interpretation of what actions constitute civil disobedience within the contours of the law in a society. It is due to this fact that scholars can argue that neither prior publicity, nonviolence, or non-evasiveness of the law is a necessary feature of civil disobedience (Brownlee, 2012). It is the communicative aspect of civil disobedience (that Rawls also alludes to) that they appeal to. If the primary purpose of a disobedient act, so the argument goes, is to communicate the injustice faced by a minority then under what conditions would that communication be successful. Under such a reading whistleblowing is justified in being non-public and non-evasive of the law.

Prior publicity will stymie the actual disclosure and thus the communication of the wrong. On the other hand, evasiveness of the law is based on an assessment whether a whistleblower by submitting to the law can expect a fair trial.

From the preceding, we notice that the act of civil disobedience is necessarily an exercise in judgement. It involves, as Koikkalainen et al. argue in this volume, a subjective assessment of the social, personal, and legal conditions, consequences, one's own strength against others and the timing of the act. Civil disobedience is not merely a classificatory conceptual category under which any practical dissenting action can be read; civil disobedience also acts as a justificatory tool that distinguishes between legitimate and illegitimate acts of disobedience and between acts that invite praise from those which are condemned.

But if the dominant conception is not applicable to understand and make sense of actual acts of dissent, and if exceptions to the norm are admitted based on the contingent needs of the circumstances, then where does one draw a line between justified and unjustified acts of disobedience? The Rawlsian scheme has so far provided a good schema to judge dissenting action and as Delmas (2018) points is also a standard used by activists and the law. Moving away from it demands justification as it may have repercussions on how we categorise and understand dissenting action. But relying heavily on it can also undermine actions that, although democracy-enhancing in nature, may not be captured within that conception. What constitutes disobedience is both a matter of theoretical enquiry as well as negotiated and contested by political actors. Theorisation and practice have occurred almost simultaneously, as Koikkalainen et al. argue in this volume, sometimes one trailing the other or influencing the other. If this is correct then the Rawlsian scheme is one, although a dominant one, among possible ways of understanding civil disobedience, and thus needs to be examined for its limitations.

Civil disobedience is a practical activity that is always constrained by the context and the circumstances and the social and political time in which it operates. Thus, by failing to appreciate its changing nature, we fail to understand the changing nature of disobedience. But if the dominant interpretation does not do justice to the conception of whistleblowing as an act of disobedience then where should one look. Interpretation of whistleblowing rests on how different theorists approach the discussion on civil disobedience and how they enumerate its functions. One common point of departure in all these interpretations lies in the understanding of what constitutes "civil" in civil disobedience. It is this category that has come under increasing scrutiny in recent times, and it is in unpacking this term that we can understand whether whistleblowing is civil.

What understanding of civility does civil disobedience have?

What understanding of civility does civil disobedience have? What makes civil disobedience "civil" is not always obvious. One can discern at least two distinct formulations of the term: (1) civil disobedience is disobedience that is performed by citizens acting in their capacity as citizens (Celikates, 2014, 2016). In this reading,

204 Manohar Kumar

civility is related to the role that citizens perform in the civic space. (2) Civil is also understood in another manner: as "civilised" behaviour, a peaceful and nonviolent form of action (Bedau, 1961; Vinthagen, 2015). Citizens are not merely the primary agents of civil disobedience, so restricting the understanding of civility as relating to citizens is bound to be problematic. This is an issue that we discuss more below. For now, I wish to highlight the limitations of the understanding of the concept of civility as explicated in the dominant understanding of civil disobedience. A more reliable and broad-based understanding of civility, one that has been highly discussed in recent times, can be found in Candice Delmas (2018). Following Rawls, she argues that acts of disobedience are civil when they are public, nonviolent, and non-evasive of the law. Civility in this understanding demonstrates not only the respect of the law but also respect for persons, by treating them as worthy of exchange and reasoning, as someone with whom one can disagree and who is equally responsive to the reason sharing and giving function of democracy. It is in this regard that disobedience is civil because it responds to and appeals to the sense of justice of the majority. This is a duty that citizens owe to each other in their capacity as citizens and as persons. They have a duty to uphold just institutions and disagree and disobey civilly when institutions are nearly just. In fact, citizens are required to explore all procedural options before deciding to disobey. In this regard, disobedience is civil in another way, it arises out of the civic duty of the citizens to uphold just institutions. Civility in civil disobedience may just as well be understood as an act performed by citizens in their civic role.

But this reading of civility has a downside. It fails to capture ordinary acts of disobedience (Delmas, 2018) and assumes a citizenry predisposed to acknowledge claims of injustice made by a minority. But as we know this rarely happens. When injustice is structural in nature, claims of justice are often overlooked in favour of prejudices and structural advantages they confer to the dominant group. That would often require a form of coercion, a nudge, a push to ensure that the claims of justice are heard, if not acknowledged. Disobedience, being a practical activity, is always constrained by the context in which it operates. As a practice, it responds to the challenges of the situation by offering considered judgements on the right course of action. The civil thing to do would then be to respond to the challenges that the context itself throws up. In what follows, I briefly take the nonviolence, publicity, and non-evasiveness aspect of civil disobedience and put it through critical scrutiny.

Nonviolence is a strict condition for the civility of a disobedient action. It is premised on the condition of respect for autonomy and equality of persons. But failing to regard an act as civil for its limited use of violence is limiting especially when it is meant to draw attention to the persistence of injustice (Morreall, 1976; Raz, 1979; Simmons, 2010). If the disobedience is motivated by concerns of freedom, equality, and respect for rights of the minority, then limited forms of coercion like picketing, blocking streets, or damage to property do not necessarily manifest incivility or disrespect for persons. They have a pedagogical function that forces individuals to take note of issues, ponder over them, and work on their second-order desires and following that sometimes to endorse those positions (Moraro, 2014). This would not have happened in the absence of coercion. Vinthagen and Johansen's piece in this volume clearly elucidates the dramatic and pedagogic function of dissent, whereby extreme measures are sometimes required to draw sustained attention.

Publicity is central to the civility of disobedience. Publicity ensures that the intentions and motivations of the disobedient are open to public scrutiny. It respects the democratic sphere as a space of reasons and that those dissenting have the obligation to provide reasons in favour of their actions. Publicity follows a duty of fair play: those accused should have occasion to defend themselves and engage in a deliberative exercise. Citizens and public officials must be offered a prior notice regarding the act of disobedience. But is prior publicity a necessity for civility? Sometimes the peculiarity of an action demands secrecy for its success. Smart (1978) and Raz (1979) argue against a strict adherence to norms of prior publicity when it goes against the very success of a disobedient action. They call for an ex post publicity. This ensures that the disobedient is able to provide not only reasons in support of their actions but also the reasons why they could not adhere to the requirement of prior publicity.

Similarly, fidelity to law has been challenged on the grounds of the burden it exposes dissenting actions to (Brownlee, 2012; Celikates, 2014; Lyons, 1998; Simmons, 2010). When legal conditions are far from just and the possibility of a fair trial or a fair hearing do not exist then evasiveness of the law is not necessarily an instance of incivility. Fidelity to law is a requirement in the Rawlsian scheme in a nearly just society where the legal and societal structures are amenable to democratic reasons and the disobedient can expect both a fair trial and a fair hearing. But real-world conditions are far from just, the justice of the law is not based on morality and chances are that disobedient voices will not be respected.

It is thus clear that any conception of civility that is sensitive to the practical nature of disobedience cannot demand an absolute adherence to publicity and non-evasion of the law. A final consideration though remains. Is civility contingent on citizenship? A recent turn in the civil disobedience literature challenges the conception of whether the proper agent of civil disobedience is the citizen (Benli, 2018; Cabrera, 2015). The anti-deportation activities by those seeking asylum, as argued by Seppälä in this volume, do represent an act of civil disobedience. In fact, her work shows that not only civil disobedience can be done by citizens on behalf of non-citizens but can also be performed by non-citizens when they seek to challenge certain domestic laws by claiming protection from human rights. Similarly Nykänen et al.'s chapter on Sámi resistance shows that even when being a citizen and accepting the laws of the land one may not always disobey as a citizen. In fact, the Sámi consider themselves Sámi first, and it is based on that identity that they disobey even if their disobedience is geared towards and appeals to the state who may consider that appeal as coming from citizens. This is also evident in Vinthangen and Johansen's piece in this volume where the act of disobedience may even be guided towards getting some of the rights of the Indigenous populations to be recognised by the state. In this way, the civility of the act cannot be merely reduced to one performed by individuals or groups in their capacity as citizens but in their capacity as persons working in a cohort claiming against some wrong.

The accounts offered earlier depart from the standard account by showing its limitations. What they offer is an understanding of civility that is sensitive to the problems that dissenters face. Against what she calls the inclusive accounts of disobedience, Candice Delmas (2018) offers an argument for uncivil disobedience. Let us call this the critical approach. In this reading, civility is seen as an expression of privilege that those in advantageous positions wield for their benefit (Delmas, 2018; Harcourt, 2012). According to this conception, the demands of civility are often in conflict with the democratic demands of the marginalised sections of the population and do not fit within their own self-conception of dissent as a tool for democratic mobilisation. It is argued that invocation of civility, by demanding adherence to mores, etiquettes, and norms of respect of the dominant class, tend to discredit and delegitimise democratic struggles (Delmas, 2018). It is those at the margins who face the burden of the demands of civility: they are doubly disadvantaged. They face the brunt of injustice and are tasked with the demand to engage in discourse that is meant to exclude them. The demands of civility limit genuine acts of dissent that though uncivil may be democracy enabling. Civility thus becomes a burden that needs to be discarded in favour of a conception of "uncivil" disobedience that is true to the democratic nature and aspirations of protest and true to the conception that activists themselves have (Delmas 2018).

The critique of civility is justified and would find general support. What is rather puzzling though is the complete disavowal of the concept of civility that the critical approach takes. That civility has a troubled past is non-disputed. It has been associated with the civilising mission and adoption of social conventions of respect, address, and etiquette without critically evaluating them. In fact, as Zurn (2013) and Reiheld (2013) have demonstrated, civility is both ambivalent and ambiguous. Civility is required to manifest respect to others, but often, it can do so with recourse to social conventions that may not always be egalitarian. But this does not require completely abandoning it. Rather, we need some form of minimal civility, or in the words of Teresa Bejan (2017), a mere civility that enables us to engage with the other. Civility can also be a virtue (Calhoun, 2000; Zurn, 2013) that "involves treating people as equally dignified subjects". It does not preclude adopting a social critical stance (Calhoun, 2000) and relies on democratic reflexivity whereby norms of conduct and democratic engagement are up for discussion and criticism (Zurn, 2013).

It is here that we notice that the critical conception of civility runs into trouble because it aligns itself with the self-conception of dissenting agents without bothering to critically interrogate their limitations. Relying on the self-conception of agents has the particular problem of grey zones and slippery slopes that Koikkalainen et al. discuss in this volume. Disobedients can "mislead by using the good name of civil disobedience for purposes that are much narrower". This is true of uncivil action generally that always seeks to draw legitimacy by claiming democratic norms.

Jennet Kirkpatrick (2008) in her work on *Uncivil Disobedience* signals the move by different uncivil forms of disobedience like lynch mobs and vigilante groups who claim legitimacy based on the constitution and popular sovereignty. This raises questions on the difficulty in separating legitimate and justified uncivil disobedience from illegitimate ones. Delmas' conception of uncivil disobedience too falls under this worry. The worry can be framed thus: by accepting the activists' self-conception and their definition of what constitutes uncivil disobedience, is Delmas not opening the door for conceptual malleability whereby even seemingly civil forms of disobedience are read as uncivil? If the error of excess in reading uncivil as civil is a search for legitimacy and thus a form of conceptual excess, isn't the error of reading the civil as uncivil an error, a form of conceptual restraint or a lack? As any conception can suffer from its excessive usage, it can also suffer by being malleable and dependent on the conception of agents performing that action. An agent may have a certain motivation and may name a certain action as representing an instance of X, but that by itself does not make it X. This is clearly evident in Nykänen et al.'s chapter in this volume, where they argue that although the members of the movement do not consider their act as civil disobedience precisely because they consider themselves as Sámi first and citizens second and do not ascribe "sovereign authority over the land and waters to the state", their strategies and methods all fall within the classical understanding of civil disobedience. Here we see a clear case of where an action that falls within the framework of civil disobedience may not necessarily be represented as such because the motivations and the intentions of the actors may be completely different. Actors may apply a different framework to frame their resistance. The action nonetheless can fall within the framework of civil disobedience. In the same vein, merely claiming that an action is uncivil does not necessarily make it to be so. It has to be clearly demonstrated that the considered action represents a genus of X. That is the critical task that the theorist has to perform. By aligning itself with the self-conception of dissenting agents the critical conception allows for far too much conceptual malleability. It does not offer a conceptual route through which we can make sense of disobedience or judge legitimate from illegitimate, and justified from unjustified forms of civil disobedience.

In Delmas's defence, it can be argued that uncivil disobedience is political in nature that signals the injustice of the civility discourse.[9] Incivility is the rejection of all that civility stands for as a symbol and expression of power. There are dangers to this move, none less than the problem of both conceptual malleability and an inability to capture the vitality of concepts that are also shaped by their use and are in the continuous process of negotiation. Olúfẹ́mi O. Táíwò (2020) argues that concepts do not lose their vitality because of the use they are subjected to. For him, a fight for "broader social structural change" requires that "we can, have, do, and must continue to negotiate alternative versions of li". The fact that civility encodes and is an expression of dominant social relations does not mean that it needs to be abandoned. Rather, we should relate to each other on terms "that embody and materialize relations of mutual respect and non-domination and collective power. That possibility is civility as self determination" (p. 1074). In other words, rather

208 Manohar Kumar

than enforcing the existing codes of civility, we need to move towards safeguarding respect and equality, values that civility protects. We need a conception of civility that enables us to engage critically with the world, not merely in nearly just conditions, that is more attuned with the social situatedness of actors contesting the injustices of the world.

To explore what such a conception of civility looks like, we need to turn towards the theory of civility offered by Anthony Milligan (2013) in his book *Civil Disobedience: Protest, Justification, and the Law*. He offers a minimalist account of civility which are kind of "basic norms that any protest must not violate or break beyond a certain point if it is to stay within civil bounds". He offers the following list:

> (i) respect for others or, if we have no fondness for the language of respect, the recognition that other humans are fellow humans, i.e. members of the same moral community; (ii) the rejection of hate-speech; (iii) the avoidance of acts which are driven by hatred; (iv) the largely successful commitment to try to avoid violence and threats of violence, although an exception may be drawn here for systemic violence in which many of us may be complicit; (v) the avoidance of cruelty; and finally (vi) the recognition of a duty of care or an avoidance of the reckless endangerment of others, although recklessness and its avoidance may turn out to be a matter of degree.
>
> *(p. 36)*

Milligan (2013) offers an "open-textured" definition that captures the social contingency of civility, and its multiple conceptions, without reducing it to an elite conception of right manners (p. 34). The conception of civility, and thus civil disobedience, that Milligan offers is not an "impossible or elitist ideal" that can only be performed by individuals of unquestionable integrity but one that is "open-textured", a concept that "can be refined and extended in various ways", that is not bound by "rigid and fixed set of preconditions" (pp. 32–33). An open-textured account, by not adhering to any single authoritative view, also offers the possibility to accommodate Delmas's concern by permitting "defensible claims of civil disobedience to be made in a far wider range of cases, with advantageous consequences for political activists". The benefit of an open-textured approach is that it not only accommodates the fact that "a claim of civil disobedience is a claim of special standing of a moral, legal or even spiritual sort" but also that it "has been and can be refined and extended in various ways." This enables the concept of civil disobedience to stay relevant to changing times and accommodate new and emerging forms of dissent.

But is an open-textured understanding of civil disobedience not too permissive. Milligan (2013) is aware of this criticism. He argues that

> plausible constraints can be set up even for an open-textured account of the concept, and the constraints themselves can be given some justification. We might think of these constraints as rudimentary adequacy conditions that

must be met if an account of civil disobedience is to be plausible. However, more than one account may qualify. Taken together, these adequacy conditions do not exclude further argument but they do help to make sense of why we still need a concept of civil disobedience, why we should not turn our backs on the concept or otherwise marginalize it.

(p. 33)

The constraints that he speaks of here are those of the norms of civility that we discussed earlier. This reading of civil disobedience is more tolerant to the context and the situatedness of the agent. By setting minimal constraints on the practice of civility this conception avoids the problem of spilling over into uncivil disobedience or into indeterminacy where real-world struggles are rendered unintelligible owing to a demanding conception of civil disobedience. Acts of disobedience arise in response to a context; an analysis of the circumstances should play a significant role in determining their justification and legitimacy. The specific mode that a disobedient action takes often depends on the social acceptance of dissent, the level of courage the dissenter can muster, the social and political rules that govern dissenting actions, and the available protections that exist within the law for dissenting actions. In societies where dissent is protected and the society, state, and the law respond favourably, the dissenter has more reasons to engage in public disobedience. Where historical evidence and social/political situations are inimical to dissenting voices an act of public dissent is a manifestation of courage and an act of last resort. A non-public dissent thereby does not become less virtuous. Disobedience, we said, is an exercise in political judgement, judgement that is a product of contingent circumstances that the disobedient is exposed to. When disobedience is evasive, non-public, and violent the question to ask is not what motivations guide those actions (motivations may be important) but rather whether the content of action is democratic. The focus should rather be on understanding, based on a judgement of circumstances, based on impartial reasons, whether the act was mandated due to the imminent injustice of the circumstances that the agent is exposed to. It should be rather inquired whether alternate and less costly pathways of action were available to the disobedient. In other words, the justification of disobedience should be read within the non-ideal circumstances in which it operates. The demands of civility should also be ascertained in a similar manner. The absence of public, non-evasive, and nonviolent disobedience is less a testimony to the character of the disobedient more of the quality of democracy.

Is whistleblowing civil disobedience?

If this reading of civil disobedience is correct then it is not difficult to see that whistleblowing does indeed qualify as an act of civil disobedience. Whistleblowing, when it uncovers grave wrongs and injustices, challenges the legitimacy of state secrecy and the reasons for which it is deployed. Delmas is correct in arguing that whistleblowing does challenge the state allocation of informational resources but

210 Manohar Kumar

is wrong in claiming that the act becomes uncivil for doing so. She calls the act transgressive in the league of vigilantism. That whistleblowing is not vigilantism is something that we have already demonstrated elsewhere.[10] But in order to defend whistleblowing as civil disobedience, I still need to show that it is not uncivil. The charge of incivility is raised on the grounds that it is not public, evasive of the law, and that it is transgressive. The transgression argument is correct to the extent that the whistleblower is not the democratic authority to decide upon both the allocation and distribution of informational resources and the authority who decides on its disclosure. But one of the objects of disobedience is to challenge the injustice around the allocation of resources (economic, social, political, informational, etc.) and the procedure through which these resources are allocated, especially when those resources have an important bearing on the enjoyment of rights and ensuring democratic structures of accountability. What we observe here is that the disclosure fulfils not only a deliberative function of overcoming deliberative inertia by injecting crucial information for deliberation, but it also reveals a democratic deficit that is produced due to secrecy. The object of disobedience is merely not to expose injustice but to challenge the procedures too through which injustice seems to be both manifested and hidden: in other words, to challenge the allocation of informational resources. In this regard, whistleblowing is civil because it fulfils a civic function, of informing citizens and right bearers of the limitation that secrecy imposes on their enjoyment of rights.[11] Even in its evasion of the law, whistleblowing is not uncivil. When the legal conditions are far from just, and the possibility of a fair trial is difficult, the choice before the whistleblower is between public, anonymous, or the non-disclosure of information. Non-disclosure has significant democratic and moral costs. When the information serves a democratic and public interest function, is backed by evidence, and is truthful, then the whistleblower is justified in disclosing it,[12] and it is unfair to expect the whistleblower to accept the burdens merely to come across as a hero.

But it can be argued that although some kinds of whistleblowing of the Snowden variety can be justified under this reading, what about anonymous whistleblowing? Is it an act of civil disobedience too? Isn't the act uncivil? Anonymous disclosure can be uncivil in the following ways: it undermines the duty to fair play; the whistleblower accuses someone without necessarily exposing their identity and standing scrutiny for their claims. The civil thing to do is to back accusations by reasons and to be able to stand scrutiny for them. It is indeed this rationale that Johan-Eerik Kukko follows in his reading of the actions of the Soldiers of Odin and Loldiers of Odin in this volume. Kukko, while finding the Soldiers of Odin unjustifiable, finds the Loldiers of Odin as an instance of uncivil disobedience. In doing so, he agrees with Delmas's formulation of uncivil disobedience where the publicity of identity is essential for an act to be civil. This is indeed a tempting conclusion that would also distinguish between anonymous and public whistleblowing. But one needs to look at finer distinctions. As I have argued here, acts of disobedience are practical acts that are guided by the circumstances surrounding those actions. In the case of Loldiers of Odin, if one reads Kukko clearly, the act of disguise is attempted more

Understanding whistleblowing **211**

for the affect that it produces and the dramatic value it has on drawing attention to their cause. By dressing up as a clown, one draws attention that one would not have been able to (say by physical demonstration). Performativity is crucial to draw attention to the cause and here identity and the publicity of the identity then attains a backseat. It is thus understandable why it becomes an act of uncivil disobedience. Here identity is not necessarily hidden due to the challenges that the disobedient themselves face. But the reading of the action would be different if the publicity of their identity is bound to invite retaliation as in the recent case of the Hong Kong protests.[13] It is the circumstances surrounding the action that plays a crucial role in determining the civility of the action. It is this aspect that is crucial to understand the anonymity of whistleblowing. Most national security whistleblowers face charges of espionage, treason and like. They are pursued by national security agencies and often do not get widespread public support or legal protections. Thus, unauthorised disclosures come at huge personal and professional costs.[14] As we have argued before, any theory of civil disobedience should account for professional and personal costs associated with disobedience.

Whistleblowers are certainly required to resort to fair play and not disclose anonymously when circumstances are fortuitous, but circumstances rarely are such. Unauthorised disclosures occur in a space of differential powers and capacities of agents. We notice that the circumstances for the whistleblowers to operate in a civil manner are not equal. Circumstances do play an important role in classifying a civil from uncivil action. Power tends to interfere with the exercise of reason, thus forcing individuals to resort to what would ideally be called an uncivil action (Estlund, 2005). In these circumstances, failing to adhere to norms of civility is not a failure but rather an attempt to equalise the power differential. It is civil, following Estlund, in a wider understanding of the concept which accommodates the context and the power differential between different actors. If the only way to make the powerful accountable is through an anonymous action, then it does adhere to a wider understanding of civility. It is indeed the protection afforded by anonymity that provides some semblance of equality whereby the whistleblower can challenge the abuse protected by power. Public disclosures are bound to invite serious repercussions, as in the case of Snowden and Manning (among many others). It undermines the possibility for ordinary agents to engage in disobedient actions. Demands of publicity are only bound to put unfair burdens on what often are conscientious actions. Civility, as upholding the norms of respect, tolerance, and equality, does not necessarily need disclosure of identity; an act can be civil when anonymous. Whistleblowing can be civil when the accusation of wrongdoing is truthful and backed by evidence, the veracity of which can be determined independently and the content has an explicit public interest value. Evidence enables the democratic space of reasons to run unabated; impartial reasons can be offered by other better placed agents in support of the unauthorised disclosures. Most often this indeed is the case. Whistleblowers are hardly in the position, physically and epistemically, to make proper judgements and offer reasons in the framework that is both accessible and understandable to all. This task is taken up by journalists, civil society activists,

212 Manohar Kumar

lawyers, theorists, and others who are better placed to judge the democratic validity of the documents. Anonymity, thus, is not a dereliction of responsibility but is rather a manifestation of social and democratic responsibility of a socially situated, albeit constrained agent who upholds the right and the just by accepting and acting within their limitations.

Conclusion

Whistleblowing has confounded political theorists and philosophers alike. At the outset, the democratic potential of whistleblowing as an act of dissent is not questioned but what rather confuses theorists is where in the genus of democratic dissent does it lie. Recent attempts to classify and categorise it as acts of civil disobedience have often taken routes that have not done justice to the specificity of the action. Attempts have been made to either fit it within existing conceptions of disobedience by admitting exceptions where required or to deny its identity as an act of civil disobedience. In this chapter, I have tried to argue that these recent attempts have mostly failed because they have not paid sufficient attention to understanding the "civil" aspect of disobedience. In other words, theorists of civil disobedience need to elucidate in clear terms how they understand civility. Civility has been broadly understood either as an act performed by a citizen as a civic duty or as following norms of non-evasiveness, publicity that demonstrate the sincerity and seriousness of the disobedient and their capacity to engage in reason with their fellow citizens. This chapter argues that the dominant understanding of civility is not sufficient to capture new and emerging forms of dissent. The dominant conception is too rigid to allow for deviations. Acts of disobedience are practical in nature that often respond to the constraints of their social, political, and economic environment. The scope and the breadth of disobedient actions and what a disobedient is able to do are also constrained by the context. The dominant reading of civility puts burdens on disobedient actions by failing to capture the challenges of the circumstances and situations they are exposed to. This is an outcome of a theorisation that has emerged in response to particular historical circumstances and consider certain disobedients as exemplars. Reasoning or theorising with exemplars often comes at the cost of a concept being too closed to allow for interpretations and change, a concept that is not accessible to ordinary actors who seek to engage with and transform the world. In this chapter, I have argued, following Milligan, that we need a more open-textured understanding of civility that is both true to the actual circumstances of disobedience and the challenges that a disobedient faces. We need to understand civility within the power relations within which different actors operate. The burdens of civility are not equal but dependent on what end of the spectrum of power relations one lies on. What is civil is less defined by rigid and unchanging norms but rather constrained by minimal requirements of upholding equality, respect, and tolerance, and it thus does not contradict a social critical stance. This chapter argues that when we read civility in a broader sense and accommodate the context and the burdens that whistleblowers face, even anonymous disclosures are not acts of uncivil disobedience. Speaking truth to power is both an exercise in judgement and an act of heroism that seeks to transcend the here and now and imagine the world as a realm of possibilities that can be transformed through political action. These political actions are various and stand testimony to the multiple ways we engage with the world through acts of dissent. It is only time that the philosophies we build around them or for them be sensitive to that multiplicity too.

Notes

1 In this chapter, *whistleblowing* means political whistleblowing, which is the disclosure of information that is protected under government secrecy clauses. This is different from civic whistleblowing, which is mostly against corruption. For a distinction between different kinds of whistleblowing, see Santoro and Kumar (2018).

2 In recent times, many forms of environmental protests, distributed denial-of-service attacks, and the march of the refugees have all been read from the category of civil disobedience (Benli, 2018; Cabrera, 2010, 2015; Celikates, 2016).

3 Wikileaks disclosure by Chelsea Manning, the PRISM disclosures by Edward Snowden, the PARIS and PARADISE papers are just some of the most famous cases of disclosure of government or corporate wrongdoing in recent times.

4 Sisella Bok (1983) and Elliston (1982) make a distinction between whistleblowing and civil disobedience as two distinct forms of dissent.

5 Not all whistleblowers are internal to the organisation they blow the whistle on. For more discussion on who is a whistleblower, see Santoro and Kumar (2018, Ch. 2).

6 Delmas (2018) equates whistleblowing with vigilantism. We have challenged this claim in detail in Santoro and Kumar (2018, Ch. 5).

7 Whistleblowing may be dictated by ideas that propagate the need for transparency and an open government. But that is one class of whistleblowers who are more ideologically tuned and whose reasons for disclosures are less to do with the content of the information and more with the idea of an open government itself. Unlike this category, whistleblowers generally are those who work within existing governmental setup and reveal information of public interest.

8 John Rawls (1999) sees civil disobedience as a "public, nonviolent, and conscientious act contrary to law usually done with the intent to bring about a change in the policies or laws of the government" (p. 181). His conception of civil disobedience is political because it is "an act justified by moral principles which define a conception of civil society and the public good" (p. 181). Civil disobedience in this conception is essentially public and communicative and is an act of last resort. The goal of a civil disobedient is to address "the sense of justice of the majority in order to urge reconsideration of the measures protested and to warn that, in the sincere opinion of the dissenters, the conditions of social cooperation are not being honored" (p. 181). Finally, for Rawls, civil disobedience does not operate outside the bounds of the law but rather expresses "disobedience to law within the limits of fidelity to law" and manifests deep respect for the law. (p. 181). It is the fidelity to the law, and the appeal to the sense of justice of the majority by undertaking disobedience nonviolently and in a public manner that makes it a civil, sincere, and a conscientious act.

9 Incivility may have important epistemic functions when it forces the other to understand the extent of injury or injustice one is exposed to. It can also enable the other to reconsider their position (Morgan, 2020) or an expression of the affective states one is exposed to due to the wrong. Amia Srinivasan (2018) argues that denying that anger has a role to play when one is exposed to systemic and continuous injustice is to deny them the possibility of expressing how they feel about the wrong. This is a form of affective injustice. For more, see Srinivasan (2018). But anger and incivility as a mode of expressing wrong, and acknowledging the wrong for oneself and the community that one belongs to is one

thing and may be justified to that extent, but whether it has the civic function that civil disobedience demands is another. For Edyvane (2020), the audience of uncivil disobedience need not be the majority or those in power but may be peers who are exposed to similar injustice. This form of disobedience may not always be meant to change law or policy or bring attention to the injustice of the law but rather to demonstrate to similarly positioned groups about the wrongness that one is exposed to. This form of address has the function of demonstrating to the group one belongs to that one is not willing to submit to injustice and unjust treatment.

10 In Santoro and Kumar (2018, Ch. 5), we discuss how the argument of vigilantism does not work in case of whistleblowing. I do not deal with this here, but I assume that whistleblowing is not vigilantism.

11 To see how secrecy impacts the enjoyment of rights, see Santoro and Kumar (2018, Ch. 3).

12 For discussion on the justification of whistleblowing, see Kumar and Santoro (2017).

13 See Smith (2019) on the struggle for anonymity by the Hong Kong protestors.

14 Whistleblowers risk losing their jobs (Alford, 2002; Johnson, 2003) and keep fearing reprisals that they need to overcome (Martin 2007). Reprisals could be of the kind of demotion and a denial of promotion (Alford, 2002; Johnson, 2003; Martin & Rifkin, 2004; Near & Miceli, 1986). In extreme cases, it can involve frame-ups, assault, imprisonment (Mansbach 2009), accusation of mental instability through diagnosis (Bok, 1980, pp. 278–279; Rothschild & Miethe, 1994). Their character can also be assassinated such as the public discussion of the gender identity of Chelsea Manning (Amoureux, 2015, p. 136). See also Santoro and Kumar (2017) for why whistleblowers have a right to protection.

References

Aitchison, G. (2018). (Un) civil disobedience. *Raisons Politiques*, (1), 5–12. https://doi.org/10.3917/rai.069.0005

Alford, C. F. (2002). *Whistleblowers: Broken lives and organizational power*. Cornell University Press.

Amoureux, J. L. (2015). *A practice of ethics for global politics: Ethical reflexivity*. Routledge.

Arendt, H. (1972). *Crisis of the republic: Lying in politics, civil disobedience, on violence, thoughts on politics, and revolution*. Harvest Book, Harcourt Brace and Company.

Bedau, H. A. (1961). On civil disobedience. *The Journal of Philosophy*, *58*(21), 653–665. https://doi.org/10.2307/2023542

Bejan, T. M. (2017). *Mere civility*. Harvard University Press.

Benli, A. E. (2018). March of refugees: An act of civil disobedience. *Journal of Global Ethics*, *14*(3), 315–331. https://doi.org/10.1080/17449626.2018.1502204

Bok, S. (1980). Whistleblowing and professional responsibilities. In D. Callahan & S. Bok (Eds.), *Ethics teaching in higher education* (pp. 277–295). Plenum Press.

Bok, S. (1983). *Secrets: On the ethics of concealment and revelation*. Vintage.

Brownlee, K. (2012). *Conscience and conviction: The case for civil disobedience*. Oxford University Press.

Brownlee, K. (2016). The civil disobedience of Edward Snowden: A reply to William Scheuerman. *Philosophy & Social Criticism*, *42*(10), 965–970. https://doi.org/10.1177/0191453716631167

Cabrera, L. (2010). *The practice of global citizenship*. Cambridge University Press.

Cabrera, L. (2015). The morality of border crossing. *Contemporary Political Theory*, *14*(1), 90–99. https://doi.org/10.1057/cpt.2014.42

Calhoun, C. (2000). The virtue of civility. *Philosophy & Public Affairs, 29*(3), 251–275. https://doi.org/10.1111/j.1088-4963.2000.00251.x

Celikates, R. (2014). Civil disobedience as practice of civic freedom. In D. Owen (Ed.), *On global citizenship James Tully in dialogue* (pp. 207–228). Bloomsbury Press.

Celikates, R. (2016). Democratizing civil disobedience. *Philosophy and Social Criticism, 42*(10), 982–994. https://doi.org/10.1177/0191453716638562

Delmas, C. (2017). Disobedience, civil and otherwise. *Criminal Law and Philosophy, 11*(1), 195–211. https://doi.org/10.1007/s11572-014-9347-9

Delmas, C. (2018). *A duty to resist: When disobedience should be uncivil.* Oxford University Press.

Edyvane, D. (2020). Incivility as dissent. *Political Studies, 68*(1), 93–109. https://doi.org/10.1177/0032321719831983

Elliston, F. A. (1982). Civil disobedience and whistleblowing: A comparative appraisal of two forms of dissent. *Journal of Business Ethics, 1*(1), 23–28. https://doi.org/10.1007/BF00382803

Estlund, D. M. (2005). *Deliberation down and dirty: Must political expression be civil?* Poynter Center for the Study of Ethics and American Institutions, Indiana University.

Gowder, P. (2005). Secrecy as mystification of power: Meaning and ethics in the security state. *I/S: A Journal of Law and Policy for the Information Society, 2*(1), 1–25. http://hdl.handle.net/1811/72714

Harcourt, B. E. (2012). The politics of incivility. *Arizona Law Review, 54*, 345–373. http://dx.doi.org/10.2139/ssrn.2020679

Johnson, R. A. (2003). *Whistleblowing: When it works – and why.* Lynne Rienner Publishers.

Kirkpatrick, J. (2008). *Uncivil disobedience: Studies in violence and democratic politics.* Princeton University Press.

Kumar, M., & Santoro, D. (2017). A justification of whistleblowing. *Philosophy & Social Criticism, 43*(7), 669–684. https://doi.org/10.1177/0191453717708469

Lyons, D. (1998). Moral judgment, historical reality, and civil disobedience. *Philosophy & Public Affairs, 27*(1), 31–49. https://doi.org/10.1111/j.1088-4963.1998.tb00058.x

Mansbach, A. (2009). Keeping democracy vibrant: Whistleblowing as truth-telling in the workplace. *Constellations, 16*(3), 363–376. https://doi.org/10.1111/j.1467-8675.2009.00547.x

Martin, B. (2007). Whistleblowers: Risks and skills. In B. Rappert & C. McLeish (Eds.), *A web of prevention: Biological weapons, life sciences and the governance of research* (pp. 35–49). Earthscan.

Martin, B., & Rifkin, W. (2004). The dynamics of employee dissent: Whistleblowers and organizational jiu-jitsu. *Public Administration Review: A Global Journal, 4*, 221–238. http://dx.doi.org/10.1023/B:PORJ.0000036869.45076.39

Milligan, A. (2013) *Civil disobedience: Protest, justification, and the law.* Bloomsbury Academic.

Moraro, P. (2014). Respecting autonomy through the use of force: The case of civil disobedience. *Journal of Applied Philosophy, 31*(1), 63–76. https://doi.org/10.1111/japp.12034

Morgan, J. (2020). Can one be rude to a shoe? Saving our humanity and the wrong of rudeness. *Philosophy East and West, 70*(4), 1094–1108. https://doi.org/10.1353/pew.2020.0078

Morreall, J. (1976). The justifiability of violent civil disobedience. *Canadian Journal of Philosophy, 6*(1), 35–47. https://doi.org/10.1080/00455091.1976.10716975

Near, J., & Miceli, M. P. (1986). Retaliation against whistle-blowers: Predictors and effects. *Journal of Applied Psychology, 71*(1), 137–145. https://doi.org/10.1037/0021-9010.71.1.137

Rawls, J. (1999). *A theory of justice.* Revised edition. Harvard University Press.

Raz, J. (1979). *The authority of law: Essays on law and morality.* Clarendon Press.

Reiheld, A. (2013). Asking too much? Civility vs. pluralism. *Philosophical Topics, 41*(2), 59–78. https://www.jstor.org/stable/43932736

Rothschild, J., & Miethe, T. D. (1994). Whistleblowing as resistance in modern work organizations: The politics of revealing organizational deception and abuse. In J. M. Jermier, D. Knights & W. R. Nord (Eds.), *Resistance and power in organizations* (pp. 252–273). Routledge.

Santoro, D., & Kumar, M. (2017). A right to protection for whistle-blowers. In D. Archibugi, & A. E. Benli (Eds.), *Claiming citizenship rights in Europe: Emerging challenges and political agents* (pp. 186–203). Routledge.

Santoro, D., & Kumar, M. (2018). *Speaking truth to power – A theory of whistleblowing* (Vol. 6). Springer.

Scheuerman, W. E. (2014). Whistleblowing as civil disobedience: The case of Edward Snowden. *Philosophy & Social Criticism, 40*(7), 609–628. https://doi.org/10.1177/0191453714537263

Simmons, A. J. (2010). Disobedience and its objects. *BUL Review, 90,* 1805.

Smart, B. (1978). Defining civil disobedience. *Inquiry, 21*(1–4), 249–269. https://doi.org/10.1080/00201747808601843

Smith, T. (2019, October 22). In Hong Kong, protestors fight to stay anonymous. *The Verge.* https://www.theverge.com/2019/10/22/20926585/hong-kong-china-protest-mask-umbrella-anonymous-surveillance

Srinivasan, A. (2018). The aptness of anger. *Journal of Political Philosophy, 26*(2), 123–144. https://doi.org/10.1111/jopp.12130

Táíwò, O. O. (2020). Civility as self-determination. *Philosophy East and West, 70*(4), 1073–1083. https://doi.org/10.1353/pew.2020.0076

Vinthagen, S. (2015). *A theory of nonviolent action: How civil resistance works.* Bloomsbury Publishing.

Zurn, C. F. (2013). Political civility: Another illusionistic ideal. *Public Affairs Quarterly, 27*(4), 341–368. https://www.jstor.org/stable/43575586

INDEX

Page numbers followed by 'n' refer to notes numbers.

Aalto, Touko 146
activism 2, 12, 59, 64, 71, 74, 142, 148,
    150, 169, 173–174, 190–191, 194;
    anti-deportation 139–140, 142, 144–145,
    148, 150–151, 205; anti-fascist 104, 115;
    cannabis 68, 77–79; civic 11
activists 20–21, 27, 29–44, 48–50, 55–59,
    61, 64, 74, 76–77, 91–92, 97, 99–100,
    105, 112–118, 142–144, 146–149, 161,
    172–174, 197, 206–207
Adhikari case 169–174
Adhikari, Ganga Maya 161, 169–170,
    172, 174
Adhikari, Krishna Prasad 169, 172;
    kidnap and killing of 169
Adhikari, Nanda Prasad, death of 172
Advocacy Forum-Nepal 164, 166,
    169–171, 173
Afghani asylum seekers 142
Aino Pennanen case of civil disobedience
    144–147
Akhil Bharatiya Vidyarthi Parisad (ABVP)
    195n15
Áltá Controversy 32–38, 44, 47–52, 56,
    59–61
Alta, Detsika Camp in 33, 49–50
Áltá-Guovdageaidnu River, dam project
    34–35, 47, 49, 53, 60; Standing Rock
    56, 60
American university liberalism 185
anarchism 70, 73
anonymous publicity 109

anti-deportation activism, in Finland
    139–140, 142, 144–145, 148,
    150–151, 205
anti-drug-war politics 64
anti-establishmentarianist momentum 96
anti-globalisation protest 111
anti-governmental movements 116
Arab Spring 188
Arendt, Hannah 1, 12, 22, 86, 122, 124,
    132, 134–135
Aristotle 15–16
artistic protesting 59–60
Aschjem, Per 37
asylum seekers 104, 109, 113, 139–140,
    142–144, 148–151
Aubry, Manon 123, 125, 127–129,
    133–134
Australian: for DCR (called a Medically
    Supervised Injecting Center or MSIC)
    66; T-Room 67

Bachman, Jonathan 114
Badiou, Alain 181
Bangladesh 179, 182, 184–185, 193;
    Awami League 183; Dhaka University in
    182; political parties in 195n7; Shahbagh
    protests 179, 182, 184; University
    protests in 182–187
Bano, Iqbal 187
Bateson, Regina 105
Beer, Andreas 111
Behdad 144

218 Index

Bharatiya Janta Party (BJP) 183, 186, 195n8
Bhattarai, Baburam 170
Bjørgo, T. 106
Bjørklund, Ivar 52
black civil rights movement 1, 21–22
Black Lives Matter 2
Bogad, L. M. 114
Bondevik, Kjell Magne 42
border-crossing developments 2
British colonialism in India 1, 181
Brownlee, Kimberley 2, 14, 20, 24, 106–108, 115, 117, 200–201, 205
Brugmans, Henri 131–132
Brundtland, Gro Harlem 33–34
Bush, George 112

campaign work 31, 43
Canada 30, 61, 65, 73–74
cannabis: activism 68, 77–79; prohibition 64, 75–76
capitalism 70, 132
carnivalism 112
Čearretsuolu island 54–55, 57, 59
Celikates, Robin 2, 14, 16, 24, 107, 115, 117, 125–126, 128, 201, 205
Chi-kuo, Mao 97
Chilwal, Ganesh, death of 167
Ching-chung, Chang 95
civil disobedience (CD): Arendt's concept of 122, 134–135; Aubry on 135; Brownlee vision of 115; component 38–39, 202; concept of 1–2, 47, 56, 58, 85–86, 92, 107, 122, 125, 127, 198, 201, 208–209; constructive 36, 44; controversial method and 148, 151; definition of 12–14, 47, 106–107, 115, 127, 134; deliberative 87, 96–97; Delmas view on 107; Finnish concept of 58; hunger strikes and theory of 48; integral federalism and 129–132; limited utilisation of 139, 151; pledge of 30; as political tool 123–129; public health 65–68; public understandings 12–14, 17, 22–23; Rawlsian definition of 14, 106–107, 115, 117, 122, 125–126, 147, 202–203, 205; theory of 48, 198, 211; whistleblowing as 199–200, 209–212
civility 2, 105, 107, 115, 117, 198–209, 211–212
civil rights movement, in United States 19
civil society 28, 32, 42–44, 85, 89, 97, 161, 163–164, 174; actors 90, 164, 166, 168, 172–173; dissenting 172–173; organisations 33, 42, 160–161, 163–164, 166, 172–173

climate-altering greenhouse effect 39
climate change 24, 38, 42, 128, 151
clown activists 105, 112–113, 115
CO_2 emissions 38, 41; see also climate change
Cohen, Gerald 86
Common Action Against Gas Power Stations (FAG) 38
communist revolutionaries 183
conceptualisation 68, 202
conflict victims 160–164, 166–169, 172–174
Conflict Victims Common Platform (CVCP) 168
conscientious acts 14
contestation 12, 125, 198
controversial method 148, 151
Cooke, Maeve 24
crimes 65, 69, 76, 160, 166, 169–170, 174, 179, 185, 188; see also violence
Cross-Strait Service Trade Agreement (CSSTA) 93–96

Dahal-Prachanda, Pushpa Kamal 170
Dalits 179, 186, 195n2; rights of 183
dam construction 35–36
Danish drug laws 67
Davidson, P.J. 67
Deatnu River 47–48, 53–54, 56–57, 59–60
Delmas, Candice 12, 14, 16, 20, 23–24, 105–107, 109, 114–115, 117, 201–204, 206–209
democracy 14–15, 19, 21, 68, 72, 74, 76, 86–87, 90, 93, 125–127, 129–131, 133–135, 203–204, 206
democratic society 19, 88, 106
demonstrations 16, 40, 48, 50, 66, 74, 77, 96, 113–114, 142–144, 187
Denmark 67
deportability 140–144
Devi, Mahasweta 186
Dhakal, Rajendra case 162
Dhar, Diksha 183
dirty and old-fashioned power stations 39–40
disobedience: actions 13, 21–22, 77, 107, 202, 204–205, 209, 211–212; justifiable civil 2, 19, 22, 67–72, 74, 107–109, 198; principled 105, 107–109, 117
dissensus 179, 181, 187–188, 194
dissent 2–3, 124, 127, 139–151, 160–161, 166, 173–174, 179–180, 182–184, 197–198, 201–203, 205–206, 208, 213; non-public 209; nonviolent 167, 172; political 181; whistleblowing as 202, 212

"Don't Send Afghans Back" protest 144
Downtown Eastside, Canada 65–66
drug policy 64–66, 69, 71–72, 74–79; law-and-order 67, 69, 75
drug users: drug consumption rooms (DCRs) 66–67, 72; injection 65–66; MSIC 66–67, 72; Tolerance Room, or "T-Room" 67
drug war 64–65, 67, 72, 75, 77–78; *see also* war on cannabis (users), marching against
Duncombe, Stephen 181
Dworkin, Ronald 1, 12, 20, 23, 86

ecosystems 32, 34–35
Einarsson, Oddvar 27–28
Ellos Deatnu! 53–58, 60
Ellseberg, Daniel 198
Elokapina 148, 150–151
environmental law 41
environmental movement 2, 30, 32, 43; Norway 27, 34
Ersson, Elin 145, 147, 150
ethnic minorities 35
European democracy 123, 126
European Economic Community 30
European Union 109, 117
evasiveness 105, 108, 201, 203, 205
Extinction Rebellion 2, 123, 125, 128, 148, 151
extremism, violent 116

Facebook 93, 105
Faiz, Faiz Ahmad 187
Fawkes, Guy 111
federalism 129, 131, 133–134; integral 123, 129–135
Fellesaksjonen mot Gasskraftverk (FAG) 38–44
feminist movement 2
fidelity 24, 125–126, 133, 150–151, 198, 200–201, 205
Finland 29, 47, 50, 53, 57–58, 60, 73–77, 79, 116, 140, 142, 144, 146, 149–151; The Aliens Act 140–141; Anti-deportation activism in 142–144; asylum/deportation policies 145, 147; Clandestine Insurgent Rebel Clown Army (CIRCA) 104, 112, 115–116; Constitution of 57–58; Criminal Code 74; Immigration Service 140, 142; Loldiers of Odin 104–106, 112–116, 210; 1972 Narcotics Act 76; no one is illegal campaign 139, 142–144, 147, 151; prohibition of cannabis in 64; river Ohcejohka 57; Soldiers of Odin

(SOO) 104, 106, 109–113, 115–117, 210; Stop Deportations network 140, 142–147, 150
Finnish people 104, 113
Fishing Act, 1989 53, 57
fishing rights 57; of Sámi 53, 57; Supreme Court decision on 58; traditional cultural 57
Fishing without a licence 57–59
force 17, 20, 37, 42, 115, 185; illegitimate use of 17; law as 20; masks use and 115; in self-defence 17; and Taiwanese 99; and vigilantism 104
Frank, V.A. 67
French anti-liberalism 129
French Ordre Nouveau movement 132
Fridays for Future school strike, by Thunberg 2

Galtung, Johan 28–29, 44
Gandhian Constructive Programme 36
Gandhi, M.K. 1, 11–12, 20, 22–23, 27–29, 31, 36, 161, 164–166, 181–182, 198; Salt March 165; satyagraha 22; strategy 28
Germany 66, 146, 196
Ghosh, Subhasree 191
global climate crisis 2
global drug prohibition regime 64, 73
globalisation 2, 24, 109, 117
Global Marijuana March, Finland 73
governance 2, 85–87, 91–92, 96–97, 100, 166, 198; participatory system of 85–86
government policy 1, 18, 75, 122
Green Action Innerdalen 36
greenhouse effect 39–40, 43; *see also* climate change
Green People's University 36–37
green voters 40
Greve, Bredo 27
Gualinga, Nina 57
Guy Fawkes masks 111, 116–117

Habermas, Jürgen 86
hacktivist communities 85, 90–91, 99
Hakkarainen, P. 74
Halla-aho, Jussi 146
Hamppumarssi 73–78
Harcourt, B.E. 201
harm reduction 65–73
harm reductionists violating drug laws 72
Hätönen, Pekka 110
Heddleston, Thomas 74
"hemp rally" in Lafayette Park 74; *see also* war on cannabis (users), marching against
Hindu nationalism 187

220 Index

Hippies 31
HIV/AIDS epidemic 65, 70, 72–73
Hobbes, Thomas 16
Holmberg, Aslak 54
Homén, Viktor Theodor 29
Horsti, K. 141
Houborg, E. 67
human rights 15–16, 69–71, 77–78,
    131, 133, 142, 144, 146, 148, 166,
    168; activists 143, 161, 163, 172–173;
    violations 160, 162–163, 166, 172–174
Hungarian campaign 29
hunger strikes 33, 38, 48–49, 51–52,
    160–161, 164, 166, 168, 172, 174, 192;
    of Nanda Prasad Adhikari 161, 169, 172;
    in Oslo 59
Hurme, T. 71
Hussein, Azfar 184
Huxley, Steven 29

immigrants, illegal 108, 117
independence referendum 127, 133; in
    Catalonia 126
India: independence movement 164–165,
    190, 193; Indian Institute of Technology
    (IIT) 187; Jamia Millia Ismalia (JMI) 187;
    Jawaharlal Nehru University (JNU)
    182–183, 186–187; University of
    Hyderabad 182; university protests in
    182–187
Innerdalen 36–38, 43–44; "Soil gives food,
    the world is starving" 36
International Crimes Tribunal of
    Bangladesh 184
International Indigenous Festival Davvi
    Šuvva 51
International Work Group for Indigenous
    Affairs (IWGIA) 50, 60
interpretations 13, 19–20, 127, 140,
    199–200, 202–203, 212
Iraqi asylum seekers 142

Jalonen, Jussi 112
Jiang, Premier 95
Johansen, J. 205
Johnston, Les 106
Jozaghi, Ehsan 66
judgement, political 18, 20, 23–24, 209
justice, conception of 13–14, 24
justification, communicative 200–201;
    rule-of-law 199–200

Kai-shek, Chiang 87–88
kansalaistottelemattomuus (disobedience of
    citizens) 56

Kant, I. 16
Kao, CL 90
Karki, Dhruba 191
Kärnä, Mikko 109
Kekkonen, Jukka 79
Khadka, Dilli Bahadur 167
Khan, Sadat 193
King Jr, Martin Luther 1, 11–12, 19, 23
Kirkpatrick, Jennet 105–106, 108, 207
Koikkalainen, Petri 202–203
Koirala, Bishweshwar Prsad 165
Koirala, Girija Prasad 170
Kotonen, Tommi 110–111
Kral, A.H. 67
Kukko, Johan-Eerik 210
Ku Klux Klan 108
Kumar, M. 20, 202
Kvaløy, Sigmund 28–30, 32, 36, 44
Kyoto Protocol 38–40

La France Insoumise 127
Lai, Ten-Herng 109
Lamsal, Tika 189
lawbreaking 65, 68, 74, 77–78, 106–108,
    115–117
legal sanctions 11–12, 18
Legislative Yuan 89, 92, 94, 96
Leviathan 16
Lin Hung-chih 95
Lloyd, David 111
Los Angeles Million Marijuana March 73
Loughlin, J. 129
"Lov is an asylum" protest in Loviisa 144

Maastricht Treaty 129
Magga, Ole Henrik 52
Mandela, Nelson 23
Manning, Chelsea 199, 211
Maoists 160–162, 167–170, 183, 185,
    190; kidnapping and murdering by
    169; movement 182, 184; rebels 166,
    169–170; revolution ,183
Mao Zedong 183
Marc, Alexandre 130–132
Marcha da Maconha 73
Marche Mondiale pour le Cannabis 73
Mareš, M. 106
Markovits, Daniel 86, 92
Martin, Rex 68, 72–76, 78
Martinsen, John Reier 61n4
Masks of disobedience 114–116
Maya, Ganga 169, 171
Mélenchon, Jean-Luc 127
migration 2, 107–109, 141–142, 144, 146
Milligan, A. 208

Index **221**

minorities 15, 50, 69, 77, 79, 105, 109, 117, 186, 202, 204
Mohaiemen, Naeem 184
Moore, Alan 111, 118
morality 15, 20, 70, 205
Mostafa 144
Movimento federalista europeo 131
Mykkänen, Kai 146

name-of-the-leader 187–189
Näre, L. 142
Næss, Arne 27–31, 35, 44
nationalism 132
National Security Agency (NSA) 197
native Taiwanese uprising 87
natural gas, electricity from 38
"Naturkraft" (The Power of Nature) 38, 41
Natur og Ungdom (NU: Nature and Youth) 38
negative publicity 151
neo-Nazi movement Nordic Resistance 109–110
Nepal: armed conflict in 160–161; Chakka Jam movement 161, 168; Commission of Enforced Disappeared Persons (CIEDP) 163; Communist Party of Maoists (CPN-M) 160; Comprehensive Peace Agreement (CPA) 162–164, 168; Enforced Disappearances Enquiry 163; hunger strikes and civil disobedience in 164–166; investigation commission 162; Seven Party Alliance 162, 168; Terrorist and Disruptive Activities Control and Punishment Ordinance 172; Tribhuvan University 182–184, 189–190, 192; Truth and Reconciliation Commission (TRC) 163–164; university protests in 182–187
Nepal, Madha Kumar 170
Nepal Maobadi Pidit Sanstha 166
Netherlands 66
new social movements 1–2, 14, 23
Nilsen, Alfred 49–50
Nixon, Richard 65
non-evasiveness 105, 108, 201–202, 212
non-governmental organisations (NGOs) 30, 67, 72, 89
nonviolence 11–13, 41, 71, 77, 105, 107–108, 125, 133, 161, 164–165, 174, 202, 204
nonviolent action/resistance 2, 11, 28–29, 36, 38, 44, 48, 60, 161, 164, 166
normative democratic theory 92, 96
Norse God Odin 109, 113, 117
North Dakota Standing Rock Sioux tribe 56

Norway 1, 28–37, 41–44, 47, 49, 51–54, 60–61, 141; Christian Democrats 42; Civil Defence Forces 34; civil society 43–44; dam construction 31–32; environmental movement 27; environmental policy 42; Mardøla 27, 30–33, 36, 43–44; Orkla Grana river in 36; Parliament 33, 37–38; Progressive Party 42; Sámi Language Act 51; social democrats 41–42; Stilla Camp 49–50
Norwegian Sámi Association (NSR) 49
Norwegian Society for Nature Conservation 32
Nussbaum, Martha C. 185
NYC Cannabis Parade 73
Nykänen, Tapio 205

Odin insignia 104, 109
Oslo protests 51–52, 60n3

Paavolainen, Teemu 104, 114
Paley, William 124
Parks, Rosa 146
passive resistance 11, 29, 182; Huxley and 29
"Passiver widerstand" 29
Pennanen, Aino 144–148, 150–151
Pennanen incident 145–146
People's Action against the Development of the Alta-Kautokeino waterways 33
People's Republic of China (PRC) 88–89, 93, 99
people who use drugs (PWUDs) 65–67, 71–72, 78–79
Perälä, J. 74
Persen, Synnøve 52, 61
personalism 132
Petri, Olaus 17
Phuyal, Komal 190
Pirkkalainen 141
pluralism 109
political activism 11–12, 15, 35, 66, 123, 126, 130, 135, 181, 189–191, 193; pedagogy of 194; protests 11, 107, 192
populism 2, 193
possibility 108
Prasad, Nanda 161, 169–172, 174
Prasad, Noor, kidnap and killing of 169–170
prohibition 65, 75–77
Proudhonian federative principle 133–134
Proudhonian theory 129, 133; of federation 130
Proudhon, Pierre-Joseph 130

222 Index

public health: civil disobedience 65–68;
 policy 70, 73
publicly 11, 13, 16, 18, 49–50, 72, 78,
 90–91, 106–108, 146–147, 149, 169,
 200–201, 204–205, 210–212
public opinion 18, 21–22, 88, 148
punishment 16, 65, 72, 78, 106–108, 127,
 135, 141, 183, 201

Quader Mulla, Abdul 183

racism 108, 193
Rancière, Jacques 181, 187–188
Rannikko, Pertti 106
Ranta, Mika 110–111
Rawls, John 1, 12–16, 18–23, 67–68,
 106–107, 115, 117, 122, 125–127, 147,
 198, 200, 202–203, 205; theory of 21,
 24; "two principles of justice 22
Raz, J. 201, 205
referendum 123, 126–127
refugee crisis 104, 110, 150
Regmi, Khil Raj 171
Republic of China (ROC) 87–88;
 Kuomintang 87–88, 95, 97
resentment 93, 179
resistance 2–3, 20, 22–23, 27–28, 41–42,
 47–48, 51–53, 55–56, 58–60, 116,
 123, 179–181, 183, 186–188, 194;
 constructive 36–37; cultural 181; forms
 of 180–182; in Máze 49; moratorium
 as form of 54–57; by Sámi protesters
 47, 205; universities and 194; university
 and 194
Resistance to Civil Government 28
Resvold-Holmsen, Hanna 30
revolution 48, 108, 111, 180–181,
 183–184, 188
Right to live protests 139, 142–143
Rimpiläinen, Tuomas 112, 114–115
Routledge, Paul 112
Rumsfeld, Donald 188
Russell, Bertrand, against nuclear
 weapons 31
Russification of Finland 29

Sainte-Marie, Buffy 51
salmon 32, 54, 57
Samenes Landsforbund–Sámi Country
 Alliance (SLF) 60n2
Sámi: activists 33, 35, 48, 56; community
 49, 54–55; constitutional rights 54;
 convention, Trondheim 35; culture 35,
 56, 59; fishers 53–54, 57–58; hunger

strikes and political action 51;
 people 33–35, 44, 47, 50, 52, 57–58,
 60n1; politics 50; population, recognition
 as ethnic minority 35; resistance 47, 205;
 rights 34–59; and traditional land-use
 rights 49
Sámi Action Group 49–51
Sámi Reindeer Herders' Association of
 Norway (NBR) 49
San Francisco 73
Santoro, Daniele 202
Sassoli, David 128
satyagraha 29, 165, 182; *see also*
 Gandhi, M.K.
Scheuerman, William E. 2, 14, 24,
 106–109, 114, 125, 132–133, 200, 202
self-determination 55–56, 99, 133
Setreng, Sigmund Kvaløy 27, 44
Shahbagh movement 184–185
Shah, Gyanendra Bir Bikram 185
Shah, King Gyanendra 167
Sharp, Gene 29
Single Convention on narcotic drugs 69
Sitaula, Krishna Prasad 170
Smart, B. 205
Smith, Christopher B. R. 70
Smith, William 86–87, 96, 99
Snowden, Edward 197, 199–201, 210–211
social: activism 1, 24; counterreactions
 55; innovation 98; media 53, 55, 57,
 89, 93, 97, 105, 109–110, 115,
 139, 145
social movements 1–2, 14, 21–22, 24,
 49, 139, 149, 165–166; and harm
 reduction 70; *see also* drug users
societal conflicts 27, 30, 35
Soini, Timo 111
Somby, Niillas A. 48, 50–52
strategy 1–2, 27–28, 38, 40, 42, 51, 67, 98,
 161, 167
Sunflower Movement 86, 89, 91–93,
 95–100; and civic hackers 94; as "Defend
 Democracy Tonight" 94; Taiwan 85

Taiwan 85, 87–94, 96, 98–99; activism 92;
 civil movements 86; civil society 89, 97;
 copyright law 91; Daybreak Project 86;
 participatory system of governance 85;
 people 88, 93–94, 96, 99; Professional
 Technology Temple (PTT) 93; society
 87, 89; United Nations Internet
 Governance Forum 98; White Terror in
 87–88; Wild Lily's movement 92
Táíwò, Olúfẹ́mí O. 207

Tammi, T. 71
Tana Fiskeförvaltning 54
Tana river fishing area 53
Tang, Audrey 86, 89, 91, 95, 97, 99–100; disobedience 99; Public Digital Innovation and Service 97; technology-empowered civic action 98
theorisations 12–13, 203, 212
theorists 12, 23, 105, 107, 115, 133, 198–199, 207, 212
Theory of Justice 19, 67, 86, 90, 96, 106
thinkers 12–14, 196
Thomas-Müller, Clayton 57
Thoreau, Henry David 12, 22, 28–29, 123–124, 181, 198
Thunberg, Greta 2, 11
Tiananmen Square student protest 180
TOJ in Ethics 67–68, 79
Tornensis, Nils Magnus 52
traditional knowledge 53–54
training 39, 41, 142, 151
Transitional Justice movement, Nepal 160–164, 166–169, 173
transparency 15, 86, 89–90, 92, 95, 98–99, 202
Traverso, Enzo 184–185
Tsai, Jaclyn 97

uncivil disobedience 3, 16, 18, 20, 105–109, 114–117, 198–199, 201, 206–207, 209–211; as cluster concept 108; Delmas on 108; forms 108, 117, 198, 207; law breaking and 108
Union of European Federalists (UEF) 123, 130–132, 134
universities 33, 42, 179–180, 182–186, 188–193; activism 189; political parties 194; protests 182–187
US Espionage Act 1917 200

"Valtion vesialue" 58
Vancouver Area Network of Drug Users (VANDU), and harm reduction 66
Vayssière 130–132
Vemula, Rohith, suicide of 183
Ventotene Manifesto 131
vigilantism 104–109, 114–117, 201, 207, 210; defence of 108; Delmas on 108; justification of 115; meaning of 106
Vinthagen, S. 205
violence 105–111, 115, 117, 140–141, 170, 173–174, 182–183, 186, 191, 193, 201, 204, 208; anarchism and 99; justification for 105; national value and 1; by police 95; political protests and 11; public opinion and 21; for self defence 20; sexual 166; SOO and threat of 109–112; State and 1
Vishwabharati 185
VKontakte 105, 111

war on cannabis (users), marching against 73–78
Wasif, Faruk 184
well-ordered society 21–22, 202
whistleblowing 107, 197–203, 219–212
white nationalism 110
World Council of Indigenous Peoples (WCIP) 50

Yami, Hisila 185
Yi-huah, Jiang 95
Ying-jeou, Ma 90, 95
Yle 110, 113

Zapatistas 112, 116
Zapffe, Peter Wessel 27–28
Ziaul Haq 187
Žižek, Slavoj 188

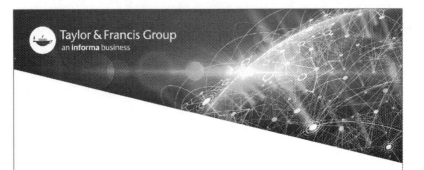

Printed in the United States
by Baker & Taylor Publisher Services